Health Industry Communication: New Media, New Methods, New Message

Edited By

Nancy J. Hicks

Senior Vice President, Associate Director North America
Ketchum
Washington, DC

Christina Mazzola Nicols, MPH, MS, MS

Vice President and Director of Research
Ketchum
Washington, DC

Caroline P. Martin

Editorial Assistant
Ketchum
Washington, DC

World Headquarters
Jones & Bartlett Learning
5 Wall Street
Burlington, MA 01803
978-443-5000
info@jblearning.com
www.jblearning.com

Jones & Bartlett Learning
Canada
6339 Ormindale Way
Mississauga, Ontario L5V 1J2
Canada

Jones & Bartlett Learning
International
Barb House, Barb Mews
London W6 7PA
United Kingdom

Jones & Bartlett Learning books and products are available through most bookstores and online booksellers. To contact Jones & Bartlett Learning directly, call 800-832-0034, fax 978-443-8000, or visit our website, www.jblearning.com.

Substantial discounts on bulk quantities of Jones & Bartlett Learning publications are available to corporations, professional associations, and other qualified organizations. For details and specific discount information, contact the special sales department at Jones & Bartlett Learning via the above contact information or send an email to specialsales@jblearning.com.

Production Credits
Publisher: Michael Brown
Associate Editor: Maro Gartside
Editorial Assistant: Teresa Reilly
Production Assistant: Rebekah Linga
Senior Marketing Manager: Sophie Fleck
Manufacturing and Inventory Control Supervisor: Amy Bacus
Composition: Cenveo, Inc.
Cover Design: Scott Moden
Cover Image: © Sebastian Kaulitzki/ShutterStock, Inc.
Printing and Binding: Malloy, Inc.
Cover Printing: Malloy, Inc.

Library of Congress Cataloging-in-Publication Data
Hicks, Nancy J.
Health industry communication : new media, new methods, new message / Nancy J. Hicks and Christina Nicols.
p. ; cm.
Includes bibliographical references and index.
ISBN-13: 978-0-7637-7892-7 (pbk.)
ISBN-10: 0-7637-7892-3 (pbk.)
1. Communication in medicine. I. Nicols, Christina. II. Title.
[DNLM: 1. Health Communication—methods. 2. Health Education—methods. 3. Marketing—methods. WA 590]
R118.H53 2012
613—dc22

2011006053

6048
Printed in the United States of America
15 14 13 12 11 10 9 8 7 6 5 4 3 2 1

Contents

Preface

The field of healthcare communications is complex, diversified, and continuously evolving. In an effort to give readers of this book a full picture of the work of practitioners in the industry, we contacted leading professionals in every industry sector. The experiences they have shared in these chapters present a robust look at the full spectrum of healthcare communications.

The book is organized into four sections representing major segments of work within the industry. "Getting Started" addresses the basics of media relations and research and planning, as well as how healthcare communications has evolved over the years. "Institutional Communications Efforts" provides compelling case studies on how associations, hospitals, and the pharmaceutical industry manage issues and build their brands. "Communicating Education Campaigns" illustrates how organizations target consumers to change health behaviors. "Communicating to Achieve Policy Change" shows the power of communication in affecting healthcare policy.

Contributors of these chapters are working professionals who have generously taken the time to share their industry experience and learning. This book has been greatly enriched as a result, and our gratitude to these contributors is immense.

As the principal authors in this process, it has been gratifying to work with our contributors and with Jones & Bartlett Learning. It has been a labor of love, and we hope that when you read this book you will understand why we are passionate about the world of healthcare communications.

Acknowledgments

The editors gratefully acknowledge the efforts of our editorial assistant, Caroline P. Martin, who tackled a great deal of logistical work with enthusiasm and good cheer. She also provided very insightful learning objectives and questions for discussion for many of the chapters in this book.

We also gratefully acknowledge the efforts of KayAnn Schoeneman, who provided research and fact checking for Chapter 1, and Denise Nguyen, who provided insight into social media measurement for Chapter 4.

About the Editors

Nancy J. Hicks has been a leader in healthcare communications for more than 25 years. She has held national positions in public relations agencies and has worked with top-tier companies in every sector of the healthcare industry. Ms. Hicks is senior vice president and head of the North America Healthcare Practice of Ketchum, Inc., a global communications firm. She is a senior counselor for healthcare clients and helps build business across the Ketchum network. She has extensive experience in strategic brand building, corporate positioning, issues and crisis management, and consumer education campaigns.

Prior to joining Ketchum, Ms. Hicks was head of the healthcare practice of Hill & Knowlton's Washington, DC office and directed the firm's national healthcare provider practice. She previously headed H&K's Atlanta healthcare practice. Ms. Hicks started her career at the Fred Hutchinson Cancer Research Center in Seattle where she promoted the work of Dr. E. Donnell Thomas who won a Nobel Prize for his pioneering work in bone marrow transplants. She headed public relations at Virginia Mason Medical Center in Seattle. She managed public relations for the eastern division of American Medical International (now part of Tenet Healthcare).

Ms. Hicks has provided leadership to a number of nonprofit organizations including serving on the boards of the National Kidney Foundation of Georgia, the National Association for Continence, the American Medical Women's Association, and the Public Relations Society of America (PRSA) Health Academy. She is a graduate of the University of Washington with a BA in English and History, and she completed a liberal arts program in London. She has published numerous articles and a book, *Branding Health Services: Defining Yourself in the Marketplace*. Ms. Hicks received the PRSA Health Academy's Lifetime Achievement Award in 2009.

Christina Mazzola Nicols is vice president-group manager in the social marketing practice of Ketchum, Inc., as well as director of research for Ketchum's Washington, DC, office. She has more than 20 years of experience in communication campaigns and marketing research, and has focused on health-related communications for the past nine years. She has conducted research in a broad range of health topics, including breast cancer, diabetes, obesity, chronic pain, seasonal flu, allergies, and heart health. Her recent speaking engagements include the PRSA Health Academy and the ExL Pharma Conference.

Before joining Ketchum in 1999, Ms. Nicols was a senior account supervisor in the Washington, DC office of Hill & Knowlton, a global communications agency. There she managed accounts for the public affairs and marketing teams, including programs for the Siemens Foundation, the National Science Foundation, and Barnes & Noble Booksellers.

Prior to her tenure at Hill & Knowlton, Ms. Nicols worked as a public affairs associate in the Dublin, Ireland, office of Fleishman-Hillard, a global communications agency, and as research manager in Fleishman-Hillard's Washington, DC, office. At Fleishman-Hillard, she developed and implemented a variety of communication programs, and designed and managed Web sites for international clients, including the first Web site for the Republic of Turkey. She was a CIPRA Award finalist for her work in developing the Republic of Turkey Web site.

Ms. Nicols holds several advanced degrees, including an MPH from the School of Public Health and Health Services at The George Washington University, an MS in Communication from Boston University's College of Communication, and an MS in Library and Information Science from the Catholic University of America. She completed a BA in Art History and English at Mary Washington College with magna cum laude distinction. She lives with her husband, Dr. Spiros Nicols, in suburban Maryland.

About the Contributors

Katherine Lee Balsamo

Katherine Lee Balsamo spent six years at agencies and worked for a major toy company before joining Aetna in 2003 as director of communications. She currently runs KLB Communications, a communications consulting business.

Michelle Davis

Michelle Davis has over 25 years of healthcare branding, marketing, and communications professional and consulting experience. Currently, she serves as the vice president of marketing and public affairs at Children's Hospital Boston, where she oversees a strategy-driven and integrated effort to build national reputation and volume for the country's top-ranking pediatric hospital. She leads a 30-member team responsible for building awareness, reputation, preference, and usage of the hospital through understanding the marketplace, digital marketing, social media, marketing promotions, communications, and earned media. Previously, she was the director of public affairs at both Tufts Health Plan and Brigham and Women's Hospital. She was also the director of marketing and community relations at Faulkner Hospital and a consultant to Hospital Corporation of America, The HealthCare Marketing Group, and the New England Life Flight. She and her teams are the recipients of over 100 professional awards in the fields of branding, public affairs, and marketing.

Steve Erickson

Steve Erickson is the Chief Communication Officer for the American College of Cardiology (ACC). In his current role, he leads all of the marketing and communication efforts for the college. A graduate of Florida State University and Syracuse University, he is a certified association executive and brings to the ACC a long career in public relations and association management. Prior to joining ACC, Mr. Erickson served as the head of the Washington, DC healthcare practice of Ketchum, Inc., an international public relations firm, and served as vice president of communication for the national office of the Arthritis Foundation.

W. Douglas Evans

W. Douglas Evans is professor of Prevention and Community Health and of Global Health, and director of the Public Health Communication and Marketing Program in the School of Public Health and Health Services at The George Washington University. He has published widely on the effectiveness of social marketing and behavior change interventions in various subject areas and global settings. His current research focuses on the use of branding strategies in public health, and evaluation methods using new and mobile media. In 2008, he published the volume, *Public Health Branding*, and is currently finishing a second book, *Global Social Marketing Research*, both from Oxford University Press. Dr. Evans is serving a four-year appointment (2007–2011) as a member of the Secretary of Health and Human Service's National Advisory Committee on Health Promotion and Disease Prevention (*Healthy People 2020*). He is also an expert panel member for the health marketing and health communication review of the Guide to Community Preventive Services. Dr. Evans consults on numerous global health programs, including branding of condom use and condom social marketing programs in Africa, Asia, Eastern Europe, and former Soviet states in collaboration with programs funded by USAID and the World Bank. Dr. Evans currently is principal investigator of a grant from the Telemedicine and Advanced Technology Research Center of the Department of the Army to conduct a pilot evaluation study of the *text4baby* mobile health intervention for Military Health Service populations. He is also principal investigator on an evaluation of the Consortium to Lower Obesity in Chicago Children's (CLOCC) 5-4-3-2-1 Go! social marketing initiative, which is aimed at reducing community obesity health risks. In collaboration with RTI, he is also co-investigator on an evaluation study of the Parents Speak Up National Campaign, a mass media campaign sponsored by the Office of Adolescent Pregnancy Prevention to promote parent–child communication about sexual activity among parents of preteen and teenage children.

Robert J. Gould

Dr. Robert J. Gould is president of Partnership for Prevention. Prior to assuming the position of president and CEO, Dr. Gould served as the director of culture/brand integration at Crispin Porter + Bogusky Group. From 2001 to 2007, he was a partner at Porter Novelli and managing director of its Washington, DC office, the second largest operation within the firm. Dr. Gould served as leader of Porter Novelli's Health and Social Marketing practice, working on antitobacco accounts that included the award-winning "truth" campaign. He also worked with the American Cancer Society, the National Cancer Institute, the National Institute on Drug Abuse, the National Heart Lung and Blood Institute, Centers for Disease Control and Prevention, and the American Heart Association. Dr. Gould was the lead researcher on the now iconic Food Guide Pyramid for the United States Department of Agriculture. Dr. Gould received his PhD in social psychology from the University of Maryland.

Phyllis E. Greenberger

Phyllis E. Greenberger, MSW, is president and CEO of the Society for Women's Health Research (SWHR). Based in Washington, DC, SWHR is a nonprofit organization working to improve the health of all women through research, education, and advocacy. Under Ms. Greenberger's leadership over the last 20 years, SWHR has turned a national spotlight on women's health, strengthening federal support for women's initiatives and forcing recognition that sex differences are a critical factor in women's health issues. Ms. Greenberger is one of the 20 most influential women in medicine today, according to *The Medical Herald*. She received a 2006 Red Dress Award from *Women's Day* in recognition of her work in leading the way in the fight against heart disease in women, and in 2010 *Women's Day* named her one of 50 "Women Who Are Changing the World." Ms. Greenberger is profiled in the book *Extraordinary Women: Fantasies Revealed* (Stewart, Tabori, and Chang, 2006), which features profiles and portraits of 58 prominent women in the United States. With Dr. Jennifer Wider, she is editor of SWHR's book, *The Savvy Woman Patient: How and Why Your Sex Impacts Your Health*, a resource guide that details differences between women and men across major health areas. Ms. Greenberger is the recipient of numerous awards and serves on the Scientific Advisory Board for WomenHeart; is a board member of the Interstitial Cystitis Association; resides on the Editorial Board for *Shape* magazine; serves on the Women's Task Force for the National Hemophilia Foundation; and is a member of the International Women's Forum and the National Association of Professional Women. Ms. Greenberger received a BA from Syracuse University and an MSW from the Catholic University of America.

Jill Griffiths

Jill Griffiths is vice president of communications for Aetna. She has been with Aetna, and formerly U.S. Healthcare, for nearly 15 years. Griffiths worked on the agency side for six years before joining Aetna.

Kathleen Harrington

Kathleen Harrington currently lives in Minnesota and works for Carol Corp., a healthcare services company focused on transitioning health systems to deliver accountable care. Most of her career was in Washington, DC, where she worked in Congress, the executive branch, the healthcare trade association, and the private sector. Her last federal assignment was as director of external affairs at the Centers of Medicare and Medicaid Services where she led the national campaign to educate and enroll Medicare beneficiaries in the new Part D prescription drug benefit. In addition she served two cabinet members, Secretary of Labor Elizabeth Dole as an assistant secretary for Government Relations, and Secretary of Labor Elaine Chao as assistant secretary of Public Affairs. Her congressional career includes service as Chief of Staff for Congresswoman Nancy L. Johnson (R-CT). She also worked in government relations and public affairs for Aetna and United Healthcare. She received her bachelor's degree from Colgate University and her master's degree from Catholic University of America.

Mary V. Hornig

Mary V. Hornig is currently the vice president, Finance and Operations, for the Society for Women's Health Research (SWHR). She came to SWHR from McGuiness and Yager, LLP, where she served as chief of staff and was responsible for the day-to-day operations and finances of both the law firm and the HR Policy Association. Previously, she was the executive director of the American Coal Foundation, the director of membership and marketing for the School Nutrition Association, and the assistant corporate secretary to the American Gas Association.

Ms. Hornig has been an association professional for over 25 years and brings significant board, governance, membership, operations, and financial management experience to SWHR. She received her BA from Cornell University and an MPA from the Ohio State University. Ms. Hornig is a member of ASAE (American Society of Association Executives), SHRM (Society for Human Resource Management), and the Finance & Administration Roundtable.

Jeff Levine

Former network TV journalist Jeff Levine is now running his own firm, JBL Media Consulting, which specializes in healthcare clients. In 1980, Mr. Levine was one of the original members of the team that launched CNN's 24-hour news venture. For the next 18 years, Mr. Levine held a number of positions at the network including correspondent in San Francisco, bureau chief in Chicago and Jerusalem, and lead medical reporter in Washington for nearly nine years. During that period Mr. Levine covered many major stories including the emerging AIDS epidemic, the Clinton healthcare reform plan, the race to map the human genome, presidential health, and the debate over tobacco regulation. After leaving CNN, Mr. Levine began consulting for top-tier healthcare clients and nonprofit organizations providing advice for drug approval initiatives, high-impact crisis situations, and social marketing campaigns. Mr. Levine has also been a featured speaker for the American Medical Association, America's Health Insurance Plans (AHIP), Prudential Insurance, Gallaudet University, and The George Washington University School of Medicine and Health. He lives in Rockville, Maryland, and is married to Susan Levine, and they have two sons.

Dennis McCulloch

A veteran of more than 35 years in news and communications, Dennis McCulloch has had a successful career in television news, public relations, politics, and government.

After graduation from the University of Missouri with a journalism degree, the writer worked 10 years as a television news producer at four stations. Mr. McCulloch served in communications and political roles in two statewide campaigns in the 1980s in Missouri. After those campaigns, he served a variety of roles when Sprint was first formed in Kansas City, starting in 1986.

Mr. McCulloch joined the Kansas City office of Fleishman-Hillard in 1989. In the next eleven and a half years, Mr. McCulloch developed a national client list for crisis counseling, public affairs, and media training, rising to vice president and head of the Public Issues Division. Among his national clients were BASF, Ocean Spray, Pioneer, Hallmark, Continental Grain, and Laidlaw.

In 2000, Mr. McCulloch joined a longtime client, The University of Kansas Hospital, as director of public and government relations. He led a strategic campaign to maintain hospital status as the region's premier academic medical center when a threat to that status was launched.

Mr. McCulloch also led a strategic media relations approach which helped lift the hospital's public image and consumer choice. He served as spokesperson during critical times for the hospital. Mr. McCulloch's tenure coincides with a dramatic turnaround for the hospital in terms of quality, patient satisfaction, and national rankings.

Jeffrey L. Molter

Jeffrey L. Molter is associate vice president for Health Sciences Communications at Emory University. In this position, he is responsible for overseeing publications, media relations, and special events programming for the health sciences center. Mr. Molter was director of the Duke University Medical Center and Health Systems News Office in Durham, North Carolina, from 2000 to 2006. He was responsible for all media and public relations for the institution. Prior to his work at Duke, Mr. Molter served as director of science news for the *Journal of the American Medical Association* in Chicago for 10 years. There he directed the weekly promotion of the medical journal and produced media briefings on a number of health issues for the AMA. Mr. Molter came to *JAMA* from the American Academy of Pediatrics in Elk Grove Village, Illinois, where he was director of communications for seven years. He began his career as a newspaper reporter in Indiana. He is a graduate of the Indiana University School of Journalism. He has lectured extensively throughout North America on a number of medical and health issues, and has received awards from several groups, including the Association of American Medical Colleges, PR Week, Public Relations Society of America, International Association of Business Communicators, and the Publicity Club of Chicago.

Jeff Nelligan

Jeff Nelligan has spent nearly two decades in the legislative and executive branch working on healthcare, budget, and tax issues. This extends from service with Congressmen Bill Thomas on the House Ways and Means and Budget Committees during consideration of the 1988 Medicare Catastrophic Coverage Act, to his tenure at the U.S. Government Accountability Office, where he served as managing director of public affairs for U.S. Comptroller General David Walker during consideration of the Medicare Modernization Act of 2003. Mr. Nelligan has worked in three cabinet departments and was the Bush administration spokesman for Medicare and Medicaid at the U.S. Department of Health and Human Services. There, he helped plan and execute national outreach on Medicare's Part D Prescription Drug enrollment effort, and campaigns on prevention and electronic health records. He's a graduate of Williams College and Georgetown University Law Center, served 14 years in the U.S. Army Reserves/Army National Guard, and is involved with his three sons in youth lacrosse.

Kristin Paulina

Kristin Paulina is a public relations specialist with 15 years experience developing and implementing communications campaigns that successfully meet objectives and deliver results for a broad range of organizations, including consumer services, health care, and nonprofit/advocacy. For the last 10 years, she has assisted Sam Brown, Inc., a public and investor relations firm with strategic public relations initiatives, corporate brand positioning, and media relations for its diverse blend of pharmaceutical and biotechnology clients. Ms. Paulina earned a Bachelor of Arts degree in Communication/Journalism with an emphasis in public relations from Shippensburg University. She is also a member of the Public Relations Society of America.

Douglas Petkus

Douglas Petkus is an award-winning communications professional with a diverse range of experience in editorial, agency, and corporate environments, and a demonstrated ability to manage and resolve complex crises and issues on a 24/7 global basis. He has deep expertise in providing executive strategic counsel and developing effective, comprehensive programs in media relations, marketing communications/product publicity, issues management, litigation communications, and employee communications. His career has been focused on healthcare communications (Rx and OTC), with added experience with food and beverage products, as well as sports and entertainment special events. Currently, Mr. Petkus is the president of Petkus Communications Consultants, LLC, a PR consultancy specializing in senior-level strategic communications counsel.

Prior to starting up his consulting firm, Mr. Petkus was vice president, Business and Financial Communications at Wyeth (acquired by Pfizer in October 2009). In this role, he directed the corporate financial/business communications function and developed the strategies to reach top-tier business media. Working across all Wyeth Divisions, he acted as the primary company spokesperson and coordinated all aspects of corporate media relations, issues management, and litigation communications. Preceding this, as vice president of Global Public Relations at Wyeth Pharmaceuticals, he led the management of all communications programs supporting commercial products and R&D organization within the company's pharmaceutical division, acted as the primary media spokesperson, and led teams handling major issues including drug litigation, negative clinical studies, product recalls/withdrawals, and regulatory affairs.

Before joining the Wyeth organization Mr. Petkus built his pharma/healthcare communications/public relations experience at blue chip corporations, including Abbott Laboratories and Schering-Plough (since acquired by Merck).

In his earlier career, Mr. Petkus was an anchorman for a local TV station in Wisconsin and progressed to several stops at well known advertising and public relations agencies in New York City, including Hill and Knowlton, Inc., where he managed accounts for major global client companies in the pharmaceutical and consumer product industries.

Richard A. Puff

Richard A. Puff is assistant vice president for Academic Health Center Public Relations at the University of Cincinnati in Cincinnati, Ohio. He directs the overall external and internal communications of the University of Cincinnati Academic Health Center. With 25 years experience in academic medicine communications, he previously served as associate director of the Medical Center News Office at Duke University Medical Center & Health System in Durham, North Carolina, and associate director of public relations at Albany Medical Center in Albany, New York. Mr. Puff also has worked as a newspaper reporter for two upstate New York dailies and in the publishing industry, producing numerous baseball titles.

Mr. Puff was a key member of the team that coordinated communications efforts following a heart/lung transplant mismatch at Duke in February 2003, which resulted in international news coverage. For those efforts, he and his colleagues were named winners of the 2004 PR NEWS Platinum PR Award in the Crisis Management category and finalists in the Media Relations category. The communications team also received an Award of Excellence from the Association of American Medical Colleges (AAMC) and an Innovation Honorable Mention Award for Crisis Communications from the Public Relations Society of America (PRSA) Health Academy.

An active member of the Association of American Medical Colleges (AAMC), Mr. Puff has served on the steering committee of the AAMC Group on Institutional Advancement and has been a judge for the group's annual communications awards competition.

A graduate of Utica College of Syracuse University with a degree in public relations and journalism, Mr. Puff has also pursued graduate studies at Rensselaer Polytechnic Institute in Troy, New York.

Kathleen Donohue Rennie

Kathleen Donohue Rennie is a partner in the McGraw Group, an integrated marketing communications firm based in Morristown, New Jersey. Dr. Rennie specializes in integrated marketing communications strategy, media relations, and editorial services. She researches, writes, and edits press materials, Web sites, annual reports, newsletters, video scripts, corporate presentations, e-communication, and more. She has taught public relations, advertising, and writing at the undergraduate and graduate levels. Dr. Rennie has a Master of Arts degree in corporate and public communications and is an accredited public relations counselor. Dr. Rennie holds a PhD and wrote her dissertation on crisis communication.

Elizabeth Sell

Elizabeth Sell is Director of Communications, Direct to Consumer and Product Group at Aetna, where she has worked since 1997. She spent two years at public relations agencies prior to joining Aetna.

Lisa M. Tate

Lisa M. Tate has enjoyed a career of more than 25 years in public affairs, healthcare advocacy, and non-profit management. Since being appointed CEO of WomenHeart: the National

Coalition for Women with Heart Disease in 2007, she has lead the organization's re-branding, increased revenue by one-third, tripled the number of community-based patient support networks in operation, doubled membership bringing it to 40,000, and increased volunteer engagement and satisfaction–the key to WomenHeart's success.

Prior to joining WomenHeart, Lisa served as Vice President, Public Affairs for the National Association of Children's Hospitals and Related Institutions. In this role she directed the association's communications, public relations, grassroots, and child advocacy programs. During her tenure, NACHRI's public affairs programming received distinctions including a Telcon Award for the Most Outstanding Broadcast for the Public Good, for a National Town Meeting on Expanding Children's Health Insurance Coverage, and an award of excellence from the American Society of Association Executives for advocacy campaigns.

Prior to joining NACHRI, Lisa managed public affairs programs for the American Academy of Pediatrics and co-founded the national Coalition for America's Children. Today, Lisa serves on the board of the Public Affairs Council, the national organization of corporate public affairs executives. She recently received The First Ladies of Distinction Visionary Award from the YWCA of Metropolitan Washington, DC She received a degree in journalism from the University of North Carolina, Chapel Hill and resides on Capitol Hill with her husband, Ragnar, and two children.

William A. Tatum

William A. Tatum is Director, Constituent Relations and Membership, at Partnership for Prevention. Prior to coming to Partnership, Mr. Tatum worked as a government relations assistant at the Alliance for Aging Research. During his tenure at the Alliance, he worked closely with the government relations manager to analyze data on geriatric policy, long-term care, and current aging issues. He also served as the National Institutes of Health Task Force Report copy editor and editor of the 2005 White House Conference on Aging research resolution. Mr. Tatum began his professional career as a lobbyist for the Consortium of Social Science Association. In this role, he monitored legislation and appropriations for the Centers for Disease Control and Prevention, Agency for Health Care Research and Quality, Assistant Secretary for Planning and Evaluation, and the National Institute of Justice. He received a BA in government and politics from the University of Maryland and an MA in government from the Johns Hopkins University.

Roba Whitely

Roba Whitely is executive director of Together Rx Access, a program that provides Americans without prescription drug coverage meaningful savings at the pharmacy counter. Ms. Whitely has dedicated her life's work to ensuring that people have access to the best in health care. Throughout her 25-year career, she has been a powerful advocate for the development and delivery of innovative healthcare solutions. In July 2004, Ms. Whitely became executive director of Together Rx, the nation's most widely enrolled private prescription savings program for lower-income Medicare beneficiaries, with nearly 1.5 million cardholders. Together Rx has helped seniors save more than $700 million on prescription medicines to date. As vice president of marketing and communications with the National Council on the Aging, Ms. Whitely enhanced the organization's strategic partnerships, healthcare initiatives, and health-focused media campaigns. Her collaborative efforts with government agencies and other stakeholder groups increased awareness of key issues linked to aging in America. Prior to joining Together Rx, Ms. Whitely served as executive director of Project Patient Care. Under her leadership, Project Patient Care conducted a study on how formulary drug substitutions affect elderly patient outcomes. Results of this research helped to inform the ongoing debate with providers and policy makers about this important issue. Ms. Whitely holds a master's degree in nutrition science from Drexel University.

Chapter 1

The Growth of Health Communications—A Story of Consumer Power and Medical Innovation

By Nancy J. Hicks

LEARNING OBJECTIVES

By the end of this chapter, the reader will be able to:

- Describe the role of the communications specialist in aiding the growth of the healthcare industry over the last half century in the United States.
- Explain how societal trends, as well as a changing media landscape, increased public awareness of health conditions and changed public attitudes towards the sharing of information about personal health issues.
- Provide an example of the shift from a national focus on care for the acutely ill to wellness.
- Describe the paradigm shift from a physician-centric to a consumer-centric healthcare system.
- Describe the role of the Internet in fueling healthcare consumerism.
- Discuss the effect patient advocacy groups have on building public awareness and influencing healthcare reform.

Introduction

Health care represents one sixth of the US economy and touches every aspect of our lives. We are living longer and better today than at any time in history. In the 1940s life expectancy was 65.7 years; today it is 77.7 years (National Center for Health Statistics, 2007). Rates for the top three leading causes of death—heart disease, cancer, and stroke—continue a long-term decreasing trend. Innovations in the science and delivery of health care have made this possible. It is an amazing story, and communications professionals are at the fulcrum of this story.

The Growth of the Profession

Communications as a function has long been integral in the healthcare industry. From the mid-1900s, hospitals were staffed with professionals who issued patient condition reports and the occasional news release about a new facility. Pharmaceutical companies similarly used communications consultants or in-house staff to announce the approval of new drugs.

Yet the growth and importance of communications in the healthcare industry has been most dramatic over the past 30 years. As opposed to the lone public relations man or woman, who often had human resources responsibilities as well, we now have large staffs in a sophisticated marketing matrix of public relations, advertising, and digital communications at major health systems. Healthcare companies that used to only have investor relations now have extensive staffs for brand and corporate communications.

Consulting companies have mushroomed in the past decade in response to industry demand. The Kennedy Consulting and Research Advisory noted that healthcare consulting is one of the few areas of growth, expected to grow at 5.3% through 2012 (Kennedy Consulting Research & Advisory, 2009). Major consulting companies such as Booz Allen Hamilton, PriceWaterhouseCoopers, and Accenture all have thriving healthcare practices.

Healthcare has long been a staple in public relations firms, but the specialty grew dramatically in the 1980s and 1990s. Most international firms such as Ketchum, Burson-Marsteller, and Edelman have large healthcare practices with a significant portion of the firms' revenues coming from healthcare clients. Within the practice of health care, there are professionals in health policy, social media, and other specialties. It is a function with depth and breadth in every major public relations firm.

In addition to the rise of health care in public relations, the 1980s and 1990s saw growth in medical advertising. In the 1970s that term would have been an oxymoron. Hospitals and physicians looked askance at advertising as beneath their professional standards. With the advent of the prospective payment system of Medicare in 1984, the age of hospital advertising began. Providers found that certain service lines, such as women's health care, were more profitable under the new reimbursement system. They reached out to consumers with advertising to tout these service lines. Advertising is now a substantial part of every hospital marketing budget.

Australia and the United States are the only countries that allow direct-to-consumer (DTC) advertising of drug products. In the United States, this began in 1997 and has been a source of great profit as well as great controversy for the pharmaceutical industry. To detractors, the ads propel consumers to seek drugs they don't need; to proponents, DTC advertising educates consumers and empowers them with information. Regardless of where one stands on the issue, there is no denying the economic impact of DTC advertising. Spending on DTC advertising increased from $220 million in 1997 to over $2.8 billion by 2002 (Sheehan, 2003). It appears this was a good investment for the pharmaceutical industry as the prescription rates of DTC drugs increased by 34% compared to a 5.1% increase in other drugs (Sheehan, 2003).

The first decade of the millennium saw an acceleration of public relations "boutique" firms that catered only to healthcare clients. Often these firms developed from expertise with the biotech sector, mirroring a repeated theme in this story—communications growing in tandem with growth in the industry. The development of biologically based drugs and the rise of companies like Amgen and Genentech is one of the great stories of medical science.

The world of academia has enjoyed a growth spurt in healthcare communications comparable to that of private industry. Thirty years ago most university communications programs did not even mention health care, let alone focus on it. Today there are 50 graduate schools that offer degrees in "health communications" (GradSchools.com, 2010). These are some of the nation's most preeminent institutions including the University of Southern California (USC) Annenberg School of Communication; Tufts University School of Medicine; Harvard University Graduate School of Arts and Sciences; and Boston University College of Communication. These universities often have alliances with private firms on communications initiatives. For example, USC Annenberg School of Communications partners each year with Ketchum on the "Media: Myths and Realities" survey.

Media Mirrors the Health Story

News organizations mirror the growth and diversity in healthcare communications. From the sole newspaper health reporter of the 1970s, who also covered sports, to the depth of seasoned health reporters at every major daily, healthcare reporting is one of the most specialized areas of journalism. According the Association of Health Care Journalists, there are over 1000 healthcare reporters in the United States (Association of Health Care Journalists, 2011). Despite the cuts in newspapers throughout the country, healthcare news coverage remains strong with online outlets supplementing traditional print and broadcast coverage. According to Technorati, there are an estimated 20,000 healthcare blogs, with such prominent journalists as Tara Parker-Pope and Katherine Hobson contributing well-read blogs in addition to print columns.

Every decade has yielded big headlines in the world of health—in the 1950s we learned the Salk vaccine would eradicate polio; President Nixon announced the war on cancer in the early 1970s, ushering in an era of progress and setbacks against this disease; the 1980s saw the first artificial heart and the advent of a new disease called AIDS. This millennium, with the human genome mapped in the 1990s, has given us the age of personalized medicine and the debut of blockbuster drugs like Avastin and Herceptin.

Perhaps nothing illustrates how communications has developed in health care than the coverage of some of these stories. In 1982, Dr. William DeVries implanted the world's first artificial heart, named the Jarvik-7 after its inventor Dr. Robert Jarvik. The recipient was a retired dentist named Barney Clark. For 112 days, the world followed the progress of Mr. Clark until his death. There were frequent press conferences throughout this period with both Dr. DeVries and Dr. Jarvik. Heart transplants continued with the next recipient living 620 days. Despite international headlines and repeated broadcast coverage, only 7% of Americans had heard of the Jarvik-7 heart by 1983 (http://www.jarvikheart.com/basic.asp?id=69). This can largely be attributed to a news era that did not have 24/7 cable and online coverage, and far less outlets for health news.

To see how news coverage has changed, you need only to look at the story of the conjoined twins, Trisha and Krishna, one of the biggest news stories of 2009. The twins, from an orphanage in Bangladesh, were separated in a 32-hour operation by a surgical team at the Royal Children's Hospital in Melbourne, Australia. The successful surgery drew worldwide attention and continues to do so as media organizations follow the girls' progress. Google news, not available in Jarvik's time, cites over 148,000 results with more than 14,000 news stories about the twins. Health news today is magnified in ways that were not possible just a generation ago.

Diseases Come Out of the Closet

The evolution of healthcare communications was fueled not only by stunning advances in medical science but by societal trends that brought an openness to once whispered diseases and a move from sick care to wellness.

It is hard to believe in an era where ads about erectile dysfunction fill the airwaves, but 30 years ago many health conditions were deemed "too personal" to discuss publicly. In the early 1970s, Betty Ford was widely praised for openly discussing her breast cancer. News organizations covered such topics with great reluctance and only when a well-known person was involved.

The shift in more openness toward diseases and conditions considered highly personal came about from the changing mores of the 1960s and 1970s with a "let it all hang out" philosophy. Even though the times favored more candor about health, these "silent" conditions would never have found a voice without effective communications campaigns.

Incontinence came out of the closet in the early 1990s. This condition, which affects millions of Americans, was never mentioned publicly, and a Yankelovich poll found that women would take, on average, 7 years to even discuss it with a physician. The condition has devastating quality-of-life consequences, yet treatments were unknown to the public.

In 1995, Bard Urological Division partnered with the American Urological Association to create Bladder Health Week and launch a landmark public education campaign on stress urinary incontinence.

The campaign received extensive media coverage, and more than one television anchor said, "This is an important issue. It's about time we're talking about it." This campaign, and others that followed, changed public attitudes about incontinence.

As new treatments for incontinence became available, drug companies created a new lexicon for clinical terms. *Urge incontinence* became *overactive bladder*, and DTC ads made this term widely used by patients. By 2004, there were five drugs on the market for overactive bladder. When Novartis was about to introduce Enablex, the sixth drug for this condition, it was clear that a creative campaign was needed to reach consumers and position the drug in a crowded market.

Ketchum worked with Novartis and the National Association for Continence to create an award-winning campaign that focused on the needs of people with incontinence who liked to travel. Research revealed that many people suffering from this condition were reluctant to travel. Enlisting travel guru Arthur Frommer, the "Where to Stop, Where to Go" campaign was launched, including a guide to well-kept restrooms in various travel destinations.

The guide was so popular that many people without the condition sought copies. The campaign generated more than 24,200 guide requests via Web site and toll-free line in just 8 months, produced a 961% increase in call volume to the Novartis Customer Interaction Center compared to precampaign levels, and stimulated a 318% increase in unique visitors to the product site, Enablex.com, compared to precampaign levels.

The campaign achieved the awareness objectives of Novartis—more than 104 million media impressions—and was another milestone in removing the stigma from incontinence.

Many other diseases, such as irritable bowel syndrome (IBS) and colon cancer, have been destigmatized by public education campaigns. The fact that Katie Couric could have a colonoscopy live on television demonstrates how far we have come in dealing openly with once unmentioned health conditions.

Health Care Becomes "Well Care"

Just as communications professionals were instrumental in opening the closet of health care, they played a major role in ushering in an era of wellness.

We so take for granted the prominence of wellness in health care that it is hard to imagine a time where this wasn't ascendant. Yet for many years our healthcare system was a sick care system. The great thrust of medical science and our highly evolved healthcare delivery system was aimed at managing acute care. Health care was all about "fixing" what was broken, not preventing that breakage.

Health maintenance organizations (HMOs), formed in the 1940s, pioneered disease prevention and wellness programs as part of their mandate to keep patients as healthy as possible.

These group health organizations were often dismissed as "group death" by the medical establishment of the 1950s and 1960s who only saw value in the sick care model.

The wellness revolution had its roots in a generational shift in values. Baby boomers coming of age in the 1970s rejected their parents' sedentary lifestyles and embraced physical activity and better nutrition. You only have to watch television's "Mad Men," where harried advertising executives in the early 1960s chain-smoked, drank three-martini lunches, and only ran to catch a train to see how far we have come in valuing wellness.

Many landmark education campaigns such as the American Cancer Society's Great American Smoke-Out were responsible for changing health behaviors. Healthcare providers were key to promoting healthy behaviors as well. Most hospitals by the 1980s were offering smoking cessation programs, stress management, and nutrition classes.

The battleship of health care was beginning the slow turn from sick care to well care. By 2004, Kaiser Permanente had launched a $40 million advertising campaign called "Thrive" (Kaiser Permanente, 2004). This landmark campaign with its emphasis on preventive care is credited with significantly building the Kaiser brand and for pioneering a new approach in healthcare advertising.

Just as consumers were taking more responsibility for their own health and providers were seeing an increasing role to help them in that process, mainstream medicine was morphing in a new direction. Alternative medicine was always popular with consumers, especially those not satisfied with conventional treatments, but it was looked down upon by the medical establishment for decades. Driven largely by consumer demand, as well as a growing body of medical knowledge, this began to change most noticeably in the 1990s.

By October 1998 the National Institutes of Health had established a National Center for Complementary and Integrative Medicine to address the increasing interest in wellness-promoting activities that are not typically addressed in conventional medical care. In the center's 2007 survey, 3.1 million adults reported using acupuncture, up from 2.1 million in 2002. Between 2002 and 2007, acupuncture use among adults increased by three-tenths of 1% (approximately 1 million people) (Centers for Disease Control and Prevention, 2007). Even the venerable Mayo Clinic had established a Complementary and Integrative Medicine Program by 2001.

The degree to which Americans embrace disease prevention and wellness is reflected in a 2009 survey conducted by the Trust for America's Health and the Robert Wood Johnson Foundation. This survey on attitudes about healthcare reform revealed Americans ranked prevention as the most important reform priority and overwhelmingly supported increased funding for programs to reduce disease and keep people healthy (Trust for America's Health, 2009).

A remarkable transformation had occurred. A country that was once indifferent to maintaining good health was now embracing it with a vengeance. By the end of 2010, more than $1 trillion dollars was spent by consumers on wellness products (Pilzer, 2007). This sea change was brought about by many factors—societal trends, medical advances—but indisputably health communications propelled wellness into a whole new level of consciousness with the American public.

Growth of Consumerism Fueled by the Internet

If communications accelerated with big developments in medical science—diagnostic and surgical innovations, personalized medicine, and blockbuster drugs—it was spurred on by a trend at least as big: the rise of the healthcare consumer.

It is hard to overstate this phenomenon and how it has affected the healthcare system. For the majority of the 1900s, consumers were passive players while physicians dominated all phases of healthcare decision making. From treatment to hospital choice, the physician voice was dominant. Patients did as they were told by their physicians, knew little about prescribed treatments, and rarely questioned them if they did.

By the end of the millennium this paradigm was changing dramatically. Fed by the Internet and multiple news outlets, consumers had access to medical information that was unprecedented. Internet sites like WebMD, launched in 1999, provided information on health and health care, including a symptom checklist, pharmacy information, blogs of physicians on specific topics, and a place to store personal information. This site received over 17.1 million average monthly unique visitors in 2007, and today it is the leading health portal in the United States (comScore, 2010). Today there are more than 200 million sites on health care including more than 19,000 health policy blogs.

Seventy-nine percent of Internet users have searched online for information on at least one major health topic, according to the Pew Internet & American Life Project. That translates to about 95 million American adults who use the Internet to find health information. Certain groups of Internet users are the most likely to have sought health information online: women, Internet users younger than age 65, college graduates, those with more online experience, and those with broadband access (Fox, 2005).

The growth of social media has further fueled outlets for health communications. Surveys indicate that 60% of Americans turn to the Internet first when seeking health-related information. At least half of this group uses social networks to consult one another on symptoms, diagnoses, and treatments. Despite the popularity of these sites, health industry groups have been slow to embrace social media. The drug industry allocated less than 4% of the $4 billion spent on direct-to-consumer (DTC) advertising to Internet outlets in 2008, and only a small portion of that was for social networking sites (Arnst, 2009).

The reasons for this "late adopter" stance can be traced to regulatory challenges with social media. Since pharmaceutical and medical device companies are required to report "adverse events" to the US Food and Drug Administration (FDA), there is a reluctance to engage in sites where there is potential for false reporting, as well as the appearance of off-label marketing. In 2009, there was an FDA public hearing on social media, which was seen as the first step toward developing regulatory guidelines for social networking sites.

In 2003, a survey of US doctors showed that 85% of patients brought the health information they gathered on the Internet to appointments (Murray, Lo, Pollack, Donelan, Catania, Lee, et al, 2003). Patients were now empowered to be active participants in their own health care.

Sometimes the instant availability of information outpaced the ability of physicians to receive medical news before their patients. In 2002, the National Institutes of Health released a long anticipated study on women and hormones. The *JAMA* publication was embargoed, but news of the study, linking hormones to a higher rate of breast cancer, leaked out to news outlets before physicians could read about the study in the journal. Many physicians were caught by surprise as worried women patients called them about the study.

Physicians are also increasingly getting their information online. Instead of reading print journals, according to a Manhattan Research Study, they are spending an average of 8 hours a week seeking professional information online. In addition, 60% of physicians use such online physician communities as Sermo or WebMD's Medscape Physician Connect (Manhattan Research, 2010).

The online revolution in health care has had profound implications for the way communicators reach consumers and professional audiences. There is no longer the distinction between old media (print, broadcast) and new media (online). Communications strategists see only "media." Top-tier print media like the *New York Times* and the *Wall Street Journal* all have widely read healthcare blogs. News placements on these sites now carry the same clout that was once reserved for national print and broadcast.

Patient Groups—Hear Them Roar

One of the most dramatic and far-reaching effects of the rise in consumerism can be seen in patient advocacy. In 1981 the first patient in the United States died of what would become known as acquired immune deficiency syndrome or AIDS. For much of the 1980s and early 1990s the diagnosis of this condition was a death sentence with thousands of men and women losing their lives.

Because the condition in the early years largely affected gay men, there was little impetus for a health policy level to find effective treatments. Gay men and their supporters mobilized, and through such groups as AIDS Coalition to Unleash Power (ACT UP) they demanded new treatments and resources for people living with AIDS. Ryan White was also a changing force in mobilizing AIDS activists.

A teenage hemophiliac, White became infected with HIV from a contaminated blood treatment and, when diagnosed in December 1984, was given 6 months to live. Doctors said he posed no risk to other students, but AIDS was poorly understood at the time, and when White tried to return to school, many parents and teachers rallied against his attendance. A lengthy legal battle with the school system ensued, and media coverage of the case made White into a national celebrity and spokesman for AIDS research and public education. He appeared frequently in the media with celebrities such as Elton John, Michael Jackson, and Phil Donahue.

Before White, AIDS was a disease widely associated with the male homosexual community, because it was first diagnosed there. That perception shifted as White and other prominent

HIV-infected people, such as Magic Johnson, appeared in the media to advocate for more AIDS research and public education to address the epidemic. The US Congress passed a major piece of AIDS legislation, the Ryan White Care Act, shortly after White's death. The act was reauthorized in 2006 and again on October 30, 2009. Ryan White Programs are the largest provider of services for people living with HIV/AIDS in the United States. They succeeded in moving this disease to much greater prominence on the healthcare agenda.

Companies like Bristol Meyers Squibb (BMS) and Gilead developed combination therapy drugs that halted the course of the disease. Today HIV infection can be managed like a chronic condition. It is no longer a death sentence; many individuals with HIV are living long and healthy lives. The most dramatic drops in both cases and deaths began in 1996, with the widespread use of combination antiretroviral therapy (Centers for Disease Control and Prevention, 2008).

During 2006 there were an estimated 28 pediatric AIDS diagnoses, compared to 195 in 1999 and 896 in 1992.(18) The decline in pediatric AIDS incidence is associated with more HIV testing of pregnant women and the use of antiretroviral drugs such as zidovudine (AZT) by HIV-infected pregnant women and their newborn infants.

Communications campaigns, like the CDC's multiyear campaign on prevention, as well as advocacy campaigns aimed at the policy level on drug reimbursement and other issues, changed the face of AIDS in this country.

Just as advocacy changed the course of HIV/AIDS, a similar trajectory was occurring with breast cancer. The number one cancer affecting women with nearly 500,000 lives lost each year, this disease did not have the industry profile or policy "urgency" that matched its devastating impact on women (World Health Organization, 2011). In 1982, Nancy Brinker founded the Susan G. Komen Foundation, named after her sister who died of breast cancer.

With the pink ribbons, Race for the Cure, and other events, the Komen Foundation put breast cancer front and center on the health issues map. Komen has raised over $1.5 billion for research, education, and health services, making it the largest breast cancer charity and private funding source for breast health and breast cancer in the world (Credo, 2009).

Today, the Komen organization is recognized as the leading catalyst in the fight against breast cancer, with more than 100,000 volunteers working in a network of 125 US and international affiliates (Eurekalert, 2009). Since 1982, Komen has awarded more than 1,000 breast cancer research grants totaling more than $180 million. Their advocacy and funds raised for research spurred the development of new treatments and prompted women to seek breast exams (Komen Grants & Awards, 2010).

Health advocacy groups have changed the face of many diseases and of legislative priorities in Congress. The Society for Women's Health Research (SWHR), founded by Dr. Florence Hazeltine, is credited with gaining parity for women in studies funded by the National Institutes of Health. Prior to SWHR's advocacy, most clinical trials of new drugs focused only on men.

Communications is at the heart of all of these advocacy groups. They had a story to tell, and in telling that story they have changed the landscape of health care.

New World: Science Breakthroughs, Boomer Tsunami, and Health Reform

If the dazzling developments in the world of health and the parallel rise of healthcare communications were not spectacular enough over the past 50 years, what is to come may outpace all of that.

Innovations in medical science, an aging population creating an unprecedented demand for health services, and the complexities of a new US healthcare system will put a premium on the value of healthcare communications.

Developments in medical technology such as gene mapping, personalized medicine, and "precision" drugs such as Fanapt, the schizophrenia drug that can target patients in whom the treatment will be most effective, open up new horizons in medical care.

Yet with these new horizons come issues of ethics and access. With the potential of gene mapping for diseases, how will patient privacy be protected, and how will this information be used in a way that does not discriminate against the patient? How will we guarantee that life-saving but extremely expensive therapies such as bone marrow transplants are available to all of our citizens? As a society we must come to grips with the ethical and policy dilemmas that advances in medical science have brought us.

Coupled with these treatment innovations, the aging of the population presents a clear challenge to our healthcare delivery system. The baby boomers will put unprecedented demands on the healthcare system. An estimated 77 million people were born between 1946 and 1964, which is defined as the baby boom era (US Census, 2005–2009). The first baby boomer turned 60 on January 1, 2006 (US Census, 2005–2009). An American turns 50 every 7 seconds—that is more than 12,500 people every day (US Census, 2005–2009). By 2015, those aged 50 and older will represent 45% of the US population, according to the AARP. By 2030, the 65-plus population will double to about 71.5 million, and by 2050 it will grow to 86.7 million people (US Census, 2005–2009).

According to a recent report by Mintel, this age group is among the most health-conscious of consumers, seeking ways to maintain vitality and wellness. Boomers place a high value on optimal health and spend annually more than $200 million on nutritional supplements and other consumer health products. In the next 10 years, US baby boomers will increase their annual spending on wellness-based services from approximately $200 million today to $1 trillion (Mintel, 2007).

They expect to live longer and healthier than previous generations and will put a huge strain on the healthcare system in doing so. Pharmaceutical and consumer health companies, device makers, and providers will be reaching out with customized communications to sell products and services to boomers.

In March 2010, the Patient Protection and Affordable Care Act was passed; it is the biggest piece of social legislation in the United States since Medicare. This law will fundamentally change the landscape of health care, affording new protections for consumers and offering sharp regulations to the insurance industry. This 2400-page law that affects one sixth of the

US economy requires skilled communications to clarify what the complex provisions mean to ordinary Americans.

A 2010 Kaiser Family Foundation poll cited that 55% of US residents are "confused" by the new health reform law, and 56% say they are unsure how the law will affect them. Exacerbating this is a timeline in which some of the most substantive parts of the bill, like the state insurance exchanges, will not be implemented until 2014 (www.kff.org/kaiserpolls/upload/8075-F.pdf, 2010). Adding to the confusion is a plethora of misperceptions about the law that are a result of the highly polarized political debate.

There are few things Americans care about as much as their health care, and close attention will be paid to all phases of the new law's implementation. Communications professionals in the healthcare industry will be called on to cut through the confusion with clear facts about the law and its impact on all stakeholders. Timely and accurate information will play a huge role in the law's success. Communications professionals have an opportunity to help their fellow citizens navigate this historic piece of legislation.

Summary

From a minor player in the healthcare industry a half century ago, to front and center of today's issues, health communications have become indispensible to the world we live in. Today health communication specialists play a variety of roles, including, but not limited to, developing health prevention and promotion campaigns, serving as advocates for patient and consumer groups, educating members of Congress about health issues, handling health crises, and developing integrated communication campaigns for healthcare corporate clients. With an expanding marketplace for healthcare products and services, a growing population in need of education and care, and an evolving media landscape that can be leveraged to connect them, the future is healthy for health communication specialists.

Discussion Questions

1. What is spurring the growth in the number of graduate schools offering degrees in health communications?
2. Explain the shift from the nation's focus on sick care to wellness. What was at the root of this shift?
3. How has the rise of Internet affected the way communicators reach healthcare consumers and professionals?
4. What will be an effect of the aging baby boomer generation on the healthcare industry?
5. What is the Patient Protection and Health Care Affordability Law? Look it up online, and describe how this law will affect you in the next 5 years.

References

AARP cited US Census data.

Arnst, C. A. (2009). Why drugmakers don't Twitter. *Businessweek*. November 19. Available at: http://www.businessweek.com/magazine/content/09_48/b4157064827269.htm. Accessed: March 4, 2011.

Association of Health Care Journalists. (2011). About AHCJ. Available at: http://www.healthjournalism.org/about-jump.php. Accessed: March 4, 2011.

Centers for Disease Control and Prevention. (2007). *National Health Interview Survey (NHIS)*. Atlanta, GA: CDC.

Centers for Disease Control and Prevention. (2008). HIV prevalence estimates—United States, 2006. *Morbidity and Mortality Weekly Report*, 3 October. 57(39);1073–1076.

comScore. *Media Metrix*.

Eurekalert.org. (2009). *Nancy Brinker to receive 2009 Porter Prize*. Available at: http://eurekalert.org/. Accessed: March 4, 2011.

Fabel, L. (2009, April 24). Credo: Nancy Goodman Brinker. *Washington Examiner*. Available at: http://washingtonexaminer.com/local/2009/04/credo-nancy-goodman-brinker.

Fox, S. (2005). *Health information online*. Pew Internet & American Life Project. Available at: http://www.pewinternet.org/Reports/2005/Health-Information-Online.aspx Accessed: March 4, 2011.

GradSchools.com. *Health communications graduate programs*.

http://www.jarvikheart.com/basic.asp?id=69. Accessed: September 2010.

Kennedy Consulting Research & Advisory. *Healthcare consulting marketplace 2009–2012*.

Komen Grants & Awards. Susan G. Komen for the Cure official page. Available at: http://cms.komen.org/komen/GrantsAwards/index.htm Accessed: March 4, 2011.

Manhattan Research. (29). Physician online communities: Physician social networking and the new online opinion leaders. January.

May, T. (2004, January 23). Kaiser Permanente will launch $40M image campaign. *Pacific Business News*. Available at: http://www.bizjournals.com/pacific/stories/2004/01/26/story5.html Accessed: March 4, 2011.

Mintel. (2007). Spending power of baby boomers. February 1.

Murray, E., Lo, B., Pollack, L., Donelan, K., Catania, J., Lee, K., et al. (2003). The impact of health information on the Internet on health care and the physician-patient relationship: National U.S. survey among 1,050 U.S. physicians. *Journal of Medical Internet Research*. 2003;5(3):e17.

National Center for Health Statistics. Life expectancy FastStats. Available at: http://www.cdc.gov/nchs/fastats/lifexpec.htm Accessed: March 4, 2011.

Pilzer, P. Z. (2007). *The new wellness revolution: How to make a fortune in the next trillion dollar industry*. Hoboken, NJ: Wiley.

Sheehan, K. (2003). *Controversies in contemporary advertising* (p. 208). Thousand Oaks, CA: Sage Publications.

Trust for America's Health (TFAH) and the Robert Wood Johnson Foundation (RWJF). *2009 Health Reform Survey*. The following analysis is based on a national research project funded by the Robert Wood Johnson Foundation and the Trust for America's Health, and conducted jointly by Greenberg Quinlan Rosner Research and Public Opinion Strategies. The national survey of 1,014 registered voters was conducted May 7–12, 2009.

US Census U.S. Census Bureau, 2005–2009 American Community Survey.

World Health Organization. (2011). *Cancer fact sheet*. Geneva, Switzerland: World Health Organization. February 2011.

The Henry J. Kaiser Family Foundation. (2010). Kaiser Health Tracking Poll May 2010. Available at: www.kff.org/kaiserpolls/upload/8075-F.pdf. Accessed: March 4, 2011.

Chapter 2

Both Sides Now: Viewing Media through the Public Relations Prism

By Jeff Levine

LEARNING OBJECTIVES

By the end of this chapter, the reader will be able to:

- Understand and explain the codependent relationship between the media and public relations.
- Describe how the evolution of technology has affected the current media environment.
- Demonstrate how the dissemination of truth can be manipulated to serve the objectives of disparate parties.
- Understand the media opportunity during both a management crisis and a management success, and know how to leverage the media and public relations industry to maximize the opportunity to the organization's benefit.

Introduction

I've looked at life from both sides now,
From win and lose, and still somehow
It's life's illusions I recall.
I really don't know life at all.

—Joni Mitchell's "Both Sides Now"

As children we're taught to tell the truth. Yet, the simple truths of childhood become stretched by the complexities of ideas and the realities of modern communications. Of course, no one tells the whole truth for fear of offending others or inviting retaliation. So while we cling to the ideal of truth in communications, we are, as Joni Mitchell ruefully observed in her 1969 song "Both Sides Now," forced to concede that "life's illusions" can outweigh the facts.

If we consider communications as a "Both Sides Now" kind of problem, we have the media arrayed at one end and public relations at the other—the former a fountain of "truth" and objective information, the latter characterized by a series of message points and arguments defending or advancing a client's point of view.

However, like the tarnished imperative to tell the truth, the reality of what media and public relations professionals do and how they do it is largely misunderstood. The argument set forth here is that the media and public relations use the same pieces of the information puzzle to arrive at different ends of the communications spectrum. Each effort may be valid, or neither may be, but there is a striking similarity in how a PR person develops a message and how a journalist writes a headline.

The reporter's story could be diametrically opposed to what a corporate spokesman writes, but the end purpose of both is to convince the reader that the last word on the page is in fact the final word on the subject. Without denigrating the efforts of either the media or PR practitioners, it's important to know how each side does its work and why, in spite of the differences, the end result is quite the same—if not in content then in approach.

For some 25-years of my professional career, I was on the media side of the bright yellow line that separates journalists from advocates and consultants. For the past decade, on the other hand, I have been a consultant on behalf of a number of prominent clients in the health-care industry. Thus, I've seen the communications landscape from both sides, and while some of what I've seen is illusory much of the experience has come clearly in focus.

There are those who see themselves on one side of the information divide or the other; it's important to see how each enterprise unfolds and why certain ideas and approaches become accepted practice.

For communications students and the public, it is critical to know how and why the two seemingly parallel lines of PR and the news media so frequently intersect. If truth is the general intent, why are both sides accused so frequently of making misrepresentations and distorting the facts? If truth is the first casualty in war, then it has been grievously wounded in efforts to grab the biggest headline or loft the client's banner.

This need not be the case, and frequently it is not. So where does good communications practice lie, and how can the depredations of language be healed?

As an approach to answering these questions, I would like to offer a series of examples, or case histories, that tell the story from "both sides"—how the media viewed the event and how public relations professionals responded. My qualifications for this analysis are based on pursuing two intersecting careers and learning how to appreciate their strengths while not ignoring their weaknesses. Truth need not be a casualty, and meaningful communications can thrive in a climate of good will. Unfortunately, no one can dispute that those conditions don't currently prevail in our public discussion.

However, the worlds of public relations and the media do have much to say to each other, and the more understanding between the two, the better the public will be served. For purposes of discussion we'll review some significant communications problems to see how successfully they were explained or if it is only life's illusions that we recall.

Finding Opportunity in a Crisis

A crisis can be viewed as an extreme disruption of normal events whose ultimate consequences are unknown. As Tolstoy wrote in Anna Karenina, "Happy families are all alike. Every unhappy family is unhappy in its own way." So it is with crises; each has a life of its own with moments both poignant and sublime.

A crisis involving a massive oil spill, the runaway acceleration of an automobile, or the discovery that a popular medication is linked to serious adverse events are all threatening circumstances requiring an urgent response. However for those engaged in reporting such events or defending those accused of causing them, a crisis is an opportunity.

As reporters comb an organization's communications architecture looking for every crack and flaw lurking in exculpatory assertions, trusted advisors scurry to patch every information leak and rationalize any inconsistencies. This codependent relationship is a regular and predictable feature of virtually every crisis that rises to the level of public attention or regulatory intervention.

The salient aspects of a crisis are the growing awareness that a problem exists, the reaction, frequently outraged, to the negative change, and, ultimately, a resolution. The 1982 Tylenol case, which left seven people dead from cyanide poisoning, is often cited as a textbook example of crisis management.

Johnson & Johnson, Tylenol's maker, was praised for rapid and complete disclosure of the circumstances surrounding the crimes as well as revamping the product to make it tamper-resistant. Though the perpetrators were never found, the idea that a corporation would speak candidly about a major threat to public health and the corporate response was laudatory. If Tylenol is celebrated as an example of the system working, it is perhaps the most special of all special corporate communications cases.

This high-profile case matured before the 24/7 news cycle became the dominant communications model. Thus Johnson & Johnson was able to disseminate its messages of action and empathy through traditional channels, which turned the story around on fixed rather than constant deadlines. This is not to say the story was controlled, but rather the more measured pace of reporting moderated the story's impact. Though CNN was reporting every development in real time, it was still a fledgling network without many viewers. All-news radio was certainly a factor, but television was the primary source for most, infusing a story with powerful pictures and dramatic narration.

If a case of Tylenol's magnitude were to break today, the story would be viral in a matter of minutes, flashed to every corner of the globe via Twitter and other Internet portals. Thus, the ability to assess a situation, develop a strategy, and present one's case to the media via press conference has given way to an information cacophony.

As if harkening back to some Golden Era of corporate communications, experts asked to analyze how a company performed in a crisis situation inevitably cite the Tylenol case as a benchmark for effectiveness and transparency. No doubt, forthrightness saved the brand and created a set of expectations for future events. However, while Tylenol was a game changer, it was also a unique circumstance.

This was certainly one of the last times that news media and corporate spokespeople stood at opposite ends of the trenches engaged in a predictable exchange of messages and reportage with the public as a beneficiary. However, the era of the information dreadnaughts is over. Technology has changed the equation to the point that a single person sending out a single Tweet can literally move the world. Anyone and everyone is a journalist. Reality shows proliferate at the expense of, well, reality.

While television news has been and will always be more television than news, major outlets like MSNBC and Fox represent opposite ends of emerging agenda journalism. In fact, they are frequently more like public relations campaigns than journalistic entities. Yes, Tylenol communications is a truth writ large in the pantheon of information. Still, those who celebrate that success must know that it can never be repeated. Another Tylenol case won't play out simply as an important news story; rather it will be a defining moment for journalists and spin doctors to present different but complimentary versions of an event, more reflective of their ends than the public's need to know.

Of course, there will always be point and counterpoint between journalists and PR people, but we have a new set of rules... or a lack of them. In place of an information marketplace where ideas can prevail, we are engaged in a kind of urban combat with verbal insurgents taking potshots from windows and darkened alleys. This is the communications equivalent of what Victorian poet Matthew Arnold described as "a darkling plain where ignorant armies clash by night."

Though this is a new world, it isn't necessarily a brave one. Still those who ply their trade as communicators must find a way to survive. The rest of this essay will chart a course.

Things Get Tense over the Present Tense

We swim in a sea of language, rarely noticing its power to arouse passions or transform the course of events. Scientific presentations, for example, offer a rational argument and, in the case of medical research, evidence to support claims of safety and efficacy. Communicators in their efforts to clarify and interest viewers and readers try to integrate emotion into academic information to make it more palatable. Typically, this involves introducing a patient anecdote to humanize the story.

This approach has become a standard that rarely draws attention—unless the patient is the President of the United States. In 1985, Ronald Reagan became arguably the world's most high-profile patient when he had surgery for a suspected malignancy. Journalists covering the story, including myself, were ill prepared for what was to become one of the most startling press conferences of that era.

After the operation Dr. Stephen Rosenberg—the surgeon at the National Institutes of Health who performed the procedure—emerged to address the national media. No doubt most of the assembled news people expected a talk full of technical detail. What they got was something quite different.

"The President has cancer," declared Rosenberg with the kind of candor rarely heard in such high-stakes situations. Rosenberg went on to say that he had successfully removed a cancerous polyp from Reagan's intestines. However, Rosenberg's straightforward statement set off a communications confrontation between the White House press office and reporters on the scene.

The political fallout of a president with cancer—even though fully treatable—was really impossible to contain. Looking back to that moment, having cancer seemed more threatening with a darker prognosis and fewer available treatments. How would the chief executive cope with this new health problem, and what would it mean for the conduct of government?

Clearly, this was a communications challenge for the president's team that hoped to dampen Dr. Rosenberg's unequivocal assessment of Reagan's clinical situation. There were many journalists on the scene, besides me, that knew Rosenberg personally and had great respect for his research to develop a cancer vaccine. Thus his words would be difficult to impeach.

What followed was almost as surprising as Rosenberg's blunt remarks. Members of the White House team began lobbying reporters with the idea that Rosenberg had misspoken. What he meant to say, according to the White House staffers, is not that the President "has" cancer, but that he "had" cancer.

That of course was a more palatable political message, but it didn't jibe with the facts, as plainly spoken by Rosenberg. No matter how much the White House wanted to spin the results, Reagan's cancer was very much in the present tense…not the past. What may have been novel information, even to some of the press corps, is that the removal of the tumor doesn't mean the disease is cured. Cancer is a chronic condition requiring long-term medical management. It isn't like a bout with influenza.

What the White House team could have done was suggest that the good news was President Reagan could live well with cancer, which he proceeded to do. That message of hope would have been a far more powerful statement than trying to blunt the medical truth.

Thus Ronald Reagan's surgery was a teachable moment on many levels. It raised the visibility of colorectal cancer, then and now a stigmatized form of the disease. It also introduced candor and clarity into the discussion, which no doubt encouraged many Americans to think about their own potential vulnerability to the disease.

Journalists got a major story made even bigger by Rosenberg's now famous four-word description of the President's condition. In the end, the White House communications team received a strong dose of reality. Simple language delivered clearly and credibly becomes an unmistakable landmark. Reporters and the public fix their course on it, and those who tack away do so at their peril.

Finding Meaning in the Message

While cynicism is the coin of the communications realm for some, others are using a more valuable currency. If, as H. L. Mencken suggested, "Nobody ever went broke underestimating the intelligence of the American public," now practitioners are doing very well appealing to our higher nature with messages that have real meaning. In fact, so-called social marketing campaigns have turned bogus public relations messages into instruments of positive change.

Few products have had such a physical and emotional grip on the public as tobacco. While advertising and PR campaigns celebrated smoking as passage into adulthood, tobacco companies were well aware that their products were both addictive and dangerous. Starting most notably with the US Surgeon General's 1964 report, evidence about the hazards of smoking was becoming incontrovertible.

To counter the science, the tobacco industry followed the advice of a public relations firm and created the Tobacco Institute to discredit and contradict legitimate scientific findings. Though the idea that the tobacco industry could present meaningful public health information was something of an oxymoron or even Orwellian in its manipulation of the facts, the Tobacco Institute was widely quoted as a source on "the other side of the issue."

The public had become as addicted to the protobacco message as it was to nicotine. Things turned dramatically in 1996 when then FDA Commissioner David Kessler and the Clinton Administration introduced regulations to control tobacco products and advertising. Kessler, a pediatrician, had been waging his own campaign against tobacco declaring smoking "a pediatric disease" that will ultimately kill many of the thousands of children who take up the habit every day.

Suddenly, a public health message was gaining traction and momentum. Though the initial regulations were overturned, hundreds of millions of dollars from a tobacco damages suit brought by the states fueled the growing antitobacco enterprise. That provided an opportunity for communications and PR professionals to develop campaigns encouraging people to improve their health rather than compromise it. Using the same sophisticated tools as their tobacco opponents, these apostles of social marketing were "selling" positive choice instead of encouraging destructive behavior.

One of the most effective antitobacco PR initiatives was the "Truth" campaign of the late 1990s. It developed an effective message suggesting the tobacco industry was deceiving and manipulating kids, not telling them the "Truth." Not a health message per se, but one that focus groups showed resonated with this particular audience.

As a medical correspondent for CNN, and later as a PR professional during this period working on the "Truth" program, the transformation that I observed in the dialogue about tobacco was truly remarkable. The tobacco industry had long scoffed at science and public health, essentially stonewalling reporters and using the Tobacco Institute to defend products linked to the deaths of hundreds of thousands of people annually in the United States.

This was little more than a Potemkin village. Now the real truth was plain to see, and, ironically, many of the same PR techniques that had built the tobacco message platform were being used to dismantle it.

From the announcement of these historic regulations to their ultimate demise in the US Supreme Court under industry challenge, I felt privileged to watch the power of science, public policy, and communications engineer a sea change in public health. The Clinton Administration lost the initial battle, but big tobacco is losing the hearts and minds of consumers. The perception of smoking as socially desirable and benign has been forever tarnished, and tobacco consumption, generally, is down in the United States.

Following legislation passed in 2009, the US Food and Drug Administration (FDA) now has the authority to regulate tobacco and this time with the grudging acquiescence of the industry.

Looking back, I worked hard to write about the tobacco issue objectively as a journalist, but I felt it was more important to tell the truth.

Antibody Anybody? Everybody!

Every PR person who has pitched a new product knows how cold the voice on the other end of the phone line can be. It is becoming increasingly difficult to interest reporters in doing stories about drugs in development until they reach the phase 3 stage of large clinical trials. Even then, it is often "wait and see" until the FDA decides what it is going to do. Nor does approval necessarily guarantee top-tier coverage unless the treatment is a game changer.

However, there are moments when a new drug's performance is so impressive that it matches, or even exceeds, its most ambitious message points. The story of Genentech's Avastin treatment—or biologic to be more precise—culminates at the meeting of the American Society of Clinical Oncology (ASCO) in Chicago in 2003. That is when researchers presented data on the first monoclonal antibody proven effective against cancer—in this case colorectal cancer, the same kind of disease that afflicted President Reagan.

Avastin uses a targeted approach called antiangiogenesis to starve the tumor's blood supply. Net result—patients in the treatment's key study lived about 30% longer than those on conventional therapy.

ASCO is the Super Bowl of medical meetings for companies in the oncology business, and Avastin was the star of the show in 2003. Coverage of Avastin's findings grew to nearly a billion media impressions, extraordinary by any measure. However, while the science driving Avastin was impressive, the PR and communications effort matched that performance stride for stride.

Avastin's development and my association with Genentech go back quite a ways. As a reporter for CNN in San Francisco shortly after the network went on the air in 1980, I received a somewhat unusual assignment. The piece would focus on Genentech, a new company that exemplified the emerging biotech industry in the Bay Area.

Stepping off Paul Berg's groundbreaking work at Stanford that led to a Nobel Prize, the company hoped to build customized versions of human antibodies that would target a disease process or mechanism in a very specific way. In effect, using smart bombs instead of carpet bombs as a treatment approach.

This was clearly an impressive concept, and I filed a story, which ran and then disappeared into CNN's 24/7 abyss. Genentech came back on my radar screen in the weeks leading up to the 2003 ASCO conference. Then a consultant for a PR firm, I was assigned as a media coordinator to promote Avastin for reporters covering the event. In this case, much of the "selling" had already been done by Genentech's forward-looking investor calls and briefings between reporters and high-level scientists involved in Avastin's research.

One of the reasons for the intense interest in Avastin from science journalists is that the treatment was the proof of principle for antiangiogenesis and in particular for its creator, Dr. Judah Folkman, who had stuck with the controversial idea for some four decades.

In a PR masterstroke, Genentech and its consultants hosted a dinner at a New York City hotel after ASCO that attracted some of the country's leading medical journalists. They came to hear Folkman and other scientists discuss Avastin as the leading edge of a new wave of cancer treatments.

The message was that cancer isn't necessarily an acute life-ending disease but increasingly a manageable chronic condition. Even though no new data points were presented since the event was preapproval, reporters took away important insights, and Genentech developed invaluable relationships with journalists that proved instrumental in the quest for coverage.

As it turned out, the problem wasn't getting coverage, but keeping up with the demand. From the *Today Show* to *USA Today*, every major news organization filed on the story in the run up to approval and well beyond.

Like the Tylenol case, Avastin is unique as a communications and public relations enterprise. Tylenol made the best of a tragic situation while Avastin successfully rode a wave of expectation in the battle against cancer.

While Johnson & Johnson's response to the Tylenol crisis was transparent and timely, and thus diffused the impact; Genentech aggressively courted media offering information about a disease-modifying treatment that heightened anticipation. ASCO provided the high point for a drama that started decades earlier.

It was a long trip from the bench to center stage at ASCO, but Genentech made the journey by realizing that good science is driven and supported by a strong communications strategy.

From Macro to Micro: Communicating in the Viral Environment

Much has been written about the declining state of major media and the ascendancy of blogs and other social media outlets. Without belaboring the obvious, the era in which a few key organizations held information hegemony is over.

While the new communications universe is still inchoate, no serious professional can ignore the effect and significance of this transformation. Every major PR agency is busily developing social media expertise, though it is still very difficult to define metrics that assess the effectiveness of placing clients in these venues. Nonetheless, the prevailing view is that not participating in social media is an opportunity missed.

Conversely, journalists are either getting information from blogs or becoming bloggers themselves. Writing in the "Neiman Foundation for Journalism at Harvard" in 2008, Paul Bradshaw observed, "From journalistic pariah to savior of the news industry, blogs have undergone an enormous transformation."

Specifically, many journalists now have more autonomy and depend less on traditional sources, including PR spokespeople. News, rather than being preedited, is becoming more of a community process, correcting and updating in real time. Thus, getting published in a blog can be easier than traditional media.

While PR people have been concerned about the loss of some of their long-standing relationships, blogs and social media are creating new opportunities. In many cases, the PR person can pitch the blogger directly who can publish the story without having to go through any editorial review.

In health care, for instance, a number of disease-state bloggers are finding an independent voice. A major media outlet reporter, who has diabetes, started a diabetes blog that is highly regarded in that community. The audience for the blog may be small but still important for clients hoping to influence diabetes patients.

Winning over this blogger may prove just as important as landing a hit in mainstream media, and the process may be easier. The challenge is to find blogs that have bona fide journalistic content that adds value for readers and consequently clients hoping to reach an audience in transformation. If a blog is seen only as a public relations tool its reach will be limited accordingly.

Whatever firewall there was between journalists and PR people is now being redefined in the blogosphere. Digital journalists are frequently more accessible and in need of more and more material to feed their stories than their traditional counterparts. PR communicators, meanwhile, are looking for new opportunities to deliver their clients' messages.

Now it is possible to speak directly to the publisher, editor, and lead reporter, all in the same person—then watch as the story is published worldwide on the Internet. Viewing the new reality, one wonders if Walter Cronkite would now conclude his nightly broadcast saying, "That's the way it was," instead of "That's the way it is."

Summary

Whatever the new trends or directions in communications may be, the relationship between the press and PR advocates will always be in flux. Like Tolstoy's unhappy family, these interactions are complex, unique but vitally important.

PR counselors have access to sources and information that reporters need. Meanwhile, reporters open the front door to audiences eagerly sought by PR clients. When these interactions work, and they often do, everyone's interest is served. It's a win–win.

On the occasions when communication campaigns serve only to advance special interests, their motives and credibility will always be in doubt. Over time, the differences will become obvious, as in the case of the Tobacco Institute or in Ronald Reagan's case, real doctors will ultimately prevail over spin doctors.

While journalists and advocates may look at each other through different ends of the telescope, they should also realize that they are engaged in the same process—with the former responding to the public interest and the latter advancing the client's agenda.

The divide may not be crossed by something as simple as Rodney King's plea, "People, can't we all just get along?" Still there are things that can be done.

Writing in the *Journal of the National Cancer Institute* in 1999 about issues in risk communication, I observed, "Risk to the scientist is ultimately a tool to measure and compare data, a statement of probability. For journalists, risk is a measurement of news value. The greater the risk of anything, the bigger the story. Is there a way of reconciling these disparate approaches?"

Safe to say the same conundrum applies today, perhaps even to a greater degree as traditional journalistic standards are tested in the new media environment. How would the Tylenol tampering case have been reported by Fox News or MSNBC, not to mention the Drudge Report? How can PR people and their clients stay in the conversation?

In 1999 I suggested that journalists and scientists make greater efforts to work together with the goal of getting the story right and in perspective. While this may be an obvious statement, it is hard to dispute. This guidance certainly applies to any kind of communications endeavor where accuracy and integrity should be the take-aways, not the type size of the headline.

It may not be possible to know the whole truth or even a fraction of reality. However, all those engaged in the process need to acknowledge that their efforts are flawed and in need of continual improvement.

Crossing back and forth along the bright yellow line as a communicator, I have seen more than my share of illusions shattered. Inevitably, though, the truth is vindicated. The workings of journalists and PR people may become increasingly strained but no less important. It is in everyone's interest to look beyond a narrow vision and in realizing a broader purpose see both sides now.

Discussion Questions

1. What are the salient features of a crisis? How can a crisis become a positive media opportunity for an organization?
2. How did the media environment during the 1982 Tylenol case affect the outcome? In what ways could a similar crisis in today's media environment result in a different outcome?
3. What was earned from the 1985 reporting of President Reagan's cancer treatment?

4. How did public relations techniques change over the years to shift public perceptions about tobacco?
5. What was unique about the Genentech case mentioned in the text? Why was it deemed a success?
6. Describe the benefits for journalists in the new viral media environment. What are the challenges in this environment for a communication professional?

Chapter 3

Research for Health Communication

By Christina Mazzola Nicols

LEARNING OBJECTIVES

By the end of the chapter, the reader will be able to:

- Distinguish between qualitative and quantitative methodologies used in communication research.
- Understand when to use various research methodologies and approaches to develop and support a health communication effort.
- Define and distinguish between different types of epidemiologic research studies.
- Define and distinguish between essential epidemiologic terms, such as incidence and prevalence.

Introduction

Planning a health communication program is a research-intensive process. Therefore, it is useful for communicators to have at least a basic understanding of quantitative and qualitative research methodologies as well as knowledge of the main types of epidemiologic studies and frequently used terms. Many of the methodologies and terms described in this chapter are referred to again in Chapter 4, which presents an exploration of the communication planning process.

As an introduction to methodologies and approaches frequently used in research for health communication programs, this chapter will explore:

- Quantitative methodologies used in communication research, including discussion about sampling strategies and sample sizes, frequently used modes of data collection and statistical procedures, and how quantitative data can be used to guide and measure a communication program

- Qualitative methodologies used in communication research, including discussion about sampling strategies and sample sizes, as well as commonly used modes of data collection such as observation, participant-observation, in-depth interviews, and focus group sessions
- Codes of ethics regarding the conduct of research involving human subjects
- Essential epidemiologic terms, such as *prevalence*, *incidence*, *mortality rate*, *proportionate mortality*, *outbreak*, *epidemic*, *pandemic*, and other frequently used terms
- The main types of epidemiologic studies, including experimental, cohort, case–control, and others

Quantitative Research for Communication

Quantitative research categorizes variables (i.e., factors of interest), counts them, and then uses statistical procedures to explain them. Numbers and statistics make up the resulting data. Communicators typically use quantitative research when they want to *measure* awareness, understanding, attitudes, or behaviors among a target audience. The most common methodology used to do this is a survey, either by telephone, online, or, less frequently, by mail. Quantitative research is typically conducted among a *representative* sample of the population the communicator is trying to reach. This representative sample is known as a *probability* sample and is one in which all members of the population have an equal chance of being selected. It is achieved primarily through random selection. The sample size should also be sufficiently large to ensure it is *generalizable*—that is, applicable—to a broader audience beyond those included in the survey.

Determining a sufficient sample size depends on the size of the target population. For example, a randomized sample of 1000 adults is typically used as a representative sample of a US adult population of approximately 230 million, and it has a fairly low margin of error of plus or minus 3.1%. The margin of error is the amount of random sampling error in a survey's results, and it should be taken into account when interpreting survey results. For example, if the survey of 1000 adults determines 54% of women and 58% of men watch television news, the four-point difference between genders falls largely within the plus or minus 3.1% margin of error. The communicator cannot know if the gender differences are real or if they are attributed to survey error, and therefore, cannot state with confidence that men are more likely than women to watch television news.

Larger sample sizes generally result in smaller margins of error, and therefore present a better chance of accurately representing the broader population. Because study participants are paid incentives for their time, larger sample sizes can be expensive to field, especially if the sample comprises professionals who require higher incentives for taking the survey. Sample sizes should be the proper size to fit the population. For example, a sample of 400 can adequately represent a population of 250,000 physicians with a margin of error of plus or minus 4.9%. A margin of error should be as low as possible, and as a rule of thumb it should be under plus or minus 5%. Margin of error calculations are based on a statistical *curve*—not a straight line—and because of the curve, a decrease in the size of the population will not necessarily lead to a proportional decrease in the sample size. For example, a sample of 400 representing a population of 2,000,000 would have a margin of error of plus or minus 4.9%, but a sample of 400 representing a population of 200,000 or 200,000,000 would also have a margin of error of plus or minus 4.9%. When planning surveys, communicators should determine necessary sample sizes before requesting vendors to submit bids for fieldwork, as vendors often base their prices on sample sizes. Margin-of-error calculators can take the guesswork out of this task, and there are several available at no cost online. Many fielding vendors, including Ipsos (www.ipsos.com) and Opinion Research Corporation (ORC) (www.opinionresearch.com), offer relatively inexpensive omnibus surveys conducted once or twice a week among 1000 general adult consumers. Omnibus surveys are usually priced per question, whereas custom surveys with more narrowly defined target audiences are priced by sample size and survey length. Surveys among consumers are typically less expensive than surveys among professional audiences. For more expensive samples, such as physicians and other health professionals, 400 can be a "magic number" for keeping a margin of error below plus or minus 5%.

Survey methodology is another factor that can affect cost. Online surveys are generally less expensive to field than telephone surveys, but experts sometimes question how adequately an online survey can represent segments of the population that are not yet fully online, such as seniors, low-income individuals, and Spanish-speaking Americans. Data collections to support federal health communication programs, such as campaigns for the Centers for Disease Control and Prevention (CDC) and the National Institutes of Health (NIH), typically rely on telephone survey methodology to ensure they adequately represent the US population. Increasingly, fielding vendors are incorporating a sample of cell phone numbers to represent households that do not have landlines. This is an important point to confirm when selecting a fielding vendor.

When analyzing the results of surveys, communicators should be aware of the statistical procedures and terms frequently used in research for health communication, as described in the following sections.

Frequency

A frequency is simply the number of people in a survey who select a particular response option. It is typically expressed as a percentage when reporting survey results. For example, 200 out of 1000 adults surveyed (20%) said they had received a flu vaccination during the past year.

Correlation Analysis

A correlation analysis measures the strength of the association between two variables in a survey. For example, if a communicator has collected data on two variables—income level and whether or not a person has had a flu vaccination—he or she could conduct a correlation analysis to determine how strongly income level is associated with getting or not getting a flu vaccination.

Cross-Tabulation

A cross-tabulation, typically called a "cross-tab," is a two-way data table that shows two variables simultaneously. In the cross-tab shown in Table 3-1, there are columns for various age groups of children and a row for the percentage of children who have had a flu vaccination in the past year, according to a hypothetical survey of parents. This cross-tab provides an easy means of comparing flu vaccination rates by age of child.

Regression Analysis

Regression analysis is useful if a communicator wants to make predictions about likely behaviors based on variables explored in the survey. While association measures like correlation analysis and cross-tabulation show the relationship between two variables only, regression analysis can show the relationships between two, three, or more variables. For example, in a survey of questions that address demographics and flu vaccination behavior, a regression analysis could quantify whether age is a better predictor of getting a flu vaccination compared to income or education level. A regression analysis could similarly be used to predict which of several messages would be more likely to persuade a target audience to undertake a desired behavior, such as getting a flu vaccination.

Cluster Analysis

The objective of a cluster analysis is to group together survey respondents with similar characteristics. The characteristics of interest are often attitudinal rather than demographic. For example, in a survey of 25 questions that address demographics, attitudes, and behaviors relating to flu vaccinations, a cluster analysis may be based on several core attitudinal questions that explore the extent to which consumers value flu vaccinations and believe they will be effective in preventing the flu. Typically three to five "types" are identified in a cluster analysis, with each respondent belonging to only one cluster. For example, a cluster analysis based on attitudes regarding flu vaccinations may yield four separate types:

- Type 1: People who strongly believe in the value of flu vaccinations and are likely to get a vaccination each year
- Type 2: People who believe they should get a flu vaccination but lack the means to get one or have other health issues that take priority

Table 3-1 **Example of a Cross-Tabulation**

	Ages 2 or younger	Ages 3–5	Ages 6–9	Ages 10–12	Ages 13–15	Age 16–18
Percentage with flu vaccination in the past year	42%	55%	44%	28%	34%	31%

- Type 3: People who never think of flu prevention because they rarely get sick, and therefore do not understand why a flu vaccination could be important
- Type 4: People who are skeptical of the effectiveness of the flu vaccination or concerned about potential adverse effects, and are therefore resistant to getting a flu vaccination

Messages targeted to each of these four clusters would appeal to the distinctly different motivations, concerns, and barriers experienced by each type. For example, Type 3 lacks awareness of why a flu vaccination could be important, and therefore a fairly straightforward informational message may be effective, whereas Type 4 may need more persuasive messages and reassurances from a trusted source such as a family physician. Communication by itself will not be effective with Type 2, as the main barrier for this type may be a lack of access rather than a lack of knowledge or motivation. Type 1, already likely to get a flu vaccination, may be even more likely if a program offers greater convenience. A cluster analysis is a useful way to develop tailored messages for a range of audiences, and when linked to demographic information, a cluster analysis can also suggest the most effective media outlets and communication channels to pursue. More discussion of this is included in the exploration of the discovery step of the communication process in Chapter 4.

While surveys are often used to gather outcome measures, such as changes in awareness, understanding, attitudes, and behavior among target audiences, they can also be useful in the discovery process, as they can identify and quantify gaps that need to be filled by communication. For example, if a communicator suspects a lack of awareness about CDC recommendations for flu vaccinations among a patient population but does not know the exact extent of the gap in awareness, a survey would be a useful tool to measure the gap. In measuring the gap in awareness, the survey data would provide a "proof point" to justify the need for the communication effort. This type of survey also presents an opportunity to generate media coverage and raise visibility about an issue or health condition. Some media outlets scrutinize survey methodology quite carefully and will decline to report surveys if they are not confident about the representativeness of the survey sample. If the communicator is planning a survey that is intended primarily for news coverage, it is important to ask a fielding vendor for credentials in this area.

Qualitative Research for Communication

Qualitative research aims to gather an in-depth understanding of human behavior and the factors contributing to the behavior. Words, pictures, or objects make up the resulting data.

Communicators typically use qualitative research early in the planning process—usually before quantitative research—to get a better understanding of the underlying causes of an issue or the motivations and barriers to achieving a desired behavior. Qualitative research offers an opportunity for in-depth exploration into a target audience's culture, lifestyle, beliefs, values, attitudes, behaviors, and preferences in communication channels. It offers essential insight into the context and environment in which audiences will see and hear the messages and materials in a communication campaign. Qualitative research can also be used for testing messages and materials, as described in the exploration of the creative development step of the communication process in Chapter 4.

The sampling strategy for qualitative research differs from that of quantitative research. In a quantitative study, the researcher uses a *probability* sample, gathered through random selection and intended to be representative of the broader population. In a qualitative study, the researcher uses a *nonprobability* sample, which is not selected at random and not intended to be representative of the population. Participants in a qualitative study are selected because they match a set of criteria that is of interest to the researcher. The researcher wants to understand a specific group of people, and therefore selects participants from that group. It is a *purposive* sample rather than a random sample. A screening questionnaire is typically used to identify study participants who qualify, based on a set of criteria that are relevant to the research. For example, a qualitative study about flu vaccination behavior may screen specifically for parents of children within a certain age range, who have not had a flu vaccination within the past 2 years. By purposefully selecting this sample, the researcher is interested in understanding a fairly narrowly defined group of people rather than gathering data that could be generalized to a broader population of parents. Sample sizes in qualitative research are smaller than in quantitative research because the goal is to elicit in-depth insights rather than to generalize to the broad population.

Commonly used methodologies in qualitative research include observation, participant-observation, in-depth interviews, and focus group sessions.

Observation and Participant-Observation

The purpose of observation is to understand behaviors in a natural (i.e., real-life) setting. Marketing professionals have long used this methodology to get a firsthand understanding of the factors influencing purchase decisions. For example, a marketing professional working for a brewery may visit a bar during happy hour to understand the factors influencing selection of a drink. He or she would want to know how strongly a friend's recommendation or the bartender's recommendation influences choice, for example. Influencer campaigns and viral marketing campaigns are developed based at least in part from insights gathered through observation. A health communication professional may visit a bar during happy hour to observe factors contributing to excessive alcohol consumption. In this context, he or she may want to know what role friends play in how much a person drinks, and if this could be a factor to leverage in campaigns advocating the responsible consumption of alcohol. In fact, the concept of peer influence and support—observed in places where people gather to drink alcohol—was the driving force behind a highly successful ad campaign in the 1990s developed by the Ad Council for the National Highway Traffic Safety Administration (NHTSA). Its central message of "Friends Don't Let Friends Drive Drunk" became the most recognized anti-drinking-and-driving slogan in the country, and contributed to a substantial decrease in alcohol-related fatalities (Ad Council, n.d.).

Some insights contributing to the development of these types of campaigns cannot be gathered through observation alone. Greater insight can be gathered through *participant-observation,* which enables the researcher to engage with target audiences and ask questions as activities occur in a real-life setting. It can be a difficult methodology to pull off, as the researcher has to balance the personal experience of interacting in a community with the required objectivity of a research professional. Collected data can include transcripts of interviews as well as pictures and videotapes of activities. Given the closeness of the interaction and the personal nature of the data, special care should be taken to protect the confidentiality and privacy of participants. This becomes especially important in areas of health research where harm may come to study participants if their identities are disclosed, as in the case of women experiencing domestic violence.

The American Anthropological Association (AAA) and the American Sociological Association (ASA) have codes of ethics regarding the conduct of research. These are both available online at their respective Web sites (www.aaanet.org and www.asanet.org). In addition to discussing procedures for ensuring confidentiality, these codes cover the informed consent process. Informed consent is an essential ethical rule for any research on humans. It stipulates participants must give their informed consent before taking part in a study. Participants must be given an explanation of the purpose of the research, how long they will be asked to participate, a description of the procedures they will undergo, any risks or discomforts they may experience, and any benefits they or others may gain from the research. Detailed information about regulations governing human research may be found on the Web site of the Office for Human Research Protections, part of the US Department of Health & Human Services (ww.hhs.gov/ohrp). These codes of ethics pertain to *all* research on human subjects, not just research incorporating observation and participant-observation. The codes are mentioned in conjunction with observation and participant-observation because research conducted in a real-life, natural setting is particularly sensitive to confidentiality and other ethical issues.

In-Depth Interviews

These are typically conducted one on one in person or by telephone. As an interview progresses, questions tend to move from the general to the specific. Within this basic format, interviews can vary in terms of the degree of formality and structure they incorporate. There are three different approaches to interviews:

- *Informal, unstructured interviews* do not follow any specific protocol or path, and they rely on an open-ended answer format that does not force participants to choose from preset response options. Questions tend to be broad, as in "What do you know about flu vaccinations?" The researcher follows the direction of the conversation spontaneously as it emerges.
- For *semistructured interviews*, the researcher has determined a basic line of questioning in advance, but still relies on open-ended questions, which enable him or her to follow new topics in the conversation as they emerge. Table 3-2 is an example of a semistructured

Table 3-2 **Example of an Interview Guide on Flu Vaccinations**

Qualitative Questions Asked of Parents Regarding Flu Vaccinations

Background Information

What is/are the age(s) of your child or children?

General Knowledge of Seasonal Influenza

Please tell me what you know about seasonal influenza...

Probe as necessary:

- What is seasonal influenza?
  - Is it caused by a virus or bacteria?
- What are the usual symptoms?
- How long does it take to develop symptoms after exposure to seasonal influenza?
- How long do the symptoms last?
- Who is most vulnerable to catching seasonal influenza?
- What time of year is seasonal influenza typically most prevalent?
- How does it spread?
  - Coughing, sneezing, surfaces?
- How long is someone usually contagious?
- How dangerous is seasonal influenza?
  - Can people die of it?

Knowledge of Flu Prevention

- What are some things people can do to prevent the spread of seasonal influenza?
- What are some of the things you teach/have taught your child or children to do?

Knowledge of Seasonal Influenza Vaccination Recommendations

- Who should get vaccinated against seasonal influenza?
  - What age groups?
  - Any other specific groups of people?
- Are you familiar with an organization or a government agency that recommends who should get vaccinated?
  - What is the name of it?
- What do the recommendations say?
- How should often a person be vaccinated against seasonal influenza?
- When is the best time to get vaccinated?

Concern about Seasonal Influenza

- How concerned are you about catching the flu during the next flu season?
- How concerned are you about your child or children catching the flu?
- Are you concerned about serious complications from seasonal influenza?
  - For you?
  - For your child or children?

Influenza Vaccination Attitudes and Behaviors

- Have you received a seasonal flu vaccination during the past two years?
  - [If no] What are some of the reasons you haven't had a flu vaccination?
- What about your child or children?
  - [If no] What are some of the reasons your child or children hasn't/haven't had a flu vaccination?
- Can you think of any other reasons why someone may not want to have their child or children vaccinated against the flu?

Likely Behaviors

- How likely are you to get a flu vaccination next fall?
- How likely are you to get a flu vaccination for your child or children next fall?
- What factors would make it more likely?
- What factors would make it less likely?

interview conducted among parents regarding flu vaccinations. The interview guide lists specific areas to probe in case these do not naturally arise in the conversation. The guide moves from general awareness and knowledge about seasonal flu to increasingly more specific areas of knowledge, attitudes, and behaviors.

- *Formal interviews*, like surveys, are completely structured, with uniform, close-ended questions that have preset response options.

Focus Group Sessions

Focus groups are semistructured interviews conducted among small groups of participants instead of individuals. Typically, a trained moderator leads a focused discussion among eight to 10 participants over the course of 1 to 2 hours. The moderator follows a discussion guide, which begins with an introduction that covers the following:

- A brief description of the nature and purpose of the research, as well as how the research will be used
- Disclosures that the sessions are being observed, audio and videotaped
- Assurances of confidentiality in reporting
- Ground rules for participants, such as the need to hear from everyone, but one at a time

Also in the introduction, participants are given the opportunity to tell the group a bit about themselves, such as information about their occupation and family. After the introduction, the discussion guide, like an interview guide, typically moves from general warm-up questions to increasingly specific questions about the topic of the research. As with the interview guide, questions in the discussion guide are open-ended, but usually include cues to the moderator to probe in specific areas. Follow-up questions often lead to in-depth insights in key areas of interest.

In-person focus groups are usually held in market research facilities that feature two-way mirrors to enable observers to watch participant reactions without intruding on the session. Many facilities offer webcasting to enable observers in remote locations to watch the session in real time online. Recruitment is often done by the facility, and participants are paid monetary incentives for their time.

Focus groups can also be conducted entirely online rather than in-person, using an online web conference platform such as Webex or Adobe Connect. Participants dial in by telephone and open the online platform through their Internet connection. Through the online platform, they can view visual stimuli, such as ads, videos, logos, prototype web pages, and slide presentations, enabling an efficient and cost-effective means of pretesting communication materials. Participants can also speak freely as they would in an in-person focus group session. However, the tendency to talk over each other is greater online than in person, so the moderator should establish ground rules about this in the introduction. A camera on the moderator's computer allows all participants to see the moderator, which facilitates a more personal experience. Because of the lack of facility costs, online focus groups are generally less expensive than in-person groups. Another benefit is that the researcher is not limited to recruiting participants from a particular geographic area, which is useful in several ways:

- It allows for greater demographic diversity, as the universe of potential participants is greater than it would be if it were limited to a particular geographic location.
- A larger universe of potential participants makes recruiting easier if the research focus is on a particular disease or health condition, especially if the condition is relatively rare.
- It facilitates efficient and cost-effective representation of people in rural areas.

The drawbacks to online focus groups compared to in-person groups include the following:

- While in-person focus groups typically occur in a special facility that diminishes the risk of external distractions, online focus group participants can be easily distracted by activities occurring in their homes or wherever they are participating.
- Researchers lose the opportunity to assess physical reactions and other cues in body language that may add insight to the analysis.
- Participants may feel isolated, and may therefore not contribute as fully as they would in person.

Combining Qualitative and Quantitative Research

As described in the previous sections, qualitative and quantitative research can be used separately and with different objectives to support a communication effort. For example, qualitative methodologies are often used in formative research to understand target audiences and guide campaign strategy, while quantitative methodologies are often used to measure various components of the campaign. However, a combined approach incorporating qualitative and quantitative methodologies can be an especially effective means of formative research intended to guide the development of a communication campaign. In particular, qualitative research can be a useful step in developing response options for surveys; they can help ensure the survey accurately reflects or captures the reality of target audiences. When researchers do not know all of the possible responses to a question, they ask open-ended questions to gather responses until they no longer receive anything new. After all possible response options have been collected in interviews, the researcher can list them on a survey to quantify which response options are most frequently selected by participants. This enables researchers to understand which factors are most important to target audiences, and therefore which factors warrant priority consideration in the communication campaign.

Table 3-2 shows questions that could be asked in qualitative research, such as individual interview and focus group sessions. The questions are open ended to capture the full range of responses or factors relevant to participants. For example, under "Influenza Vaccination

Attitudes and Behaviors," the researcher asks, "What are some of the reasons your child hasn't had a flu vaccination?" to understand all the possible barriers to flu vaccination.

In Table 3-3, which shows an example of a survey questionnaire on flu vaccinations, Question 6 uses the list gathered through qualitative interviews to present response options to participants. The question also includes an "other" response option in case the interviews, conducted among a relatively small group of people, did not capture the full range of relevant responses. Also in Table 3-3, Question 3 quantifies the level of parental concern discussed in the interviews, and Questions 4, 8, and 9 quantify parents' degree of knowledge in several key areas of prevention. Question 7 quantifies the behavioral intent of taking a child for a flu vaccination if offered in a convenient location. A regression analysis incorporating responses to this question and demographic factors could be used to predict which types of parents (e.g., by age, income, education level, gender, etc.) are most likely to respond to the offer of a convenient location. Communication efforts could then be targeted to the most likely segments to maximize the effectiveness of the program and increase its likelihood of success.

Table 3-3 **Example of Survey Questionnaire on Flu Vaccinations**

Quantitative Questions Asked of Parents Regarding Flu Vaccinations

1. How many children do you have who are 18 years of age or younger?
   - None [End survey]
   - One
   - Two
   - Three
   - Four
   - Five
   - Six or more
2. Please indicate *the age* of each child you have who is 18 years of age or younger. Please specify the age of up to six children. [Number of response lines should correspond with the number specified in Q1]

   I have a child who is ___ year(s) of age
   [The blank should be a drop box of number options from "less than one" through "18"]
3. How concerned are you that your child or children may catch influenza ("flu") within the next 6 months? Please select a single response.
   - Very concerned
   - Somewhat concerned
   - Only slightly concerned
   - Not at all concerned
   - Not sure
4. How long is a child who has influenza ("flu") contagious and able to infect others? Please select the single best response.
   - Beginning 1 day before symptoms develop and up to 3 days after becoming sick
   - Beginning 1 day before symptoms develop and up to 5 days after becoming sick
   - Beginning 1 day before symptoms develop and up to 7 days after becoming sick
   - Beginning 1 day before symptoms develop and for longer than 7 days after becoming sick

(continues)

(continued)

Table 3-3 **Example of Survey Questionnaire on Flu Vaccinations**

Quantitative Questions Asked of Parents Regarding Flu Vaccinations

5. Within the past 2 years, have you taken your child who is [pipe in age from response in Q2] years of age to get an influenza vaccination ("flu" vaccination or "flu shot")? [Repeat question for age of each child specified in Q2]
   - Yes [Skip to Q7, but only after going through each child listed in Q2]
   - No
6. Why not? Please select the single best response. [Repeat question for each "no" response in Q5] [Randomize list, except for "other"]
   - The influenza vaccination isn't effective.
   - The influenza vaccination isn't necessary.
   - My child doesn't like needles.
   - It's too expensive.
   - I don't have time.
   - I don't know where to get the influenza vaccination.
   - It's recommended for children who are younger than mine.
   - It's recommended for children who are older than mine.
   - My child doesn't need the influenza vaccination.
   - Other: Please specify ___________________
7. If the influenza vaccination ("flu" vaccination or "flu shot") were readily available at locations such as schools, shopping malls, grocery stores, or public parks, how likely would you be to take your child or children to be vaccinated against the flu this fall? Please select a single response.
   - Very likely
   - Somewhat likely
   - Somewhat unlikely
   - Very unlikely
   - Not sure
8. The Centers for Disease Control and Prevention (CDC) currently recommends the influenza vaccination ("flu" vaccination or "flu shot") for which age group of children? Please select the single best response.
   - Children age 6 months to 2 years
   - Children age 6 months to 5 years
   - Children age 6 months to 10 years
   - Children age 6 months to 15 years
   - Children age 6 months to 18 years
   - All children under the age of 18 years
   - None of the above
   - Not sure
9. In your opinion, when is the *best* time to get the influenza vaccination ("flu" vaccination or "flu shot")? Please select the single best response.
   - September or October
   - November or December
   - January or February
   - March or April
   - None of the above
   - Not sure

This type of analysis can also help communication professionals determine the segments that are *least* likely to respond to the offer of a convenient location, prompting professionals to develop alternative strategies for educating and persuading these segments.

Essential Epidemiologic Terms

Health communication professionals are often tasked with translating scientific study data to the lay public and often rely on these data to guide campaign strategies, tactics, messages, and materials. Therefore, it is useful to have at least a basic understanding of the main types of epidemiologic studies. To understand these scientific studies as well as the broader context of public health, health communicators need to have a working knowledge of frequently used epidemiologic terms.

Table 3-4 defines two essential epidemiologic terms that are often confused: prevalence and incidence. *Prevalence* measures the existence of current disease. It is simply the proportion of the total population that is diseased. *Incidence* is the occurrence of new cases of disease that develop in a population over a specified time period. Incidence measures the frequency with which new disease develops.

Program uses for prevalence and incidence are also outlined in Table 3-4. In the discovery step of the communication planning process, explored in Chapter 4, health communication professionals may be interested in understanding the extent of a health problem, especially if the health problem is driving the need for the communication program. Prevalence and incidence both contribute to an understanding of the extent of a health problem. *Prevalence* is useful for estimating the need for a program, based on how many people currently have the disease or health condition, and for allocating resources to support the program. However, prevalence is not useful for determining likely causes of a disease or health condition, as it looks at existing cases. By studying existing cases, researchers lack the ability to look back in time and study the factors that led to the development of the disease. Therefore, prevalence by itself is not especially useful for developing or measuring prevention programs. *Incidence* is useful for determining the likely causes of a disease, as researchers study only new cases of the disease, and can therefore study the factors that lead to the development of the disease. Because it measures new cases of a disease or health condition over a specified time period, it is useful for evaluating the effectiveness of a prevention program.

Table 3-5 defines other frequently used epidemiologic terms health communication professionals can expect to encounter in literature pertaining to health and medicine. Many of these terms are particularly relevant to professionals working in the area of infectious diseases, such as seasonal and H1N1 influenza.

Additional epidemiologic terms can be found on the CDC Web site in a section devoted to the Excellence in Curriculum Innovation through Teaching Epidemiology and the Science of Public Health (EXCITE!). The glossary is available at http://www.cdc.gov/excite/library/glossary.htm.

Table 3-4 **Definitions of Prevalence and Incidence**

Term	Definition	Program Uses
Prevalence	*Prevalence* measures the existence of current disease. It is simply the proportion of the total population that is diseased. There are two types of prevalence measures: *Point prevalence* is the proportion of the population that is diseased at a single point in time and can be thought of as a single snapshot of the population. It can be expressed by the following mathematical formula: $\frac{\text{Number of existing cases of disease}}{\text{Number in total population}}$ *Period prevalence* is the proportion of the population that is diseased during a specified duration of time, such as a single calendar year. It can be expressed by the following mathematical formula: $\frac{\text{Number of existing cases of disease}}{\text{Number in total population}}\ \text{During a period of time}$	Useful for estimating the need for a program and allocating resources. Not useful for determining likely causes of diseases, as it looks at existing cases. By studying existing cases, researchers lack the ability to look back in time and study the factors that led to developing the disease.
Incidence	*Incidence* is the occurrence of new cases of disease that develop in a population over a specified time period. Incidence measures the frequency with which new disease develops. There are two types of incidence measures: *Cumulative incidence* is the proportion of a population that becomes diseased over a specific time period. It can be expressed by the following mathematical formula: $\frac{\text{Number of new cases of disease}}{\text{Number in a population}}\ \text{Over a specific time period}$ *Incidence rate* is the occurrence of new cases of disease that arise during person-time of observation. It can be expressed by the following mathematical formula: $\frac{\text{Number of new cases of disease}}{\text{Person-time of observation in population}}$ Person-time is a unit of measurement that looks at the number of persons and their time contribution in a study. It is the sum of individual units of time that the persons in the study population have been exposed or at risk to the disease or health condition being studied. The most frequently used person-time is person-years.	Useful for evaluating the effectiveness of a prevention program. Also useful for determining likely causes of diseases. By studying new cases of the disease, researchers can study the factors that lead to developing the disease.

Source: Aschengrau, A., & Seage, G. R., III. (2008). *Essentials of epidemiology in public health*. Sudbury, MA: Jones and Bartlett.

Table 3-5 **Other Frequently Used Epidemiologic Terms**

Term	Definition
Morbidity	Disease; any departure, subjective or objective, from a state of physiological or psychological health and well-being.
Mortality	Death. *Mortality rate* is a measure of the frequency of occurrence of death among a defined population during a specified time interval. *Age-adjusted mortality rate* has been statistically modified to eliminate the effect of different age distributions among different populations. *Age-specific mortality rate* is limited to a particular age group, calculated as the number of deaths among the age group divided by the number of persons in that age group, usually expressed per 100,000. *Cause-specific mortality rate* is from a specified cause, calculated as the number of deaths attributed to a specific cause during a specified time interval among a population divided by the size of the midinterval population. *Crude mortality rate* is a mortality rate from all causes of death for an entire population, without adjustment.
Proportionate mortality	The proportion of deaths among a population attributable to a particular cause during a selected period. Each cause of death is expressed as a percentage of all deaths, and the sum of the proportionate mortality for all causes must equal 100%. These proportions are not mortality rates because, in proportionate mortality, the denominator is all deaths instead of the population among whom the deaths occurred.
Outbreak	The occurrence of more cases of disease, injury, or other health condition than expected in a given area or among a specific group of persons during a specific period. Usually, the cases are presumed to have a common cause or to be related to one another in some way. Sometimes distinguished from an epidemic as more localized, or the term less likely to evoke public panic.
Epidemic	The occurrence of more cases of disease, injury, or other health condition than expected in a given area or among a specific group of persons during a particular period. Usually, the cases are presumed to have a common cause or to be related to one another in some way.
Pandemic	An epidemic occurring over a widespread area (multiple countries or continents) and usually affecting a substantial proportion of the population.
Endemic	The constant presence of an agent or health condition within a given geographic area or population; can also refer to the usual prevalence of an agent or condition.
Cluster	An aggregation of cases of a disease, injury, or other health condition (particularly cancer and birth defects) in a circumscribed area during a particular period without regard to whether the number of cases is more than expected (often the expected number is not known).
Exposure	Having come into contact with a cause of, or possessing a characteristic that is a determinant of, a particular health problem.
Attack rate	A form of incidence that measures the proportion of persons in a population who experience an acute health event during a limited period (e.g., during an outbreak), calculated as the number of new cases of a health problem during an outbreak divided by the size of the population at the beginning of the period, usually expressed as a percentage or per 1000 or 100,000 population.

(continues)

(continued)

Table 3-5 **Other Frequently Used Epidemiologic Terms**

Term	Definition
Case-fatality rate	The proportion of persons with a particular condition who die from that condition. The denominator is the number of persons with the condition; the numerator is the number of cause-specific deaths among those persons.
Agent	A factor (e.g., a microorganism or chemical substance) or form of energy whose presence, excessive presence, or in the case of deficiency diseases, relative absence is essential for the occurrence of a disease or other adverse health outcome.
Host	A person or other living organism that is susceptible to or harbors an infectious agent under natural conditions.
Carrier	A person or animal that harbors the infectious agent for a disease and can transmit it to others, but does not demonstrate signs of the disease. A carrier can be asymptomatic (i.e., never indicate signs of the disease) or can display signs of the disease only during the incubation period, convalescence, or postconvalescence. The period of being a carrier can be short (a transient carrier) or long (a chronic carrier).
Vector	A living intermediary that carries an agent from a reservoir to a susceptible host (e.g., mosquitoes, fleas, or ticks).
Risk	The probability that an event will occur (e.g., that a person will be affected by, or die from, an illness, injury, or other health condition within a specified time or age span).
Risk factor	An aspect of personal behavior or lifestyle, an environmental exposure, or a hereditary characteristic that is associated with an increase in the occurrence of a particular disease, injury, or other health condition.

Source: CDC. Excellence in Curriculum Innovation through Teaching Epidemiology and the Science of Public Health (EXCITE!), Glossary of Epidemiology Terms.

Introduction to Epidemiologic Studies

Health communication professionals are likely to encounter the terms outlined above when they conduct literature reviews among peer-reviewed articles in health and medical journals or when they gather data from the CDC and other health information Web sites. They may also encounter discussion of various types of epidemiologic studies, described in Table 3-6 (Aschengrau & Seage, 2008). Although health communication professionals are not likely to conduct these types of studies in support of their communication programs, they may rely on data from studies conducted by epidemiologists and other scientists, and they may also be responsible for reporting the results of these studies to the public. Therefore, it is useful to have a basic understanding of the various types of studies and how they are used.

Experimental studies are also known as trials, such as the clinical trials conducted by pharmaceutical studies to demonstrate the efficacy and safety of a medication and secure its approval by the US Food and Drug Administration (FDA). Experimental studies investigate the role of a factor, such as a medication or a preventive health intervention, in the prevention

Table 3-6 **Main Types of Epidemiologic Studies**

Type of Study	Characteristics
Experimental	Studies preventions and treatments for diseases; investigator actively manipulates which groups receive the agent under study.
Observational	Studies causes, preventions, and treatments for diseases; investigator passively observes as nature takes its course.
Cohort	Typically examines multiple health effects of an exposure; subjects are defined according to their exposure levels and followed for disease occurrence.
Case–control	Typically examines multiple exposures in relation to a disease; subjects are defined as cases and controls, and exposure histories are compared.
Cross–Sectional	Typically examines relationship between exposure and disease prevalence in a defined population at a single point in time.
Ecological	Examines relationship between exposure and disease with population-level rather than individual-level data.

Source: Aschengrau, A., & Seage, G. R., III. (2008) *Essentials of epidemiology in public health*. Sudbury, MA: Jones and Bartlett.

or treatment of a disease or health condition. In an experimental study, the researcher assigns participants to two or more groups that either receive or do not receive the medication or intervention. Groups that receive the medication or intervention are called treatment groups, and those that do not receive it are called control groups. Experimental studies are considered the most scientifically rigorous of all study types (Aschengrau & Seage, 2008).

In experimental studies, researchers actively manipulate which groups receive the medication or intervention under study. In *observational studies*, however, researchers passively observe as nature takes its course. They look at exposures that occur in natural settings rather than in the controlled environment of a scientific lab. Exposures may include substances encountered in the environment or on the job, personal behaviors such as dietary habits or the use of seat belts while driving, and other factors that influence health. The two main types of observational studies are cohort and case–control studies. A *cohort study* examines one or more health effects of exposure to a single agent. Participants are defined according to their exposure status and are followed over time to determine the incidence of health outcomes. Cohort studies can be prospective (looking forward), retrospective (looking backward), or ambidirectional (in both directions). In a prospective cohort study, participants are grouped on the basis of past or current exposure and are followed into the future to observe health outcomes. In a retrospective cohort study, both the exposures and the outcomes have already occurred when the study begins, and therefore, the researcher does *not* follow participants forward to observe future outcomes, but studies only prior outcomes. An ambidirectional cohort study has both prospective and retrospective components. A prospective cohort study has advantages over a retrospective cohort study and a case–control study in that researchers can usually gather more detailed data on exposures, as they have more control of the data collection process and can gather data directly from participants (Aschengrau & Seage, 2008).

In a *case–control study*, participants are selected on the basis of whether they have or do not have the disease or health condition under study. Those who have the disease are called cases, and those who do not are called controls. The study is conducted by comparing the exposure histories of cases and controls. A case–control study is by definition retrospective, as researchers must look back in time to gather and analyze exposure histories of participants. Case–control studies are frequently conducted when little is known about a disease, as they offer the opportunity to evaluate a variety of exposures. They are particularly useful for studying rare diseases, as participants are readily identified based on disease status, whereas in a cohort study, they are identified by exposure status, and it is uncertain whether or not they will develop the disease. The retrospective nature of this type of study contributes to an important disadvantage in that it is often difficult for researchers to determine which occurred first, the exposure or the disease. Therefore, it is difficult to establish that a particular exposure *caused* a disease or health condition, as an exposure must have occurred *before* a disease as a criterion for having caused it (Aschengrau & Seage, 2008).

Cross-sectional studies and ecological studies are additional types of observational studies. A cross-sectional study examines the relationship between a disease and an exposure among individuals in a defined population at a point in time. This type of study can be thought of as a snapshot of a population that measures the prevalence of an exposure in relation to the prevalence of a disease or health condition. An ecological study evaluates the association between exposure and disease using the population rather than the individual as the unit of analysis. These two types of studies are considered less scientifically rigorous than cohort and case–control studies for two main reasons:

- In cross-sectional studies, researchers cannot tell which occurred first—the exposure or the disease. Therefore, this type of study cannot establish that a particular exposure *caused* a disease or health condition.
- The lack of individual-level data in an ecological study leads to a limitation known as the "ecological fallacy," which means the association between exposures and health outcomes at the population level does not necessarily represent the association that exists at the individual level. (Aschengrau & Seage, 2008).

Despite their limitations, these types of studies are frequently used because they are relatively inexpensive and can be conducted fairly quickly, using preexisting data.

Summary

Communicators typically use *quantitative* research when they want to *measure* awareness, understanding, attitudes, or behaviors among a target audience. The most common methodology used to do this is a survey, conducted among a *representative* sample of the population the communicator is trying to reach. This representative sample is known as a *probability* sample, and it is one in which all members of the population have an equal chance of being selected. It is achieved primarily through random selection. Larger sample sizes generally result in smaller margins of error and therefore present a better chance of accurately representing the broader population. Online surveys are generally less expensive to field than telephone surveys, but experts sometimes question how adequately an online survey can represent segments of the population that are not yet fully online.

Statistical procedures and terms frequently used when exploring survey results for health communication research include *frequency*, *correlation analysis*, *cross-tabulation*, *regression analysis*, and *cluster analysis*. Regression analysis is useful if a communicator wants to make predictions about likely behaviors based on variables explored in the survey. A cluster analysis can be a useful means of grouping together survey respondents with similar characteristics, especially attitudinal characteristics.

Communicators typically use *qualitative* research early in the planning process—usually before quantitative research—to get a better understanding of the underlying causes of an issue or the motivations and barriers to achieving a desired behavior. Qualitative research offers essential insight into the context and environment in which audiences will see and hear the messages and materials in a communication campaign. It can also be used for testing messages and materials.

The sampling strategy for *qualitative* research differs from that of quantitative research. In a qualitative study, the researcher uses a *nonprobability* sample, which is not selected at random and not intended to be representative of the population. Participants in a qualitative study are selected because they match a set of criteria that is of interest to the researcher. The researcher wants to understand a specific group of people, and therefore selects participants from that group. It is a *purposive* sample rather than a random sample. Sample sizes in qualitative research are smaller than in quantitative research because the goal is to elicit in-depth insights rather than to generalize to the broad population. Commonly used methodologies in qualitative research include observation, participant-observation, in-depth interviews, and focus group sessions.

Health communication professionals are often tasked with translating scientific study data to the lay public and often rely on these data to guide campaign strategies, tactics, messages, and materials. Therefore, it is useful to have at least a basic understanding of the main types of epidemiologic studies, which include experimental and observational studies. Specific types of observational studies include cohort, case–control, cross-sectional, and ecological studies. To understand these scientific studies as well as the broader context of public health, health communicators need to have a working knowledge of frequently used epidemiologic terms, including *prevalence*, *incidence*, *mortality rate*, *proportionate mortality*, *agent*, *outbreak*, *epidemic*, *pandemic*, *attack rate*, and case-fatality rate. In working step by step through the communication planning process outlined in Chapter 4, communicators will encounter many of the qualitative and quantitative research methodologies as well as the epidemiological terms discussed in this chapter.

Discussion Questions

1. Explain the different applications of quantitative and qualitative research in health communications planning.
2. How does the sampling method for quantitative research differ from the sampling method used for qualitative research?
3. How can cluster analysis be used to develop tailored communication efforts for distinct target audiences?
4. What are the pros and cons to online focus groups?
5. Explain the difference between prevalence and incidence. Which is better suited for developing a prevention program? Why?
6. What are the six main types of epidemiological studies? How are they different?

References

Ad Council. (n.d.). *Drunk driving prevention (1983–present)*. Available at: http://www.adcouncil.org/default.aspx?id=137. Accessed: August 15, 2010.

Aschengrau, A., & Seage, G. R., III. (2008). *Essentials of epidemiology in public health*. Sudbury, MA: Jones and Bartlett.

Chapter 4

The Communication Planning Process

By Christina Mazzola Nicols

LEARNING OBJECTIVES

By the end of the chapter, the reader will be able to:

- Identify and describe steps in the communication planning process, including:
  - Discovery
  - Objectives
  - Strategy
  - Creative development
  - Measurement
- Describe and use tools and resources within each step of the planning process.

Introduction

An effective communication program begins with a thorough planning process. *Before* embarking on a campaign, the communicator needs to be able to answer several essential questions:

- What is driving the need for communication?
- What are the objectives of the communication effort?
- What does success look like, and how will it be measured?
- Who are the target audiences, and why should they care about the communication?
- How will the communication reach them, and with what messages?

Working through a planning process will help the communicator answer these and other questions to develop a more targeted and effective campaign. Several examples of planning processes are available to communication professionals, and they vary in the number of steps they include. Planning processes developed by communication firms and advertising agencies tend to have five essential steps, described as follows:

1. ***Discovery***: The first step in the planning process involves research and analysis to understand the environment in which the communication effort will be implemented, including the legislative context, media landscape, economic factors, relevant upcoming events, and cultural background pertaining to the topic. The competitive landscape is another key area for exploration, including competitors' messages that will vie for "mind share" among the target audiences. Perhaps most importantly, this first step in the planning process will include research about target audiences—who they are, what they care about, how they make decisions, and where and how they spend their time.
2. ***Objectives***: In the second step of the process, the communicator develops *measurable* objectives. The emphasis here is on *measurable* objectives because too many communication campaigns introduce measurement at the close of the campaign, when it is usually too late to achieve any meaningful measure of effectiveness. Measurement, which is the fifth step in the planning process, is inextricably linked to—and should flow from—the communication objectives.
3. ***Strategy***: Developing communication strategy typically involves considerations about the four *M*s of communication: message, messenger, media, and moment, and the four *P*s of marketing: product, price, place, and promotion.
4. ***Creative Development***: The development of messages and materials, including visual elements, print materials, videos, and interactive games, occurs in the fourth step of the planning process. This step also includes the pretesting of messages and materials among target audiences, typically through in-person focus groups or online surveys. Pretesting is a useful means of gathering audience feedback about messages and materials before finalizing them for use in the communication effort. The ultimate test of the effectiveness of messages and materials, however, is captured in the fifth step of the planning process, campaign measurement.
5. ***Measurement***: This final step in the planning process is intended to demonstrate the effectiveness of the communication effort and suggest ways to improve it moving forward. This step links back to the measurable objectives developed in the second step of the planning process. Communicators can demonstrate success in achieving campaign objectives through *process* measures, which measure how well the campaign was conducted, and *outcomes* measures, which measure the extent to which the campaign changed awareness, understanding, attitudes, or behavior among the target audiences. The rise of online communication and social media has necessitated new forms of measurement, such as the number of "fans" a brand has on Facebook and the number of "followers" who "retweet" a message through Twitter.

Some planning processes separate objectives from strategy to create a six-step process, and others break out target audience research as a separate step. The planning process developed by the National Cancer Institute (NCI), within the National Institutes of Health, contains just four steps:

1. Planning and strategy development
2. Developing and pretesting concepts, messages, and materials
3. Implementing the program
4. Assessing effectiveness and making refinements

While the NCI process combines discovery, objectives and strategy into its first step of planning and strategy development, the two different organizational approaches cover much of the same terrain. The NCI process, titled *Making Health Communication Programs Work*, and commonly known as "The Pink Book," is available online at http://www.cancer.gov/pinkbook. It is a tremendous resource for communication students and professionals. The current version of the Pink Book was developed in accordance with CDCynergy, a planning process originally created for use within the Centers for Disease Control and Prevention (CDC) that has been made available to professionals outside the agency. Whereas the NCI planning process focuses specifically on health communication, CDCynergy focuses on planning public health interventions, in which health communication may be just one component. While it may not be relevant to all of the types of communication efforts explored in this book, it is a robust planning process that may be useful to health communication professionals in various roles and settings. CDCynergy is available in a multimedia CD-ROM format through the CDC Web site at http://www.cdc.gov/healthmarketing/cdcynergy/.

Communication planning is a research-intensive process. Therefore, it is useful for communicators to have at least a basic understanding of quantitative and qualitative research methodologies as well as the main types of epidemiologic studies and frequently used terms. These methodologies and terms are described in Chapter 3, and many are referred to in the following exploration of the communication planning process.

The five steps of the communication planning process are explored in greater detail in the following sections, beginning with discovery, and moving through objectives, strategy, creative development, and measurement.

Discovery

As mentioned in the overview of this chapter, the discovery step of the planning process focuses on conducting research to understand the environment in which the communication effort will be implemented, including the legislative context, media landscape, competitive environment, economic factors, relevant upcoming events, cultural background, and target audiences' attitudes, actions, and preferences. These various research components are often incorporated into a situation analysis. The scope of a situation analysis can vary by program and organization, but it often contains the components outlined below. Each component outlined below has a basic description, a list of key research questions, and resources useful for secondary research (i.e., research using existing data sources). When secondary research does not provide the needed information, primary research (i.e., original research) should be considered, using the qualitative and quantitative methodologies described in Chapter 3.

Assessing the Challenge

Description

A challenge assessment examines the factors that are driving the need for the communication program, including business challenges and opportunities as well as health problems. It considers what is needed to solve the problem or leverage the opportunity to its fullest potential. In addition, this type of assessment looks at stakeholders—people and organizations likely to be affected by the problem or opportunity—and what they stand to gain or lose.

Key Questions

- What is driving the need for communication?
  - Is it a problem that must be resolved, an opportunity to fill an unmet need, or a combination of both?
  - If a health problem is driving the need for the communication, what is the prevalence and incidence of the health problem? See Table 3-4 for definitions and uses, as it is important to understand the difference between these terms.
- What will it take to solve the problem?
  - Can it be solved by communication, or does it require a policy change or a new product?
- Will there be winners and losers in the resolution of the problem?
  - What is at stake for people and organizations involved? What might they gain or lose depending on the outcome?

Resources

The following resources are useful for obtaining information about businesses and business challenges:

- Hoovers: This database provides information about public and private companies, including information about key business units and products, biographies of executives, top competitors, industry insights, and financial information. It is available by subscription online at www.hoovers.com.
- SEC filings: All companies, foreign and domestic, are required to file registration statements, periodic reports, and other forms electronically through the SEC's EDGAR database, available at http://www.sec.gov/edgar/searchedgar/companysearch.html. Anyone can access and download this information for free. All publicly traded companies in the

United States are required to file annual and quarterly reports, known as 10Ks and 10Qs respectively. In addition to company history, organizational structure, executive compensation, information about subsidiaries, and audited financial statements, the 10K filing contains a section on anticipated concerns or problems the company may have in reaching their financial goals. This can be a useful place to look for information pertinent to a SWOT (strengths, weaknesses, opportunities, and threats) analysis, particularly regarding company weaknesses and threats in the marketplace.

- Business publications: The *Wall Street Journal* and other major business publications are available in full-text through the Factiva database (http://factiva.com). These are a terrific source of company and industry news. In addition to business news outlets, the local newspaper where the company is based usually provides more in-depth coverage than any other media outlet. Factiva and LexisNexis (http://www.lexisnexis.com) include full-text coverage of most of the daily newspapers in the United States.
- Analyst reports: Research analysts at brokerage houses, investment banks, and research companies regularly publish reports on companies, industries, and markets, and often provide the most detailed information available. These reports are a tremendous resource because they offer expert opinion on how well a company is positioned in the marketplace and insights into key competitors. Analyst reports are available for individual purchase per report at Yahoo Finance (http://screen.yahoo.com/reports.html).

The following resources, produced by the US Department of Health and Human Services (HHS) and available at no cost online, provide information about diseases and health conditions, including prevalence and incidence data for the US population:

- National Center for Health Statistics: The Web site provides statistics by topic, including by disease or injury, by population or demographic, and by lifestyle factor. It provides data and reports for the major surveys conducted by HHS, including the National Health and Nutrition Examination Survey (NHANES) and the National Health Care Surveys (NHCS), such as the National Ambulatory Health Care Survey (NAMCS) and the National Nursing Home Survey (NNHS). These are available at http://www.cdc.gov/nchs/. Also within the National Center for Health Statistics Web site is *Health, United States*. An essential reference source for health statistics, it covers causes of death, prevalence and incidence of specific diseases, health-related behaviors such as smoking, and health conditions. It is available at http://www.cdc.gov/nchs/data/hus/hus09.pdf.
- Healthfinder: This site serves as an *A–Z* index and entry portal to a variety of government agencies, professional and nonprofit organizations, and educational institutions that provide health information and statistics. The site is available at www.healthfinder.gov.
- HRSA Community Health Status Indicators: The database provides county profiles covering basic demographic data, health measures, birth and death measures, environmental health indicators, health risk factors, and access to care. The database contains more than 200 measures for each of the 3141 US counties. It is available at http://communityhealth.hhs.gov/HomePage.aspx.

- *Morbidity and Mortality Weekly Report (MMWR)*: The *MMWR* contains data on specific diseases as reported by state and territorial health departments and reports on infectious and chronic diseases, environmental hazards, natural or human-generated disasters, occupational diseases and injuries, and intentional and unintentional injuries. It provides updated reports on seasonal influenza each year, with a final report at the close of the season. It is available at http://www.cdc.gov/mmwr/mmwr_wk.html.
- Child Health USA: This resource covers 55 pediatric health status indicators, including statistics pertaining to childcare, infant mortality, vaccine-preventable diseases, and hospitalization, as well as health behaviors, such as smoking and physical activity. It contains a state data section with statistics for a limited number of indicators. It is available at http://mchb.hrsa.gov/mchirc/chusa/.

Information about treatments for various diseases and health conditions can be found in the following resources:

- National Guidelines Clearinghouse: The clearinghouse is a public resource for evidence-based clinical practice guidelines. Users can browse guideline summaries by topic or organization or search for them using keywords. A feature enables a comparative analysis of guidelines on similar topics. It is available at http://www.guidelines.gov/index.aspx.
- The Merck Manuals Online Medical Library: The online version of the *Merck Manual*, available in Merck's online medical library, contains information on disease states and management, with diagnosis and treatment of common clinical disorders arranged by organ system, etiology, or specialty. Merck provides the content of the *Merck Manual* on the Web for free. Registration is not required, and use is unlimited. The Web site is continuously updated to ensure that the information is as up to date as possible. It is available at http://www.merck.com/mmpe/index.html.

In addition the government resources listed above, WebMD provides in-depth reference material about various diseases and health topics, commentaries, and patient communities. The content is written specifically for consumers and incorporates multimedia, such as slide presentations and videos. Users can browse health topics organized from *A* to *Z* or use the search feature. The site is available at http://www.webmd.com/.

Competitive Analysis

Description

A competitive analysis examines the marketplace position of the product and the concept or behavior the communicator is attempting to promote, including its status relative to its competitors and how it fits in the overall environment of its target audiences.

Key Questions

- Who or what are the chief competitors to the product, concept, or behavior the communicator is attempting to promote?

- What are the strengths, weaknesses, opportunities, and threats (SWOT) for the product, concept, or behavior the communicator is attempting to promote relative to its competitors?
  - *Strengths* may include financial resources, expertise within an organization, key product claims and differentiators, alliances and partnerships with other organizations, distribution channels, brand recognition, media visibility, and credibility among target audiences and those who influence the target audiences.
  - *Weaknesses* may include the comparative lack of financial resources, expertise, product differentiators, alliances and partnerships, distribution channels, brand recognition, media visibility, and credibility.
  - *Opportunities* are the circumstances that could make the product, concept, or behavior the communicator is attempting to promote more desirable. These may include the unmet needs and desires of target audiences, new legislation and regulations, demographic and cultural trends, important upcoming events, the misfortunes of competitors, and the efforts of potential allies and partnering organizations.
  - *Threats* are the circumstances that could make the product, concept, or behavior the communicator is attempting to promote *less* desirable. These may include the circumstances outlined above as potential opportunities. The most important threats to consider are often the strengths of competitors and the possibility of opposition by organizations interested in or affected by the situation.
- How are the communicator's product, concept, or behavior and its competitors portrayed in media coverage and blogs?
  - A media analysis, described in a later section, is a useful way to compare visibility or "share of voice," message penetration, marketplace perceptions, topics driving coverage, and tone of coverage.
- What organizations are doing or have done a similar communication effort?
  - What successes have they achieved?
  - What challenges have they encountered?
  - What are the key insights to consider for future communication programs?
- What organizations are likely to support or oppose the proposed communication program?
  - What level of visibility does the organization have? Is it nationally known or local?
  - How well connected is it politically and culturally?
  - What resources is the organization able to leverage in its support or opposition of the product, concept, or behavior the communicator is attempting to promote?
  - What is the extent of the organization's reach among the target audiences? Does it have local chapters that actively participate in communities? Does it provide services or information directly to individuals in the target audience?
  - Do target audiences and their influencers consider the organization credible?
  - If the organization is opposed to the proposed communication effort, is it possible to negotiate or reach a better understanding with the organization? What would be required in doing so? Is the communicator prepared to make the necessary compromise?

Resources

The following resources are useful for obtaining information about the marketplace positions of products and companies:

- Hoovers: Hoovers provides information about 65 million companies. Profiles include a history and description of the company, its business units, key products, and subsidiaries; contact information and biographies of executives; lists of key competitors; financial reports, including stock performance, revenues, and market value; selected insights from analysts; relevant industry information; and basic company statistics, such as number of employees. The service is available by subscription at http://www.hoovers.com.
- Analyst reports: As noted in the "Assessment of the Challenge" section, analyst reports are a useful means of obtaining expert insight into the marketplace positions of various competitors within a sector or industry.

The following resources may be used to prepare an analysis of previous communication efforts:

- PubMed: PubMed is a free cataloging and indexing service developed and maintained by the National Center for Biotechnology Information (NCBI) at the US National Library of Medicine (NLM). The service offers more than 20 million citations for biomedical literature from MEDLINE, life science journals, and online books. Citations may include links to full-text content from PubMed Central and publisher Web sites, but often a user will need access to an academic or medical library to download the full-text articles. In addition to indexing medical journals such as the *New England Journal of Medicine* and *JAMA*, PubMed indexes communication, social marketing, and health policy journals such as *Health Communication*, *Social Marketing Quarterly*, *Health Affairs*, and *Health Education Quarterly*. Many of the journals indexed by PubMed contain evaluations and assessments of communication programs and other interventions developed to solve public health problems. These types of articles typically describe the degree of success a program achieved using specific strategies and tactics under specific circumstances. Many of the articles focus on research studies conducted to determine the effectiveness of the program or intervention, and therefore, it is useful to have a basic understanding of the various types of studies described in Chapter 3, Table 3-6. The database is available at http://www.ncbi.nlm.nih.gov/pubmed.
- PRSA Anvil Awards Database: Members of the Public Relations Society of America (PRSA) have access to the PRSA database of Silver and Bronze award entries, which provide useful case studies of successful communication programs and campaigns. The case profiles outline the campaign's challenge, strategies and tactics, creative elements, and measurement. The database is available at http://www.prsa.org/Awards/Search.

For information about medications on the market and in the pipelines of pharmaceutical companies, the following resources are useful:

- *Physicians' Desk Reference*: The reference contains the package inserts of prescription medications, grouped and listed by manufacturer. It lists active and inactive ingredients for most drugs on the market. There is a separate PDR for nonprescription drugs and dietary supplements. It is available by subscription at http://www.pdr.net/login/Login.aspx.
- PhRMA New Medicines Database: The Pharmaceutical Research and Manufacturers of America (PhRMA) offers free access to a database of medicines currently in clinical trials or at the US Food and Drug Administration (FDA) for review. The information contained in the database was derived from Wolters Kluwer Health's Adis R&D Insight and is published with permission under license with Wolters Kluwer Health. The database is searchable by drug, indication, company name, or status (e.g., phase I, phase II). It is available at http://newmeds.phrma.org/.
- ClinicalTrials.gov: ClinicalTrials.gov offers up-to-date information for locating federally and privately supported clinical trials for a wide range of diseases and conditions. The database offers free access to tens of thousands of trials sponsored by the National Institutes of Health, other federal agencies, and private industry. Studies listed in the database are conducted in all 50 states as well as internationally. It is available at http://clinicaltrials.gov.

Media Analysis

Description

A media analysis can be a useful component of a competitive analysis. It examines the media environment of the communicator's product, concept, or behavior relative to its competitors. Specific factors to examine may include overall visibility or "share of voice," message penetration, marketplace perceptions, topics driving coverage, and tone of coverage.

Key Questions

- What is the visibility or "share of voice" of the communicator's product, concept, or behavior in media coverage relative to its competitors?
  - How much coverage has it received in the past year or two?
  - How much coverage have competitors received?
  - What types of media outlets tend to cover it?
  - Is it a national story or a local story?
- What topics tend to drive media coverage? Topic drivers may include financial stories, such as quarterly results, news of research and product innovations, features about individuals grappling with a health condition, and news about legislation and regulation affecting the product, concept, or behavior.

- What are the marketplace perceptions of the product, concept, or behavior?
  - What messages have been reported—positive as well as negative?
  - What are analysts and other experts saying?
  - What are editorial and op-ed writers and bloggers saying?
  - What is the tone of the coverage—mostly in favor of the product, concept, or behavior, or mostly critical of it?

A quantitative media analysis is a tool that allows communication professionals to compare coverage of competitors using a standardized methodology. Indicators of the quality of coverage, such as tone, message penetration, caliber of media outlet, and the inclusion of quotes of stakeholders and experts, are quantified using a point system. The analyst uses a score sheet to assess news articles, blogs, editorials, and op-eds over a specific time period, such as a year or 6 months. Coding is typically done in an Excel spreadsheet to facilitate basic statistical analysis. Each article is given a score, and the average of article scores over the time period can be used as an indicator of the quality of coverage. The coverage of several competitors can be compared using this methodology to determine strengths and weaknesses in the marketplace position of each. A quantitative media analysis can also be used as a process measure, as described in the measurement section of this chapter. An example of a score sheet for media coverage pertaining to a pharmaceutical product is shown in Table 4-1.

Resources

- Factiva: A product of Dow Jones Corporation, Factiva offers full-text access to more than 28,000 leading news sources from 157 countries in 23 languages, including regional and industry publications, Web, and blog content. The service offers advanced search tools and automated alerts, with timed or continuous delivery to e-mail, RSS, or mobile devices to help users stay on top of the latest news about a company, product, or issue. Factiva is a useful all-in-one source for conducting media scans and analyses on companies and issues. In addition to providing newspaper coverage from virtually every market in the United States, it contains transcripts of national television news. It does not, however, provide transcripts of local television news. If local television news is an essential part of a campaign that should be accounted for in the media analysis, an additional monitoring service should be used for this, such as VMS (http://www.vmsinfo.com). Factiva is available by subscription at http://www.factiva.com.
- LexisNexis: The Nexis database contains content from more than 20,000 full-text global news sources, company and industry intelligence providers, and biographical and reference sources. The Nexis archive of content dates back to the 1970s for many sources, which makes it useful for research into case histories, such as crisis communication situations and product launches. Like Factiva, Nexis offers advanced search tools and automated alerts. Nexis is available by subscription at http://www.lexisnexis.com/new/.

Table 4-1 Example of a Score Sheet for a Quantitative Media Analysis of a Pharmaceutical Product and Its Competitors

Competitive Media Analysis—Pharmaceutical Sector
Algorithm Framework for Corporate Reputation Coverage

Article Selection

Headline: ______________________________

Publication: ______________________

Reporter: ______________________

Date

Code for month (e.g., 4 for April, 5 for May, 6 for June)

Company Featured

1. Company A
2. Company B
3. Company C
4. Company D

Topic of Coverage (Choose as many as two; no points assigned)

1. Corporate business story—merger/acquisition, stock performance, financial results
2. Specific product on the market
3. Research findings/data publication or presentation
4. Drug pricing
5. Medicare Part D drug benefit
6. Marketing/advertising practices
7. Litigation/lawsuits
8. Legislation—state or federal
9. FDA regulation/activity
10. Philanthropy/community engagement
11. Pipeline—either overall pipeline or specific product in pipeline

Reach and Audience (Choose one; maximum 15 points)

1. National television—15 points
2. Major business publications (*Forbes*, *Fortune*, *Businessweek*, *Barron's*)—15 points
3. National news weekly magazines (*Newsweek*, *Time*, *US News*)—15 points
4. National newspapers (*WSJ*, *NYT*, *USA Today*, *LA Times*)—15 points
5. News wires (AP, Dow Jones, Reuters)—10 points
6. Other top 50 newspapers—10 points
7. Trade publications—10 points

Positive Messages (Choose as many as relevant; 5 points for each message; bonus 10 points if 3 or more messages)

1. Message relating to product attributes—therapeutic benefits/efficacy
2. Message relating to product attributes—side effects/safety issues
3. Message relating to price
4. Message relating to business performance
5. Message relating to marketing/advertising practices
6. Message relating to research findings/trials/data publication or presentation
7. Message relating to jobs/employment/employees
8. Message relating to philanthropy/community engagement
9. Message relating to litigation
10. Message relating to regulatory approval/new indication

(continues)

(continued)

Table 4-1 **Example of a Score Sheet for a Quantitative Media Analysis of a Pharmaceutical Product and Its Competitors**

Negative Messages (Choose as many as relevant; –5 points for each message; bonus –10 points if 3 or more messages)

1. Message relating to product attributes—therapeutic benefits/efficacy
2. Message relating to product attributes—side effects/safety issues
3. Message relating to price
4. Message relating to business performance
5. Message relating to marketing/advertising practices
6. Message relating to research findings/trials/data publication or presentation
7. Message relating to jobs/employment/employees
8. Message relating to philanthropy/community engagement
9. Message relating to litigation
10. Message relating to regulatory approval/new indication

Expert quote (Choose as many as two; 30 points maximum)

1. Article includes quote by company spokesperson (15 points)
2. Article includes expert/consumer quote in support of company (10 points)
3. Article includes negative expert/consumer quote about company (–10 points)

Overall Tone of Coverage (Choose one; 15 points maximum)

1. Very positive—15 points
2. Positive—10 points
3. Neutral—0 points
4. Negative— –10 points
5. Very negative— –15 points

Placement (Choose one; 10 points maximum)

1. Neutral/positive article on first page of first section of paper or cover story of magazine (10 points)
2. Negative article on first page of first section of paper or cover story of magazine (–10 points)
3. Neutral/positive article on first page of other section of paper (5 points)
4. Negative article on first page of other section of paper (–5 points)

Headline Mentions (Choose one; 15 points maximum)

1. Featured company neutral/positive mention in headline (15 points)
2. Featured company negative mention in headline (–15 points)

Total Points: 140 possible points per article, including bonus

- Google News: Google provides a free search engine of news articles appearing within the past 30 days on various news web sites. Google News aggregates content from more than 25,000 publishers around the world. The service provides the headlines but not always full-text access to articles, as many publishers require subscriptions to view full-text content. While Google News can provide a quick comparative scan of headlines for various competitors, it is not as precise as the Factiva and Nexis databases for conducting in-depth or quantitative media analysis. Google News is available at http://www.google.com.

Legislative and Policy Analysis

Description

A legislative and policy analysis examines existing laws and regulations affecting the communicator's product, concept, or behavior, as well as bills and proposed regulation that may have a future effect. This type of analysis also considers the positions of key lawmakers and policy influencers involved.

Key Questions

- What are the existing laws, regulations, and policies that affect the communicator's product, concept, or behavior?
  - Are they controversial or contested?
  - How might they change in the future?
- What recent bills have been proposed that will affect the communicator's product, concept, or behavior?
  - What individuals or organizations are driving the legislation?
    - Who are the sponsors and co-sponsors in Congress?
    - Are there external organizations driving the legislation?
  - Is there bipartisan support?
  - Do other organizations or individuals have strong opinions about the proposed legislation?
    - What organizations or individuals are likely to support and oppose the proposed legislation?
  - Is the issue driving the legislation front-page news or a front-burner political issue?
- What is the economic impact of the proposed legislation?
  - What segments of consumers will be affected?
  - Who stands to win or lose, and what is at stake?

Resources

- Trade associations: Trade associations representing various industries typically include a summary of their legislative and political activities and interests in the government affairs section of the Web site. They often provide issues analyses and summaries of legislation they are supporting or opposing.
- THOMAS: The Library of Congress THOMAS Web site is a free resource for federal legislative information. THOMAS provides several options for finding bills, resolutions, and other congressional information. Users can search bill summaries from the 101st (1989) through the current Congress, public laws by law number, House and Senate roll call votes, legislation by sponsor, activity in Congress, and committee information. The database is available at http://thomas.loc.gov/.

- State Net: State Net has evolved over the past several decades from a computerized tracking system of bills proposed in the legislatures of the 50 states to a comprehensive source of legislative intelligence and in-depth reporting by legislative experts. State Net monitors every bill in the 50 states, District of Columbia, in Congress and every state agency regulation. It is available by subscription at http://www.statenet.com.
- LexisNexis: LexisNexis also offers state bill tracking on a pay-as-you-go basis rather than an annual subscription, which can be convenient for infrequent users. State bill tracking reports track legislative developments for all 50 states. Bill tracking reports for current legislation are typically available 4 to 5 days after action, with the exception of California, Pennsylvania, and Colorado reports, which are available within 48 hours of an action on a bill. These reports include a summary of pending legislation from introduction through enactment or veto, and chronicle the stages of the bill's legislative processes. The service is available within the LexisNexis Legal database.
- Policy-related media—Newspapers and newsletters such as *Roll Call, National Journal, The Hill*, and *Congressional Quarterly* publications offer insightful commentary in addition to legislative news. These publications are useful for determining the issues, people, and organizations that are driving proposed legislation. Most are available on Factiva and LexisNexis.
- Foundations, policy organizations, and think tanks—Organizations such as the Brookings Institution, the Heritage Foundation, the Kaiser Family Foundation, RAND, the Robert Wood Johnson Foundation, the Urban Institute, and the Commonwealth Foundation often provide on their Web sites commentary, position papers, original research, and news about various issues pertaining to health policy. Policy makers view these institutions as credible resources, and they frequently rely on them for perspectives and research data as well as testimony in hearings.
- Institute of Medicine (IOM): The IOM is an independent, nonprofit organization that works outside of government to provide unbiased and authoritative advice to policy makers and the public. Established in 1970, the IOM is the health arm of the National Academy of Sciences. The IOM publishes in-depth reports on a variety of issues affecting health and medicine. The reports are searchable by topic and date, and are available at http://www.iom.edu/Reports.aspx.

Target Audience Analysis

Description

A target audience analysis examines primary audiences (i.e., the audiences the communicator needs to reach to achieve changes in knowledge and/or behaviors) as well as secondary audiences (i.e., intermediary audiences that influence the primary audiences). This type of analysis considers the audience size; how the product, concept, or behavior being promoted may affect the life of individuals within the audience; demographic and lifestyle factors, knowledge levels, attitudes and beliefs; and preferences in media and other channels for message dissemination. The analysis also explores how the audiences perceive the benefits associated with the product, concept, or behavior, and any barriers the audiences face in realizing those benefits. Arguably, the target audience analysis is the single most important analysis in the discovery process, as the communicator will not be able to influence the audience's attitudes, beliefs, and behaviors unless he or she thoroughly understands the factors that will facilitate change.

Key Questions

- How is the target audience defined?
  - Is it defined by a disease or health condition? Demographic factors such as gender, age or geography? Or by knowledge levels or attitudes?
- What is the size of the target audience?
  - Does it represent a broad population or is it a narrowly defined segment?
  - If it is a broad population, are there "sweet spot" segments that represent significant areas of need or opportunity?
- What product, concept, or behavior is the target audience currently using that the communicator hopes to replace?
  - How strongly does the target audience feel about or rely on the current product, concept, or behavior?
  - How difficult or easy will it be to replace the current product, concept, or behavior?
- What demographic factors influence the target audience's decisions regarding the product, concept, or behavior? Demographic factors, such as age, gender, marital status, race and ethnicity, income, and education levels frequently influence health decisions and health status. For example:
  - Women are often the chief decision makers on health issues affecting their families, and are therefore a popular target audience for health communication professionals.
  - Income and education levels are key determinants of knowledge of health information, access to health care, and other important factors influencing health status.
  - Age is also a key factor, as, for example, younger people tend to experience fewer health problems, and therefore may not devote a lot of time or thought to health decisions.
  - With regard to race and ethnicity, African American and Latino communities are often more likely than other races and ethnicities to encounter health disparities, particularly in terms of access to health care. They may also be more difficult to reach if they do not use media as frequently as others, and may therefore require additional or alternative outreach components and resources within the communication effort, such as communication through trusted community organizations.

- What attitudes influence the target audience's decisions regarding the product, concept, or behavior? These may include:
  - Attitudes specifically about the product, concept. or behavior, such as fears of adverse effects, concerns about cost, enthusiasm or anticipation
  - Cultural beliefs and personal values, which may include religious beliefs and cultural traditions
  - Dreams and aspirations, which may include career goals, social aspiration, financial security, and opportunities for children
- What lifestyle factors influence the target audience's decisions regarding the product, concept, or behavior?
  - Will the product, concept, or behavior offer a lifestyle benefit such as convenience or improved quality of life over what the target audience is currently using or doing?
  - Does the product, concept, or behavior complement existing activities and lifestyle factors?
  - Will the target audience have to give up an enjoyed lifestyle factor to embrace the product, concept, or behavior?
- What is the geographic concentration of the target audience?
  - Is it rural or urban? Audiences in rural areas can be more difficult to reach than those in urban areas, as there are fewer media outlets and channels for outreach.
  - Which designated market areas (DMAs) are most heavily populated by target audiences? These should be the priority for the communication effort.
- What upcoming events could contribute to the target audience's interest in the product, concept, or behavior?
  - Would the target audience be most receptive during a special occasion, holiday, or commemoration day?
  - What other moments in time present opportunities for reaching the target audience? For example, as described in Chapter 10, Aetna developed a campaign to encourage consumers to take stock of their health insurance at specific times in their lives, including when they are getting married, expecting a child, or graduating from college.
- What are the audience's perceptions about the benefits to be derived from the product, concept, or behavior?
  - Is the audience aware of the benefits?
  - Does the audience value the benefits?
  - Does the audience believe the product, concept, or behavior will deliver the benefits promised?
- What barriers may prevent the target audience from realizing the benefits of the product, concept, or behavior? Barriers may include the following:
  - The monetary cost (i.e., price) of obtaining the product, concept or behavior

- Nonmonetary costs, such as the time it takes or having to give up favorite activities or foods
- Lack of access
- Lack of knowledge
- Cultural norms, prohibitions, and/or taboos
- Competitive alternatives to the product, concept, or behavior

- What individuals or organizations influence the primary target audience?
  - What type of relationship do they have with the primary audience?
  - Can they be recruited as partners in the communication effort?
  - What dissemination channels do they offer in reaching the primary audience?
- What are the audience's preferences in media and other channels for message dissemination?
  - What traditional media outlets does the audience read or view? (e.g., television, newspapers, or magazines?)
  - What Web sites does the target audience visit regularly?
  - Does the audience engage in social media, such as Twitter, FaceBook, LinkedIn, and other sites?
  - Does the audience follow and interact with blogs? Which blogs are most important for the audience?
  - Does the target audience actively seek health information? What sources does it rely on most frequently?
  - Are there venues at the point of purchase or point of decision that could be used as channels for message dissemination? (e.g., supermarkets are point-of-purchase venues often used for disseminating messages about food and nutrition)

Resources

When physicians represent the target audience, the following resources are useful:

- *Physician Characteristics and Distribution in the U.S.*: Published by the American Medical Association (AMA), this book is a complete source of statistical data about the physician supply in the United States. It includes extensive data on trends, characteristics, and distribution of physicians, as well as analysis of professional activity by self-designated specialty and geographical region. There is a separate section on primary care specialties. The book is available for purchase at the bookstore on the AMA web site (http://www.ama-assn.org/).
- PERQ/HCI Focus Journal Readership Studies: PERQ/HCI tracks physician readership of major medical journals. The readership survey is segmented by physician specialty, including internal medicine, OB/GYN, oncology, and neurology. The study report includes how frequently physicians read each journal as well as their reading habits (e.g., cover-to-cover, skim pages). Readership data can be purchased at http://kantarmediana.com/healthcare/expertise.

Resources providing information about consumer audience segments include the following:

- US Census: The US Census Web site (http://www.census.gov/) provides a wealth of data about the US population, including general population characteristics (e.g., age, gender, race, marital status), and social and economic characteristics (e.g., income, education level, occupation). The site provides data at the national, state, county, and city levels.
- PubMed: Described previously in the "Competitive Analysis" section, PubMed provides citations to journal articles about studies conducted among various audience segments. These insights can be useful in understanding audience attitudes regarding a health condition or proposed intervention, including their perceived benefits of and barriers to achieving a desired health-related behavior. PubMed is available at http://www.ncbi.nlm.nih.gov/pubmed/.
- The National Health and Nutrition Examination Surveys (NHANES): Conducted by the National Center for Health Statistics (NCHS) and the Centers for Disease Control (CDC), NHANES assess the health and nutritional status of adults and children in the United States through interviews and direct physical examinations. NHANES data enable researchers to estimate the proportion of the US population with a selected disease or risk factor; monitor trends in selected behaviors, exposures, and diseases; and study the associations among diet, nutrition, and health. Reports and data sets are available on the CDC Web site at http://www.cdc.gov/nchs/nhanes.htm.
- GfK MRI (formerly Mediamark Research Inc.): The database of consumer behavior and attitudes is based on *The Survey of the American Consumer*, conducted twice annually among approximately 13,000–14,000 consumers per survey wave. The two survey waves are combined each year into a "doublebase" representing 26,000–28,000 consumers annually. The database includes product usage, media consumption, demographics, sports and leisure activities, as well as attitudinal data on various topics. Data can be segmented by demographics, attitudes, and life stage. Virtually any variable in the database can be cross-tabulated against another, providing a vast range of ways to define and target audience segments. For example, researchers can define an audience segment based on a specific attitude or health behavior, and then run cross-tabs against the definition to determine the segment's media preferences in television, radio, magazines, newspapers, and online. This approach enables researchers to target the media outlets that will be most effective in reaching their target audiences. The database provides MRI data trends back to 1998 in selected categories. The database is available by subscription at http://www.gfkmri.com/.
- Teenmark: Also from GfK, the Teenmark database is based on a survey among more than 3600 US consumers age 12 to 19. Like the MRI database, Teenmark includes data on product usage, media consumption, demographics, sports, and leisure activities, including dating habits and hobbies. The database also includes attitudinal data in a wide range of topics, such as health, food and diet, finance, music, media, technology, fashion, stresses, self-perception, goals and aspirations, volunteerism, personal values, and socializing. The database is available by subscription at http://www.gfkmri.com/ProductsServices/TeenMark.aspx.

- Scarborough Research: Scarborough Research measures the lifestyles, shopping patterns, media behaviors, and demographics of American consumers locally, regionally, and nationally. The database contains specific regional market data for the top 77 local media markets to supplement what can be obtained through MRI. Categories include automotive, banking and financial, beverages, business-to-business, computer and Internet use, drug and grocery purchases, health care, home improvement, household shopping, media, restaurant, retail, sports, telecommunications, transportation, travel, and voting. The database is available by subscription at http://www.scarborough.com/.

Objectives

After developing a thorough understanding of the environment in which the communication effort will be implemented, including the legislative context, media landscape, competitive environment, and target audiences' attitudes, actions, and preferences, the health communicator is ready to develop measurable objectives for the communication program.

The emphasis here is on *measurable* objectives because too many communication campaigns introduce measurement at the close of the campaign, when it is usually too late to achieve any meaningful measure of effectiveness. As each program objective is determined, it should be linked directly to a measurement methodology.

Creating Measurable Objectives

Communication objectives are typically aimed at achieving a change in the awareness, understanding, attitude, or behavior of a target audience within a defined time period. For example, if an audience is predominantly unaware of new CDC recommendations for flu vaccinations, the focus of a communication campaign over the coming year will likely be to generate awareness of the new recommendations. If an audience is aware of the new recommendations, but doesn't understand the importance of them, the campaign will likely focus on explaining why the new recommendations are necessary. Alternatively, an audience may be aware of the new recommendations and understand them, but may disagree with them. In this case, the campaign will likely focus on persuading the audience to change an attitude. For example, a segment of parents may have heard the CDC recommends flu vaccinations for children older than 6 months, and may have seen research showing the benefits of the flu vaccination. However, these parents may feel the flu vaccination is simply not necessary, as their children rarely get sick, or they may feel the vaccination is not worth the perceived risk of adverse effects. Therefore, a campaign to move parents to the desired behavior of getting flu vaccinations for their children would have to focus on changing their attitudes rather than on increasing their awareness. A change in behavior is usually the ultimate goal of a communication campaign, but it can take some time to achieve, depending on where the audience is in terms of awareness, understanding, and attitudes. Figuring out where the audience is in this spectrum is the key to developing reasonable campaign objectives.

Research is typically needed to assess current levels of audience awareness, understanding, attitudes, and behavior, and in turn, to develop the objectives of the communication program. It is generally a good practice to check first for existing research (i.e., secondary research) on target audiences. If existing research sources do not offer the needed insights, the communications professional should conduct original research (i.e., primary research). Omnibus surveys can be an inexpensive and efficient means of surveying target audiences to determine their current levels of awareness, understanding, attitudes, and behavior. Chapter 3 provides more detail about conducting surveys, including omnibus survey services.

Well-formulated campaign objectives typically commit to achieving a defined percentage change in audience awareness, understanding, attitudes, and behavior within a defined time period. Examples are shown in Table 4-2.

Determining a reasonable percentage of change for a campaign objective can be difficult. If the communication program is not new, objectives can build on the achievements of previous years. To develop objectives for new campaigns, communications professionals can review evaluations of previous campaigns that are similar in scope and content and aimed at comparable target audience segments.

To estimate the levels of message exposure that will yield desired changes in awareness, understanding, attitude, and behavior, some health communicators use a "rule of halves" approach proposed by McGuire in 1984. McGuire's hierarchy of communication effects suggests that for any given placement of a message in a media outlet seen by a target audience, 50% of the audience will be exposed to it; 25% will have specific recall of the message to achieve awareness; 12.5% will understand how the message effects them; 6.25% will have a change in attitude resulting from the message; 3.12% will have the intention to act; and 1.56% will at least try a behavior change as a result of the message (McGuire, 1984). This approach is generally used only as a "rule of thumb" when more specific measures are not available, as it has seldom been tested in campaign evaluations. The key lesson learned in this hierarchical model is that changes in behavior are much more difficult to achieve than changes in awareness, and communicators should not overestimate likely behavior change in their objectives.

Table 4-2 **Example of Measurable Communication Objectives**

Awareness objective	Increase awareness of new CDC recommendations for flu vaccinations by 40% among mothers of children older than 6 months in 2011.
Understanding objective	Increase understanding of the benefits of flu vaccinations by 20% among mothers of children older than 6 months in 2011.
Attitude objective	Decrease by 10% in 2011 the number of mothers who believe flu vaccinations are not necessary for their children.
Behavior objective	Increase by 5% the number of mothers who get flu vaccinations for their children older than 6 months in 2011.

In addition to objectives pertaining to changes in audience awareness, understanding, attitudes, and behavior, communicators often develop objectives relating to the process of conducting a campaign. Many of these process measures are specifically about earned media (i.e., media coverage achieved by working with reporters to develop articles), including:

- Number of articles achieved in earned media efforts
- Audience reach, through circulation and viewership
- Tone and overall quality of earned media coverage
- How frequently campaign messages appear
- How frequently campaign spokespeople are quoted

Process measures can also relate to activities with partnering organizations. Objectives in this area may specify how many partnering organizations will sign on to the campaign within a defined time period, how many events they will co-host, and how many materials they will disseminate to target audiences. To formulate process objectives, communicators either build on the achievements of previous years or review evaluations of previous campaigns that are similar in scope. The scale of these objectives and measures generally depend on the size and composition of the target audience.

Recommended means of measuring audience and process objectives in communication programs are explored later in this chapter.

Strategy

Communication strategy does not have to be complicated. In fact, "the simpler the better" is usually the rule. A well-stated communication strategy should fit neatly into a single statement, outlined as follows:

> *The communication program will target [whom], to help them understand, believe, or do [what], by informing them of [messages], through [messengers and channels], to result in [objectives].*

The Four *M*s of Communication

To complete the strategy statement, communicators need to think through the four essential *M*s of communication:

- Develop a *message* that resonates with a defined target audience.
- Determine the most credible and persuasive *messenger*.
- Drive the message through the most effective *media* or channels.
- Deliver the message at the *moment* when the audience will be most receptive to it.

Naturally, the strategy should support the objectives of the communication program. A communication campaign designed primarily to raise awareness will likely differ in important ways from a campaign designed primarily to change behavior. One of the differences may be in the "richness" of the media selected for disseminating the message. The degree to which a medium is considered "rich" or "lean" is based on how well it is able to convey information to the audience. Information may be straightforward facts or more complex emotions and opinions. According to media richness theory, communicators use four criteria to rate a medium's ability to convey information, including its ability to:

- Relay immediate feedback.
- Provide multiple cues such as body language and visual images in addition to text.
- Tailor information to the audience.
- Transmit the emotions of the communicators (Daft & Lengel, 1984).

A campaign designed to change behavior may require a rich medium for disseminating messages, as a behavior change often requires a substantial commitment from the audience. To make a behavior change, audiences may need feedback to reassure them they are doing something beneficial and worthwhile. They may need information tailored specifically to them to eliminate any confusion or misunderstanding they may have about the behavior. They will likely need multiple cues for reinforcement, such as visual images of others doing the behavior as well as text explaining how they can do the behavior too. Audiences may also need emotional support to convince them to try the behavior, especially if it is something they have never tried before. These types of needs require a high degree of richness in media selected for the campaign. Face-to-face communication is considered the richest of media, but it is not practical for mass communication campaigns. Some forms of social media, especially those supporting multimedia formats and interactive components, can provide richness through their ability to deliver multiple cues, emotions, and feedback from communicators as well as the online community. Tailored information is also possible through interactive components that collect information from individuals through surveys and provide recommendations based on the information provided.

An awareness campaign may not require as much of a commitment from the audience, and therefore may not require the same degree of richness in a medium, especially if the message is fairly straightforward. Table 4-3 provides an outline of some potential differences in message, messenger, media, and moment between a campaign intended primarily to raise awareness and one intended primarily to change behavior. These potential differences are hypothetical and are *not* based on evaluations of specific campaigns; instead, they are intended as general guidelines for thinking about how the four *M*s should be tailored to communication objectives.

Communicators should incorporate the research gathered and conducted in the discovery phase of the planning process into decisions about the four *M*s and campaign strategy. For example:

- Insights from the challenge assessment can drive decisions about the content of the messages as well as stakeholders—individuals as well as organizations—that may serve as credible messengers.
- A competitive analysis often yields clues about what is needed to make messages stand out from the crowd.

Table 4-3 **Potential Differences in Four Ms Between Campaigns to Raise Awareness vs. Change Behavior**

Four *Ms*	**Awareness Campaign**	**Behavior Campaign**
Message	Message aims to *inform* the audience about a new product, concept or behavior.	Message aims to *persuade* the audience to try a behavior.
Messenger	Messenger aims to *capture the attention* of the audience. Messenger should be someone who *stands out* from the crowd.	Messenger aims to *reassure* the audience that the behavior is beneficial and worth doing. Messenger should be someone the audience *identifies with and trusts*.
Media	"*Leaner*" media may be sufficient to generate awareness, especially if the message is straightforward. Strategy may emphasize breadth over depth.	Media should be "*rich*" enough to provide feedback, multiple cues, tailored information, and emotions. Strategy may emphasize depth over breadth.
Moment	Moment can be *broadly defined* as any time the audience has a few minutes to absorb the message. Strategy may emphasize repeated messages throughout a typical day, such as during the morning commute and again at the grocery store on the way home.	Moment needs to be *more specific* to when the audience feels the need to make a behavior change, when it feels most confident about making a change, and/or when the audience will have support from family and friends for the behavior change. Strategy may emphasize fewer messages delivered at the most opportune times.

- A media analysis can be useful in determining message tone and content as well as the outlets and channels most likely to convey the messages.
- The legislative and policy analysis can spur thinking about secondary audiences who are in positions to influence the primary audiences of the campaign.
- The target audience analysis is essential in determining all four *M*s, including audience preferences in message tone and content, media, messengers, and moments. Insights into how the audience views the product, concept, or behavior being promoted can help determine if the message tone should be humorous or serious. Message content should address the benefits and barriers the audience associates with the product, concept, or behavior. An understanding of audience media preferences and usage helps pinpoint the most effective dissemination channels. Insights about the audience's trusted advisors and influencers can drive decisions about messengers to be recruited for the campaign.

The Four *P*s of Marketing

The four *P*s of marketing—product, price, place, and promotion—represent another approach or framework commonly used in developing communication strategy. The essentials of the four *P*s are outlined as follows:

- *Product* is the product, concept, or behavior being promoted in the communication program.

- *Price* is what the product, concept, or behavior will cost the target audience. Price can be monetary or nonmonetary. Examples of nonmonetary costs can be psychological (e.g., the stress or anxiety of trying a new behavior), social (e.g., stigma associated with a product or behavior), related to convenience (e.g., distance required to travel to obtain the product), or related to physical discomfort (e.g., initial soreness with exercise).
- *Place* refers to where the audience will purchase the product, encounter the concept, or do the behavior. It also refers to the general availability of the product, concept, or behavior.
- *Promotion* considers many of the factors explored in the four *M*s of communication, including message tone and content, messengers, media, and channels to be used in the campaign. It also refers to the positioning of the product, concept, or behavior, including how benefits are presented to the target audience. In addition, promotion pertains to communication tactics used in the campaign, which typically can include some combination of paid media (i.e., advertising), earned media (i.e., media coverage achieved by working with reporters to develop articles), social media activity, outreach through partnering organizations, events, and direct mail.

Chapter 15, which presents a case study of the Chicago *5-4-3-2-1 Go!* program, illustrates the use of the four *P*s in strategy development and their implications for campaign measurement. The case shows, for example, how *promotion* and *product* strategies can directly reach individuals and nudge them to change nutrition and physical activity habits for the better. The case also explores how the *price* of getting children active can be reduced through community sports and recreation programs in local neighborhoods (integrating *place*) at times convenient for busy working parents.

Creative Development

After outlining communication objectives and strategy, communicators can begin creative development of messages and materials. It is usually a good idea to start with a creative brief, which is intended to guide the work of the team that will handle the writing and creative design of messages and materials. Table 4-4 outlines the information typically included in a creative brief. Much of this information can be found in research conducted during the discovery phase of the communication planning process.

Message and Materials Testing

The creative development process can involve three separate phases of research: an early formative phase, followed by qualitative testing of messages and materials, and ending with a quantitative test through a survey methodology. Constricted budgets and timelines often mean the first two phases are combined.

Table 4-4 **Sample Creative Brief**

Project Management Details
Project Name: Date: Prepared by: Phone: E-mail: Design Lead: Business Lead: Timing: Release Date:
Project Objectives
What is the message, material, or creative design trying to do? What is the format of the deliverable? (e.g., fact sheet, video, logo, message set, website design template) How will it be disseminated?
Audiences

Who are we trying to reach?
    What is the primary audience?
    What are the secondary audiences?
 	
What do they think, feel, say, or do now?
 	
What do we want them to think, feel, say, or do in the future?
 	
What are the key insights about the audience that could impact receptivity to the message, material, or creative design?

Value Proposition
What benefits will audiences get from the message, material, or creative design? What are the main ideas it is trying to convey? How will the audiences use the message, material, or creative design?
Competitive Landscape
What are some examples of competitive products? How are audiences currently using them? How well have they been received? How can they be improved?

(continues)

(continued)

Table 4-4 **Sample Creative Brief**

Brand Personality
What is the preferred tone of the message, material, or creative design? (e.g., humorous, serious, sympathetic, authoritative)
What unique qualities should it convey?
Parameters and Mandatory Elements
What elements must be included to be considered a success?
What are the technical specifications?
Does the deliverable have to complement an existing design or work in conjunction with something else?
Is there anything that must be avoided because it is "taboo" or off-limits?
Success Factors
What does success look like?
How will we measure it?

Phase One

The first phase is purely formative and qualitative, conducted through interviews or focus group sessions, to determine initial concepts for messages and materials that will resonate with target audiences. This phase explores some of the key sections of the creative brief, including the value proposition, aspects of the brand personality, and audience reactions to existing competitive products.

Phase Two

The second phase is qualitative message and materials testing, which explores audience reactions to messages and materials after they have been developed. This type of testing is typically done through in-person or online focus groups, but "online immersions" are becoming more popular. In an online immersion, participants try out the messages and materials in their daily lives and report their experiences, perceptions, and attitudes in a password-protected Web site set up specifically for the study. Participants' reports can be in the form of online diaries or blogs, photo essays, and conversations with other participants, depending on the format and composition of the messages and materials being tested. For example, if a health communicator has developed guidelines for selecting healthy foods in a supermarket and recipes for healthy and easy meals, participants can report their experiences with the materials through photo essays depicting their purchases, diaries outlining the challenges they face in eating healthy each day, and videos of themselves and family members using the recipes to prepare healthy meals. The key benefit of the online immersion methodology is that it assesses behavior—actual use of the messages and materials—rather than just gathering perceptions of messages and materials in focus group sessions. Doyle Research (http://www.doyleresearch.com/), a qualitative research firm based in Chicago, specializes in online immersion studies and other innovative methodologies. Another resource is PluggedIn (http://www.pluggedinco.com/), a company that provides research professionals with software for hosting market research online communities that can be used for short-term or long-term immersion studies.

Questions for message and materials testing typically focus on the following topic areas:

- Clarity and call to action
- Appeal and credibility
- Personal relevance
- Behavioral intent

Examples of questions in each of these areas are listed below. These can be used in interview or focus group guides as open-ended questions, or they can be adapted for survey questionnaires by reworking each question into a statement and having participants use a five-point Likert scale to indicate the extent to which they agree or disagree with the statement. Table 4-5 shows an example of how questions can be adapted to a survey format using a five-point Likert scale.

Table 4-5 **Example of Message and Materials Testing Questions in Survey Format**

On a scale from 1 to 5, where 1 indicates that you strongly disagree, and 5 indicates that you strongly agree, please tell me the number that indicates how much you agree or disagree with each of the following statements.

	Strongly Disagree 1	Somewhat Disagree 2	Neutral 3	Somewhat Agree 4	Strongly Agree 5
Overall, I liked this brochure					
I learned something new by reading this brochure					
The information in this brochure is important for me to know about					
I was interested in this brochure's topic					
This brochure was easy to understand					
I would read this brochure if I saw it posted online					
I trust the information in this brochure					

(continues)

(continued)

Table 4-5 **Example of Message and Materials Testing Questions in Survey Format**

On a scale from 1 to 5, where 1 indicates that you strongly disagree, and 5 indicates that you strongly agree, please tell me the number that indicates how much you agree or disagree with each of the following statements.

	Strongly Disagree 1	Somewhat Disagree 2	Neutral 3	Somewhat Agree 4	Strongly Agree 5
I like the way this brochure looks					
This brochure is convincing					
This brochure is confusing					
This brochure grabbed my attention					
This brochure makes me think more about [TOPIC]					
I plan on looking into this topic					
I plan to visit the Web site mentioned in the brochure					
I plan to do [ACTION] within the next [TIME PERIOD]					

Clarity and Call to Action

- What is the main idea this message is trying to get across?
- How well do you think the main idea comes across?
- What action is the message prompting you to take?
- Is it easy to read?
- Are there any words that are unusual or unfamiliar?
- Is there anything confusing, unclear, or hard to understand?

Appeal and Credibility

- What feelings do you have in reaction to this message?
- Is your reaction mostly positive or negative?
- Is this an appealing or unappealing message?
- What makes the message appealing or unappealing?
- Is this message believable or not?
  - Why or why not?
- What additional information would you need to believe this message?

Personal Relevance

- If you saw or heard this message, would it get your attention?
  - Why or why not?
- Are there any words or phrases that would be more likely to get your attention?
  - Which ones and why?
- Are there any words or phrases that you would remove?
  - Which ones and why?
- Do you feel this message was written for someone like you?
- How would you improve this message?

Behavioral Intent

- Does this action sound like something you would be able to do?
- How easy or difficult would it be to do?
  - What makes it hard to do?
  - What would make it easier to do?
- Would you consider doing this?
- How likely are you to try doing this within the next week?

Phase Three

The third phase of research is a testing of "near-final" messages and materials in an online survey to get a quantitative validation of audience preference. This methodology is often used for choosing a final version of a message, tagline, logo, video, or print advertisement from among two or three semifinalists. Knowledge Networks is a research firm that specializes in online surveys for testing a variety of materials, including videos, artwork, print ads, and brochures (http://www.knowledgenetworks.com/).

Measurement

The final step in the planning process, measurement, is intended to demonstrate the effectiveness of the communication effort and suggest ways to improve it moving forward. This step links back to the measurable objectives developed in the second step of the planning process. Communicators can demonstrate success in achieving campaign objectives through (1) *outcomes* measures, which measure the extent to which the campaign changed awareness, understanding, attitudes, and/or behavior among the target audiences, and (2) *process* measures, which measure how well the campaign was conducted. The rise of online communication and social media has necessitated new forms of measurement, such as the number of "fans" a brand has on Facebook and the number of Twitter "followers."

Outcome Measures

Outcome evaluations with an experimental design, such as comparing a control group that is not exposed to the campaign to a treatment group that is exposed, are rare in communication campaigns (see Table 3-6 in Chapter 3). Given the proliferation and reach of online and social media, it would be difficult to ensure the control group has not been exposed to the campaign. Experimental designs can be more expensive to implement as well. For these reasons, they are not common in mass communication efforts. However, Chapter 15, about the Chicago *5-4-3-2-1 Go!* program, demonstrates how an evaluation with an experimental design can be implemented. For example, participating parents randomly received either in-home counseling (treatment), *or* no counseling (control) to enable evaluators to determine the effectiveness of the counseling component.

Outcome measures for communication campaigns are more typically in the form of pre- and postcampaign surveys to measure changes in audience awareness, understanding, attitudes, and/or behavior. Even with a pre- and postcampaign survey, it can be difficult to isolate the effect of the campaign. The evaluation survey needs to establish that the audience heard the messages specifically through the campaign and not through a different effort or source, which can be challenging because audiences often do not remember exactly where they heard or read a message. Therefore, whenever possible, it is usually more effective to gather feedback directly at the point of contact with the audience. For example, if the communication campaign directs audiences to call a hotline or go to a Web site, try to incorporate a brief survey at the end of the call or on the Web site to gather feedback.

Process Measures

Process measures, which are intended to measure how well the campaign was conducted, are the most common form of communication measures. They typically quantify various components of the campaign, such the number of people reached through media outlets, the number of events co-produced with partnering organizations, or the number of visitors to a Web site. Process measures also provide a qualitative assessment of campaign components, such as the tone of media coverage about the campaign, including reactions from bloggers.

Process measures can include the number of impressions and audience reach for earned media, click-through rates and cost-per-thousand (CPM) for paid media, page views and time spent on a page for web sites, the numbers of Twitter followers and Facebook members for social media, and various levels of engagement for partnership efforts. Table 4-6 shows a more extensive list of process measures for common campaign components.

Social media measurement is an emerging discipline, and several tools—some of them free and others requiring payment—are available to communicators. Most of the tools try to measure four levels of audience interaction with the campaign:

- Exposure: How many people were exposed to campaign messages? Exposure measures can include the number of unique visitors to a Web site, the number of tweets per minute in response to a campaign message, or impressions of campaign mentions in online media.

Table 4-6 **Examples of Process Measures Used for Various Campaign Components**

Activity Type	Process Measures

Web site development	• Visits to the Web site from organic, referral, mobile, and paid advertising
	• Page views and goal completion rates (number of subscribers to e-newsletters, materials downloaded, etc.)
	• Low bounce rates from search for targeted phrases
	• Number of visitors that visited for more than two pages
	• Time spent on page
	• User satisfaction survey data on:
	  • Content (accuracy, quality, freshness)
	  • Look and feel (visual appeal, readability)
	  • Navigation (organization, layout, click-throughs, options)
	  • Search (relevance of search results, organization of search results, how well search narrows down a topic)
	  • Transparency (how quickly information is made available)
	  • Site performance (how quickly pages load, lack of error messages, consistency of speed from page to page)

Paid media (e.g., print and online advertising)	• Audience reach (based on circulation) • Value-added placements secured at no charge • Click-through rates or cost-per-thousand (CPM) for online banner ads • Click-though rates (CTR) and cost-per-click (CPC) from paid campaigns

Earned media (e.g., national and regional media outreach	• Volume and reach of media coverage; number of impressions resulting from media outreach efforts
	• Media analysis of messages delivered and depth of penetration of key talking points in coverage:
	  • Number of talking points/messages cited
	  • Frequency and accuracy of messages
	  • Spokespeople/partners quoted
	• Number of target audiences reached as a result of media outreach
	• Online stories/postings with direct links to Web site
	• Drop-in articles and matte release placements
	  • Number of articles placed
	  • Audience reached (based on circulation of target journals)
	• Interviews secured for spokespeople

Social media	• Increased referral traffic to Web site • Increased traffic to Web site via Facebook and Twitter • Facebook members to group "likes" • Twitter followers • Increased number of links to site from social media • Positive mentions in social media • Number of blog posts and online articles • Number of comments per visitor to blog post • ShareThis (http://sharethis.com/) metrics with number of shares for specific content • Number of views on social publishing sites, such as Scribd *(www.scribd.com)* and SlideShare (http://www.slideshare.net/) • Number of YouTube *(http://www.youtube.com/)* views

(continues)

(continued)

Table 4-6 **Examples of Process Measures Used for Various Campaign Components**

Activity Type	Process Measures
Partners and stakeholder outreach	• Number of organizations that agree to partner • Partner organizations that link to the Web site on their homepage • Toolkits and materials distributed to partners • Drop-in articles placed in partner publications • Sessions or workgroups added to partner events • Speaking engagements at partner events • Promotion/placement of content on partner Web sites, in member publications, and through social media outlets • Number of video material embedded in Web sites of partner organizations • Number of referrals to Web site generated by partner promotion • Partner participation on regular conference calls/webinars • Partner "check-in report" to assess the engagement from the perspectives of the lead and partner organizations

- Engagement: How many people engaged with the campaign? Engagement measures can include the number of Twitter followers or Facebook fans, the number of repeat visitors to a Web site, the number of comments to a blog post, or the number of searches conducted in search engines for the campaign brand.
- Influence: How many people told friends and family members about the campaign? Influence messages can include the number of "retweets" of campaign messages (i.e., the number of tweets forwarded to others) and the number of links to a Web site from blogs and other social media.
- Action: How many people did something as a result of the campaign? Action measures can include sales generated through the Web site or other campaign channels, the number of people who sign an online petition, or the number of people who sign up to participate in a program.

Commonly used tools for measuring social media are outlined as follows:

Free Tools

- *Technorati* (http://technorati.com/): The leading blog search engine and directory, Technorati.com indexes more than a million blogs. Technorati tracks the authority and influence of blogs, and provides a current index of the most popular blogs in a variety of categories.
- *Social Mention* (http://www.socialmention.com/): Social Mention is a social media search and analysis platform that aggregates user-generated content from across the Web into a single stream of information. Users can track and measure what people are saying about a brand, company, product, or topic across the Web's social media landscape in real-time. Social Mention monitors 100+ social media properties directly including, Twitter, Facebook, and YouTube.

- *Google Trends* (http://www.google.com/trends): Users can enter up to five topics and see how often they have been searched on Google over time. Google Trends also shows how frequently topics have appeared in Google News stories, and in which geographic regions people have searched for them most.

Paid Tools

- *Radian6* (http://www.radian6.com/): Radian6 provides a "listening platform" to help companies and organizations understand and participate in the conversations happening about their brands throughout the Internet and across social media. Users can scan millions of blogs, tweets, online news sites, video and image sharing sites, discussion boards, and other social media venues to track brand mentions or discussions of their messages. Radian6 also analyzes social media conversations for tone, level of engagement, audience reach, and other metrics.
- *Sysomos* (http://sysomos.com/): Sysomos is also a "listening platform" that helps users monitor and analyze social media conversations about their brand and messages. Its Media Analysis Platform (MAP) provides automated tone analysis and key influencer tracking of social media conversations, and Heartbeat provides real-time monitoring.
- *Cymfony* (http://www.cymfony.com/): Cymfony helps users evaluate what is being said about their brands in traditional and social media. The service provides market influence analytics by scanning and interpreting "millions of voices" in social and traditional media. Its listening and influence platform, Maestro, integrates technology with expert human interpretation to deliver intelligence on consumer preferences, competitor strengths and weaknesses, and other information critical to a company's reputation, brands, products, and employees.

Summary

An effective communication program begins with a thorough planning process. Several examples of planning processes are available to communication professionals, and they vary in the number of steps they include. Planning processes developed by communication firms and advertising agencies tend to have five essential steps—discovery, objectives, strategy, creative development, and measurement.

Discovery involves research and analysis to understand the environment in which the communication effort will be implemented, including the legislative context, media landscape, economic factors, relevant upcoming events, and cultural background pertaining to the topic. The competitive landscape is another key area for exploration, including competitors' messages that will vie for "mind share" among the target audiences. Perhaps most importantly, this first step in the planning process will include research about target audiences—who they are, what they care about, how they make decisions, and where and how they spend their time.

In the second step of the process, the communicator develops measurable objectives, which are typically aimed at achieving a change in the awareness, understanding, attitude, and/or behavior of a target audience within a defined time period.

Strategy is developed as the most effective way of achieving campaign objectives. Developing communication strategy typically involves considerations about the four *M*s of communication—message, messenger, media, and moment—and the four *P*s of marketing—product, price, place, and promotion.

The creative development of messages and materials, including visual elements, print materials, videos, and interactive games, occurs in the fourth step of the planning process. This step also includes the pretesting of messages and materials among target audiences, typically through in-person focus groups or online surveys. Pretesting is a useful means of gathering audience feedback about messages and materials before finalizing them for use in the communication effort. The ultimate test of the effectiveness of messages and materials, however, is captured in the fifth step of the planning process, campaign measurement.

Measurement is intended to demonstrate the effectiveness of the communication effort and suggest ways to improve it moving forward. This step links back to the measurable objectives developed in the second step of the planning process. Communicators can demonstrate success in achieving campaign objectives through *process* measures, which measure how well the campaign was conducted, and *outcomes* measures, which measure the extent to which the campaign changed awareness, understanding, attitudes and/or behavior among the target audiences.

Discussion Questions

1. Identify the five essential steps to the planning process, and explain why the planning process is essential to an effective communication campaign.
2. What is the focus of the discovery phase of the planning process? Briefly describe each of the components of a thorough situation analysis.
3. Why is it important for objectives to be measurable? Define process measures, and describe how communicators formulate process objectives.
4. Describe the four essential *M*s of communication. Explain how the four *P*s of marketing are used to develop a communications campaign.
5. Describe the three phases of research conducted during message and materials development. What type of information can be assessed during these phases, and how does it affect the development of the creative?
6. What is the purpose of the measurement phase of the planning process? Define outcome measures, and describe how they are different from process measures.

References

Daft, R. L., & Lengel, R. H. (1984). Information richness: A new approach to managerial behavior and organizational design. *Research in Organizational Behavior, 6*, 191–233.

McGuire W. J. (1984). Public communication as a strategy for inducing health-promoting behavioral change. *Preventive Medicine, 13*(3):299–319.

Chapter 5

Health Professional Associations: Finding the Balance between Profession and Business

By Steve Erickson

LEARNING OBJECTIVES

By the end of the chapter, the reader will be able to:

- Identify the main functions of a medical professional association and understand how communication supports those functions.
- Understand the knowledge and skills needed to implement effective communication programs in a medical professional association.
- Differentiate between and identify key components of public affairs, marketing, and member communication programs.
- Identify and discuss essential components of a strategic communication plan.
- Discuss strategies for balancing the often competing organizational objectives of a medical professional association.

Introduction

This chapter will serve as a best practices guide for health communication professionals from the perspective of practitioners working in the setting of medical professional associations. Health communication in the medical professional association setting requires practitioners to use a full range of communication skills, including public relations and public affairs expertise, marketing communication, reputation management, media relations, member communication (using both traditional and new media), and market research. Medical professional associations represent both the continuous advancement of the profession and the business of their members. Communicators in this setting must find a balance between the member and societal goal of improving the profession (and the quality of care given to patients) and the practical goals related to the business of health care.

For health professional associations in the United States and their members this is a time of dramatic business, technological, and regulatory change. Communicators are required to adapt to rapidly changing environments while striving for message and brand consistency for their organizations.

While communication and marketing have always been central to the success of health professional associations—indeed to all associations—the importance of fast and accurate communication is growing in this time of rapid change. New communication technologies are supplanting traditional channels, and one-way communication to members and other stakeholders has evolved into multidirectional and interactive communications driven by the emergence of social media. Medical professional associations are increasingly required to provide an information-filtering function for their busy members.

Member communication lies at the heart of the marketing and communication function within the professional medical association. Communicating the value of membership and providing opportunities for interaction between the association and its members can help to achieve strategic objectives. Association members place a high value on publications, both peer-reviewed scientific publications as well as organizational publications. Communication practitioners are using traditional channels, such as print publications, as well as Web-based and social media tools to communicate with members.

Although health professional associations differ from one another in their programming and approach, most share a common commitment to enhancing the knowledge and skills of their members and contributing to the advancement of the medical sciences. Both of these functions contribute significantly to improving the health of society at large. Many health professional associations play a direct role in the publication of new science through peer-reviewed journals and research presentations at scientific meetings. A core function of medical societies is to translate emerging science into information that can readily be used in the practice of medicine. This translation is accomplished through the creation of clinical guidelines and standards and broad offerings in continuing medical education. Communication plays a direct role in the advancement of the profession using media relations, promotion of educational offerings, and the development of online resources for members.

In addition to the focus on advancing the profession, medical associations also represent the business interests of their members. In a time of great technological and regulatory change this advocacy role has been elevated. Medical association communicators must work hand in hand with regulatory and legislative specialists to develop and implement public affairs campaigns to protect the viability of medical practices. Media relations, relationship building with like-minded organizations, and helping members communicate directly with elected officials are all part of these public affairs efforts. While advocacy efforts often focus on the business of health care, they must be conducted within the context of providing patient access and value.

Like most associations, medical professional societies use a business model that offers members and other consumers a wide variety of programs and services. Communication practitioners in many medical professional associations also participate to a significant degree in marketing. Practitioners provide promotional support for membership recruitment and retention, attendance at association meetings, educational products and services, and online resources. Knowledge of market research and association marketing strategy is essential.

The overlapping goals of professional advancement and business advocacy will be illustrated by the inclusion of a case study of the American College of Cardiology's involvement in the recent health system reform debate. The case study will detail a public affairs campaign designed to secure for the college "a seat at the table" in discussions and negotiations for health system reform, while at the same time ensuring the continued support of its membership in a time of rapid change. As shown in the case study, the college achieved campaign success through several factors, including:

- Effective segmentation and involvement of key stakeholder groups
- Research aimed at understanding the awareness, knowledge levels, and attitudes of these stakeholders
- The creation of targeted messages and effective channels to reach them

Introduction to Health Professional Associations

Professional societies emerged during the late Renaissance, when scientific organizations developed around the collection and dissemination of knowledge. The earliest of these organizations, the Academia Secretorum Naturae, was organized in Naples in 1560. "Candidates for membership had to present a new fact in natural science as a condition of membership," but otherwise membership was open (Bergen, 1987).

Some societies were formed by groups of scholars with the aim of exchanging knowledge and ideas. Others were founded by royal fiat to set standards of education and practice in the public interest. Still others found roots in the elitist ethos of medieval guilds.

The growth of professional societies was bolstered by the philosophy of Enlightenment, prominent during the 1800s, which reflected the division of labor and a reverence for scholarship. The educated classes could now spend more time developing fields of scientific specialization and organizing and recording information into growing bodies of knowledge for the benefit of future generations. This advancement of recorded science heralded the development of professionalism (Magner, 2002).

A few professional societies developed early in the history of the United States. Benjamin Franklin founded the American Philosophical Society in Philadelphia in 1743, and the American Academy of Arts and Sciences got its start in 1780 in Boston. The pace of development slowed during and in the years immediately following the American Revolution, but another brief growth spurt came in the mid-1800s with the American Statistical Association, the American Psychiatric Association, and the American Medical Association being formed.

Over time the growth accelerated and professional societies began to concentrate on the dissemination of new information and the development of standards. These societies also performed some of the economic protection duties of trade associations and the guilds from which they evolved.

Currently in the United States, there are hundreds of active medical professional organizations. A benchmarking report from the American Association of Medical Society Executives (2010) shows nearly 150 US medical professional societies at the county, state, and national levels. The average number of professional members of these organizations is more than 4000. The average number of employees is 16, and the average operating budget is more than $3 million.

The push and pull between standards of professionalism and economic considerations has continued as professional societies have grown and matured. In an article in the *Journal of the American Medical Association*, Pellegrino and Relman (1999) argued, "Today the dominant influence on professional associations is economic, and the tension between self-interest and ethical principles is greater than ever." Physicians and their professional associations must now choose more definitively than in the past what is most important to them: ethical commitment versus economic considerations. Associations that allow economic considerations to completely dominate their policies may now have to shed any pretense of being moral enterprises.

Certainly, this underlying philosophical tension in an era of significant change, combined with the growing complexity of professional societies, makes for challenging and engaging work for health communicators. Communication practitioners who represent medical professional organizations use every communication tool at their disposal, including public relations and public affairs expertise, marketing communication, reputations management, media relations, member communication, and market research.

An Era of Fundamental Change for Healthcare Professionals

Health care——and healthcare professional associations—in the United States are experiencing a time of unprecedented change on several fronts—scientific, business, regulatory, and technological. Communicators who represent these organizations must adapt to a rapidly shifting environment, while providing a message and brand consistency that maintains the support of key stakeholder groups.

American healthcare stands at a critical crossroads. Healthcare costs per capita in the United States have surpassed those of most other developed countries, and costs are continuing to rise. National health expenditures as a percentage of GDP have risen from about 5% in 1960 to approximately 16% in 2007 (Centers for Medicare and Medicaid, 2009). Unfortunately, these high and ever-rising costs have not enabled greater access to medical care. The nonelderly uninsured population in the United States has reached 45 million with annual increases of more than 2 million per year since the turn of the century (Kaiser Commission on Medicaid, 2008).

These higher levels of expenditures do not necessarily result in either longer life expectancy or more years of good health for Americans as compared with citizens in other developed countries.

There is a wide difference between best practices and the actual level of care delivered. A RAND study found that on average Americans received only 55 percent of the care that would be suggested by accepted clinical standards. One can also find significant variations in medical practice, costs, and quality of care from one region to another in the United States. Dartmouth research on Medicare found there was no basis in medical theory for these variations and, in fact, that higher cost in a region did not correlate with higher quality (Porter & Teisberg, 2006). Consumer unhappiness is matched by dissatisfaction on the part of healthcare professionals. Surveys found both doctors and nurses spending one-third to one-half of their time on paperwork, with the overall estimated percentage of healthcare expenditures for administration tracked at a whopping 30% (Porter & Teisberg, 2006).

In 2010, the passage of the Patient Protection and Affordable Care Act (PPACA), the most sweeping social legislation since the 1960s, ushered in what could be fundamental changes in access, insurance reform, and care delivery. The United States is experiencing a significant shift from private practice delivery of health care to hospital and systems-based care. Health information technology is becoming the foundation for evidence-based care. Current payment models based on quantity of care are moving to payments based on performance and health outcomes. Our workforce is increasingly independent and mobile, leading to a desire for health coverage that is portable. The move toward increased individual control over healthcare decisions and spending is part of a global trend of health consumerism.

These fundamental legislative and regulatory changes are likely to have a major effect on how healthcare providers care for patients, how they administer their practices, and how they report clinical data. Health provider members are looking to their professional associations to provide guidance on such issues as the validity of performance measures as well as offering practical business solutions about how to realign the practice of medicine to comply with new regulatory requirements. A number of medical societies have taken a leadership role in the development of performance improvement measures that contribute to a continuous improvement in quality without becoming unduly burdensome to those providing the care (Sgrignoli, 2006).

The Growing Importance of Communication and Marketing

Individuals with marketing and communication skills have always been an important part of the success of medical professional organizations, and of associations in general. This importance has increased owing to a number of environmental factors, including the growing percentage of association revenues that must be derived from nondues sources and the increasing interconnectedness between associations and the key stakeholder groups on which they depend.

In many associations, the term *communication* refers to the management function that guides the organization in carrying out sound policy decisions and responsible practices through a program of two-way communication with its publics. This management function also helps secure the financial, volunteer, governmental, and public support needed for the association to accomplish its mission.

Many medical professional societies employ some form of integrated marketing communication program that combines public relations, media relations, advertising, sales promotion, direct marketing, public affairs, and other communication disciplines. Marketing and communication professionals employ similar skill sets, and in associations there is much overlap in intended audiences. Many organizations find an integrated structure reduces duplication, enhances message consistency, and produces cost savings. There is, however, a wide variation in the degree of integration and in the level of centralization in the marketing and communication functions. The complexity of the communication program and whether or not it is carried out by association employees or outsourced to outside firms depends on the size of the organization and its management philosophy.

Communication and marketing activities in professional medical associations are most effective when they are driven by a strategic communication plan that flows directly from the organization's mission and overall strategic plan. The strategic communication plan will likely include some or all of the following elements:

- Organizational goals for the communication function
- Relevant research to guide the development of communication
- Key messages of the association
- Target audiences
- Communication strategies
- Communication channels for message delivery and feedback from target audiences
- Evaluation mechanisms (Hyde, 1997)

Established communication theory suggests that a symmetrical model of communication will be more effective than an asymmetrical model; that is, a communication approach that emphasizes interaction and dialogue between an organization and its publics will be more effective than one that emphasizes the one-way delivery of messages (Grunig & Grunig, 1992). Advances in communication technology, such as Web-based channels and social media, can help facilitate this kind of two-way interactive communication. A brief checklist for planning communication programs is provided in Table 5-1.

Table 5-1 **Checklist for Planning Communication Programs**

Checklist for Planning Communication Programs	✓
Conduct internal and external analysis and research.	
Set program goals.	
Identify and define target audiences.	
Develop objectives and communications strategies for each target audience.	
Implement the program internally and externally.	
Evaluate results.	
Modify the program as necessary.	

Connecting with Members

Providing value to the membership is the driving force for medical professional associations, and as a result, interactive communication with members is a core function implemented by the marketing and communication staff. Association members need to be aware of, support, and participate in the wide range of activities offered by the organization.

Communication practitioners have the opportunity of using a full array of channels to foster interactive communication with members, including peer-reviewed journals, member magazines and newsletters, meeting exhibits, Web-based communication, e-newsletters, member resource centers, local and regional chapter resources, and, more recently, social media tools.

Many association members place a high value on publications, consistently citing them as a major reason for membership. In medical professional associations, peer-reviewed scientific journals also serve the specific goal of advancing clinical science. These journals enhance the reputation of the association as a scientific resource and can serve as a vital frontline public relations tool. Scientific research published in journals can be a significant source of information for the media and the general public as well.

The clinical nature of peer-reviewed journals makes it likely that the production process will have high member involvement and a specialized publications staff with scientific expertise. Other periodicals that are more organizational in nature—magazines, bulletins, newsletters, and e-newsletters—are most often produced as part of the communication function.

All publications should have a formal editorial mission statement, which usually involves a series of management decisions, including the type of content, editorial responsibility and control, business goals, and subscription and advertising policies. Association publications can be a key source of revenue for the organization, and at the very least may be able to cover all costs of production. The communication practitioner should coordinate the various publications of the association to be sure they are contributing to the overall strategic direction and are not giving members either too little or too much information.

The explosive growth of online communications has made association Web sites a hub for member interaction and communication. The marketing and communication staff may be solely responsible for Web-based communication or share that responsibility with the information technology department and other areas of the organization.

Web-based communication has evolved to provide innovative social networking opportunities between members and other members and between members and the association. Association communicators are monitoring and providing information to public social media sites that are applicable to their membership as well as building proprietary social networks and tools that allow members to build communities, share information easily, and cooperate on the publication of new information. A brief checklist for planning association publications is provided in Table 5-2.

Table 5-2 **Checklist for Planning Association Publications**

Checklist for Planning Association Publications	✓
Identify the need for the publication.	
Identify financial and organizational goals.	
Evaluate different types of publications.	
Assess the preferences and needs of key audiences.	
Determine the editorial mission.	
Develop a management system for producing the publication.	

Communicating the Science and Advancing the Profession

The communication practitioner working in a medical professional association will have a major responsibility to help members fulfill the longstanding contract between medicine and society. Medical professionals operate in a wide variety of situations, but they share a common role of healer and a common commitment to an ethical approach to the practice of medicine that dates back to the writings of the ancient Greek physician, Hippocrates.

The principals to which medical professionals aspire have been categorized most recently in the Medical Professionalism Project in 1999. The project, a joint effort of the American College of Physicians, the American Society of Internal Medicine Foundation, the American Board of Internal Medicine Foundation, and the European Federation of Internal Medicine, aimed to "ensure that the healthcare systems and the physicians working in them remain committed both to the patient's welfare and the basic tenants of social justice." Several of these principals relate directly to the role of medical professional associations and the work of the communication practitioner (Cox, 2002).

Commitment to Professional Competence

Medical professionals are committed to lifelong learning, including maintaining a level of competence necessary to provide quality care. Medical professional associations provide a wide array of continuing medical education offerings and board certification resources in print, online, and in face-to-face educational settings. Communication practitioners help make members aware of the resources available from the association and make the public aware of their members' commitment to professional competence.

Commitment to Improving Quality of Care

Medical professionals, both individually and through their professional associations, create and implement systems to measure and improve quality. These systems, which may include the development of data registries for measurement and the setting of standards for care, seek to reduce medical errors, increase patient value and safety, minimize the overuse or underuse of medical resources, and optimize the outcomes of care. Communication professionals play a key role in driving member and public support for continuous quality improvement and evidence-based medicine. For example, the American College of Cardiology, long a leader in continuous quality improvement of cardiovascular care, has conducted a multiyear campaign to make quality care the focus of healthcare reform efforts (see the case study later in this chapter).

Commitment to Scientific Knowledge

Medical knowledge is constantly changing based on new scientific findings, and the presentation, evaluation, and translation of this new science into medical practice constitutes a major responsibility of the medical professional association. Peer-reviewed research is often presented in association medical journals and at major scientific sessions. The communication practitioner is intimately involved in the dissemination of emerging science to members and the public. Much of the media relations outreach conducted by communication professionals centers on new research findings, and many scientific sessions held by medical professional associations including working newsrooms where journalists can receive the latest scientific information and interact with the researchers.

Advocating for the Interests of Health Professionals and Their Patients

In addition to their role of advancing the profession, medical professional associations often play the role of more traditional trade associations by conducting government relations and advocacy activities. In the United States, federal and state governments, as payers, providers, and regulators of health care, play a major role in the business and professional lives of healthcare providers. Medical professional associations, therefore, must be actively involved in regulatory and legislative processes that have a significant impact on the ability of health professionals to provide care.

The role of professionalism has an impact on the advocacy activities of a medical professional association because the goals of advocacy must benefit society as a whole as well as the specific business interests of the members. In the text, *Professional Practices in Association Management*, Janis L. Tabor, CAE, writes:

> *The most successful government relations programs couch issues in the context of the overall business and professional community and society in general—the framework in which government decisions are made. When laws and regulations are well thought out and properly applied, they can stimulate growth and improve services to the public. Conversely, the actions of uninformed lawmakers and regulators can adversely affect an industry or profession, thus denying services to society* (1997).

This is true of associations in general and perhaps even more applicable to associations for healthcare professionals.

Government relations programs are varied but usually include some combination of the following components:

- Preparing issues identification reports and analyses
- Providing information to legislators and regulators
- Interacting directly with government officials
- Developing and providing legislative testimony
- Creating and participating in coalitions
- Guiding member involvement with governments at local, state, and federal levels

Some professional associations also become involved in the development and implementation of political action committees to raise and contribute funds to candidates for office.

Communication practitioners, while usually not directly involved in managing the government relations program, are often active partners in advocacy efforts. Communicating the association's advocacy views to lawmakers, members, and the general public can be crucial to success in achieving government relations goals. Regulatory issues can be complex, and the communication practitioner must package the information in a way that can easily be understood by both the expert and the layperson. Outreach to the public may be through extensive media outreach or even paid advertising if resources allow.

Providing information to members about relevant laws, regulations, and legislation can be the most visible part of any government relations program. This capacity to reach members quickly with essential information also can be used to mobilize large numbers of members in a grassroots effort to respond to particular legislation or regulations.

Communicators assist in preparing members to advocate on the behalf of the profession by providing presentation and media training, writing speeches and talking points, and conducting periodic government affairs conferences that include the scheduling of visits between members and lawmakers.

Marketing to the Customer Base

Medical professional associations employ a not-for-profit business model that relies on member dues plus nondues revenue derived from marketing a wide variety of offerings to members and other consumers. While the strategic goals of associations differ from their for-profit counterparts, they share the same principles of marketing—introducing products and services that fill a particular need within a targeted group of consumers.

Most associations strive to be market driven—that is, oriented toward understanding and meeting the needs of members and other consumers as opposed to simply offering products and services. The marketing function typically includes:

- Market research to understand consumer needs
- Developing products and services to fill these needs

- Setting the price or the relative value that consumers may be willing to pay
- Determining the optimal channels to distribute the product or service to the intended consumers
- Using promotion techniques to make the offering known and desired by the intended audience

Association communicators may be involved in all aspects of the marketing plan in a system of centralized marketing, or they may be limited to involvement in the promotion aspects of the plan in a system of decentralized marketing. Many communicators help to implement some hybrid variation between these two extremes (Hignite, 2000).

Marketing and communication strategies are employed for a wide range of revenue-producing activities in the medical professional association. Membership recruitment and retention is vital to the continued health of the organization because members provide a steady influx of support to help accomplish the organization's goals. Publications, through subscriptions and advertising, can provide an important source of revenue while giving voice and increasing the reputation of the profession. Scientific sessions and educational programs not only advance the clinical science but also provide steady sources of income for the association. A wide variety of other products, from self-assessment programs to practice management tools help to meet needs of the members and add to the economic vitality of the association.

The nature of the association business model dictates that building positive long-term relationships with members will result in increased rates of retention, discretionary spending, and referrals. This emphasis on the long-term value of the member/consumer can be expressed as the total revenue generated by the average association member versus the cost of delivering programs and services over the average lifetime of the member.

Association marketing and communication operations employ both traditional promotional channels such as direct mail and telephone marketing along with newer tools such as e-commerce on the association Web site and e-marketing channels.

Ongoing evaluation of marketing activities, much like ongoing evaluation of general communication activities, can help the association communication practitioner gauge the return on investment in communications and continually improve the marketing and communication strategies and tactics used to achieve the association's objectives (American Society of Association Executives and the Holmes Corporation, 2002).

A Case Study: Putting Quality First in Healthcare Reform

This case study describes how the development of a strong public affairs campaign—based on communication research and delivering targeted messages through focused channels to highly segmented audiences—helped an organization provide substantial input to regulatory and legislative decision making during a time of significant legislative reform (Erickson, 2010).

In the spring of 2007, staff members and cardiologist leaders of the American College of Cardiology (ACC) could sense the first rumblings of what would become a nationwide focus on healthcare reform in less than 2 years. ACC leaders were concerned reform would be focused only on cost-cutting and cost-shifting, the same short-term solutions that had buried previous attempts at reform and not focused enough on fundamentally improving the quality of the system. The ACC, long involved in programs of quality improvement to translate the latest science into practice, was in a position to mold healthcare reform in a way that would simultaneously improve quality while reducing costs.

It was in this environment that the communication staff at ACC was asked to develop a public affairs campaign approach that would help to give the college "a seat at the table" during health system reform, while at the same time ensuring the continued support of its membership in a time of rapid change. Established communication theory suggested campaign success would be based on effective segmentation and involvement of key stakeholder publics; research aimed at understanding the awareness, knowledge levels, and attitudes of these key publics; and the creation of targeted messages and effective channels to reach them.

Fast forward to 2010 and the passage of the Patient Protection and Affordable Care Act (PPACA), sweeping social legislation that will result in be fundamental changes in the delivery of health care in the United States. The ACC is now involved on a daily basis with the implementation of healthcare reform. ACC proposals for payment reform were included in legislation as it was being written. The organization's CEO and its elected cardiologist leaders are frequent featured speakers at healthcare reform conferences. The ACC is quoted often in the media regarding healthcare reform, and ACC editorials are being printed in newspapers across the country. ACC print and online advertisements appear in political publications aimed at policy makers. Members of the organization receive at least weekly updates on the progress of reform and can visit a special Web site and an online blog to see all of the college activities on their behalf. Perhaps most importantly, improving the quality of the healthcare system has become an accepted goal and part of the passage of reform, along with the reduction of costs and an increase in coverage for uninsured and underinsured Americans.

Campaign Foundation Included Strategic Planning and Membership Support

To be most effective within existing resources while still competing in a cluttered communication landscape required the ACC to adhere to a targeted methodology including:

1. Using a variety of research techniques and repeating research over time to measure progress
2. Achieving member consensus before reaching out to other target audiences
3. Targeting audiences and reaching those audiences with research-based messaging
4. Getting maximum leverage from cost-effective tools (including earned media, speaking engagements, exhibits and Web-based tools) and using sparingly the more expensive tools of advertising

Because the ACC is a member-driven organization, a high-level panel of member leaders was selected in the fall of 2007 to begin work on a series of ACC principles for healthcare reform. The completed draft, *Quality First: the American College of Cardiology's Blueprint for Reform*, was unveiled in February 2008 at a Health System Reform Summit in the organization's Washington, D.C., headquarters.

In the Quality First Blueprint, the ACC announced it was "taking a leading role in healthcare reform efforts… around a new standard of healthcare delivery centered on increasing the quality of care and ensuring great patient value." Under the organizing principle of "Quality First," the ACC outlined six principles to reform the current healthcare approach into a system that:

1. Provides universal coverage
2. Provides coverage through an expansion of public and private (pluralistic) programs
3. Focuses on patient value—transparent, high-quality, cost-effective, continuous care
4. Emphasizes professionalism, the foundation of an effective partnership with empowered patients
5. Ensures coordination across sources and sites of care
6. Includes payment reforms that reward quality and ensure value

The Quality First Blueprint document noted that while coverage and financing are extremely important, cardiovascular professionals could have the most impact on the last four principles, which focus on reforming delivery and payment systems to improve the quality and cost-effectiveness of care.

Audience Research Provided Campaign Direction

Because communication theory suggested a campaign would be most successful if it was targeted at specific stakeholder audiences, ACC staff recognized that a campaign to the general public would be too broad. The stated goals of participation in health system reform and member support would suggest a campaign targeted to two specific groups: ACC members and "inside the beltway" policy makers, including members of Congress and their staff.

Initial intelligence about these groups suggested that a small group of ACC member leaders would be more supportive of system reform than would be the rank-and-file members who were busy with their practices and already struggling with low reimbursement rates. Intelligence about the policy makers in Washington, D.C., suggested ACC would be thought of as just another in a large list of physician groups more concerned with increasing payments than with long-range reform aimed at increasing value and quality for patients. Formal research conducted with each of these groups revealed a somewhat different landscape.

Findings from a quantitative survey of members (distributed via registration bags at ACC's annual meeting) found overall very positive support for the principles outlined in the Blueprint document, and yet this support for quality-based reform was tempered by the current reality of a reimbursement system that creates disincentives for providing quality care.

The ACC also participated in a congressional omnibus survey of policy makers (conducted by Harris Interactive and featuring telephone interviews of congressional staff members and aides representing approximately one in five Capitol Hill offices), finding support for the quality-focused health system reform among the members of this target audience.

When similar questions regarding system reform were compared for the two groups, not surprisingly, the ACC found its members were more supportive of self-regulation approaches and that policy makers tended to favor government regulation.

In general, these surveys described an environment among target audiences that would be receptive to ACC proposals for reform. Specific findings indicated messages to members would have to balance the need for significant reform with the current economic obstacles, and messages for policy makers would need to emphasize the commitment of the profession to self-regulate.

Targeted Messaging Employed to Reach Key Stakeholders

The issue of healthcare reform is one of significant complexity, and the ACC would have to deliver messages about its proposals for reform in an increasingly cluttered communication environment. The stakes were high for the organization and its members, and messages around healthcare reform would have to be direct and easily understandable.

ACC communication staff turned to a message-mapping process that would simultaneously create a storytelling structure for campaign messages while organizing messages in an easily accessible one-page format.

The message map provided campaign planners with a comprehensive yet easy-to-access communication tool. The one-page format allows anyone in the organization to answer any question and quickly bridge to more than one message. The message map is designed so that no matter what question a person is asked, he or she is never more than 10–15 seconds away from delivering the core message.

The message map features three message tiers: The first tier, called "Home Base," is the primary message that fully addresses the issue at hand and becomes a positioning statement for the campaign. The second tier contains "satellite messages that form a logical story and act as sound bites that amplify and support the Home Base positioning." The final tier offers supporting points and evidence to support each satellite message. These messages can support more than one second-level message.

The process for developing the message map was a brainstorming session in which participants answered a series of questions designed to tell the story of ACC's involvement in healthcare reform. This process included capturing and prioritizing answers to questions such as:

- What are the current problems with the healthcare system?
- Why is the ACC in a position to propose solutions for reform?
- What is the ACC doing now to solve the problem, and what additional strategies does it propose?

Campaign Implementation Used a Wide Variety of Channels

Tactical implementation included the creation of campaign materials, and both traditional and Web-based communication channels, media relations efforts, campaign advertising, speaking engagements, and campaign promotion at other events. The communication campaign was implemented in tandem with direct lobbying activities.

Building directly on the positioning statement developed in the message mapping process, ACC created a wealth of campaign materials under the banner of Quality First and the positioning statements "Transforming Health Care from the Inside Out" and "Setting a New Standard for Health Care Reform." Materials included fact sheets, posters, and exhibit materials.

The Quality First Web site featured up-to-date content on the campaign's activities, as well as the college's advocacy and quality efforts. Over the course of the campaign the Web site became more robust and user-friendly as usage has increased and healthcare reform efforts have become more detailed.

The Lewin Report is an online blog by ACC CEO Jack Lewin and forum intended to foster discussion about healthcare reform. The online publication continues to grow in readership, averaging more than 1000 hits each month. Coordinated posts with annual meeting events and connection with social media tool, Twitter, led a record 2566 visitors to *The Lewin Report*. The blog features a monthly "guest post" from ACC member leaders.

The Quality First Campaign was launched with a press conference at the National Press Club in Washington, D.C. At the press conference, the ACC released findings from a national survey revealing the American public's dissatisfaction with the current healthcare system and the need for doctors, especially cardiologists, to be involved in the reform movement.

Following the introductory press conference, the Quality First message had been spread through intensive media relations activities. Highlights include more than 69 health policy hits, 22 op-eds, seven ReachMD interviews, a *Newsweek* advertorial as well as a radio media tour including a Colorado-area audio release airing on 39 stations.

The ACC also developed an online and print advertising campaign aimed at the policy makers and running in such publications *RollCall, Politico, The Hill, National Review, CongressDaily AM,* and *National Journal.*

In addition to the Health Care Summit referenced in the creation of the Blueprint document, the Quality First message has been presented in multiple speaking engagements and healthcare-related events. ACC leaders spoke at more than 34 national and international conferences, and the Quality First message was presented at more than 27 ACC local chapter meetings.

Quality First campaign exhibits and presentations were prominent at the ACCs Annual Scientific Sessions where attendance regularly tops more than 25,000 ACC members and other key stakeholder groups.

Quality First and health system reform were driving themes for the ACC's annual legislative conference, during which ACC members come to Washington, D.C., to educate Congress about the ACC's important work in improving quality and promoting evidence-based care. Participants held nearly 250 meetings with their national representatives to discuss the need for health system reform and incentives to encourage the adoption of health information technology. In addition, participants communicated the importance of long-term reform to the Medicare physician payment system.

Campaign Achieved Intended Impact

The Quality First Campaign has been an unqualified success. The American College of Cardiology has indeed had a prominent seat at the table during the healthcare reform debate. ACC President, Doug Weaver, M.D., was invited by the Obama administration to the President's first formal briefing on healthcare reform in March 2009, the only representative of a medical specialty physicians' organization to be invited. ACC staff and member leaders are frequent speakers at events where policy makers gather to discuss healthcare reform. The ACC is quoted widely in the media on health reform issues. Specific ACC proposals for quality improvement and value-based payment reform were included in final approved legislation.

Equally clear is the continued support the ACC has from its membership for its active role in healthcare reform. In a quantitative survey of membership conducted in June 2009 (an online survey with approximately 10% response rate), more than 70% of ACC members indicated that the organization was headed in the right direction with its reform activities. The smaller percentage of ACC members recommending a different direction were almost equally split between those asking for more concentration on payment reform and those asking for more focus on quality improvement.

The Quality First Campaign continues, but now it is making a transition to foster the grassroots implementation of the principles found in the Blueprint report—a focus on patient value, professionalism, coordination across sources and sites of care, and value-based payment reform. The ACC is implementing on a pilot basis a Web-based community of cardiology practices, primary care practices, hospitals, and payers that will implement these quality improvement principles on a local, regional, and national basis.

The success of this public affairs campaign conducted with relatively limited resources can be attributed to a foundation of research, strong and consistent messaging, cost-effective use of resources, and a targeted approach to reaching stakeholders. For the Quality First campaign, there were three distinct elements that contributed to campaign effectiveness and that can be considered learning points from this case study:

1. Strong, consistent messaging allowed the campaign to stay focused, even in a rapidly shifting environment.
2. Targeting audiences ensured cost-effective use of resources and contributed to campaign success.
3. Closely coordinating more generalized communication strategies with more personalized lobbying efforts increased the success of both efforts.

Summary

This chapter has outlined the essential practices of communication professionals who work in the setting of the medical professional association. Communications professionals in this setting employ a wide variety of skills and help medical associations represent both the advancement of the profession as well as the business of the members. The importance of communication for medical associations is increasing in a time of rapid change for the healthcare system.

Elements of a communication program for a medical professional association may include communication with members, key stakeholders, and the public; providing medical education and the advancement of medical science; advocating for the business interests of members so they might provide better access to care for their patients; and the marketing of products and services that contribute to the financial success of the organization.

Discussion Questions

1. Describe the two main and sometimes competing objectives of a medical professional association.
2. Describe the elements that are used to develop a strategic communication plan.
3. Describe the typical components that make up a government relations program.
4. The case study in this chapter illustrated several factors that contributed to the success of the Quality First Campaign. Describe these factors.
5. Describe the benefits of using a message-mapping process in the Quality First case study.

References

American Association of Medical Society Executives. (2010). *Benchmarking project.* Washington, DC: American Society of Association Executives.

American Society of Association Executives and the Holmes Corporation. (2002). ASAE's essentials of the profession learning system. *Strategic Marketing*, Module 4, 49–91.

Bergin, T. G. (Ed.) (1987). *Encyclopedia of the Renaissance*. New York: New Market Books.

Centers for Medicare and Medicaid Services. (2009). *National health expenditures and their share of gross domestic product 1960–2007*. Baltimore, MD: CMS.

Cox, H. C. (2002). Medical professionalism in the new millennium: A physician charter. *Annals of Internal Medicine, 136*, 243–246.

Erickson, S. (2010). Quality first: A public affairs case study. *Journal of Communication in Healthcare*, 3(2):87–97.

Grunig, J. E., & Grunig, E. L. (1992). Models of public relations and communication. In J. E. Grunig (Ed.), *Excellence in public relations and communication management* (p. 292). Hilldale, NJ: Lawrence Erlbaum Associates.

Hignite, K. (2000). Marketing as a mindset. *Association Management,* September.

Hyde, B. (1997). Public relations. In J. B. Cox (Ed.), *Professional practices in association management* (p. 265). Washington, DC: ASAE & the Center for Association Leadership.

Kaiser Commission on Medicaid and the Uninsured/Urban Institute. (2008). Analysis of 2001–2008 ASAEC supplements to the CPS. Number of nonelderly uninsured Americans 2000–2007. Washington, DC: Henry J. Kaiser Family Foundation.

Magner, L. N. (2002). *A history of the life sciences.* New York, NY: CRC Press.

Pellegrino, E. D., & Relman, A. S. (1999). Professional medical associations ethical and practical guidelines. *Journal of the American Medical Association, 282*(10):984–986.

Porter, M. E., & Teisberg, E. O. (2006). Redefining health care (pp. 21–29). Boston: Harvard Business School Press.

Sgrignoli, D. (2006). Physicians still highly value professional medical societies. *Product Management Today,* December.

Tabor, J. L. (1997). Government relations. In J. B. Cox (Ed.), *Professional practices in association management* (p. 250). Washington, DC: ASAE & the Center for Association Leadership.

Chapter 6

Building a National Brand for a Children's Hospital

By Michelle Davis

LEARNING OBJECTIVES

By the end of this chapter, the reader will be able to:

- Understand the importance of gaining consensus and alignment of key board members and hospital leaders when launching a brand-building initiative.
- Use a SWOT (strengths, weaknesses, opportunities, and threats) analysis to assess the capabilities of the organization and identify key areas that need strengthening.
- Engage an external branding expert to facilitate the strategic branding process and provide objectivity in finding the right brand positioning.
- Implement a brand-building strategy that can evolve and adapt in a digitally networked and rapidly changing market.
- Engage leadership, as well as employees, along the journey to ensure brand-building success.

Introduction

Few hospitals in the country truly have "national" recognition among the general populations. Exceptions are Cleveland Clinic, Mayo Clinic, and Johns Hopkins Hospital. There are slightly more than 50 freestanding children's hospitals across the country, and with the exception of St. Jude's Hospital, none of them have national reputations; however, they are very well known in their respective regional service areas. By many measures, Children's

Hospital Boston (Boston Children's) is in a leading position among pediatric hospitals. It has been listed as one of the top two hospitals in *U.S. News and World Report* for the past 20 years. It has the largest research program and the highest caliber of scientists among its peers. It also trains and retains more physician scientists than any other children's hospital. Its affiliation with Harvard Medical School makes its training programs the most sought after in the world. The clinical innovation and basic science research generated from the hospital is world changing, including the first successful heart surgery on a child for a congenital defect, the first successful remission of pediatric leukemia, and the first successful treatment of a fetus in utero for a heart defect. All of these factors contribute to reputation, but how can the communication function leverage these assets to achieve national recognition?

This chapter is intended to provide guidance to communicators who want to take steps to leverage their institutional assets in enhancing reputation. The steps and approach outlined in this chapter can be applied to any hospital seeking to build its reputation whether on a national, regional, or local level or among targeted audiences. The chapter outlines a 7-step process to build a hospital's brand, including how to do the following:

- Gain census and alignment of leadership.
- Assess capabilities to expand the brand and determine areas that need strengthening.
- Find the right brand positioning.
- Develop brand strategy and getting leadership to buy in.
- Engage employees in the journey.
- Implement strategy in a digitally networked world.
- Adjust to a rapidly changing market.

Building a Reputation Requires Commitment

The focus for many academic medical centers (AMCs) over the past decade has not been building a brand or enhancing a reputation but maintaining financial health, responding to capacity and access issues, expanding quality and safety initiatives, making the transition onto an electronic medical record system, building clinical programs and expertise, and expanding research funding. Branding and marketing are sometimes seen as "dirty words" by many in the physician leadership who feel that a hospital has no need to actively promote itself, especially if the hospital is already at maximum capacity for patients. A common and legitimate question is: Why would we promote ourselves if we can't even get our current patients through the door in a timely manner?

Board, administrative, and clinical leadership have to be ready to market the hospital and be willing to go under the microscope before it engages in what is really a "journey" of self-exploration that is likely to take years, not months. Leadership may or may not like the answers they get during the process. Maybe the supposed marketing problem is that the operational systems to get patients through the doors are ineffective, or that clinical staff are perceived as being unfriendly to referring physicians who want to be treated with respect. These are common problems for many AMCs and why community hospitals are often successful in attracting patient volume from the better known AMCs in their markets. A solid marketing audit will raise these and other issues, and require more than just communications tactics to solve.

A serious effort to build reputation requires institutional focus, prioritization, and resources. However, the rewards of a strong and growing reputation are many and include:

- Retention and expansion of market share
- Recruitment of high-quality physicians, scientists, and employees
- Strong platform for friend and fundraising
- Strong attraction for grant funding
- Better able to withstand crises, such as medical errors, if there is an element of trust and a preconceived positive impression of organization
- Better able to attract media coverage
- Better positioned to pursue legislative and advocacy agendas
- Improved staff morale and investment in mission
- Willingness for customers to pay for quality of service

On the downside:

- Quality and services must live up to reputation or there is a risk of disappointing customers
- A higher profile requires more transparency on bad as well as good news
- Expectations of involvement from external forces (community-based partners, public agencies) increases

The Seven Steps

The following are seven steps to identify, improve, and communicate a brand and its positioning.

Step 1: Leadership Must Be Involved

Leadership—from the board of directors down—must become involved in a branding effort to make the underlying changes needed to maximize the brand (improving service, benchmarking quality, expanding access, changing care delivery models, or reducing price as several major examples) and to garner the resources necessary to build a brand that is ready to promote.

In a healthcare environment, it can be challenging to enlist ready-made brand champions at the board level. While many external board members inherently understand the necessity of a strong brand presence, many do not come to the board with direct brand, marketing, and communications experience. Hospital boards are typically populated by leaders with financial, management, and legal expertise.

Recruiting an executive-level marketing expert onto the board can help to provide the expertise and advocacy needed to begin building a meaningful branding effort. If recruitment of such a member of the board is not an option, you will need to focus on finding a board member with a natural inclination toward marketing and begin educating him or her about the field. Establishing an advisory group with this individual at the lead and involving brand experts from the community at large would provide a strong basis at the top from which to champion the effort.

It is also imperative that the top leaders of the organization (the CEO, president, and COO at Boston Children's) be actively involved and make an explicit commitment to improving the institution's brand. At Boston Children's the initiative for the brand started with the board chairman, who is a successful real estate entrepreneur, owns shopping malls, and is savvy about retail marketing. He and the CEO, an actively practicing surgeon, and the president and COO, formed the senior Brand Steering Committee.

Step 2: You'll Need Help

Next to having strong leadership support, it is important to find an external brand expert to help you through the process of analyzing your brand positioning. Literature and experience dictate that it is difficult for the internal marketing leaders to successfully conduct a brand audit and develop strategy for several reasons, including the lack of outside perspective and credibility of seeing a number of different brands in action outside the conservative hospital environment. Also, if and when there is bad news to deliver, internal marketing leadership is in a tough position to deliver that news.

There are several factors you should take into consideration when engaging an expert.

What Kind of Support Do You Need?

Do you already have a good handle on your brand position and instead are looking to develop a marketing strategy to spread your brand reputation? Many in-house public affairs and marketing (PAM) leaders hire full-service advertising agencies to assist in rebranding efforts. While there are some advantages to having an advertising agency as a partner, it is important to remember that an advertising agency's business model is to sell "advertising." Therefore, they are likely to put forth a costly paid media campaign, and not put as much emphasis on less costly and very effective public affairs tactics, such as earned and social media tactics. Mission-driven nonprofits often are better positioned to generate publicity and engage communities online. AMCs, such as Boston Children's, are particularly fortunate to generate clinical research and great patient stories. For instance, in 2008, researchers at Boston Children's developed the first lines of induced pluripotent stem cells (iPS), a discovery that was deemed as one of the breakthroughs of the year by *Science* magazine. This discovery garnered significant media attention.

Consider Hiring an Independent Brand Strategy Expert

If you need expertise to determine your brand positioning strategy then an independent brand strategy expert would be helpful. If you do not hire a person or company that specializes in brand strategy, you will need to assemble separate teams (creative, media buying, search engine optimization) to implement the strategy and/or rely on internal resources. In today's "virtual" world there are many affordable resources with low overhead that can be coordinated to implement a multifactorial communication strategy. On the plus side of this approach, you can recruit the best talent suited to the job. On the negative side, you will have to take on the role of account supervisor to coordinate all of these vendors—the role that a one-stop advertising agency would play.

Interactive marketing is a key strategy in today's digital world. It is imperative to have someone who understands how to best exploit that medium.

Rebranding Is Expensive

Hiring outside help can be out of reach for some smaller and less-well-funded nonprofits. In these situations, it might make sense to seek pro bono expertise. To develop a pro bono partner, start by identifying a company whose work you admire and has the right complement of competencies (advertising, media buying, earned media, interactive marketing) and then determine if there are connections between your board members and the targeted company's leaders. You could also contact the company directly and ask for advice, eventually seeking more substantial support. A tour of the facility and a description of its mission and communications goals may create a willingness to provide pro bono support if the company is not already overcommitted.

Beware a Pro Bono Relationship

Agencies often use pro bono accounts to meet their own needs to express creativity and may not be focused on your business goals. It is difficult to criticize and demand changes when you are at the recipient end of a pro bono relationship. And, second-tiered staffers are often assigned to service this account as first-tier staffers are understandably focused on paying customers. On the other hand, pro bono staffers are often more passionate and interested in your mission, and may spend more and not less time on your account.

Regardless of your approach to getting outside perspective and advice, make sure that you have a qualified expert who is persuasive, patient, and politically savvy. That person or team will play a crucial role in helping senior leadership to understand the concept of branding; the importance of establishing a brand position, strategy, and messaging; and the need to make appropriate investments in staff and resources.

Step 3: Use a Selection Process to Refine and Clarify Goals

The process of meeting with outside experts will help to refine the key questions that need to be addressed as part of the engagement.

Basic questions can include:

- What is the organization trying to achieve?
  - Reputation building
  - Volume building

- Who are the key audiences you want to reach?
- What behaviors and actions do you want those audiences to take?
  - Seek treatment? Find employment? Give money?
- What selection criteria are important for these audiences when choosing a hospital, physician, or center?
- How does your entity fill these key criteria?
- What is the current brand position of the entity?
- What are the entity's key competitors, and how do they compare along the same criteria?
- What are their strengths and weaknesses relative to your organization and your key audience's needs?
- What opportunities does your organization have to uniquely connect with its targeted audiences, either because of its unique strengths or because of unmet demands in the market?
- Given those opportunities, what is a successful national brand position to project?
- What strategies will help build brand?
- What resources are needed and available?
- How could you garner support among leadership?

Step 4: Intensive Information Gathering

Once the outside branding expert (OBE) has been engaged, a very intensive information gathering process should ensue. Components of that process can include, but are not limited to the following methods.

One-on-One Interviews

Conducting one-on-one interviews with key constituents, including internal and external audiences, is critical. In the case of Boston Children's, there was a specific interest in finding alignment among senior leadership for the need for a national brand-building effort and in understanding the opinions of healthcare leaders across the country.

To get these perspectives, the OBE engaged in 1-hour internal interviews with board members, hospital clinical and administrative leadership, and leaders at our educational partner, Harvard Medical School. For an external perspective, "medical opinion leaders" were interviewed on the phone and in person, when possible. This list included:

- Renowned pediatric specialists across the country
- Administrative leadership at other pediatric hospitals throughout the nation
- Sales leadership at global medical device companies
- Directors of foundations
- Local business leaders

- High-level donors
- National healthcare consultants who have worked with a variety of pediatric hospitals

In total, 100 interviews were conducted over the course of 3 months.

There was surprising insight and agreement in these interviews, and the actual words used to describe Boston Children's and its strengths and weaknesses were invaluable to producing a persuasive narrative.

Focus Groups

Focus groups are also a quick and effective way to gather feedback from key constituents. At Boston Children's, internal focus groups were conducted among nursing leadership, physicians, scientists, young physicians and scientists in training, and support staff at the lower tiers of the organization. Focus groups of patients were also conducted at Boston Children's and two of its presumed competitors.

Quantitative Research

Large quantitative surveys are costly, but they can be helpful if there is a need to provide validation of an important assumption that has been questioned or challenged by leaders within the institution. For instance, there may be a general perception that an organization is already well known within a geographic area (e.g., Boston, Massachusetts, New England, United States), but reality may differ. Or there may be statements being made about perceptions of patients and their customer service experiences that need to be validated with patient satisfaction surveys.

The need for statistically significant information should be weighed against the often substantial expense of gathering that data and the extended timeframe required to gather that information. Brand managers should ask themselves whether the study will provide any new information that is pivotal to strategy or whether it will significantly help in selling a key component of the strategy.

In the case of Boston Children's, the OBE recommended relying on the above mentioned "qualitative" methods of gathering information (i.e., one-on-one interviews and focus groups), citing that large quantitative studies were not necessary at this point and might be restrictive to thinking, as we were still determining the major perceptual elements of what determines a pediatric hospital's reputation. In addition, the hospital had previously conducted local, regional, and national studies on consumer awareness and attitude as well as for referring physicians. Over the years, the trends had not changed significantly, and there was confidence that the trends still held.

Internal Information Gathering

Scour existing sources for information that might be relevant to your audit. Make sure you understand the short- and long-term strategies of the institution. Does your hospital want to aggressively expand its volume? In what service lines (e.g., clinical departments or diagnoses)?

What new technologies and science are being invested in? What new physicians are being recruited into the organization? What geographic areas are currently represented, and what is your current market share in those markets? Are there opportunities for growth? You also need similar information on your competitors. Comparative volume data is available through analysts and trade journals, and information about new technologies and science is often available on the Web sites of competitors.

Other potential sources of rich internal information are patient and family satisfaction surveys and performance measures for access to an institution, such as the number of rings until the phone is answered, wait times for the next available appointments, or wait times within the emergency department.

At Boston Children's, there was an interest in measuring the hospital's clinical and scientific levels of innovation relative to its peer hospitals. The public affairs and marketing staff gathered competitive performance metrics, such as a comparison of publications in top science and medical journals, an analysis of active clinical trials, the number of patents and licenses issued, listing of clinical discoveries, and clinical outcomes measures. One of the unique aspects of pediatric care is that it is extremely difficult to track outcomes as there is no central repository of information, such as there is with Medicare for adults, and the pool of children with medical problems is much smaller compared to adults, making clinical outcomes more challenging to collect and compare.

Site Visits

The consultant made site visits to Boston Children's presumed top competitors, comparing facilities and customer service experience. She was able to visually document the look and feel of these facilities and experience firsthand service differentiators.

Marketing and Communications Audit

The public affairs and marketing team also looked at the promotional efforts among peer children's hospitals, including online presence, earned media (i.e., publicity), collateral material, and advertising. They also looked at similar materials for national hospital brands, such as Cleveland Clinic and the Mayo Clinic.

It took approximately 6 months to complete the entire information-gathering process.

Step 5: Synthesize Findings and Develop Brand Blueprint

While gathering feedback and information, you should begin to get a sense of where your organization fits into the landscape compared to similar type providers. You may be the provider with the most advanced technology and treatments, or perhaps you are well known for your compassionate bedside nursing. Maybe you have the most modern facilities and most service-oriented culture, or perhaps you lack the amenities, but are located in a convenient urban location with the most culturally diverse and competent staff. Understanding your unique brand offering is the essential first step in developing a "brand blueprint," which is the road map for any branding effort.

Based on the information-gathering process, you may now have a unique perspective on where there are weaknesses in the organization and how it performs, or a lack of cohesiveness in leadership's vision of the future, goals, and strategies. This is very powerful and important information to uncover. The role of your OBE is to raise these red flags, which will likely not be news to many leaders. Addressing these issues can sometimes paralyze an organization, but sometimes they can be easily addressed at the highest levels of the organization once uncovered. For example, at Boston Children's, there is a partnership with another hospital that is comarketed by both institutions. However, there's been a longstanding debate as to whether a certain clinical service is part of the collaboration or is under the sole direction of Boston Children's. While the two services were functioning collaboratively on the ground, there was a constant "rub" about whether to actively market the services jointly. The public awareness and marketing team was able to raise the issue to leadership who were willing to discuss and resolve it at the highest level. Not only did this help the marketing effort, but it also helped to operationally push deeper collaboration between multidisciplinary services.

Ultimately, you want to come out of the information-gathering and synthesizing process with a brand blueprint (or road map for communicating your institution). This road map consists of several interlocking components including a brand idea or insight, brand platform, brand offering, brand messaging, an elevator pitch, brand strategy, brand expressions, and a graphic identity manual.

- *Brand blueprint*: The operating principles of the brand: strategies and concepts for the helm to use in assessing if activities are on brand/off brand, and to brief outside resources on how to appropriately express the brand in what they create. The brand blueprint includes all of the components listed below.
- *Branding idea or insight*: Single, central organizing concept of the brand that is the enduring, differentiating and compelling idea.
- *Brand platform*: The blueprint articulated in simple, inspiring language for the workforce to use a tool to guide their decisions, behaviors, and pursuit activities so they build the brand.
- *Branded offering*: Diagrammatic depiction of organization's assets, products/services, and outcomes—the "what" that the organization offers to the world.
- *Brand messaging*: Simple language to capture the major components that make up the brand and proof points to support claims. The messaging is used consistently throughout all communications.
- *Elevator pitch*: Pretend you are in an elevator and have 30 seconds to explain who you are in the most succinct and powerful terms (see Box 6-1).
- *Brand strategy*: How are you going to communicate that brand? What are the strategies and tactics you are going to use to shape or reshape the perceptions with key audiences?
- *Brand expression board*: Real or mockup examples of how your brand is expressed through various communications tools—digital, print, signage, and facilities.
- *Graphic identity manuals*: The "nitty gritty" specifics on how your brand should be communicated, including the use of your "logo lock," typographies, colors, photography, and videos.

Box 6-1 Example of Boston Children's Elevator Pitch

Boston Children's is the best pediatric hospital in the world because its science-driven approach pushes the boundaries of pediatric care.

- It has the greatest cluster of pediatric hospitals, medical centers, and programs.
- It has the Pediatric Institute of Innovation and Discovery, the greatest pediatric research center in the world.
- It has the greatest level of partnerships with the top research, biotech, and health-care organizations in Boston, working together to improve children's health.
- Bright, compassionate, and determined people work in an intense culture of innovation and achievement.

Developing a brand blueprint is probably the most difficult part of the process, as senior leadership in a nonprofit hospital generally does not spend time discussing brand positioning and is probably not familiar with the process. At Boston Children's, one of the most challenging aspects of the discussion was letting go of the hospital's four-part mission (care, teaching, research, and community) when defining its brand position. In fact, the top leadership met for more than 8 hours to "wordsmith" the right brand platform. The process of discussion with an outside consultant who pushed for a unique and "ownable" brand position helped to inculcate the brand into the leadership's strategic thinking.

Graphic Identity

One of the most obvious expressions of your brand is your name and logo. Changing a name and logo is a major endeavor and should be undertaken with care and skepticism. The first question to ask is how much "equity" does your organization have in its name? Do your customers know who you are? What is their level of positive association with your organization's name? Does your name express the most important components of your brand? Are there parts missing? Can those parts simply be added?

There will likely be many and conflicting opinions about your name and logo. Many logos fall into the trap of looking trendy. A logo that was groundbreaking and fresh when designed in the 1970s now looks like it was designed in the 1970s. Boston Children's logo, a nurse holding a small child, was developed in 1914 and had a classic and traditional look that did not reflect the forward thinking research that occurred in the hospital. However, the logo's image is very popular and well known within the hospital, and it conveys a powerful sense of trust and experience.

Before you change anything, it is a good idea to assess the full cost of making those changes and getting consumer feedback. At Boston Children's, it was estimated to cost at least $3 million to make a change to the name and logo. Making that level of investment would have been a hard sell internally and externally given the financial challenges facing health care.

If you are going to proceed with a name and logo change, test current and new options with your targeted publics through focus groups. An experienced graphic design firm should be familiar with this process and be able to help you with the testing. Getting unanimous agreement on name and logo is nearly impossible, given the variety of opinions and personal preferences. Whether you stay the same or change, it will take fortitude and a thoughtfully presented case to justify your decision. Prepare your leadership for the reality that everyone will have an opinion and they will all be different.

Brand Strategy

Focus areas. One key component of developing your brand strategy at a hospital is to decide what to market. This sounds simple, but it is no small achievement. At Boston Children's, there are 266 programs, centers, institutes, clinics, and services; more than 1000 active medical staff, many of whom are the world's experts in their clinical discipline; and another 1000 scientists. It is impossible to effectively promote so many services because of overwhelming resources that would be needed and the confusion in the marketplace caused by so many messages.

Your brand strategy should focus on those clinical services that distinguish you in the marketplace. At Boston Children's, five clinical focus areas were selected in areas of major interest (heart, cancer, brain, bone and spine, and transplant) and where there was superior performance in the delivery of care and new discoveries. These areas warrant extra promotional focus (digital and social media, paid and earned media, collateral materials, and assignment of service line managers). For instance, during the redesign of the Web site, these areas were the first to undergo the redesign and receive massive support in developing new content, videos, and social media platforms. This focus allowed resources to be used more effectively.

Audience and geographic identification. As mentioned previously, there are very few hospitals that truly draw nationally. Therefore, it is important to specifically define your geographic reach, whether by state, town, or zip code. This can be based on a careful analysis of your current market share versus that of your competitors, coupled with a SWOT (strengths, weaknesses, opportunities, and threats) analysis. This information will help you understand where you have opportunities for growth. However, do not forget to carefully consider where there may be threats to your current base of customers. Put yourself in your competition's shoes: What weaknesses could you exploit to attract patients and their families?

Also, precisely define your audiences. In the case of Boston Children's, it was too costly to try to reach every American citizen, so the hospital focused its strategy on reaching medical opinion leaders as well as parents whose children were facing an illness or those who were impassioned about staying updated generally on pediatric health. These parents were most likely to get their information online.

Open brand. In this digital era, brands are shifting from "closed" to "open" brands where consumers of your service can instantaneously rate their experience through online sites such as Yelp or social media sites such as Facebook. Gone are the days when you could tightly control your brand image through "messaging" that was blasted out through advertising and publicity. National brands are now expected to be "lighthouse" brands, guiding the way for others to an ideal or solution. For Boston Children's, that means leading clinicians and parents toward achieving the best health care for their patients and children, respectively.

This required a paradigm shift from the previous communications approach, which was to trumpet the hospital's accomplishments. Instead, the goal was to lead the way in advancing pediatric health and sharing information, which means giving credit to other hospitals and individuals for their contributions. This change in direction was both challenging and invigorating for communications staff. It forced them to reach outside the walls for news and developments that were relevant to key audiences. This provided a wealth of engaging information to report on.

In July 2009, Boston Children's launched a popular pediatric health information site called Thrive. It has had 400,000 visits (280,000 unique visits) since its inception and has won several awards for its reporting. The goal of the blog was to both publish Boston Children's specific findings but also to stay current with the daily news cycle to provide commentary on breaking pediatric health topics, such as new genetic findings in autism, allergies, sex texting, and other developments with teenagers and technology.

To achieve this and to integrate all communications efforts, the public affairs and marketing staff began daily "huddles," where owners of key outlets (intranet, Internet, Facebook, Twitter, Earned Media, etc.) meet to discuss Boston Children's announcements, breaking national news topics, and a possible role that the hospital can play in responding to those stories. While there was some skepticism about the need for daily meetings (9:00 a.m. everyday and they last about a half hour), they have become a department mainstay with growing attendance.

There are several other strategies under development to build national reputation that involve a national event for opinion leaders, a digital engagement site, and school-based distribution program. As these efforts are still under development, it would be premature to discuss them. However, a common theme among all of them is that Boston Children's is strong enough to be a "lighthouse" brand. It requires moving the hospital away from being a "closed" brand that trumpets its successes only and engages in one-way community, to an organization that recognizes others successes and invites engagement from the outside world.

Digital. The Internet is the most effective tool for building reputation and volume for your organization and should receive significant time and resources. It is also a competitive space that requires a deep understanding and expertise of what drives visits, how to engage visitors once they are online, and how to convert them into action (e.g., make an appointment, give money, add themselves as a "friend"). In addition, social media sites, such as Yelp, Amazon, eBay, and Zapatos are successfully recruiting consumers to rate their products and services, which have high credibility with other visitors to the site.

Six years ago, Boston Children's had invested significantly in its Web site, adding 1100 pages of content with descriptions of diseases, diagnosis, and treatment. This was largely responsible for the site's success in drawing visitors. Currently, there are 2 million visits per month, approximately 50% of which go to the disease and diagnosis section of the site.

While Boston Children's had the most active Web site among its peers, none of these children's hospitals have national reputations. True benchmarks for national players in health care are the Cleveland and Mayo clinics, whose Web site visits eclipse those of other hospitals. Determining the right benchmark is the best starting point for determining the resources that will be needed to reach that benchmark.

At Boston Children's, a talented manager of Internet marketing was promoted to a new director's position and charged with increasing traffic to the site, increasing engagement, and building traffic to focus on clinical areas mentioned above. He identified a digital marketing and development company with whom to partner. Together, they laid out a strategy that focused on the following:

1. Enriching the content on the site
2. Adding digital videos as the population shifts from readers to viewers
3. Vastly improving the searchability of the site
4. Sharply defining the prime audience as being parents of sick kids
5. Turning up the focus on clinical innovation to reflect the new brand
6. Drawing visitors to the national focus areas of the hospital
7. Pulling visitors in from basic health information to services that may be of use to them
8. Prominent integration with social media tools, such as Facebook
9. Making sure the site was using the most current search engine optimization techniques to increase the likelihood of traffic

The scope of the project is immense, and it requires major support from clinical leadership and medical staff to review content. To secure that support, the Boston Children's Internet team made several presentations to senior leadership explaining its goals in revamping the site and asking for support. Interesting operational issues beyond the site were raised as a result of this process including:

- When multiple departments treat a disease, such as headache, and are not fully coordinating care, where do you refer the patient first?
- Who is responsible when multiple clinical departments are involved for reviewing copy?

Senior clinical leadership agreed to a system for resolving these issues, which involved assigning a coordinating physician to take ultimate responsibility for reviewing the data, and having any conflicts come to an executive-level decision-making body at the hospital.

A key strategy in building ranking in Google and other search engines is the provision of useful and well-organized content. To update and supplement the thousands of pages of content at Boston Children's, the senior editor and writer in the department, who previously focused on print communications, was reassigned to oversee the content development process. Fifty top diagnoses with the potential to draw national volume were identified. A format for all sections was developed, which included adding innovations that were unique to Boston Children's. A cadre of Web writers was retained to update the content.

A 2-year schedule was developed to address all of the diseases and their diagnoses. At this writing, the Web site is under development, so the jury is out as to its ultimate success. However, when the site is launched, it is likely to be one of the richest and best organized sites at a children's hospital in the country. A launch campaign is being developed that will entail paid and unpaid media, as well as full promotional social media.

Step 6: Sharing Findings

Brands are managed at the helm by the corner office with one single individual charged with implementing it across the organization. In a perfect world, everyone else expresses the brand under the guidance of the helm. As mentioned previously, in nonprofit health care organizations, at best the words *brand* and *marketing* are often poorly understood, and at worse they are viewed as unethical. Therefore, using a branding process to educate leadership is essential. They must buy into the importance of building and maintaining a brand in order for the effort to receive the level of support it needs.

It is crucial to determine in advance how you plan to share your findings, particularly if there are findings that are controversial in nature. For instance, you may find that there are issues with access or customer service, or perceptions around quality that are important to the marketing of your organization because they shape your product but are not directly under marketing's control. It is important to create a safe and confidential environment in which honest discussion and debate can ensue.

In the case of Boston Children's, the board chair, CEO and president, and COO were given the first debriefing. It took three 2-hour meetings. There will be a tendency to want to rush through the information. If possible, try to get the time needed to have comprehensive discussions about the findings. This is an important educational moment for hospital leadership, who traditionally spend most of their days focused on quality and safety, research, teaching, finance, and other agendas. They need to become comfortable and well versed in branding terminology. What is a brand position versus brand messaging? They also need to begin to understand that key decisions about brand strategy are the responsibility of—and important to—the highest level of the organization.

In the case of Boston Children's, the first 2 hours of debriefing focused on important operational and alignment issues that the hospital needed to deal with in order to retain its number one ranking among children's hospitals. Those issues included continuing to improve customer service, continuing to overcome the natural tendency toward operating in clinical silos in an academic medical center, and continuing to push the boundaries in clinical innovation by investing in the translation of basic science to the bedside. It was clear that many of the challenges that internal leadership had been struggling to address were visible to external opinion leaders. To senior leadership's credit, they embraced this perceived "chink in the armor" as a way to motivate internal clinical and administrative leadership to redouble their efforts to make the changes that were essential to maintaining the hospital's ambitious vision of offering the world's most advanced pediatric care.

During the 6 hours of presentation time with leadership, the consultant used a 183-slide presentation with quote after quote from outside sources. There was great consistency between the comments, regardless of whether they were from an inside or outside source. The use of actual quotes was extremely persuasive in shaping the narrative about the hospital's brand. Sections for such a presentation could include:

- What was the perception of your institution?
- Who are your top competitors?
- How does your reputation compare to competitors?
- What are your top respective strengths and weakness?
- Who has top ranking perceptually?
  - Why?
- What were the most important criteria that your key audiences use to judge you relative to other choices?
- Where does time and effort need to be invested to achieve your branding goals?
- What is the unique proposition that would be meaningful to your targeted audiences?
- How can you position your institution to take advantage of that unique proposition?
- Who are the important audiences that needed to be targeted?
- Is your name working for you or against you?
- What are the important positioning attributes need to be in a name, meaning, how is clinical innovation and discovery best represented?
- What about the logo?
- What are the big ideas that could help rapidly build national name?
- What is the overall strategy for building brand?

Following discussions with top leadership, there was a decision to share the information in a half-day retreat session with board, clinical, and administrative leadership, which would include brainstorming sessions to enlist idea generation and involvement. The strategy for building a national brand through marketing and public affairs tactics was not addressed. Instead, the team focused on what could be done through operations and the culture to make real changes to the "product" that was delivered.

The goal of the retreat was to reengage leadership in the important work that needed to be done and leave with a very specific set of actions to achieve that work. Retreat participants formed smaller teams and rapidly brainstormed possible actions in response to topics, including improving customer service, achieving better institutional alignment, and accelerating clinical innovation. The group as a whole then responded to those ideas and established a to-do list coming out of the retreat. The session was facilitated by the outside consultant who hired several professional facilitators to help lead those sessions.

Engaging leadership in the process in a meaningful way is an important step in developing consensus and support for the plan. This is probably the most important part of the process, and careful thought should be given to the best way to proceed.

Educating Leadership—The Four Ps of Marketing

The retreat with an experienced outside consultant, who had worked with some of the country's largest brands, served as an educational session for leadership, who began to understand that branding wasn't just about "advertising" or "promotion"; it is also thinking about the "product," "place" of distribution, and "price."

As discussed in the previous section, "the product"—the quality and service of the hospital's health care—received feedback from the brand information-gathering process. In the past 5 years, Boston Children's had been putting an emphasis on the "place" of delivering care, opening up a new center in a western suburb and planning new, improved and expanded facilities in the north and south. There was also a keen awareness that the "place" or facilities that were the hub of the hospital's inpatient care were aging and needed investment. A new inpatient clinical building addition was in progress that would allow the hospital to convert double to single rooms, which is an absolute imperative in pediatric care where entire families spend time around the clock with their hospitalized children, and where there is an increased need for additional staff and equipment because of the fragility of sick children and to minimize the chance of the spread of infectious disease.

"Price," which is generally set by the finance department and not easily transparent because of the complexity of healthcare finance (i.e., health care purchased through insurers in private and public markets), was not a consideration in the initial discussions. However, as time progressed and the marketplace quickly shifted it became increasingly important as discussed in the section called "Understand the Brand Context before Launching."

Start at Home—Employees, Patients, and Families as Ambassadors

Employees, patients, and their families are obviously ambassadors for the hospital who are able to credibly and virally spread the word about the brand. The public affairs and marketing vice president was appointed to sit on the new Patient and Provider Experience Committee. A new position, the director of patient and family communications, was created, and the manager of public affairs was promoted to the position. He was responsible for working with clinicians to follow the pathway of a patient through the hospital (before, during, and after) and making sure online, printed, and onsite communications were added and updated to help patients better navigate the system and understand the full benefits of services available to them.

The hospital already had a fairly active set of communication tools for employees, including an intranet site, monthly newsletter, quarterly open meetings with the CEO and COO, a faculty e-newsletter, digital television screens, screen savers, and all-user e-mails, on occasion.

The national branding consultant suggested the development of cultural principles and maxims for employees to capture and feedback the unique aspects of working at Boston Children's. Fifty employees from different areas of the hospital were recruited for focus groups and brainstorming sessions. Values and maxims were developed focusing on the key attributes that make the hospital a top leader, edited by creative staff, and recirculated to original participants for prioritization and comment.

The result was a genuine list of attributes that capture what makes the organization unique. However, in the meantime, a new customer service endeavor was taking shape, and there was overlap between service standards and the principles and maxims developed. Concerned about creating confusion and looking like the "flavor of the month," public affairs and marketing staff and customer service leadership met and combined the efforts to develop "Who We Are (our principles) and How We Behave (a combination of service standards and maxims)." The result was a clear and memorable motivational document for employees. The documents are now in the process of being reviewed by the Patient and Physician Experience Committee.

Examples of the "Who We Are" principles include:

- *Love kids*: Everyone comes here to work with or around kids. They are either devoted to caring for sick children, supporting caregivers, or making discoveries that will improve the health of children.
- *Love science*: We believe great science drives great care. We use science-based approaches, scientifically tested treatments, and produce innovations using the most rigorous scientific methods. We are the leaders in pediatric sciences.

Examples of the "How We Behave" maxims include:

- *Excellence*: Exceed expectations. See a problem, fix a problem. Achieve excellence without arrogance.
- *Respect*: Cherish differences as learning opportunities. Treat others with empathy and compassion. Put yourself in their shoes.

Step 7: Understand the Market Context before Launching

Every brand is a perceptual lens by which people make judgments about a product or service. Affecting the view from that lens is the external environment in which that brand is being projected. Your central brand "concept" (e.g., Volvo = safety; BMW = German engineering; Subaru = adventure) is like DNA and will always remain the same until you consciously make a major shift, but how it is presented may change depending on the environment in which you are offering your product. Be cognizant of rapidly changing dynamics in the market when you are promoting your brand.

As Boston Children's prepared to launch its brand, a major transformation of the market was underway led by Massachusetts, the first state to pass health reform and gain universal access to health insurance. Federal healthcare reform passed soon after. As predicted, once the "access" issue was addressed (97% of Massachusetts residents are covered by health insurance), the focus shifted toward the cost of care. In Massachusetts, the governor, legislature, and business and advocacy groups called for transparency and price reductions. The Massachusetts Attorney General's office published prices charged to the major insurers.

Children's was one of the most costly because of the resource-intensive nature of pediatric care mentioned above.

Boston Children's reduced its prices by more than $80 million dollars, but there was still a differential for pediatric secondary and some tertiary care provided by Boston Children's. It became even more essential for Boston Children's to demonstrate its value in order to justify the higher costs. However, at the same time, the hospital did not want to appear to be wasting money with expensive advertising given the price sensitivity of the market.

To communicate its value and stay consistent with its brand, the hospital used the equation: value = quality, service, and innovation/price. This new marketplace dynamic also required that brand launch be done without expensive fanfare and that more time should be given for the brand to organically grow. Fortunately, the proposed reputation-building activities (an event, a patient/family-oriented Web site and major improvements to the current site) were all geared toward providing value to targeted audiences.

Measurement

Setting up measurements in advance of your campaign will help you document and demonstrate progress, which will help to build long-term support for branding efforts. While it is difficult and costly to obtain "outcome" measures, there are several options, and the Internet provides instantaneous and detailed data. Possible measurements include the following.

At Boston Children's, a pre- and postsurvey of "medical opinion" leaders is currently in the first phase (presurvey) of measurement, and postmeasurement will occur within an 18-month period. In addition to asking about awareness, the survey investigates qualities that make a children's hospital a top performer, competitors, and sources of influence in reputation building. There are also questions about specific clinical focus areas. Large quantitative surveys are a good standard for measurement as they can capture statistically significant shifts.

Another measurement gold standard is being able to *capture referrals* into a hospital that are the result of branding efforts, such as a news program on epilepsy treatment. This can be done through call center or front desk staff who ask how patients and families heard about the hospital, clinical service, or doctor, or it can be done through an online appointment-scheduling function.

There are countless *Internet measurements* using data-capturing analysis programs (Web Trends, Google Analytics, Omniture) that can tell you how many unique visitors to a site, page views, time on the site, geographic location of visitor, video views, or donations. Another measure you can use to benchmark your organization against that of others is hiring a company to *track earned media hits* and the quality of those hits.

Creating a *"brand" dashboard or report card* with all these measures will help to quantify the value that a strong marketing and public affairs strategy brings to an organization, but it will not likely capture all of the intangible benefits of a strong brand, such as the ability to attract top-notch staff or funding.

It Is a Marathon, Not a Sprint

When the writers first agreed to write this chapter, they assumed that they would be well into implementation and ready to report on success. However, the effort has required nearly a year and a half of research, synthesizing, review, debate, and revision. The major initiatives mentioned above will require at least 18 months of implementation, and a few years of start up. As such, building a national reputation with limited funds requires time—3 to 5 years. In retrospect, building a commitment to a long-term process and to continual involvement of leadership is essential.

Summary

Building a brand nationally requires commitment and understanding from the top leadership of an organization. In the nonprofit hospital arena, it also requires educating leadership about the process of branding and its importance. Many misunderstand branding as only addressing names and logos and do not understand the importance of brand positioning.

Finding a brand position is best achieved by an outside party who is unbiased and can effectively communicate the strengths, weaknesses, opportunities, and threats in the marketplace. An analysis of brand should not focus only on what needs to be communicated, but also on any weaknesses in meeting the brand promise from a customer service perspective. A brand audit provides a credible opportunity to focus the organization on important operational issues. It can provide the impetus for change.

The right brand position should intuitively feel like the right fit. When it is articulated and reduced to the essentials, it will provide a valuable road map for all communications. However, getting agreement on the right name and logo for an organization could be challenging and is likely to garner diverse opinions.

In this day and age, new media (digital and social media) is an essential component of building a brand and must be a key component of a strategy. Reorganizing staff to take on that role can be challenging, but it offers new opportunities.

In the end, undergoing a branding or rebranding process is one of the most rewarding experiences an in-house marketing leader can undertake and, if done right, will help to elevate the importance of the function within the organization.

Discussion Questions

1. Describe how to get hospital leadership involved in the branding effort if there is a lack of marketing expertise on the board.
2. Why is seeking external branding expertise a good idea when developing a branding strategy? What should you consider before engaging an external expert?

3. Identify and describe the research methods used for gathering information that guides the strategic branding process.
4. Define the term *brand blueprint*, and describe its components.
5. Explain how the concept of "open brands" affects the task of a communications specialist in today's digital era.
6. Why is engaging leadership critical to the brand-building process?

Chapter 7

Crisis Communication in the Health Sector

By Jeffrey L. Molter and Richard A. Puff

LEARNING OBJECTIVES

By the end of the chapter, the reader will be able to:

- Define the term *health crisis* and identify the multiple causes of such crises.
- Prepare for a health communication crisis and prevent a crisis before it happens.
- Understand the role of a communications specialist in the event of a health crisis.
- Effectively manage a health communications crisis.

Introduction

In February 2003, a teenage girl received a heart and lung transplant at Duke University Medical Center in Durham, North Carolina. Unfortunately, an unthinkable mistake had occurred: the transplanted organs were the wrong blood type. A media firestorm ensued placing the university, its doctors, and staff into its most severe crisis to that date.

This highly unusual and tragic medical error also began a tumultuous period for Duke's communicators. However, Duke's media team helped the institution restore public confidence and trust by collectively facing the hard questions from hundreds of news media across the globe, including *60 Minutes* and *U.S. News & World Report*. In fact, Duke's response to this situation even resulted in improvements to the nation's organ donor and transplant systems.

Afterward, polling showed Duke's reputation remained intact. A *Forbes* magazine article said Duke's handling of this situation was reminiscent of one of the most celebrated public relations victories—Johnson & Johnson's handling in October 1982 of the random poisoning of a few capsules of Tylenol, which killed seven people in Chicago. (J & J recalled millions of bottles, introduced new tamper-resistant packaging, and handled a great deal of media coverage.)

In addition, *PRWeek's Book of Lists 2003* noted Duke in its "5 Communicators We Listened To." It commented: "Seventeen-year-old Jesica Santillan underwent a heart and lung transplant that proved fatal due to a blood-type mismatch. Within days, remorseful Duke doctors were on *60 Minutes* to explain how the mishap occurred, conveying that anything of the sort would not occur again."

What Is a Health Crisis?

In the health communications arena, with all the advances (and controversies) in medicine, science, health, and clinical care, it is likely that a practitioner will encounter several crises in a career. Some will last a short while; others might create history.

The important items to remember are these: crises happen, you have to deal with them, your company or institution must deal with them, and you must strive to help recover your institution's reputation as soon as is humanly possible.

What is a crisis? The Institute for Crisis Management in Louisville, Kentucky, has a cogent definition:

> *a significant business disruption that stimulates extensive news media coverage. The resulting public scrutiny will affect the organization's normal operations and also could have a political, legal, financial, and governmental impact on its business.*

A health crisis can be caused by many things, including natural disaster, accident, human error, management error, conflict-of-interest violation, disagreement between your institution/client and another competitor, governmental or regulatory agency action against your institution/client, criminal act, or lawsuit. But that list just scratches the surface. There are dozens of other situations that could arise at any time that could cause your institution to jump into crisis mode.

In this chapter, we'll provide many of the essentials needed to prepare for and deal with a crisis. At the end of the chapter we'll provide a detailed case study of the organ transplant mismatch. But there also are many crisis examples everyday in the media. Expectations for medical perfection are high in our world's fast-paced 24/7 culture; advances over the past 30 years have led people to expect successful outcomes all the time, not some of the time. That did not happen a generation ago. When a medical error occurs, there is an immediate hunger now by others (media, regulators, government, patients, etc.) to learn what happened, why it happened, and who is responsible. Health communications professionals help to handle and ameliorate these situations and help restore trust and respect for their institutions or clients.

Here's a headline on an error at a leading West Coast hospital: "Hospital error leads to radiation overdoses." An October 13, 2009, *Los Angeles Times* news report said: "After Cedars-Sinai (a prominent Los Angeles hospital) reset a CT scan machine in February 2008, more than 200 brain scans on potential stroke patients were performed at eight times the normal dose of radiation, the hospital says."

Think for a moment how you would respond to this situation. The doctors there were trying to improve care for their patients. But problems ensued when they reset the machine to override preprogrammed instructions from the manufacturer. What do you disclose? How do you try to fix the problem? How do you help your hospital's patients? Your institution? Finally, how can you prepare for any lawsuits that might ensue?

As you read this, go to the Web and type the words *medical error*, *patient safety*, or a similar term into any search engine. You'll have no problem finding issues or events health communications professionals are currently dealing with across the globe.

Health crises often have different speeds in which they become a big concern. Some are "smoldering." That is when a serious problem not generally known inside or outside the company could generate negative new coverage if or when it goes public.

Another is "sudden." That's a disruption in the company's business that occurs without warning and is likely to generate news coverage.

In addition, a crisis is not always about your institution's bad news or misfortunes. It could be a health issue (an epidemic, pandemic, natural disaster, etc.) that your institution has to deal with. The overall news could be bad, but even when your institution is thrown into chaos, positive news can be generated when your institution rises to the occasion.

In summary, a health crisis is any issue—if not well handled—that can damage your institution's/client's reputation, and yours as well. Health communications professionals' jobs are to make the situation better and to help restore or burnish reputation. Trust is "king" in our business.

Before a Crisis Happens: Being Prepared

If you learn anything from this chapter, it should be that preparation is essential to survive and thrive in a health crisis. The leaders of many institutions think that bad things will not happen to them. Even when a crisis occurs, the prevailing thought by many is that they can "control" the situation and continue to go about their regular work. Too often it's thought that the situation will "fly under the radar." In a crisis, there are many things (and some people) you won't have control of. You must be prepared in advance to have a game plan, and you must persevere to keep your institution true to that game plan.

Your game plan should include:

- Prepare a crisis response plan.
- Prevent crisis situations before they happen.
- Know your company, client, or institution's "culture."
- Know your media spokespersons.

Prepare a Crisis Plan

Here's a brief summation of our crisis communications plan when we experienced the organ transplant mismatch at Duke. However, there are many good crisis plans out there; do some homework and find a couple from health and nonhealth institutions to learn from.

1. Notification of situation or event to communications lead, or second in command.
2. Notification of institution leaders and staff, and ancillary management (in our case, Duke University).
3. Rapid response to collect information concerning the situation. This includes, but is not limited to, discussions with senior management, assigning communications staff to the situation; assigning staff to command center; and discussions with outside agencies (e.g., state Department of Health, emergency management, Red Cross). Assign communications staff to various areas to collect information and data and also monitor the situation.
   a. Bring in additional staff or assistance as needed.
   b. Arrange for alternate work area or computer access if situation warrants.
4. Convene staff, consolidate information, and formulate plan to release information to the news media. Vehicles could include: news releases, Web sites, news conferences, and social media.
   a. Select key communications staff to provide information and coordinate interviews as needed or warranted
5. Maintain lines of communication with senior management and ancillary organizations (parent company).
   a. Have staff maintain accurate record of media calls and chain of events.
6. Discuss need for dissemination of information internally. Work with internal communications staff to produce and disseminate messages.
7. Continue updating leaders as situation progresses.
8. Maintain flow of information as situation continues. Update media and internal audiences as needed or warranted.
9. Monitor staff for signs of stress depending on length of situation. Rotate fresh staff.
10. Anticipate second-day coverage of situation. Continue providing updates to both media and internal audiences.

Many organizations create comprehensive crisis communications plans in order to be prepared for any crisis. Go to the microsite for the crisis communications plan for Emory University's Woodruff Health Sciences Center in Atlanta (18,000 employees; large health system and research enterprise; professional health schools and a primate center, too). It is especially helpful to create a comprehensive crisis communication plan in cases where non-communications personnel may have to assume the role of communicator. This may be in the case of a natural disaster (e.g., hurricane, tornado, etc.) when communicators could be lost, incapacitated or unable to perform duties, or when key staff are off-site and unavailable at the moment of crisis. Creating a comprehensive plan and sharing it with key leaders in advance is essential in preparing for a crisis.

Prevent Crisis Situations Before They Happen

Many crisis situations can be managed or even avoided with persuasive public relations counsel. This doesn't mean communications expertise can make a problem magically disappear; it means provide counsel to deal with an issue immediately, provide the necessary information to the media and others if necessary, and manage the issue into becoming a one- or two-day story instead of a problem that drags on and becomes a crisis, or even eliminate the situation before it escalates into a true crisis.

This area is where a communications professional earns his or her keep. Senior management needs to get the best possible information, counsel, advice, and recommendations from communications experts in order to make the best decisions, even when they want to avoid the issue and think it can be managed by not saying much.

In this way, a communications professional serves as the conscience of an organization. Most experienced public relations practitioners can spin tales of advising senior management against taking a specific action that would have resulted in negative public reaction and thus avoided a crisis. This is another reason why communicators must play the role of critical advisor to senior management. It is much easier to provide advice before something blows up than jumping into action after the problem has gotten out of hand.

Think of the Tiger Woods image crisis at the end of 2009. Where were his counselors when he had his driving "issue?" When he had his mistress issues? He had a big problem to begin with, but his handlers made it worse by not being more open and dealing with it. Instead, the issue snowballed into a full-blown crisis. You need to deal with problems right up front, get them behind you quickly, tell the truth and be transparent (the media will find out anyway), and begin a recovery plan as soon as possible.

Of course, trying to convince leaders to divulge bad news is not popular with them. But you must insist, when appropriate, to strongly encourage them to take this course. Communication professionals must speak up, provide counsel, push for follow through, and stay on leaders (even when it is not immediately appreciated) to help them make the proper decisions to prevent, lessen, or deal with a crisis in order for it not become all consuming to the institution. Just remember Tiger.

Know Your Institution's Culture

Every institution is susceptible to a crisis. However, how a crisis mixes with your institution's "culture" is important to know before one occurs. What kind of culture do you work in? Is your company, public, private, government; open and transparent, or tightly held and close-lipped; polite or bullish? It is important to understand your organization's culture and not let it get in the way of dealing with a crisis. You can't change the culture, but you can alter how the outside world perceives you during a crisis.

For example, you might have a top leader who in a crisis would not be an appropriate spokesperson because he or she is too brutish or too meek. Sometimes you need to put the strongest leader out front as a spokesperson, not the top leader. Uncaring, unfeeling CEOs discussing how you are dealing with a crisis only reinforces negative attitudes about your organization. Same goes for a spokesperson who is too polite or offers up too much information. If you must make your top leader available to the media, you have to prepare him or her to be honest, transparent, empathetic, caring, and strong. Those might not be the attributes of your organization's culture or your leader, but they need to be your spokesperson's attributes when presenting to the media and others.

That means engaging in media and platform training before a crisis occurs so you can help your spokesperson use the best of your culture, become a strong and coherent mouthpiece for your organization, and avoid parts of your institution's culture that don't translate well via the media in a crisis situation (e.g., large money-driven drug company).

Know Your Institution's Key Leadership (Media Spokespersons)

Having a good, honest, and close relationship with your senior management, legal, and risk management teams in advance of a crisis—and knowing who will be your key spokespersons or information providers—is key to surviving and thriving in a crisis. They have to trust you, and you have to trust them. Get to know them and build that trust before a storm hits. Let them know what you'll need from them during a crisis, and that you'll prepare them and also cover their backs during difficult interviews. It is truly a team effort during a crisis.

Who will be your lead spokespersons? Will it be your CEO or others? Is he or she willing to do the job? Is he or she strong enough, tough enough, and courageous enough to do the job? Will he or she do a good job? Will he or she be trusted by the company or the board? Will he or she get the necessary help from others on the team to do a good job?

These are all questions you need to have answers for in preparing for a crisis, not when the crisis is at hand. You'd be surprised how many institutions haven't planned on who is out "front" when a crisis erupts. Work on all those questions in advance, and have the proper spokespersons trained and ready for a crisis. Again, some leaders aren't always the best spokespersons. Make sure your CEO is trained and ready to go, but also plan to have others prepared, too. Ask the CEO to assure other spokespersons that this is a team effort and that they are supported as well.

Before a crisis hits is also the time to make sure your key spokesperson understands the importance of the role. It is as critical as the management decisions that are made during a crisis.

In addition, plan to have more than one spokesperson available and trained for a crisis. Today's news cycle is 24/7, so the requests will not stop at the end of the night. During the Duke organ transplant crisis, our communications team should have asked for an additional spokesperson or two during the media barrage. Our spokespersons did a fine job, but there were too many media requests for them to handle at first. Some media didn't get their needs met—and punished us by saying "Duke was unavailable for comment." We were too slow to immediately meet their demands and had to play catch-up as the crisis continued.

Being a spokesperson in a crisis is also a very tough job and drains your energy quickly. We'll never forget our hospital CEO executing a tough conference call during the crisis, after having done many other interviews. He had done a great job throughout the crisis, but was exhausted. He laid his head on top of the phone for a couple of moments to compose himself. It was a moving moment; it showed how much strength it takes to be a spokesperson during a crisis and how it tests every ounce of one's resolve.

Having additional spokespeople to assist is good for your institution's image, because they can take your messages and deliver them promptly—instead of having no one available and letting people assume you don't care, don't want to talk, or have something to hide.

Have Your Spokespeople Prepared

Two of the most important words in your lexicon should be: media training. Having 50 years in the healthcare communications business between the two of us, media training is as important today as it was 20 years ago. It is absolutely imperative to have spokespeople practiced and prepared, and media training is the way to accomplish this to ensure a good performance during a crisis.

Practicing in front of the camera, being asked tough questions, and reviewing interview performance as many times as possible will pay off in the long run for your spokespersons and your institution.

Create a training program for all of your key spokespersons. It is recommended to use outside trainers to do this (health professionals respond to this better and take it more seriously), but if necessary produce your own in-house media training program. Go to the microsite for information given to Emory spokespeople when they go through media training. Whatever you do, have a media training program in place at your institution so you have spokespeople trained regularly and are always prepared. It is a great insurance policy.

Know Your Media

Media perceive crises differently than health organizations. Understanding your local, regional, and national media landscape is important when a crisis erupts. Studying how the media might portray your organization in a crisis situation in advance may help you when a real crisis happens. Will they be fair? Will the crisis situation ruin your relationship with them after the crisis is over?

Media want to tell a story quickly and are competitive; you want to manage the story once you have the facts and maintain relationships after the crisis. Focus on which reporters are the most important to your organization, which ones might need TLC in order to maintain good working relationships during and after the crisis, and look for ones that you may have not worked with before but are drawn to your crisis. Even if you have a great relationship with a reporter, a crisis changes how you will interact with that reporter during this event.

Quickly draw up a plan on how to serve key local media as well as national media (in case your crisis crosses state lines). They are two different audiences and can cause tension for your communications operations during a crisis. Local media don't like it when national media take your attention away from them; they feel it is their story. Conversely, national media come in and don't always know who you are and what you do, so you need to explain things to them more carefully. Treat them both well, and understand they are different animals and should be treated as such.

As a crisis unfolds, also identify and understand your key audiences. What media does your board, your community, your patients, your employees, your competitors, and other key stakeholders pay attention to? This is important to make sure you take care of this media very carefully, as what they write will have a lasting impact on how people perceive how the crisis was handled. Assign key communications staff to monitor and communicate with these key audiences and closely follow what they pay attention to in the media.

These key internal audiences will need follow-up communiqués directed at them from your organization to place perspective on the crisis and what you are doing to handle it as the situation progresses. After the crisis is over, return to these key internal audiences for insight on how to improve handling a crisis.

Role of Communications in a Crisis

When an institution has communications professionals at the table during a crisis, they stand a much greater chance of surviving, thriving, and recovering from the event. Communicators *have* to be at the table, period. As a communications professional, you must insist that someone be there when decisions are made during a crisis. We have to tell it like it is (often unpopular) and help leaders engage in a reality check at all times. We have to serve the best interests of the institution. And sometimes we just have to make people do their jobs (e.g., doing interviews, explaining to other stakeholders what happened).

Many health institutions have suffered when they believed communications was secondary to effectively dealing with the crisis. Organization leaders who do not believe communications are essential in a crisis process do so at their own peril. We've seen leaders lose their positions when they haven't effectively handled a crisis, and often it was what was communicated (or not communicated) that sent them packing. You spend years to build trust; without key communications counsel to protect it, it is easy to lose that trust and is very difficult to reclaim it down the road.

When a Crisis Happens

Many communicators equate a portion of their jobs with that of emergency physicians: when trouble happens, they jump into action. There is a certain adrenaline rush when a crisis happens; you wish it wasn't happening, but you're glad that you're there to help your institution or organization extricate itself from the problem.

One of the most important, and occasionally the most difficult, thing to do is to recognize when a crisis could rear its head or even has begun. It is important for a communicator to be an integral part of any organization, have their finger on the pulse of the daily operation, and know what is happening or about to happen. Knowing how the public, your employees, regulators, or news media will react to a situation will provide the astute communicator with the ability to predict whether impending actions by their organization could instigate a crisis situation. The best way of handling a crisis, of course, is averting one in the first place.

Sound the Alarm

Embedded in every veteran communicator's mind is a memory of when the phone rang, an e-mail arrived, or someone walked into their office to give them information that they instantly recognized as the start of a crisis. A good communicator will quickly know the impact the news will have once it reaches a specific audience. In the Duke organ transplant mismatch case, when the phone rang at almost midnight following the young girl's transplant and we heard that something had gone wrong with the procedure, it was clear that we would soon be in crisis mode with this difficult issue. It is important for communicators to sound the alarm and notify senior administrators of a situation that they deem could be hazardous for their institution.

Frequently this first alarm is triggered by a junior-level public information officer who happens to be on call during off-hours and receives the initial inquiry or alert. An astute staff assistant also often receives first notice. The point is, anyone on the communications team can be the first to realize that something is amiss. Teach them all, including yourself, to be aware.

Fact Finding

Once a communicator has an indication that a problem has started, it is paramount to begin learning all that is known about the situation. In medical institutions, a phone call or visit from the PR person is often the last thing a busy doctor or administrator wants, but it is vital to speak to the people at the center of the issue to learn as much as possible. Getting information second- or third-hand can be dangerous as each telling of the story can change, personal biases can be introduced, and facts quickly become misinformation. As the situation plays out, the last thing a communicator wants is to be surprised by new information that should have been previously shared.

This is the time when you need to know everything that went on and, as best as can be determined at that point, how and why it happened. Also important is learning such things as what the regulatory ramifications are (what needs to be reported to state and national agencies), whether any laws were violated, and what the accepted standards of care may be. This is the time when a communicator becomes very knowledgeable about specific medical conditions and treatments, healthcare business practices, laws, and regulations.

It is also important to begin gathering other types of information. For example, with the transplant mismatch, we assigned one staff person to gather detailed information on lung transplants at Duke along with researching significant transplant errors at other institutions throughout the country. With this information we were able to better understand the institution's lengthy transplant history and track record in addition to learning what troubles occurred at other hospitals.

Gather the Team

Healthcare organizations often will declare an emergency situation and bring together key representatives from administration, medical and nursing staffs, risk management, legal, security, compliance and communications, to name just a few. Many institutions practice and follow an emergency response system that was developed in the military and stipulates that an "incident commander" is identified and takes control of a situation. In these cases, the incident commander will often call together a group of people needed to work a situation as soon as it is recognized as a true or potential crisis. The incident commander does not necessarily need to be the highest ranking official. The team needs to gather quickly and share information about what has happened or could happen in the immediate future.

It is sometimes difficult for people to be open and honest at these times, but it is vitally important that everyone share all information and be as candid as possible. All facts must be tossed onto the table so everyone knows and understands the situation so appropriate steps can be taken.

The chief communications person also has his or her own team to assemble. For smaller institutions this could be just the one or two other people on staff. The communications crisis team also can include people from other offices.

Frequently, lead communicators will hold back information from their communications team members thinking that the situation hasn't reached the point where others need to know. Some may even feel that the fewer people who know, the less chance the situation will become public. But consider this: It would be better to fill in your colleagues who will be working closely with you on a crisis situation while things are still relatively peaceful than later when the story is breaking and the situation has reached full crisis mode.

Research

In addition to learning everything you can about the situation at hand, you also should consider how others have handled similar situations. Very early in the transplant situation, we contacted several other institutions who previously faced similar issues. It was helpful and reassuring to hear colleagues at different medical centers recall their situations, hear details about the specifics, and learn how they handled the case and how their local media reacted. Great information was gleaned during these discussions that helped us think through the possible scenarios and how we could best address the situation. This is another reason why relationships with colleagues at other institutions are very important. You'll also find most communicators very helpful to their brethren in a jam. We've all been there before and have appreciated the help others have given us.

Plan a Strategy

As you gather the intricate background details about the situation at hand, you will already be contemplating the strategy needed to address it. Very early on you will begin working out the best response to the situation and drafting a comprehensive communications plan. The sooner you begin to put this down on paper, the better. It can change as new information is learned or with input from others. Eventually you will need to present it to the organization's senior leadership and advocate for the response you believe is warranted.

Your plan should include an overview of the situation, the issues that could present problems for your institution, the suggested response strategy, goals, tactics, key talking points, spokespeople, and ways to assess the plan. The plan can be adapted as the situation changes. It is truly a living document that must be able to adapt to an evolving situation.

Execute Your Plan

Trust your plan. Fully execute it once you have buy-in from senior leadership. It should be shared among those people immediately involved in handling the operational issues associated with the crisis situation along with your communications colleagues. But don't consider that once your plan is reviewed, approved, and set that it is set in stone. It needs to be flexible and easily altered.

Reassess and Repeat

Your plan should be considered your operating principles rather than a roadmap or recipe for success. It is difficult in crisis situations to simply refer to the next step in your plan. Situations change and require constant reassessment. Change can come hour by hour or day by day. Rarely is it possible to lay out a lengthy plan for a crisis and follow it without change.

Effective Communications Keys

Focus on How Your Institution Is Fixing the Problem

Beyond recognizing and admitting a problem at your institution, the most important thing that can be done is to identify ways that the problem is being addressed. Your key audiences will be focused on how the issue is being addressed and the steps that are being taken to ensure that a similar situation won't happen again.

Most people will be accepting of a situation when an institution publicly recognizes that it has happened and accepts responsibility for the situation. There is only a short window of time, however, for an institution to accept responsibility and begin an honest discussion of the issue.

Before long the conversation has to transition into fixing the problem. The quicker that this phase is entered, the better it will be for the organization. Details about how an institution is fixing the problem will move the discussion forward more quickly; remember time is of the essence.

Effective Spokespeople

One of the most critical decisions in any crisis is deciding who your main spokesperson will be. The nature of the crisis and the institutional culture will often be the driving forces in this decision. Major crisis situations will dictate that the senior most officer of an institution should be the face and voice of the institution. An effective leader demonstrates control and caring, concern and compassion, and can quickly lead an institution out of danger. In the transplant mishap, the CEO of Duke Hospital, the senior most administrator at the hospital, was quickly selected to serve as the institutional spokesperson. Above everyone, he was the person responsible for leading the inquiry and corrective action plan following the transplant. He was the captain that directed the course of action and clearly took responsibility for everything associated with the case.

Keep the Media at Your Front Door

Your relationship with members of the news media is very important. Every interaction you have with a reporter is judged and remembered. While there certainly are members of the media who will never appreciate assistance from public relations professionals, most will value honesty and honest efforts. They usually will understand when you can't get specific information they request, as long as they feel they've been treated fairly. However, when they begin to feel their requests are being ignored or not taken seriously, they will immediately begin to seek other sources. In a medical case, for example, reporters will quickly turn from the official spokesperson or institutional leadership and try to connect with staff nurses or other employees. Doing so could result in incorrect information getting to the reporter or details that violate federal privacy regulations.

By working closely with reporters in an honest and open fashion, you can keep them at your "front door" so they don't try to circumvent official channels and seek "back door" information. However, reporters are typically very resourceful people and won't wait by your side for every crumb of information. They'll go find information themselves. Strong, trusting relationships and honest interactions with them will go a long way in keeping the lines of communication open with them and your organization.

Get All the Bad News Out at Once

There is an innate desire among most organizational leaders to offer only a limited amount of information about negative situations. If a reporter asks a question about only one aspect of an issue, that's all that leadership often wants to discuss. "Wait until they ask about the other things before we answer," is a frequent refrain. Well, if the information is available to you as spokesman, consider getting it all out at once. Reporters will probably dig it up the next day and now you have a story with legs, one that will continue playing in the media as new details emerge.

By getting all the facts out at once, you have a better chance of trimming the length of the story. You also will earn respect by being open and honest with reporters. While your institution's leadership may not be happy about releasing all details—and your general counsel's office may also argue against the strategy for a variety of legal reasons—you need to advocate for this type of disclosure. Learn to work and bargain with counsel in these and other instances to reach good outcomes for your institution. Remember, communicators need to push to get all the bad news out there. Though this is difficult, your institution's leadership will appreciate it when the story fades away a day or two later rather than continuing to resurface when new details emerge. This is taking control of the story and something for which communicators must advocate.

Anticipate What the Reporters Will Need

A classic step in working a crisis situation is preparing for the questions that reporters will be asking you or whoever is designated as the institution's spokesperson. Throughout our transplant crisis we prepped our spokespeople for their interview by doing mock interviews and asking a series of questions that we thought media were most probably going to ask. It helped that we were both former reporters and tried to approach the issue as we thought a typical reporter would. There were times when we even played the role of a belligerent reporter just so our spokespeople would not be thrown off if they encountered such a reporter. By throwing many of these questions out to our spokespeople it gave them a chance to think about their answers, practice what they might want to say, and then craft stronger answers. While our spokespeople were well experienced in speaking with reporters, it still helped make them more comfortable when discussing a very difficult situation. Anticipating what reporters will need also includes more than just answers. Television reporters, for example, might want a location to do a stand-up interview different from the location of their sit-down interview. Having a location ready will make both your job and their assignment easier. Anticipating the need for specific facts and figures that reporters could be seeking is also wise.

Communicate Internally as Well as Externally

Employees deserve to hear news about their institution—especially bad news—from their leadership rather than seeing it first in their newspaper, reading it on a Web site, or hearing it on TV or radio news. Sometimes a wise way of breaking a bad news story is to distribute a memo from senior leadership to your employees and then distribute the memo to news media. The message remains consistent and you've proactively gotten the story out to all media at the same time. It often will help control the message and limits the story from taking off in a frenzy. Your staff will also appreciate hearing the news from their institutional leaders.

Also consider other specific internal audiences who might need certain information about the situation. For example, your development office might benefit from receiving specific talking points so they can either communicate in advance with major donors and prospects or be prepared to answer questions when those key individuals call to inquire about the situation. Your institution's board members are another key audience. Sometimes this group will be ahead of a breaking issue, but sometimes this is not the case. Consider special communications with this important group before communicating with news media or as quickly as possible when a story breaks. Board members also can be important advocates for an organization and are people news media frequently turn to with questions. A board member who learns of a negative issue through the questions of a reporter may be ill-prepared to respond and could also answer questions in ways that hurt rather than help recovering from a crisis. Likewise, legislative representatives also need to be considered. This can be especially true in cases where the institution involved is a state or federally funded organization. State and federal representatives will be very interested in learning about critical issues directly from the institution's legislative staff or senior leadership.

Crisis Observations

No Two Crises Are Alike

There are a number of things to consider whenever you find yourself in the middle of a crisis. While these may not be the most important issues to keep in mind, they are nonetheless important to consider and will often have a hearing in how you handle crisis communications.

An organ transplant mishap at another hospital could come with a completely different set of circumstances that will make that crisis entirely different from the one that occurred at Duke University Medical Center. You certainly need to investigate other similar situations whenever something happens that could turn into a crisis for your organization, but keep in mind that even slight differences in circumstances could cause you to use different strategies or handle the situation differently.

A Crisis Plan Will Not Tell You What to Do

The importance of having a crisis plan cannot be stated enough. But following a crisis plan through an actual crisis like it was a recipe for your evening meal is not enough for you to deal with a crisis.

A crisis plan will help you think through a crisis. Crises often happen so quickly and consume you to such an extent that the last thing you will have time to do is pull your notebook off the shelf and read 90 pages of an exquisitely written plan. If you even have a few moments to dust if off, you will probably only be able to glance at key sections, lists, and bullet points. You'll be ahead of the game if it helps remind you of some key things to consider or provide a list of people to think about communicating with.

This is another reason why it is important in quiet times to review your crisis plan so it remains fresh in the back of your mind when you're confronted with a crisis situation.

No Crisis Plan Can Prepare You for Every Situation

Another fallacy of a well-written crisis plan is that it will prepare you for any crisis situation. It simply will not. No one can plan for every situation. Yes, you can estimate with some certainty what the most likely scenarios will be, but unless you have a crystal ball that actually works you will not be able to foresee every situation and the myriad different circumstances that could unfold.

In our situation at Duke, there was no way that we could have anticipated that a family representative would ask to speak before 80 reporters and a dozen and a half television cameras—some of which were transmitting the news conference live. We also could not have predicted that the patient's family would post images of our nurses with Jesica in her critical care bed following surgery on their Web site. These were issues that could not have been included in any crisis plan.

If Something Bad Happens, the Media Will Find Out About It

One of the hardest decisions that ever face a public relations practitioner is whether to be proactive and release information about an incident before news media learn about it. When the possibility is posed to senior leadership, the usual reaction is: "Let's not, it'll probably fly under the radar." It is indeed rare that any serious situation "flies under the radar" and escapes detection by the news media, although it can happen. The more serious a situation, the more likely that it will become known to those outside your institution. The larger your institution—and therefore the more people who may hear internally about an issue—the more likely it will become known to those outside your institution. It is wiser to operate under the premise that the news media will pick up the issue than to think they will not, so be prepared to respond and prepare your leadership that the information will get out.

If you don't proactively release details of the incident at hand, you should at the very least, have everything ready as if you were announcing it. Then, when the first media inquiry comes about the incident, you will be ready to move on the issue with a moment's notice.

As discussed previously, no two crises are alike. As true as that is, you can benefit from the experience of another communicator who faced a similar situation. The circumstances of their situation may be slightly or significantly different, but surely there will be some lessons learned that you can consider.

This also lends itself to the issue of networking. It is a lot easier contacting someone who you've met or spoken with previously to ask them for information or counsel about a prior issue that they dealt with than it is calling someone who does not know you. This shows the importance of being involved in public relations and communications organizations—both locally and nationally and especially those related to the healthcare industry—in which you establish relationships with colleagues. You never know when you will need them or they will need you.

Throughout our careers, we have always been overwhelmed by the generosity of colleagues at institutions throughout the country. Even when we had never met, communicators have always been willing to provide us information about situations they have been involved with and offer counsel and support during our crisis. This has always been one of the genuine benefits of working in this industry.

It's OK to Say "I Don't Know"

Whenever a reporter asks you a question, especially during a tumultuous situation, you expect to have an answer. Your desire is to have already thought of the question beforehand and rehearsed the perfect answer. However, that does not always happen. You're bound to get hit with a question for which you have no answer. At this point, remember that it is alright to say those three difficult words: "I don't know."

One of the prime ways a spokesperson can get in trouble during a media interview is to try to answer a question when they do not have the needed information. Speculation, especially in time of crisis, is never a good thing. Reporters will understand if you do not have the information at hand and will appreciate it even more when you get the information to them later. This will not only save you from speculating about something, but it will also prevent you from providing incorrect information that you will only have to correct later. This becomes even worse if the information is transmitted immediately to the public via broadcast or Web stories. Reporters will be frustrated and ticked off and you will be embarrassed. No one wins.

Transparency Is Essential

"Being transparent" has become an overused cliché. However, for the communicator in the midst of a crisis, there is value in understanding the need for transparency. In crisis periods, everything an institution and its spokesperson does and says will be closely scrutinized. Your troubles will be multiplied if a reporter discovers that you have been deceptive in any way.

In the Duke transplant mismatch, the institution openly talked about its reporting of the mistake to regulatory agencies and its process of reviewing the event to learn why it happened. When the factors involved in causing the incident became known, hospital leaders widely discussed the details in the hope that other hospitals would learn from the situation and similar incidents could be avoided. This openness (transparency) greatly assisted Duke in recovering from the mishap.

There is clearly a difference in being transparent during a crisis situation and simply providing every shred of information the news media requests. There are ways of helping news media—and internal and other audiences—understand the process of an incident review, for example, while withholding preliminary findings until it is appropriate to release them.

The more an institution can be transparent with news media, the better it can communicate its key messages and the quicker it can work through crisis situations.

Truth Is Mandatory

It seems foolish to say that the truth is mandatory. Just as there is no crying in baseball, there's no lying in communications. The truth is always the only way. Not only is the truth a basic tenet of our industry, providing false information will come back to haunt you in ways a hundred times worse than if you had just told the truth in the first place. The news media will certainly learn that they have been lied to and your reputation, something more important than any ability you can bring to the table, will be ruined, reducing you to an ineffective communicator.

No public relations practitioner should ever be asked or directed by an institution's leadership to purposefully lie or deviate from the truth. Your crisis will quickly evolve into something different if you are faced with the directive to lie about something or issue false information. Lying will certainly make a bad situation worse and is never an option.

Always Expect the Unexpected

While there is no way to anticipate everything that could come your way during a crisis, it is always safe to expect the unexpected. Something always seems to happen that you had no idea would occur. This could be labeled as one of the hallmarks of a crisis. Talk to any communicator who has faced a crisis and you will surely hear "we never expected" in their description of the case.

How can you prepare for the unexpected? Well, there really is no way other than to be nimble and ready to think quickly on your feet. Be able to adapt to a changing situation. Have a strong staff and a supportive leadership. Turn to your network of colleagues. Don't be afraid to say "I don't know" and then find the answer. And, above all else, whenever you say anything, make certain it is truthful. These are among the essentials to successful communications whether or not it is during a time of crisis.

Case Study: Dissecting the Duke Hospital Organ Transplant Mismatch

In February 2003, Dr. James Jaggers, respected chief of pediatric cardiac surgery at Duke University Hospital, transplanted a heart and lungs into 17-year-old Jesica Santillan in a rare and difficult procedure. He had performed over 100 heart transplants. Toward the end of the procedure, he was notified by an immunology lab technician that the girl's type O blood did not match the type A donor organs.

How could this have happened?

Jesica was well cared for and kept alive until a second transplant was performed 2 weeks later. Unfortunately, she died 2 days after the second transplant. This case study will provide an overview of what happened and lessons in how to respond to the media crisis when a medical error occurs.

Jesica Santillan was born in Mexico. As a young girl, she was taken to a doctor who told the family she'd need a heart transplant (she was later diagnosed with restrictive cardiomyopathy, which makes the heart muscle enlarged and stiff and requires a heart and lung transplant). The Mexican doctors thought this could best be done in the United States. The family had heard about Duke Hospital in Durham, North Carolina. Duke had a long history of successful solid organ transplants; in addition, this was also near where the family had relatives.

Jesica and her family illegally crossed into the United States in 1999 and made their way to North Carolina. By January 2002, Jesica's name was added to the national waiting list for a donor heart. Five months later, she was added to the heart-lung waiting list in need of a procedure that is performed on no more than seven children each year.

Prior to entering the Duke system, a local building contractor had read a newspaper account about Jesica's plight and noted the family was living in an old trailer without air conditioning. The contractor, who also spoke Spanish, befriended the family and established a charity called Jesica's Hope Chest to mobilize local contractors and builders to construct houses that would be sold with the proceeds benefitting Jesica and her family. He also gained limited power of attorney over the child and assumed the role of family advocate.

The First Operation

On February 6, 2003, an adolescent heart-lung became available at Children's Hospital in Boston, and the New England Organ bank was alerted. Two patients in North Carolina, an adult and a child, appeared to be a match. The Carolina Donor Services was called and then in turn called Duke. The call eventually got to Dr. Jaggers, chief of pediatric cardiac surgery (a child was first on the list at Duke). That patient was too sick for a transplant. Jaggers asked if Jesica could have the organs.

Jaggers did not have his list of waiting patients with him when the call from Carolina Donor Services came. He also didn't recall discussing blood type. A Duke coordinator called the New England Organ Bank and asked them to verify that Jesica could be a suitable recipient. However, donor organ banks only have access to hospital wait lists; they couldn't—at that time—match run lists and thus had no way to determine Jesica's blood type.

The organs were sent to Duke anyway on February 7. Jesica was prepped and the transplant started around 5 p.m. About 10 p.m., near the end of the surgery, a technician in the Duke immunology laboratory was conducting a routine ABO blood check on the patient and suddenly realized that Jesica was type O and the donor was type A, an obvious mismatch.

He called the operating room and alerted Jaggers, who at that time was starting to close. Dr. Jaggers would later recall when he heard of the mismatch from the lab, his reaction was "almost like a death and dying reaction. It's that deep, sort of sinking feeling, you know, that there's absolutely nothing you can do about it."

The surgical team began plasmapheresis treatment to try to prevent rejection. Immediately after the surgery, Jaggers went to the family and told them what happened. He took responsibility for the error and told them he and the hospital were going to do what was needed to keep her alive and would make every effort to locate another set of organs. Instead of being removed from the waiting list, Jesica remained at the top of the list because of her dire medical condition.

Pediatric heart-lung donations are uncommon, and there is a lengthy list of waiting recipients. This case raised numerous issues, including: how could a problem like this happen at an elite hospital; whether foreign nationals should receive transplants ahead of American citizens; who should pay for such transplants in foreign nationals; whether patients should receive a second transplant; and potential problems with the US transplant system (see questions for discussion at the end of the chapter).

Duke communications' first involvement with Jesica's transplant came the morning of February 7, prior to the transplant. We were contacted by a medical staff member who overheard the family advocate contact local media to alert them to the impending transplant. Prior coverage existed on the girl's need for a transplant. We immediately contacted the advocate and offered assistance with working with the media. It was also communicated to the family advocate that news reporters and cameras were not permitted in the hospital without escort from our office to ensure patient privacy and confidentiality. We also verified the family advocate had been able to speak on behalf of the family.

The day after the transplant, with our lead communicators having learned about the mismatch, we had another conversation with the family advocate. He wanted additional assistance in responding to media inquiries concerning Jesica. After a discussion, it was agreed only to release a condition for Jesica and not to mention any mismatch with the transplant. This was the advocate's decision.

On Wednesday, February 12, in interviews arranged by our office, Jesica's family told reporters that she was rejecting the organs and needed another transplant, but at no time did the family mention the mismatch. The Duke Medical Center news office continued to provide a condition and stated that Jesica was being treated for organ rejection, in accordance with the family's wishes.

Start of the Crisis

This highly unusual and tragic medical error began a tumultuous period for Duke and its communicators. On February 14, the mismatch was made public. The family advocate (unbeknownst to Duke officials or communicators) contacted the local CBS television affiliate and told a reporter that Dr. Jaggers had informed the family following the transplant that there was a mismatch. The story broke at 11 p.m. that evening. Our office had been following developments closely that week and, once the story aired, we anticipated being deluged with calls. But there were only inquiries from just two local media outlets, most likely due to the story breaking during the weekend and in the midst of an ice storm that hit the area.

On Monday, February 17, a decision was made by Duke Health system and hospital administration to confirm the mismatch. The news office issued a news release stating there was a mismatch and detailed numerous changes in transplant protocols that had already been made to ensure there would not be a repeat of the mismatch. National media picked up this story and the media deluge began.

A media firestorm erupted with a national and international spotlight suddenly turned on Duke. After working closely with the family and their advocate for 10 days and following requests to safeguard their privacy, Duke was suddenly confronted by an angry family advocate who had permission to sit in on medical conferences. The advocate began freely disclosing medical information to the media, frequently within minutes of it being presented to the family, and a public adversarial relationship ensued. Hundreds of daily inquiries from US and international media poured into the Duke news office with dozens of satellite trucks parked around the clock in front of the hospital.

Prior to the initial interviews the family conducted, we had obtained written permission to release detailed medical information about Jesica, which allowed us to speak publicly about her care. (This event occurred 9 weeks before the Health Insurance Portability and Accountability Act [HIPAA] privacy rules took effect.) Duke Hospital's CEO, Dr. William Fulkerson, was selected to be our primary spokesperson. On Tuesday, February 18, he conducted many one-on-one interviews, including with CNN, CBS, NBC, ABC, and NPR. We decided to conduct as many one-on-ones as possible and to avoid group interviews. The downside to this was that it was impossible to accommodate every reporter. Fulkerson did a stoic and marvelous job of trying to conduct as many interviews as possible and spoke candidly and openly about the situation. Our news office fielded and answered many other requests from reporters both on the scene and nationwide. Interest in this story was also especially high in Latin and South America.

The Duke news office continued to release daily updates on Jesica's condition using our news Web site. In addition to being a source for the media, many Duke employees followed developments there, too. Traffic on the site increased at such a rate that our automated system detecting the number of unique visitors stopped counting soon after the crisis started.

Throughout these interviews, we had two main messages: 1. Duke took full responsibility for the mismatch, and 2. we pledged to learn from the mistake to help prevent other similar incidents from happening.

Other key messages included:

- Our thoughts are with the family.
- We are investigating the cause.
- Staff is working diligently to keep Jesica alive and comfortable.
- Staff is assisting family.
- Jesica remained on the United Network for Organ Sharing (UNOS) waiting list for another set of organs.
- Duke has a long and successful transplant history.

A New Development: The Second Transplant

On February 20, 13 days after the first transplant, another set of organs became available for Jesica through the regular donor process. This time the organs were triple-checked to make certain they were the right blood type. This required a series of checks and balances that had been added to the hospital's system following the mismatch.

That day Duke decided to hold a news conference to announce the second transplant and provide an update on Jesica's condition. The speakers were Dr. Fulkerson and Dr. Duane Davis, director of heart and lung surgery at Duke who assisted in the second transplant (the family wanted—despite everything going on—to have Dr. Jaggers perform the second transplant, too).

We decided early in the crisis to have Dr. Jaggers focus his attention to care for Jesica and not to be part of Duke's media relations initiative.

The room was filled with 20 television cameras and more than 60 news reporters. Later in the day we announced to the media we had self-reported the incident to the North Carolina Division of Facility Services, the state agency that investigates medical mistakes and regulates healthcare facilities. We also held a second news conference on Friday, February 21, to provide an update on Jesica's condition after the second transplant. At this time, her condition began to deteriorate.

Complicating both news conferences were appearances by the family advocate. Both times he learned about the event from the media and, at the conclusion of each event, requested and received an opportunity to speak with the media.

Unfortunately, at 1:35 p.m. on Saturday, February 22, Jesica was pronounced dead. She remained on mechanical ventilation until 5 p.m. to provide her family with an opportunity to say good-bye. At that time, their priest said that the family felt it was time to remove the equipment. The medications were ceased, her heart stopped at 5:07 p.m., and she was completely disconnected from all mechanical assistance.

A news release announcing her death was distributed at 5:15 p.m. (we had decided to wait until she was disconnected from all life support before releasing news of her death). At 3 p.m. that afternoon, however, the family held a news conference to say that Jesica was dead.

The day Jesica died, we issued another news release outlining the case. The goal was to demonstrate to the media we were sharing all the details we could about the case, that we were not hiding any facts, and we were working to prevent a similar situation from ever happening again.

From the first operation on February 7, Jaggers had focused his attention on Jesica and her family and had not been available for media interviews. Once Jesica died, the Duke news office discussed the multitude of requests from the media to speak with him. It was determined the most efficient and practical strategy was to release a video message from Jaggers. We knew video could have substantial impact for Duke at this juncture of the crisis.

Jaggers taped a brief message at the University's TV studio. While we counseled him, the heartfelt message was in his own words (see complete statement on the microsite). The evening of Jesica's death, a copy of the tape was hand delivered to the dozen television news trucks still at Duke. A copy of the statement also was made available to stations throughout the country via two satellite feeds. The video and text statement also was placed on our Web site and provided to print media as well.

In his message, Jaggers stated that his heart was with the family, how sorry he was, and that he shared their grief. He explained the tremendous effort the Duke staff made to try to keep her alive and find another set of organs. He very briefly explained the donor process and emphasized its complexity, but he was very clear that human errors were made. As the lead surgeon he accepted full responsibility for what happened. He closed by saying that hopefully we'll be able to learn from this situation and make the transplant system better and avoid a similar situation in the future.

Media Coverage and Tone

The Duke news office had a very extensive media tracking system that was useful to determine the type and tone of news coverage Duke received in order to begin to recover as an institution. Prior to the transplant mismatch, there had been between 600 and 800 news stories about Duke Medical Center each month with 98 percent of the media mentions deemed positive about Duke. However, in February 2003, there were almost 6000 news stories about Duke, with 5300 about the Jesica case. Of all the news stories, 79.2% were negative (see chart on microsite). Our job was to turn that number back to positive territory again.

Hospital Response to Regulators and Duke's Road to Recovery

During all of the media hoopla, another important desire for the communicators was to assist the institution with communicating the hospital's response as the regulators began to come into the facility and investigate.

Our hospital response was as follows:

- Immediate changes in transplant protocols
- Root-cause analysis (to find out what went wrong)
- Cooperation with external reviews and create and execute corrective action plans: North Carolina Division of Facility Services, Centers for Medicare and Medicaid Services, United Network for Organ Sharing, and The Joint Commission
- How to improve our crisis response

We worked with leadership to produce news releases and answer the media in interviews on all regulatory agency visits and reviews, as well as UNOS-revised transplant protocols. We also kept employees informed. The Duke news office helped Duke Health System leadership with meetings with local newspaper editorial boards to mend fences after the crisis, and to reestablish sound relationships with local media.

Following Jesica's death, the news office communications team played a pivotal role in Duke's arduous task of restoring patient confidence and maintaining staff morale as the institution restored full regulatory accreditation. By offering full disclosure of the investigation surrounding the mismatch, accepting full responsibility for the error, and facing the hard questions, we helped the institution restore confidence in the Duke University Hospital and Health

System as a safe place for patients and repaired its reputation in the local community, the nation, and among the medical community. Furthermore, Duke's actions resulted in significant improvements in the nation's organ donor and transplant systems.

National Reputation Recovery: 60 Minutes, Forbes, US News and World Report

Three major news placements particularly helped Duke recover and ultimately repair its reputation with a number of constituencies. The first was when a producer at CBS-TV's *60 Minutes* called our health system CEO to say they had seen all the coverage of the organ transplant mismatch and wanted to tell the story in a more balanced and rationale way than had been communicated during the heat of the ordeal. They said they'd be fair to us and tell a balanced story, but they wouldn't shy away from the problems that occurred during the mismatch.

After some intense discussions and helpful advice from a number of individuals, it was decided to work with *60 Minutes* to ultimately produce a 13-minute segment on March 16, 2003, titled "Anatomy of a Mistake" (see microsite for transcript of the broadcast). We spent a great deal of time opening up our institution to them, meeting their production needs, and providing access to key individuals in the story for interviews, including the transplant surgeons and the CEOs of the organization.

What followed was a great communications result from a calculated risk. Millions of people saw what happened when a "hospital admitted what few hospitals ever admit; it had made a mistake, a tragic mistake." Millions of people saw our organization become transparent, honest, and open as we talked about the mistake—including what needed to be done to fix this kind of problem. Callers to Duke thanked us for being forthcoming and praised the organization's bravery to do this type of interview.

Then *Forbes Magazine* called. They said they found the broadcast fascinating and asked if we had done something brilliant or crazy. We cooperated with them, too, and provided information and access to key players in this story. "Duking it Out" appeared on June 9, 2003 (see microsite for the article), noting that "a transplant tragedy garnered worldwide coverage and threatened the reputation of a renowned hospital. What to do?"

The article detailed how we handled the event and said the result of the admissions was reminiscent of one of the most celebrated PR victories some 20 years ago: Johnson &Johnson's handling of the random poisoning of a few capsules of Tylenol, which killed seven people in Chicago.

"J & J waged the recall of 31 million bottles, debuted new tamper-resistant packaging, and fielded a blitz of press coverage. J & J's chief at the time, James E. Burke, even appeared on *60 Minutes* to discuss the case, in December 1982," the article recounted.

A crisis communicator also noted in the article that Duke's response was "the perfect example of why you're always better off telling the story instead of ducking and hiding."

While working on the *Forbes* story, *U.S. News and World Report* called and said they were interesting in putting together a thorough report not only on our story but how the entire national organ-transplant system might have played a major role here, too.

Again, we worked with veteran reporter from *U.S. News*, Avery Comarow, to help tell the story of what happened and what could be done to fix mismatches like this from happening again in the world of medicine. "Jesica's Story: One Mistake Didn't Kill Her—the Organ Donor System was Fatally Flawed" was an 11-page special report in the Best Hospitals issue of the magazine that appeared on August 4, 2003.

This story was exhaustive (see microsite for article) and provided all the details of the story from Duke and many other experts. It also included timelines, multiple photos, and interviews with several key Duke health professionals. We even provided the listed charges for Jesica's care (approximately $900,000) and noted Duke took care of the costs. We got the whole story out there, showed compassion and caring, and noted we wanted to learn from all of this for our sake and others as well.

At the end of the article, a cutline under a picture of Duke Hospital said: "Postmortem: Despite the Jesica Santillan tragedy, Duke remains one of the nation's most highly regarded hospitals."

The communications professionals at Duke's Medical Center news office had done their jobs to help resolve a crisis and restore the reputation of the institution. We were tired but proud of what we had done. At the end of this ordeal, we even got permission to provide a modest bit of one-time compensation to the key communications staff involved to reward them for their work. It was well earned.

Lessons Learned

There were numerous lessons learned for almost every Duke employee during the transplant mishap. For the communications office, the valuable lessons included:

- *Eliminate internal bottlenecks.* Early in the crisis, the communications office relied on several people outside the department to gather information. In some instances, the details were slow to come in or were incomplete causing our efforts to slow. We quickly realized we needed to remove this bottleneck and allow our staff direct access to the information we required. Once we achieved this we were able to move at the speed necessary to address our issues.
- *Be able to work with your legal counsel.* This is important and is not always easy; however, it is essential to strike a good working relationship to deal with the crisis. Legal strategy often does not synch with communications needs, but usually the two professions can find an adequate middle ground to support your institution.

- *Need for a Spanish-speaking spokesperson.* One of our biggest problems was failing to have an available spokesperson fluent in Spanish. With Jesica being a native of Mexico, there was significant interest in the story from Latin and South American news media. We would have been able to better communicate our key messages to these news outlets had we had a person on staff or available to us who was fluent in Spanish.
- *Rotating on-call staff.* Two days after the transplants story was picked up, the on-call person on our staff came into work and was completely sluggish from having only several hours of sleep during the last two nights. He said he had been receiving pages and phone calls about the situation almost around the clock. It was then that we realized that our normal routine of having one person on call for a week at a time was not going to work during this situation. At that moment we changed to having one person on call for only a 24-hour period. This allowed each person to share in the workload of handling after-hours calls and no one would have to handle this chore for more than one day at a time. This kept everyone in the office fresh and relieved those scheduled for a weeklong on-call stint of an impossible burden.
- *Recognize issues with your staff's morale.* The weeks during which we dealt with the transplants crisis were very stressful for our staff. The mere responsibility of communicating with internal and external audiences was a monumental task. But hearing numerous news reports critical about the institution took a heavy toll on our staff's morale. We tried to keep our colleagues as upbeat as possible throughout the crisis. We also brought in representatives from Duke's Employee Assistance Program to speak with each staff member whether or not they showed any signs of stress. Each person seemed to appreciate someone to speak with and decompress during and after the situation.
- *Keep your staff well-fed.* With all the work required of our staff in handling the crisis communications, no one had sufficient time to run out for lunch or dinner (most of our staff were in the office well before and after our normal work hours). Very early on, our administrative assistant was assigned the task of arranging for lunch and dinners to be delivered to our offices. While the food was standard fare—pizza, Chinese, sandwiches—it was a welcome relief to simply run down the hall to grab some food and not worry about taking the time to leave the office when much had to be done. It was one less thing communicators had to worry about and allowed everyone to concentrate more on the problems at hand. It also brought the staff together in impromptu meetings where we could update everyone on the situation and share ideas for a few minutes while we ate.
- *Enjoy the small victories.* There were many difficult moments for the Duke Medical Center news office during the transplant crisis. During one of these, our day brightened when we received several e-mails from former patients offering kind words about the extraordinary care they had received at the Duke Medical Center. Several supportive messages also came from colleagues from other medical centers across the country. We began printing out the messages and taping them to the wall in our hallway. Within a week or so, a wall about 20-foot long was covered floor to ceiling with encouraging messages. Each of our staff members and many other Duke employees were buoyed by the many messages that helped us get through a rough time.

Working with an Agency During a Crisis

When a crisis begins to brew, communicators and leaders often wonder when help from the outside—like a public relations agency—might be beneficial to either help curtail the issue or keep the problem from completely overwhelming the organization.

It is always a tough call; many organizations think they can handle the impending crisis. Others think the cost is too much to bear and rationalize that the problem will blow over soon, and any extra public relations help will not be worth it.

Nevertheless, organizations with a crisis have very little time to think about when to pull in a PR agency, and sometimes they do not know to whom to turn because they don't have a formal relationship with an agency. This can be an institutional risk if your health organization is not prepared to take on additional help to deal with a crisis.

It is a wise idea to have a relationship with an agency in case you need them. You must know them, rely on them, and trust them in an emergency. It is worth the money in the long run to your organization. Duke spent thousands in agency fees to help deal with this crisis. Without that extra help, the Medical Center and University would have spent much more in money (and time) in trying to fix the problems we had to deal with.

In our Duke organ transplant mismatch crisis, we had the good fortune of having sound and courageous counsel in the likes of Kent Jenkins, a savvy former *Washington Post* reporter and crisis PR counselor from Burson-Marstellar in Washington, D.C. Kent provided us with excellent writing skills, sound advice, moral support, and assistance with senior leadership to gather their confidence and to convince them to let us do our jobs to help alleviate the crisis.

Our PR agency quickly became part of the Duke team, and this assistance helped bolster our confidence and created a solid ensemble between the two groups. During this ordeal, we became colleagues and friends. We were in this together.

Senior management saw this, and noted we offered the same counsel and advice, in addition to similar recommendations on how to ameliorate this crisis. That provided our leadership with the advice and confidence they needed in a PR crisis operation. We were able to back each other up and not second-guess each other, too.

Changing Media Landscape

Throughout the crisis at Duke with the organ transplant mismatch, new media was not a significant concern for the Duke news office. The situation occurred just as the social and new media environments were beginning to become formidable forces in communications. At the time there was no Twitter. Blogs, as we currently know them, were less than a year old and still a year removed from becoming the established force they are today. Social networking sites such as MySpace and Facebook would not be launched until later in 2003 and in early 2004, respectively.

In today's media landscape, reporters increasingly reply on social networking sites and blogs for news and information. More and more often, events that become crises for institutions begin with a blog post, tweet, or Facebook mention.

But just as the communications teams did not have to worry about the instant worldwide distribution of behind-the-scenes commentary from the transplant mismatch, the Duke staff also could not take advantage of using new media to help in spreading its message. The Duke news Web site was the only direct-to-the-public vehicle available at the time to provide messaging unfiltered by news reporters. (A steady stream of information about the transplant was posted on the Duke University Medical Center news Web site as soon as the event went public and was a significant tool used to communicate Duke's key messages.)

Had the transplant mismatch happened today, Duke communicators would most probably be forced to deal differently with the crisis. The situation very likely would have become public well before the family's disclosure of the situation a week after the transplant occurred on the local CBS television affiliate. Anyone close to the family or even a staff member at Duke Hospital could have anonymously posted details of the mismatch on any number of social networking or news sites. Numerous blogs probably would have sprung up during the first day or two of the crisis. Facebook pages dedicated to Jesica's plight or critical to various issues associated with this case—such as organ transplantation allocation, illegal immigration, uncompensated medical care, just to name a few—would most likely have been created and spread among the millions of site visitors. The images of Jesica in her intensive care bed that suddenly appeared on the Jesica's Hope Chest Web site would probably have been supplemented by YouTube videos.

Several of the images of Jesica that appeared on the Jesica's Hope Chest Web site spread quickly to traditional news media before they were removed. Duke staff pictured in some of the images did not know they were being photographed and became upset that they were visible in photos posted on the Internet. The images also were taken without hospital permission and in violation of hospital policy prohibiting photography in a critical care unit.

Had today's social media been in existence in 2003, it undoubtedly would have influenced news media coverage and community—local, regional, national, and international—perception of the crisis as it unfolded. Many more people would have had access to information about the crisis as it played out, and details would have reached people much faster than going through traditional news media. In addition to dealing with hundreds of news media, Duke communicators would have had to focus similar attention to monitoring and responding to citizen journalists from around the globe.

The new media landscape, however, would have provided the Duke news office staff with other vehicles for reaching millions of people with its story of what happened. For example, instead of only transmitting video of Jesica's transplant surgeon Dr. James Jaggers following Jessica's death via satellite to television news stations throughout the United States, YouTube and other video sharing sites could have rapidly made his heartfelt words of apology available to hundreds of thousands of people.

Box 7-1 Timeline of a Crisis

Friday, Feb. 7	Medical Center news office (MCNO) is notified that "Yesica Santillian," a 17-year-old patient in the pediatric intensive care unit, was going to receive a heart and lung transplant and that a friend of the patient's family, who allegedly has power of attorney for the patient, was going to invite the two media outlets to the hospital to watch the transplant. A public information officer (PIO) investigates and explains Duke's media policies to the patient's friend. The transplant surgeon decides against having media in the operating room.
Friday, Feb. 7	First media inquiries concerning the impending transplant are received.
Saturday, Feb. 8	The MCNO on-call PIO is informed that the organs were "incompatible," and the family was notified of the situation by the transplant surgeon.
Saturday, Feb. 8	A PIO speaks with the family friend, who asks the MCNO to handle all media inquiries on the situation.
Monday, Feb. 10	Reporters from the Franklin Times, WRAL-TV, and the *News & Observer* contact the MCNO for condition updates.
Wednesday, Feb. 12	A WRAL-TV reporter reaches the PIO handling the situation saying that he understands that Jesica has rejected her transplanted organs. The MCNO arranges an interview with Jesica's family and the family friend. The MCNO releases the following statement: "Jesica Santillan, 17, remains in critical condition today at Duke University Hospital. Our medical and nursing staffs are doing everything possible to keep her comfortable following the rejection of her transplanted heart and lungs. At this point, our priority is to help Jesica and her family through this difficult time. She continues to be listed on the national waiting list for new organs.

Box 7-1 Timeline of a Crisis *(continued)*

	In fact, she is at the highest priority to receive a new heart and lungs from organ donation organizations nationwide. We hope that a suitable donor can be found. Duke Hospital is continuing a careful review of the sequence of care for Jesica."
Friday, Feb. 14	A scheduled meeting at Duke Hospital involving hospital administrators and the family friend is canceled when the family friend arrives with an attorney and a TV news crew. The purpose of the meeting is to deliver a letter to the family friend alleging misrepresentation of power of attorney, violations of hospital policy about taking photographs of Jesica in her ICU bed, soliciting other families for contributions to his charitable organization, and intimidating behavior.
	A WRAL-TV 11 p.m. evening news segment reports that "family says hospital put in organs that didn't match." The report quotes "a family friend" as saying that "(the doctor) said he made a mistake and that he was sorry." The story details that the organs were blood type A negative and that Jesica is blood type O positive. "Duke hospital released a statement saying Jesica is once again on the national waiting list for new organs. The hospital says it continues to keep a careful eye on her and also is carefully examining all aspects of her care up to this point. They hope to find a suitable donor soon."
Saturday, Feb. 15	Local television reports on the family friend's accusations that organs with the wrong blood type were transplanted into Jesica.
Sunday, Feb. 16	*News & Observer* article headlined "Mistake Alleged in Blood Match."
	Representatives from Carolina Donor Services, New England Organ Bank, and the United Network for Organ Sharing alert the MCNO PIO that their organizations had received calls from a *News & Observer* reporter.

(continues)

Box 7-1 Timeline of a Crisis *(continued)*

Monday, Feb. 17	*News & Observer* article headlined "Donor Site: Organs Labeled."
	Meeting is held at Duke involving senior administration, caregivers, and the MCNO among others to discuss the situation. Decision is made to issue a news release concerning the situation. News release titled "Duke University Hospital Implements Additional Transplantation Safeguards" and backgrounder titled "Organ Transplant Programs at Duke" is distributed statewide by the MCNO at 5:26 p.m.
	Inquiries continue to come in from local media including the Associated Press. A reporter from CNN in New York calls late in the day to say that CNN is thinking about covering the situation.
	A PR agency representative arrives at Duke.
Tuesday, Feb. 18	The family friend appears on *Good Morning America*.
	Inquiries come from CNN, NBC *Nightly News*, ABC *World News Tonight*, CBS *The Early Show*, CBS *Evening News*, CNN *Connie Chung Show*, Telemundo, CBS *NewsPath*, NPR, *New York Times*, CBS Radio, CNN Radio, AP Radio, Associated Press, *Good Morning America*, *Boston Globe*, and NHK Japan, in addition to numerous local and regional media outlets.
	Dr. William Fulkerson, head of Duke Hospital, is identified as primary spokesperson. At 1 p.m., a media training session is held to prepare Dr. Fulkerson for his interviews. An MCNO PIO will handle all other interview requests. Beginning at 2:30 p.m., Dr. Fulkerson conducts an on-site interview with NBC *Nightly News* and satellite interviews with ABC *World News Tonight*, CNN's *Connie Chung Show*, and an ISDN interview with National Public Radio.
	Calls begin to come in from people asking how they can donate organs for Jesica.

Box 7-1 Timeline of a Crisis *(continued)*

	Throughout the day, more than 100 media outlets request information and/or interviews regarding Jesica. Many of the reporters call multiple times through the day with additional questions and seeking updated information.
Wednesday, Feb. 19	Interview requests continue to come in from across the country and internationally (Mexico and Columbia). Most requests are handled by the MCNO with a limited number handled by Dr. Fulkerson.
	News release titled "Review of Blood Type Mismatch for Jesica Santillan Continues" distributed by MCNO nationwide at 8:47 p.m.
	MCNO is notified shortly before midnight that another set of organs might have been found for Jesica.
Thursday, Feb. 20	News release titled "Organs Located for Jesica Santillan" issued nationwide by MCNO at 7:28 a.m.
	News release titled "Jesica Santillan Out of Surgery; Update Briefing at 1:30 p.m." issued by MCNO statewide at 10:30 a.m.
	News release titled "Jesica Santillan Receives New Heart-Lung Transplant" issued by MCNO nationwide at 1:30 p.m.
	Briefing Update held at 1:30 p.m. with Dr. Fulkerson and Dr. Duane Davis, chief of transplant surgery. Twenty television cameras and representatives from more than 40 media outlets are present. Briefing is broadcast live on CNN and on local ABC, CBS, NBC, and Time Warner Cable news affiliates. At the end of the briefing, the family representative requests and is granted permission to make comments to the media. He offers comments and responds to media questions for more than one hour.
	News release titled "Jessica Santillan Condition Update" issued by MCNO and distributed nationwide at 4:46 p.m.

(continues)

Box 7-1 Timeline of a Crisis *(continued)*

	News release titled "Duke Hospital Self-Reports DFS Visit" issued by MCNO and distributed statewide at 6:41 p.m.
	Hundreds of phone calls from media requesting information and interviews concerning Jesica again come in to the MCNO throughout the day. Inquiries, which began at 4 a.m., continue through 2 a.m.
Friday, Feb. 21	Update titled "Jesica Santillan Condition Update" issued nationwide by MCNO at 7:38 a.m.
	Advisory titled "Jesica Santillan Briefing Update at 1 p.m." issued nationwide by MCNO at 11:45 a.m.
	Update titled "1 p.m. Status Report Update on Jesica Santillan" issued by MCNO nationwide at 12:58 p.m.
	Briefing Update involving Dr. Fulkerson and Dr. Karen Frush, chief medical director for children's services, is held at 1 p.m. Briefing is attended by representatives from nearly 40 media outlets. The family friend again addresses media for 45 minutes at the end of the formal briefing.
	News release titled "Duke Releases Letter to UNOS Concerning Jesica Santillan" issued nationwide by MCNO at 6:20 p.m.
	During the evening two men who are believed to be from a primetime television program are asked to leave the PICU by Duke officials and security.
	Hundreds of phone calls requesting information and interviews again come in to the MCNO throughout the day. Inquiries, which began coming in at 4 a.m., continue through 2 a.m.
Saturday, Feb. 22	Jesica is pronounced dead at 1:25 p.m. At approximately 3 p.m., the Santillan family attorney holds a news conference at a hotel across the street from Duke Hospital announcing that Jesica had died.

Box 7-1 Timeline of a Crisis *(continued)*

	News release titled "Jesica Santillan Dies at Duke Hospital" is distributed nationwide by the MCNO at 5:15 p.m.
	News release titled "Statement From Dr. James Jaggers Concerning Jesica Santillan" issued nationwide by MCNO at 7:13 p.m. Video tape of statement simultaneously hand delivered to media remote trucks on the Duke campus. Satellite feeds of the statement provided at 8 p.m. and 8:30 p.m.
	News release titled "Chronology of Events Regarding Jesica Santillan" issued nationwide by MCNO at 8:06 p.m.
	Hundreds of phone calls are received by the MCNO throughout the day seeking updates, additional information, and interviews.
Sunday, Feb. 23	News release titled "Statement From Karen Frush, M.D., Concerning Care of Jesica Santillan" issued by MCNO and distributed nationwide at 10:05 p.m.
Tuesday, Feb. 25	Conference call is held at 3 p.m. involving Dr. William Fulkerson, Dr. Karen Frush, Dr. Ira Cheifetz, and Dr. Eva Grayck. Participating are reporters from the Associated Press and local news media.
Wednesday, Feb. 26	Statement from Ralph Snyderman, M.D., chancellor for health affairs, posted to the dukemednews.org Web site at 10:02 a.m.
	Release titled "Letter From Pediatric Intensive Care Unit Caregivers at Duke University Hospital" distributed nationwide at 2 p.m.
	Producers from *60 Minutes* on site to discuss the possibility of taping a segment of the program. The producers meet with various administrators, physicians, and staff through Thursday, Feb. 27.
Sunday, March 16	CBS airs *60 Minutes* segment titled "Anatomy of A Mistake" reviewing the transplant mismatch.

(continues)

Box 7-1 Timeline of a Crisis *(continued)*

Monday, June 9	*Forbes* publishes article titled "Duking it Out: A Transplant Tragedy Garnered Worldwide Coverage and Threatened the Reputation of a Renowned Hospital. What to Do?"
Monday, July 28	*U.S. News & World Report* publishes article titled "Jesica's Story: One Mistake Didn't Kill Her—the Organ Donor System Was Fatally Flawed."
Sunday, September 7	CBS airs a repeat of their *60 Minutes* segment from March and includes a brief update at the conclusion of the segment.

Discussion Questions

1. Are all healthcare crises "bad news" stories? Can you suggest an example of other types of events that could occur that are not bad news for you or your organization—but still requires crisis communications?
2. Can you think of a recent healthcare crisis that would be considering a "smoldering" situation?
3. Discuss how a communications professional can serve as the conscience of an organization.
4. How would you prefer your chief executive officer serve as a spokesperson for your institution during a crisis?
5. Accepting responsibility during a crisis is a critical component of a response. How would you argue on behalf of this response if your institution's chief legal counsel was against accepting any responsibility for the situation?
6. Referring to the case study in this chapter, how would you have reacted as chief communicator if healthcare leadership refused to confirm the transplant mismatch occurred and did not want to respond to media inquiries?
7. If you were leading communications during this case study, how would you have reacted to the family advocate's request to speak to news media during both news conferences?
8. How would you incorporate new communications technologies, such as Facebook, Skype, blogging, and Twitter, into your communications plan if the transplant mismatch situation happened today?

Chapter 8

Hospital Media Relations in a Time of Change

By Dennis McCulloch, The University of Kansas Hospital

LEARNING OBJECTIVES

By the end of this chapter, the reader will be able to:

- Identify and describe the eight basic rules for success in hospital media relations.
- Understand the importance of aligning the public relations initiatives of an organization with its business and strategic objectives.
- Develop tailored media stories that leverage patient stories and visuals to expand coverage and ensure success.
- Describe the essential components of successful media trainings and briefings.
- Develop a news release and pitch.

Introduction

After graduation from the University of Missouri with a journalism degree and 10 years as a television news producer, the writer decided he preferred using communication skills for advocacy. After two political campaigns, he worked with corporate video at Sprint before joining Fleishman-Hillard in 1989. For more than 11 years there, he developed the public affairs and crisis practice, which introduced him to health care and animal health clients. When his wife was diagnosed with cancer,

McCulloch looked for a position that would keep him home, and he joined a long-time client, the University of Kansas Hospital, as director of public and government relations. He joined the academic hospital in the beginning of a major change in governance, culture, and image.

People often assume a hospital public relations job is about attending golf tournaments and other charity events—no heavy lifting required. They could not be more wrong.

The job requires thorough knowledge of not only the hospital operation but also of every media outlet of importance in your market. It requires management of a staff and budget, management of an agency and, most importantly, managing up to top-level executives.

The public relations or media relations function is in upheaval, not because of that function but because of disarray in the media industry.

Newspapers are evolving. Viewership for national and local television newscasts are dropping. Other than public radio, it is rare to even find radio news. Media relations are changing from wholesale, where stories are pitched to "retail" news outlets to reach the public, to retail, where social media is combined with traditional media to reach the public directly.

But the wholesale approach will never go away completely. There will be fewer outlets, and they will be more selective with higher thresholds for inclusion. However, this will only enhance the role of "third-party credibility" in the outlets that are left. They will still provide an aura of authenticity.

These changes require the modern media relations professional to both know the basics and to think outside the box.

The Eight Basic Rules

Rule 1: Make News

What is important to people at your hospital or on your campus, may not mean anything to the person across the street. Media outlets do not exist to publish whatever is on the mind of the organization, no matter how important it is to a CEO.

News is basically two things: change and controversy. Generally, media professionals are pushing change and reporters are pushing controversy. A metropolitan daily newspaper has to inspire readers to keep or begin subscribing so advertisers will pay to keep the presses rolling. Broadcast outlets have had that approach for years. They want stories that will excite or interest the most number of readers, viewers, and listeners. More and more news outlets are following public surveys of what the public wants, rather than "journalistic standards" of what the public "needs" to know.

Media relations professions should know media thresholds for news better than the editors and producers themselves. It is a difficult task in this changing media world. Stories that would have had a certain pick up 20 years ago, now are dismissed with "It's interesting, but…."

Does that mean that the media professional is restricted to major stories? No.

It *does* mean that he or she needs to think about what makes any story newsworthy. The fact that a hospital is performing the first operation of its kind in Indiana is not in itself making news. But the fact that for the first time, thousands of Indianans won't have to fly to California for the procedure might make it news worthy.

If a story is important to the organization, it is the media professional's job to keep working to find an appropriate outlet for the story.

Example: The University of Kansas Hospital was not the first hospital in the market to use robotic surgery. So, it is easy to say there is no news. However, by asking more questions to find the angle, we found that the hospital was the first to use it for more than one specialty (we had five) and that we had more fully developed the hybrid rooms to use with both robotic heart surgery and interventional catheterization.

Rule 2: Align Media Relations with Strategic Direction of the Hospital

If the organization's niche is orthopedic, why go out of the way to promote stories on pediatrics? The strategic direction of the hospital—where the hospital is investing resources, focusing its advertising and Web site—must be the media relations focus as well.

At least half of the effort in media relations should be in proactive media relations to promote the strategically important areas of the hospital. Merely answering the phone when it rings is only part of the job. Obviously, it is desirable to take advantage of media opportunities when they come in a variety of areas. But the proactive work should be concentrated on the areas the hospital leadership had decided are the strategic direction of the organization.

Example: We get several inquiries from both national and local reporters asking general questions about the latest developments in medicine. We could answer them in several ways, but our first approach is to look in those areas where the hospital has its focus, such as cancer or heart disease.

Rule 3: Understand the Media Outlet Before You Pitch the Story

One of my most embarrassing moments came with a chief executive I had flown to New York for a series of interviews. At the end of what I thought was a constructive interview with a leading business magazine, the reporter said "I don't know why you are here. We don't cover organizations like yours." Obviously, my organization had not done its homework.

So tailor your pitch, verbally or in writing, to the publication. If pitching a story to a nursing publication, make sure nurses that have a prominent role in the program are being pitched. Don't expect the reporter to interview physicians.

There are many types of media of interest in hospital media relations.

Medical Journals

These journals are highly prestigious and most have stringent guidelines for inclusion of an article, primarily on research, but there are those that focus on good patient care practices. Publication in research journals should be encouraged. It can add credibility to the capability of the organization, especially if it can be leveraged for coverage in the consumer media. Many academic medical centers have many published physician researchers. The biggest task is often simply finding out what articles are being submitted or published in respected journals. Staff members should be encouraged to publish, and they should keep the media relations staff apprised of when the publication appears.

Many of these publications are timed for major meetings and national public relations firms handle releases. Often the publication itself handles national distribution to key reporters. It is up to the local media relations person to get the credit in the home media market.

If the timing of an article is known, this information can be shared with a local reporter on an embargoed basis.

Trade Media

These are magazines, newsletters, Web sites, and so on that are designed for reading by others in the medical field. While the articles are targeted for the industry, they can often be leveraged into coverage by consumer media. Also, trade publications stories assist with hospital recruitment messages.

National Consumer Media

This is the gold standard of media coverage. This is the *New York Times, Wall Street Journal, USA Today, Newsweek, Time,* and others of this level. Why is this more coveted than *60 Minutes?* The hard copy of these major publications carries tremendous weight and respect in a way that trumps broadcast media. These print outlets are also having a tough time in the new marketplace. Remember *Life*, the national magazine? Its death was a forerunner of what has happened to all national media, as unifying national media is lost.

Daily Newspaper

This used to be the backbone of quality media coverage. But, the combination of the recession and declines in readership has put daily newspapers in jeopardy. Still, they probably will reach more people per story than social media and will be reproducible for marketing clips. Just like the national media, it was thought at one time the metropolitan newspaper would lose out to the weekly suburban papers, but it turned out that a combination of factors is driving all of them to cut back or fold.

Small Dailies and Weekly Papers

Weekly papers used to be the staple of suburban communication, but they too are dying out. The key to dealing with those papers that are left (and sometimes the Web sites that have succeeded them) is to find a link to the community they serve. Find patients who live in the suburban or rural paper's city to focus on those patients instead of the metropolitan hospital. Find physicians' hometowns, either where they were born or where they are currently living to bring that angle to the hometown paper.

Regionally, be aware that there are hospitals in local markets throughout any state. Why should a local editor run a story about a distant hospital when it is the local hospital that is advertising in the newspaper? There is no reason to expect a weekly publication 100 miles away to run a story unless they have a solid reason. Are there referring physicians in the local market that are excited about the new program? Is one of the physicians involved from that local area?

Another thought for academic institutions to broaden a story's appeal is to use the academic titles and aspects of the story beyond the local market. Instead of using the story to promote the hospital with Dr. Jones procedure at XYZ Academic Hospital, recast the story at Professor Jones, MD, at XYZ School of Medicine. That way the story is less threatening to the local hospital.

Radio

This is another medium that, apart from National Public Radio, has declined in outlets. When the federal government stopped requiring news as a license requirement, radio news outlets plummeted. Those calling themselves "News Talk" generally have a lot more talk, most from a political point of view, than they do news. However, there are still some real news programs in prime time, which in radio means the morning commute. For a live guest on one of these shows, a physician would have to be ready to go on the air as early as five o'clock in the morning. Needless to say, finding a physician to do this is difficult.

If you can get a legitimate news radio interview, the physicians will have to understand that this means being recorded on tape or live on the air. In other words, the voice is critical. Foreign-born physician accents in a newspaper interview and sometimes on television are often acceptable, but for radio there must be more clarity in the voice. An interview over the phone for radio needs to be done in a quiet room on a landline, not a mobile phone.

Another warning about radio stations concerns weekend programs. Many station turn low-rated Saturday and Sunday time slots over to sponsored talk shows, programs where the host generates his or her own ad revenue from promoting his own business. Ratings for these programs are slight for the effort involved. So are the stations "public affairs" programs, which will often run in the worst weekend times, but often tape during reasonable hours.

If there is a radio talk show that is seeking guests, do the research before agreeing to any interview. There are many shows with a point of view, and it may not be friendly to medicine (H1N1 shots, vaccines and autism) or medical research (stem cells). Know a show and host's approach before booking a guest. Also know that most talk shows have an older audience, which may mean it is not a place to talk about birth control and fertility but may be a perfect audience for Alzheimer's or arthritis.

Television

When I began at the University of Kansas Hospital in 2000, the four news stations in Kansas City each had an active full-time medical reporter. Now, only one does, while a couple of others fight valiantly to get their stations interested in medical stories. I remember consultants coming into television stations in the 1980s saying medical news is what the public wanted, and everyone rushed to do it. So, what changed? My personal belief is that lackluster medical reporting, combined with the monotony of daily medical story requirements, eventually caused medical stories to wear out their welcome.

While it is an axiom that television is a visual medium, this is something that needs to be explained repeatedly to physicians. They need to know how to sit (at the back of the chair, slightly leaning forward) because frankly, because most physicians will slump in a chair as if they have had the worst day of their lives. They need to understand that of all media, television is the most general and the least precise. Explaining things in their simplest forms is a difficulty for many physicians, who believe a 30-slide presentation is their idea of simplifying. A public relations professional will have to be the enforcer to make sure these things happen. While there is sometimes initial resistance to this counsel, they tend to thank you later.

Also, think about building news as well as pitching news. Maybe a story starts in a small weekly and that comes to the attention of a daily paper or a wire service. Maybe a blog leads to a newsletter that leads to a trade magazine. It is no longer taboo to send another media's work to another outlet (as long as the two are not competitors.) Major newspapers for years have combed small weeklies looking for stories. There is nothing wrong with pointing it out for them.

Another aspect of building news is that even when stories don't run, editors, producers, and reporters have heard the pitch. They know something positive is happening at the institution. This can provide a foundation for future stories.

Example: We have often sparked general news coverage by focusing on the nursing aspect for a local or regional nursing publication, and then leveraging that coverage for consumer or trade media.

If a story is rejected, don't hesitate to ask why, not in an accusatory way, but to help understand what the news threshold is. Often a reporter will say "If it only had *X*, I'd jump on it." You may have *X* but don't know it.

Rule 4: Be Opportunistic

It is easier to inject your organization into a story the media is already interested in than open up a new interest in an editor or producer. In other words, look for healthcare stories in the news and be proactive in pitching your organization to be a part of them or reacting quickly when the media calls.

These opportunities can be wide ranging. There can be stories of medical advancements, research breakthroughs, and the like in the news. Generally, you can ask physicians when the major conferences are coming up in their fields and a Web site check can give an idea of the important stories. (It is not unusual to find one of your own physicians making a presentation and you knew nothing about it.) Armed with this information, you can lay groundwork with media about a potential story, one that can be localized.

Monitoring local and national media Web sites can also give you heads-up of stories of interest allowing you an opportunity to localize. A breakthrough announced in the British journal *Lancet* can be an opportunity to offer a local physician or patient to react.

But these opportunities are not limited to medical stories. Every celebrity or politician who announces an illness is an opportunity to leverage through the local media. Every heart problem of former Vice President Cheney was an opportunity to have a cardiologist explain the problem. Every sports injury is an opportunity to trot out an orthopedist, even on sports radio.

Sometimes strategic judgment calls have to be made. While generally, you do want to build goodwill with reporters by responding when they want a story, that doesn't mean you have to plunge physicians into controversial areas such as embryonic stem cells, abortion, euthanasia, or other politically hot topics. Nor does it mean you need to provide an expert's opinion on controversial lawsuit topics.

Physicians may want to jump into topics on their own. The general rule of thumb is they can speak out, as long as they are expressly speaking for themselves and not for the organization. Trying to muzzle a physician who wants to talk will only lead to conflict and will often result in the physician not being cooperative in distancing the organization from his or her personal views.

Example: When the H1N1 pandemic was declared, all hospitals were in pretty much the same boat in terms of waiting for the new vaccine. But, we knew through media contacts by our agency that CNBC wanted to do the story somewhere else than the usual East Coast venues. We knew we had our ongoing staff flu shot effort for the seasonal flu ready to switch to H1N1 as soon as supplies came in. I worked with our pharmacy director, who paged me as soon as the first shipment of medicine arrived. I, in turn immediately called the agency, who called CNBC. We were the first hospital to respond that we had H1N1 vaccine in house and were going to start using it on staff. CNBC immediately got on a plane, rented a local satellite truck and in two days, we were live across the country on CNBC and MSNBC. Being opportunistic worked. (One side note: living by breaking news means dying by it as well. We lost at least two live reports that day because of the false report of a boy up in a weather balloon.)

Rule 5: Blame Roone Aldridge

The creator of ABC's Wide World of Sports started something that pervades all medical reporting today. You didn't just get to see the demolition derby winner interviewed after the event; often you would see a vignette with the two-time champion at home with his dog scampering around. The "up close and personal" expanded to Olympic coverage and then to ABC News when Roone headed it.

The message for medical media relations: You need patients, and you need visuals. Even early developments in the research labs need potential patients to say how excited they are about the potential for this research and what it can mean down the road. Often the patients will be able to articulate better the potential for the new knowledge than the discoverer who will put everything as if he or she is submitting every answer for peer review.

Visuals are more important for television, but good visuals can uplift a story in any medium. Simply putting the patient in an exam room can get you by, but you need to think creatively. Maybe the discovery could someday free the patient from a plethora of pills. Take the media to the patient's home to see the shelf full of pills. That will illustrate the story and may result in expanded coverage.

How do you get patients? Ask. Better than 90% of the patients we ask are thrilled to be part of the story. Often, for HIPAA (patient privacy law) purposes, it is easier to have the physician's nurse make contact with the patient first and then have media relations join the conversation if they are interested. Ask physicians and nurses for patients who are articulate.

Remember patients and visuals are not limited to media stories. The relationships established are valuable for Web sites, annual reports, fund raising, and internal commutations.

Example: Our hospital developed a program for awareness, assessment, and advocacy of women's heart health. Everybody does screenings, but when we found women willing to be followed throughout the assessment process, reporter interest came alive.

Rule 6: Manage Communications

Frequently, the biggest communications challenges are inside the hospital.

It often is like the cobbler's children having no shoes. There is so much focus on communicating with the media, that it is easy to give short shrift to communicating with management and with people involved in the story. You cannot communicate with these internal audiences too much in order to (1) encourage them to let you do your job, and (2) contribute to the process.

Very few hospitals themselves are so big that the person in charge of media relations shouldn't have access to the top executives. This doesn't mean reporting directly to the CEO, only that he or she needs to know directly what is happening in key stories. A large multinational corporation can have layers of people between the leader of the department actually doing the work of media relations and the top executive. I once worked for a department where the director worked for a noncommunicator vice president, who reported to a senior vice president who reported to an executive vice president who reported to the president. By the time any message got upstairs it was so filtered it was inconsequential.

But individual or even small groups of hospitals, which are the bulk of the hospital providers today (even big systems like HCA have individual CEOs in hospitals and often individual communication people), should not be so big that communications is filtered like that.

This is not to say that a media relations professional should bypass their boss to go directly to the CEO. Any use of such communications should be select and strategic. The best way is for the head of media relations to regularly meet with the CEO and have all the people in between in the reporting structure present. Establish a good relationship with those in the positions ahead of you so your voice can be heard. Good executives help you craft your message to top management so they will be more effective. Remember, it is not the CEO's job to take time to be educated on what you are doing; it is your job to take the time to educate the CEO.

What do you communicate? One of the key things is to manage expectations. Every executive wants stories he or she cares about on the front page of every newspaper and the lead story on every broadcast outlet. At some point, top executives need a Media 101 class about news thresholds, key media audiences, and appeal beyond the confines of the hospital.

There are many other items that need to be communicated throughout an organization in order to have effective media relations.

An organization must have rules to determine how media calls are handled throughout an organization, around the clock. How are patient conditions calls handled on nights and weekends? How are other media requests handled off hours? The standard plan here is to have a policy where all media requests go through one department and that the one department be reached off hours through pager or mobile phone by the switchboard.

Can patients talk directly to the media, including inviting news media directly into their patient rooms? Generally, this is a bad idea. Nurses should be instructed to turn away any arriving media personnel. It is a good idea to brief all area news media on this policy. The downside is that a hospital is not a motel, and patient care must be the sole function of the patient rooms. If a patient can be moved to a common area, then an interview can be set up. This policy also gives patients time to really think about their decision to talk to the media, and many don't really want to do it. Another problem this avoids is a patient using your hospital to raise money for a fund whose integrity you can not vouch for.

Can a hospital endorse a vendor or vendor's product in an interview or ad? Vendors and their public relations firms are often very aggressive on this. Every organization has to do its own policy on this, but a good compromise is that the organization's name can only be used for objective, not subjective, information. In others words, an organization's name can be used to say it is a client and that because of using the product some metric improved X percent. However, the name cannot be used to say the product is "great" or "the best" or any other superlative.

Example: We experienced an 8-day media siege during a tragic situation involving a brain dead child. Local and regional media followed the story extensively. The hospital came out of that tragic situation with our reputation intact because the chief executive, risk management, nursing, physicians, and even campus police communicated and cooperated smoothly. That meant we did not make the situation more difficult for ourselves by giving out inaccurate information, and we avoided unnecessary confrontations with emotional family members.

Rule 7: Train (or At Least Brief) Spokespeople

It is vital that anyone representing any organization know the basics before any news interview. Media training or briefings will never guarantee a good interview (and run away from any trainer who guarantees that!), but it is essential to increase the odds of your message getting through.

Know What You Want to Say

It sure sounds simple. But it is the most common mistake in media interviews. "I will just answer the questions they ask" can be a disaster, but most often is just wasted media opportunity. What is the strategic reason you are doing the interview? What is the message you want to get across? Who is the physician representing, himself, his practice, his specialty, or the hospital?

Know Who You Are Talking To

This is more than avoiding jargon. It is knowing that you are not talking to the reporter, but rather, the reporter's audience. The reporter is your conduit.

It is not unusual for a reporter who regularly covers medical stories to begin using medical terms in his interviews with physicians. This can be a trap if the interviewee is not prepared. If the physician responds in kind, the reporter can find no useable quotes to use with his or her audience. Understand who the reporter's audience is. Most broadcast outlets and daily and weekly newspapers are speaking to the broad general public, so it is important to put things in terms that audience can understand and relate to. A trade publication allows a subject to be more technical.

A side note: Often physicians will decline interviews because they do not feel they are experts in the field. This problem can usually be overcome by explaining a consumer media interview is far, far different than presenting a paper to a conference. The media is looking for someone to translate and to make something technical relevant to its general audience, not to have it diagrammed.

Know the Basic Rules of Consumer Media Interviews

- Don't go "off the record." Media professional may have trusting relationships that allow them to go off the record, but the interview subject generally does not. Off the record means something different to each reporter, and it is a game the physicians or other nonmedia people should not play.
- Don't play with "exclusives": This is again the province of the media professional and when executives, physicians, or others try to play this game, it often results in friction with other media. This is far different than respecting an individual reporter's enterprise (a story he or she developed), which should be respected as exclusive. But, if there is no reason to make a story exclusive, don't.
- Appearance should be appropriate and not distracting: There are experts who will tell women to wear red, men to wear blue, and so on. If a CEO is on a media tour of major outlets, this is relevant. But, for the most part, just make sure clothing does not distract. Women's jewelry should be subtle, as should men's ties. The white coat is a fixture for a physician.
- Take advantage of the first and last questions: Ninety percent of the time, the first question is a very general question that should be seen as a blank canvas for the interviewee to fill with the prepared messages. Almost every interview ends with "Is there anything you'd like to add?" Again, this is another blank canvas to fill by repeating the key messages. I can't tell you how many times it is this answer that has wound up being aired in a broadcast interview because the subject is relaxed and thoroughly comfortable by this time.
- Repeat, repeat, repeat: In normal conversation, it is rude to repeat your point. It is as if you are saying "I think my listener is stupid." In media interviews, repeating the messages is

accepted and even desired. The interviewee may say it better the third time than the first. If the reporter hears the key points repeatedly, it is more likely to the message gets through. Many physicians, especially researchers, have very precise minds and have trouble with this concept.

- Pause and think: With the exception of live television (and to a degree even then) interviewees should know that they are not held to the same standards as presidential candidates on *Meet the Press*, where questions and answers fly as if it was a gunfight at the OK Corral. If a subject doesn't know how to respond to a question, it is not inappropriate to pause a few seconds to think about the answer before a response is given.
- Time-out: Again, with the exception of live television (and again, to a limited degree even then), if a subject has to cough or sneeze, or even forgets their train of thought, simply say "I've got to sneeze," or "I need to start over," and do it. Nearly all medical stories are nonconfrontational, and most reporters are happy to have you take the time to explain it correctly and clearly.
- Refer other questions to the appropriate people: Your physician or other executive is there in a particular role as described above. If questions veer from that role, or if there is a dreaded "bait and switch" (where the interview was set up for one subject but the reporter just wanted to get in the door to ask other, more controversial questions), simply state you are not the person to appropriately respond to those questions and pledge to get the correct person to the reporter. I once had a reporter ask to talk about liver transplants, but about five questions in started asking questions about surgery residents downloading pornography on hospital computers. My associate jumped in to say that the physicians do not monitor computer use and that we would be happy to get him to the correct person. Fortunately, when the reporter realized he wasn't going to get his big moment, he lost interest in the story.
- No humor or sarcasm: Sometimes, in the course of an interview, a subject will crack an obvious joke or witty remark. But, medical stories tend to discuss real life or death experiences and humor in cold print may come across as being insensitive. Often a reporter will think including it will be a favor to the subject, to "humanize" the interviewee, but the remark may be seen as insensitive, especially in the very serious world of disease. However, when a glitch in an update from antivirus software McAfee knocked down hospital computers for a few hours, I was able, after assuring everyone that patient care had not been compromised, to quip that it was a good day to be a spokesman for Norton software, McAfee's prime competitor. It helped get the message through that the problem was caused by the big national company and not by our own systems.
- No beginning, middle, or end to an interview: Everything within earshot of a reporter is on the record. Even after a camera or tape recorder is turned off, anything said still has the potential to make it into a story. Business reporters have told me they get good lines from top executives in conversations while they are being walked to elevator to say goodbye. Also, respect publishers, editors, and so on in social settings, because things they hear in these venues often turn into stories.

- Can't review the story before it airs: This is one of the most difficult ones for physicians to grasp. Many are used to professional publications where they get final approval of the text. This is not the case in consumer media, and they need to understand this before the embarrassment of asking for script approval from the reporter and throwing a pique when the request is turned down. However, reporters are open to the request to "fact check" a story for technical accuracy. A reporter who would show offense at being asked for text approval will often be happy to fact check a story. I have had fact checks run the gamut from just making sure a technical name for a procedure is right to hearing the entire story. In either case, it is better than nothing.

Rule 8: Monitor All Interviews

This is an essential part of media relations. It protects everyone involved. However, some people, especially physicians, can resent being "spied upon" during interviews.

The first step is to make sure your top executives follow this policy. It will be difficult to get physicians, who are generally not hospital employed, to comply if the top brass if ignoring the procedure.

To get buy in, you have to put the reason for media relations to monitor interviews in terms of benefiting the interviewee.

First, it provides the interviewee with a witness for being misquoted or misrepresented by a reporter. While this does not happen as often as physicians think it does, it plays to their fears and media relations becomes a comforting presence. (Actually, my personal experience is my presence in an interview has more often resulted in my telling a physician he or she was not misquoted than telling a reporter that the story was inaccurate.)

Also, media relations can jump in when a reporter goes on a different track beyond what was prepared. The physician can be assured media relations will be the "bad cop" who jumps in to say, "This is not the appropriate person for that question," or "We haven't researched all the facts of that and will get back to you."

Media relations can also be of service to the interviewee when photos or other materials or requested. When media relations is on the call, physicians and physician staff don't have to take time to follow up on those issues because media relations will be there to handle it.

A great benefit of monitoring the call is to make sure messages are remembered and offered. It is appropriate to jump in if a message is missed and ask "Doctor, wasn't it a patient who first requested this?" or some other appropriate question to prompt the subject to get back to the message.

Another thing to remember is that many reporters do not want to look stupid, so you must be willing to. When, in listening to an interview, you know the physician is speaking over the head of the reporter and the reporter's audience, it is appropriate for a media relations person to jump in (even on a taped television interview) to say something along the lines of "Would you mind explaining how that works (or what that means, or how I can explain that to my mother?)" That will be a cue to the physician or other source to simplify the answer, increasing the odds of the reporter understanding the subject.

The Basic Tool: News Release

Whether you call it a news release, or an advisory, or a blog, there will always be a need to tell reporters or the public what is going in clear language.

A personal note, as a former television producer, I always resented the term *press release* or *press conference*. I used to make interns stand on a chair to tell me where the "printing press" was if they handed me a script with "press conference" in it. There are no presses in broadcast outlets or Internet sites. Media release is acceptable, but I have always preferred "news release." It may not be a big deal to every broadcast outlet, but why risk offending any?

There are many ways to do a news release, and sometimes we worry too much about whether to single-space, double-space, or use 1.5 spaces with double space between paragraphs.

It does need to say if the information is embargoed, and have a contact name, phone number, and/or e-mail address for further information.

The most common mistake in a news release is to "bury your lead," or "lede" if you prefer. This means you make the reporter or editor dig three paragraphs down before they find the news. If the most important thing about your story is that your hospital has become the first in the Midwest to perform a procedure, make sure that is up front. Don't tell a corporate or chronological story. Don't lead with a physician's name unless that name has a major significance in your desired coverage area.

Think of classic Associated Press style with the most important thing first so if only one sentence was printed, it would tell a cohesive important story. In reality, with today's shrinking papers, you may only get a reporter or editor to read one sentence before making a quick judgment on one of a hundred news releases.

Interviewing physicians and creating quotes from their comments is preferred. However, often the media relations professional will write the quotes in the interest of time. If there is trust with a highly quoted executive, they will prefer you drafting their quotes. (However, the "quotee" does need to approve the quote before the release is distributed.) This is comparable to being a speechwriter, except the content is in little bite-sized portions.

Try to tell the story in one page, certainly no more than two. However, there will be those complex stories that run longer.

It is sometimes a good strategy to do more than one release on a subject. Have the breaking news announcement in one release, but compile a background release or fact sheet to present the additional information. Breaking the information up into more than one release makes the information more user-friendly.

Sometimes with a clinical trial or a journal publication, or even winning an award, the presenting organization will sometimes insist that you send out their release verbatim. This is not a problem. There is no rule against submitting a companion release that may better explain the announcement for your target audience and allow you to quote local people. Think of your release as a memo attached to the national release, tailoring it to your needs.

There are two major pains concerning news releases. One is the approval process. Any time lawyers are involved, prepare to fight for clarity and completeness. Attorneys have a necessary role in your organization, but they shouldn't have the ultimate role. Your work in image development, crisis communication, or promotion is just as important and should be considered along with attorneys.

There are many dangers in the approval process. One is the plethora of hands all making changes to make the end product unreadable. Physicians and researchers have a tendency to put in items more appropriate for a medical journal than a news release. Each has his or her quirks. I have worked with one executive who demanded that the word *that* be stricken from all written communications.

Another danger is losing changes as it undergoes multiple drafts. With the Track Changes features in word processing, you can save everyone's changes. It is important that someone in communications keep the master document. It is helpful to put draft numbers at the top of the document and to make it clear that you are keeping the master copy. Ask them to use the Track Changes mode, but someone invariably will rewrite the release, forcing you to go over it line by line to find the changes.

One of the advantages of the memo approach with a national release is that it saves approval time.

The other problem with a news release is distribution. Sending to named reporters, editors, and producers is a must, but what if that person is on vacation or out sick? As a safeguard it is wise to send a second copy to just the newsroom of each outlet.

Then, it is important to find out in what format the news outlets want to receive the information. Today, most publications find e-mail attachments acceptable. (Some, fearful of a computer virus, still prefer cut and paste in the body of the e-mail.) There are still weekly papers out in rural areas that prefer a faxed copy. Sometimes it is more trouble than it is worth customizing distribution, but every edge counts when seeking coverage.

The Pitch

There is no one way to pitch a story directly to reporters, editors, and producers. Sometimes, it is easier to pitch a story on the phone than go through the time and approval hassle of a formal written news release. Often, when jumping on breaking news stories, such as the disease of a celebrity, time is of the essence, and pitching your experts quickly is essential.

There is simply a balancing act to calling reporters to pitch stories and not being a pest. Don't waste a reporter's time. Make sure you believe the story is relevant for the reporter. Then make your pitch. Try to concisely explain why readers, listeners, or viewers would be interested and what you have to make the process work. In that latter category, emphasize visual possibilities as well as patient and physician availabilities.

Don't ask a reporter to guarantee coverage of an event. Sell the story as important and someone will be there, but reporters are often at the whim of breaking news. You can push, but know the limits and maintain professional dignity.

"New" Media Still Requires "News"

With the rush to social media distribution, there is no reason to abandon the established principles of public relations. Social media merely extends those principles.

You shouldn't use Twitter to send out an item that isn't interesting, helpful, or strategic, any more than you should send out a non-newsworthy release to reporters. You will get more followers on Twitter and Facebook (or whatever might replace them by the time this book is published) if you hold their interest with legitimately interesting stories. Twitter and Facebook allow you to put in that exciting AP lead line and connect it to the full story on your Web site. You Tube allows you to interview physicians and others to compliment the story.

You can use companion releases, audio interviews, or video to add to the story. You can focus more on the patient.

The downside to video shot on a flip video is the audio quality. You can get a quality camera with a microphone input and editing software for under $1000. (Many department heads who have added video recommend editing on an Apple computer. The software is more user-friendly than PC editing.)

It takes an entire new mindset to think of shooting your own video and using social media to help distribute directly to consumers, but remember that good, well-written stories are the key, no matter what distribution you use.

Complaints Are an Art Form

Think about it. A physician generally goes to 4 years of medical school, a 3–5 year residency and often, years of practice. A reporter comes in and spends 20 to 30 minutes with the physician and the patient. The reporter goes back, writes the story, and hands it to an editor or producer who was not privy to the conversation with the physician and patient. That editor or producer edits the story, sometimes with the reporter's input and sometimes not. Often in a newspaper, a layout person may cut more to fit in the available space.

Given all that, it often seems like a miracle that *anything* in the story is right, much less if any one or two things are wrong. So, basically, expect an inaccuracy in almost any story.

Do not going charging in with guns blazing at the media outlet (and make sure the executives and physicians know not to do that as well).

First, was the story inaccurate, or was the "tone" of the story upsetting? You generally should not complain about the tone of the story, unless you can conclusively show a pattern of abuse in that area. If, for example, other hospital stories are run without talking to competitors, but your hospital stories always quote competing institutions, you have a case to evaluate bias in reporting.

It is always best to see if the reporter can fix things before going to the editor or news director. However, as in every profession, sometimes inaccuracies are so outrageous you have to go to the top quickly. Remember to keep your focus on errors and serious omissions, not "It made us look bad."

Summary

Media relations professionals are walking right on the fault line as a media industry earthquake is occurring. We are living in a world of constant change.

While outlets may come and go, the basic principles (have an interesting story, humanize it, explain it clearly and concisely, and hope for the best) are true whether the *New York Times* is replaced by a blogger or if *60 Minutes* becomes a flip video on YouTube.

Also true is that the best people in media relations will be on top of what is happening and will know and understand the media better or at least as well as the people in the media. With that kind of professionalism in place, media relations will survive this period stronger than ever.

Discussion Questions

1. Why do media outlets exist today? What must media professionals consider in order to get stories picked up by these media outlets?
2. Describe proactive media relations and the importance of implementing proactive public relations work.
3. What types of media outlets are relevant to the practice of hospital media relations? Describe the pros and cons of each.
4. Discuss the importance of managing communications efforts inside a hospital as well as outside a hospital. Describe why it is important to manage the expectations of top executives.
5. What is a news release, and how is it used to inform the media outlets and public of your story? What are the key components of news release? Why is a good pitch important to develop?

Chapter 9

An *A* to *Z* Guide for Communicating the Launch of a New Pharmaceutical Product

By Douglas Petkus

LEARNING OBJECTIVES

By the end of this chapter, the reader will be able to:

- Use key terms related to the launch of new pharmaceutical products.
- Develop a sense of the corporate communications professional's role in bringing new pharmaceutical products to the marketplace.
- Define the stakeholders and key audiences of a pharmaceutical product launch.
- Identify the skills required of communications specialists that will enable their success within the pharmaceutical industry.

Introduction

While issues are what pharmaceutical companies want to avoid, new products represent just the opposite: they are the lifeblood of the industry and the key to long-term growth and future business success. While the corporate communications professional plays a significant role in helping companies manage issues, he or she is also an integral player in supporting new products—from discovery in the lab to marketing to physicians and use by patients.

This chapter provides an *A* to *Z* guide for the communications professional who has the challenge of being part of the team that helps to bring a new pharmaceutical product to the marketplace.

A

If you are a communications major reading this textbook, it's not likely you have acquired a mastery of *arithmetic*. You'll need to brush up on your math proficiency if you are working on publicity or educational materials relating to a new pharmaceutical product. The basis for regulatory approval of any new product is scientific data. These data are presented by the clinical researchers working in the lab in the form of numbers—numerical information that demonstrates why a certain product is safe and efficacious. There are terms you'll need to understand, such as *adverse events*, *statistical significance*, and *P* values, all of which are part of the statistical analyses of any given medicine, and each is presented as a measurement or numerical quantity. Without a basic understanding of these numbers and their significance, you will be lost and won't be very helpful when asked to develop a press release, Q&A document, or media statement. The lesson here is simple: don't ignore math as you compile your elective academic requirements. Take a course in basic statistics to help you understand some of these terms. If you can't be trained as a scientist, at least you should have a basic knowledge of their language.

B

Watching a television commercial or listening to a radio advertisement for a prescription medicine can be confusing. What makes it so is the complicated language that usually is heard toward the end of the particular message, the information about side effects and the parameters for safely using a particular product. For a communicator, this language is called "fair *balance*," and it's one of the key lessons to be learned when putting together materials to help reporters understand how and why a particular product should be used. The challenge for the communicator is how to present this information in a factual, yet unscary fashion that meets the FDA requirements and keeps the company out of potential legal trouble. Transparency, accuracy, and clarity are the keys to successfully communicating this fair balance information. The last thing in the world you want to do is create a sense that the product has no side-effects (not true), but, on the other hand, you need to make sure that you present information that is seen in context with the potential benefits of any given medicine. It is up to the physician or medical practitioner to make the judgment regarding the risks and benefits of a new medicine. It is up to the communicator to make sure all of the important information is presented so an appropriate evaluation can be made.

C

One of the key decisions that needs to be made regarding communications support for a new product is when it should begin. The last thing you want to do is create expectations about a new therapy when it isn't 100% certain that the product will make it to market. On the other hand, it is also important to *condition* the marketplace to make sure the doctors, patients, investors, media, and other key constituents totally understand the benefits possessed by a product and why it will be an important addition to the "medicine chest." There's no real formula for when communications about a new product should begin. A good rule of thumb is creating a communications timeline that begins once a product is submitted for approval to the governing regulatory body. In the United States, that's the Food and Drug Administration (FDA). Companies cannot and should not send its package of scientific data to the FDA until they are certain there is a decent chance for approval. There should be sufficient clinical data regarding safety and efficacy, and there should be a defined need for the product so that the regulatory body understands why it even needs to review the product. The job of the communicator, while all of this scientific rigor and review is underway, is to condition the key targets for the product so there is complete understanding about the positive impact the medicine could have *and* how best to use it safely.

Unless there is a defined need for a product (e.g., to treat a condition for which there's no effective treatment currently available), then it will be difficult for the product to be successful and less chance that patients will benefit. There are many components to this conditioning effort: doctors, patients, government officials, employees, media, investors, and stock analysts. So you can see the challenges that lie ahead for the communications professional. If you think about the ultimate objective—conditioning all of these audiences so they have a full understanding about a product before it is available—you'll see it's an important step in the process. Without this understanding, no one benefits: doctors, patients, or the company.

D

It may sound odd, but playing *defense* is also part of providing communications support for a new product launch. There are two reasons: first, there is likely competition out there that would like nothing better than to undermine your efforts to support the new product; and second, what if something goes wrong? What if you need to defend the company or its research efforts if the product launch doesn't go as smoothly as you hope? The process that needs to be incorporated into any communications plan to support a new product launch is known by a variety of terms; *crisis communications* or *issues management* are the most common. But, whatever you call it, there is clearly a need to be prepared for a worst-case scenario that you can never predict. For the communicator, this means taking all of the usual precautions—developing tough Q&A documents with the toughest possible questions; working through the different scenarios that may occur for optimum preparedness; and most importantly, making sure the company's senior management is totally cognizant of what could go wrong—so that there are no surprises should any of these worst-case scenarios actually happen.

E

One of the most important, but often overlooked, audiences when developing a communications support plan for a new pharmaceutical product are the *employees* of the company. Building a foundation of understanding regarding a new product needs to start from the bottom. In the case of a pharmaceutical product, it will pay off in the long run to make sure your own company's employees are totally conversant about the potential that a new product brings, both the positive and the negative. If and when you find yourself in a situation when you are developing a communications support plan for a new product, make sure that you include an internal or employee component. Employees should be the first to know, so the timing of message delivery is important. Make sure your internal targets are made aware of the news before you issue a press release or post information to the company's Web site. Often the most effective way to achieve this early notification is via a message from the company's top executive "to the troops." You'd be amazed how effective this type of "top-down" communication can be in improving overall company morale, not to mention establishing a connection between senior management and the company's biggest supporters—its own employees.

F

Another consideration for development of a new product communications strategy is whether the product is a *first* or *follow-on* compound. Depending on the product's status, the communications approach should be different. When the new product is the first in its category or a totally new class, it will be important to do three things:

1. Establish a need for the product.
2. Fully explain the disease state for which it will be used.
3. Explain why this particular product is different and unique.

You can only be first in a specific category once, so take advantage of this status. If the product is a follow-on, meaning there are similar products in the category or it is a slightly improved version of an existing product marketed by the company, the communications challenges are a bit more daunting. The focus of the communications effort needs to be on the reasons why the product is better than the competition or the existing version. Usually, the best way to achieve this is to rely on science. If there are compelling clinical data that substantiates the need for the product, that should be the key information to impart to target audiences.

G

One thing to avoid when developing new product support materials is using the word *great*. A dinner can be great; a spouse or a ball game can be great. A new pharmaceutical product, on the other hand, should not be described as great; resist the urge. It is more appropriate to use terms such as *effective*, *safe*, and *novel* to describe a new pharmaceutical product.

H

Remember that your most important audience when developing materials to support the launch of a new prescription medicine are *healthcare practitioners*. This is a key distinction because in today's modern world, doctors aren't the only group who seek information about new products. There are nurses, managed care providers, nurse practitioners, patient advocacy groups, opinion leaders, and pharmacists. All of these groups are involved in the business of health care and will benefit by receiving information about new pharmaceutical products.

I

The *investment* community is what we generally call the world of financial analysts and *investors*, the latter group comprising those who buy the stock offered by the pharmaceutical companies who are developing new medicines. Members of this "community" are an important audience for information about new products as they often recommend purchase of a particular company's stock based on the firm's new product pipeline. The investment community, as you would imagine, is most interested in a product's earning potential. As you develop your communications plan to support a new product launch, it will be important to put the investment community at the top of your list of key audiences. This group needs to receive product information, and arranging conversations with company executives will prove beneficial in generating optimum understanding of a new product's attributes.

J

Journalists are perhaps the most significant conduit to consumer, financial, and physician audiences when a pharmaceutical company launches a new product. When compiling a media list, it is important to include the broadest possible range of outlets: print, broadcast, and Web-based media. Today, news cycles are around the clock; no longer are we slaves to deadlines. Thanks to the digital news world, a deadline occurs virtually every minute.

When developing a media plan to support a new product launch, it is important to divide your effort into three parts: education, breaking news, and in-depth coverage. The education phase should take place well before the product comes to market, to alert reporters that there is a disease category with unmet needs and that a company is working on a product that could potentially address those needs. The breaking news phase is exactly what it appears to be, the actual announcement of news concerning the product, important data, its regulatory approval, or its actual marketplace availability. In the in-depth phase, opportunities need to be identified for expanded coverage of how the new product is effecting the therapeutic category, helping patients or serving as an revenue driver for the company that developed the new product. It is also the phase when long-lead publications (e.g., magazines) should be targeted. In any of these situations, reporters will be able to understand the product and its benefits if the materials they are provided are clear, concise, and accurate. Also, providing access to company or third-party spokespersons who can provide some additional information will usually enhance coverage.

K

Kainotophobia is the fear of change. If a communicator suffers from this malady, healthcare communications might not be the right career choice. This is especially true when developing a plan to support the launch of a new product. The key thing to remember when planning for a new product launch is to be flexible. Develop plans based on several scenarios so you are prepared for any situation. Otherwise, a change in strategy, patient targets, or indications (how a product is recommended for use) will set you back and put you in a catch-up situation. Executive management and product management will expect communications support to be ready for anything.

For example, not every new product will be subjected to public scrutiny at an FDA advisory meeting. This is a public hearing when products and scientific data supporting its approval are discussed by a group of independent experts. Preparation for this meeting needs to be a part of any product support effort, even if it's not guaranteed that the meeting will take place at all.

L

One of the most important lessons to be learned by a corporate communications executive is the importance of developing alliances with key groups within the company. One of the most significant business partners you can have is the *legal* team. This group of inside lawyers serves as the compliance expert for the company. They make certain all communications materials meet the appropriate legal guidelines, whether the materials are developed by the communications department or not. The primary objective of a company lawyer's intervention is to determine that any public communication will not make the firm vulnerable to potential lawsuits. Company lawyers also teach employees how to communicate responsibly to one another. History shows that even innocent e-mails are used in litigation, when senders and recipients never envisioned that a plaintiff's attorney would attempt to convince a jury that the communication was inappropriate.

M

New product launches within a pharmaceutical company are driven by *marketing* experts, known as product management. These individuals usually have earned an MBA degree (masters in business administration) and have the primary responsibility for the sales success of a new product. The optimum time for a communications professional to begin working with a marketing executive is prior to the drug's submission to the FDA for approval. It is during this time when gaining understanding of the drug's clinical (scientific) profile, including the data that supports its safety and efficacy, is critical. In addition, learning about the disease for which the product will be indicated (approved), as well as the current products it will compete against for market share are important steps in the process. Without this information, the communications professional will be unable to prepare the materials to be used by external audiences (e.g., media, patients, physicians, government officials) to learn about the product's attributes.

In addition, it is during this preapproval timeframe when the communications team begins identifying medical experts who will eventually be tapped as information resources for the product and the disease it will treat. These key opinion leaders will be asked by media, patients, and other physicians to provide information about the product and its role in treating the malady for which it has been approved.

N

One of the most overlooked audiences in a company's efforts to promote a new prescription drug are *nurses*. In today's world of modern health care, a nurse has taken a broader role in managing a patient's treatment. The same holds true for pharmacists. The message here is that a communications professional needs to include nurses and pharmacists when developing its audience target list. Whether it is through development of materials that are sent directly to these professionals or materials that are sent to trade presses serving these groups, don't limit your information or educational efforts to just physicians.

O

Promoting new prescription drugs, through advertising or materials targeting media or other audiences, can only discuss use of the specific product from the context of its approved use (or indication). Communicators can never forget this tenet (the lawyers won't let you) or risk an FDA warning letter, something you never want to receive. But in the real world, prescription drugs aren't always used solely for their approved purpose. Medical professionals use their discretion to prescribe a product for a nonapproved or *off-label* usage. They are able to do this because their knowledge of the drug's mechanism of action or its clinical data package gives them confidence that it may be effective in treating an off-label ailment. For the communicator, caution is advised when considering discussing this information with a reporter. It is usually best to frame all conversations within the context of the approved use and refer the media representative to a third-party professional (a doctor not affiliated with the company) to discuss the nonapproved use for the product.

P

Once a new product has been introduced to the marketplace, its sponsor (the company) usually spends a significant amount of money to *promote* the product. This promotion takes many forms, but the most common is paid advertising through traditional (magazines, newspapers, television, and radio) or nontraditional (digital and social media) methods. The work performed by the communicator is also part of this promotional effort—with a big difference. Promoting a new product through advertising is paid; it represents what the company is saying about its own product. Of course, even though the advertisements are based on scientific clinical data and approved by the FDA, questions about their credibility can be raised. The efforts of the communicator are enhanced when the materials they develop to educate audiences about the new product include third-party endorsements, which are statements from medical professionals not affiliated with the company who support the use of the new product for its approved purpose. It is essential to identify and work with these independent professionals when developing press material. It's always preferred to present information where others speak up in support of a product or service versus when the product's developer makes the statements that support the product.

Q

When information about a new product is released to the public it will elicit *questions* from a broad range of constituencies. It is the communicator's job to prepare for all of these questions. It is essential to think about every possible question that could be posed by media, patients, and physicians. The end result of this effort, known as a Q&A document, comes in handy when answering questions from these audiences. It is important that everyone in the company who comes into contact with key constituents uses the same information when providing answers. The last thing you want to do is create confusion by providing varying replies.

R

Another important business partner for the communicator is the individual from *regulatory* affairs; these are the internal experts on the product's labeling and packaged insert information. These coworkers are probably the most knowledgeable as it relates to the scientific clinical data used to support a product's approval, as well as the product's side effects, bioavailability, and potential impact from concurrent use with other pharmaceutical products (drug interactions). All of this information is required for inclusion in press materials and is known as "fair balance." The issue for the communicator is attempting to interpret this technical information so it can be understood by the reader. The problem is you might not be permitted to stray very far from the verbatim language (the lawyers and regulatory experts might not allow it).

S

It was mentioned earlier that communicators need to come to work possessing some mathematics skills. The same holds true for *science*. The communicator with a basic scientific background will benefit when developing materials to support the launch of a new pharmaceutical product. Remember that the approval for any new product is contingent on FDA review of the scientific clinical data provided by the company. A communicator will be unable to discuss these data with reporters or other important audiences without an understanding of the significance of this scientific information.

T

Practice makes perfect for the communications professional when preparing for the launch of a new pharmaceutical product. *Training* your media spokespersons, senior executives, and helping with sales force preparation is one of the keys for a successful launch. Identifying both an internal and external spokesperson will provide optimum flexibility and credibility. Taking the time to rehearse every possible scenario and considering the toughest possible questions will help you be ready for just about anything. Finally, developing three to five key messages about the product's attributes and learning how to deliver these messages in virtually any situation will enhance efforts to deliver the most positive impact possible. Keeping it simple, considering all possibilities, and staying on message will create the perceptions you seek. Don't forget: perception is reality.

U

Approaching the launch with a sense of *urgency* is a must. You only launch a new product once—there are no second chances. Develop a strategy that meets the needs of the product marketing effort, execute it flawlessly, and create a plan to measure your success. The latter is especially important in a corporate environment. Senior executives need to understand what the objectives are for any given communications support plan so they will recognize success when the plan is fully implemented. Unless you outline the criteria for success, it won't be easily discerned.

V

When developing communications tools for a new product launch, don't forget *video* and *visuals*. A significant number of your targeted media outlets are either broadcast outlets or Web based. In either case, there is a visual element that is the essence of the communications vehicle. Without developing a video package or compiling broadcast sound bites featuring both internal (company) and external (third-party) spokespersons, you'll be missing an opportunity for the broadest possible reach and exposure.

W

The *World Wide Web* has changed the way communicators target media. The term traditional media has become an anachronism. Remember that the 24/7 news cycle is alive and well. The days of the 6 p.m. deadline are over. Fewer reporters honor embargoes, and when you disseminate your press release or information package, it takes mere seconds for the impact to be felt. Getting it right the first time is more important than ever. The rapid uptake of the information you provide increases the importance of instant media monitoring, but it also allows for rapid corrections and instantaneous evaluations of the impact of media exposure on key audiences. The influence of social media outlets like Twitter and Facebook as well as the "blogosphere" is still being determined. What we can say is that these outlets are having an impact, so they need to be part of your media outreach target list. Because social media and bloggers are clearly different, you need to treat these outlets with extra care. The immediate impact of a negative blog or tweet can reverberate throughout an organization, and the responsibility for this type of "coverage" falls on the communicator.

X

The *X-factor* in all of your efforts to launch a new product is that the timing, messaging, and targeting is in the control of the communicator. It is an advantage that can be leveraged but one time, so execution of the strategic communications plan needs to be flawless. The start of the launch effort is probably the final piece the communicator can control. Once the information you disseminate reaches its target audience, the perceptions for your product will be shaped by others. That being said, the communicator shouldn't just sit on his or her hands and watch the world pontificate about the new product. Be proactive; reach out to target audiences to determine if your messages are resonating and that there's an understanding regarding the product's significance. Follow-up can make a difference in coverage that is perfunctory and coverage that is perfection. The latter outcome is possible only through hard work.

Y

While the first moments of a new product's launch are critical toward establishing its ultimate acceptance and success, supporting a product's marketplace introduction should be a *year-round* effort. Products go through seasonal cycles, when prescriptions or buying habits fluctuate. A communications plan should be designed to take these patterns into consideration. Your communications plan and the product's marketing strategy will determine how your tactical approach should adapt to these realities. You will find, however, that a constant flow of information and "noise" about your product will help more than hurt over the long run. There is plenty of competition for the attention of consumers and physicians. Keeping their attention beyond the launch will help maintain the momentum achieved on day one.

Z

It is important to know the difference between a being a product advocate and a *zealot*. The last thing a product communicator wants is to be perceived as a "flak," a pejorative term used to describe an overzealous public relations professional. Reporters, bloggers, and tweeters expect you to be a resource for information about a new product, not a salesman. The product's "newness" dictates that an expert be available 24/7 to provide information and answer questions; that's the job of the communicator. Accept this role and execute it with diplomacy, courtesy, and professionalism.

Summary

Corporate communications professionals play a significant role within the pharmaceutical industry in bringing new products to the market. Therefore, it is critical for communicators to gain a basic understanding of the terms and phrases used within the industry. Additionally, communicators should develop an understanding of needed skills beyond the scope of communications, as well as how to leverage internal experts, to succeed. This chapter provides an easy-to-use *A* to *Z* guide for the pharmaceutical communications professional who is challenged with bringing a new pharmaceutical product to the marketplace.

Discussion Questions

1. List the pharmaceutical communications specialist's key audiences. Which audience is the most important, and why? Which audience is the most overlooked, and why?
2. Differentiate between a *first compound* and a *follow-on compound*. Explain the communications approach for each.
3. Who are the key business partners for the communications specialist? Describe how communicators benefit from developing positive relationships with these internal experts.
4. What skills, outside of the communications field, must a communications professional possess in order to be successful within the pharmaceutical industry? Why are these skills important?
5. How has the Web changed the way communicators target media?

Chapter 10

Plan for Your Health: A Public Education Campaign to Build Awareness and Gain Consumer Preference

By Jill Griffiths, Elizabeth Sell, and Katherine Lee Balsamo

LEARNING OBJECTIVES

By the end of the chapter, the reader will be able to:

- Understand how marketing research can unearth insights into consumer behavior and lay the foundation for long-term strategic communication plans.
- Discuss how to create win-win scenarios by properly aligning with strategic partners to bolster reach of campaign messages.
- Leverage survey data, events, and spokespersons to pique key media interest and increase visibility of public education campaigns.
- Recognize how public education and health communication campaigns need to evolve and adapt over time to remain relevant to target audiences.

Introduction

This chapter will examine a multiyear public education campaign implemented by Aetna to educate consumers about health benefits and financial planning, and help them get the most value from their health plans. Specific initiatives will be highlighted in the *Plan for Your Health* case study, some of which are broad in terms of target audience, and others that appeal to specific niche populations.

What was the rationale for creating *Plan for Your Health*? Simply put, the world of health insurance is a complex one, and many consumers openly admit to being confused when it comes to their health benefits. Adding to their uncertainty are employers who may change the health benefit options they offer their employees annually, and the recent growth of "consumer-directed" health plans, which transfer more responsibility for managing one's health benefits and related spending to the consumer. A combination of these factors fueled Aetna's desire to educate consumers.

In fact, Aetna saw an opportunity to become a "first mover" in the industry by helping consumers understand health benefits, and see the connections between health benefits and financial planning. The company conducted foundational research in the form of a consumer survey among women, the primary decision makers on healthcare issues, to confirm the need for a greater understanding of health- and financial-benefits knowledge.

Based on the results of the survey, Aetna partnered with the Financial Planning Association (FPA) to launch *Plan for Your Health*, with the Web site www.PlanforYourHealth.com as the centerpiece of the campaign. Aetna and FPA selected a celebrity spokesperson to help add sizzle, and executed a media relations strategy to build awareness of the initiative.

The site contained general information on health benefits, such as a glossary of health insurance-related terms, and useful tools to help consumers make the most of their health plan. One of the most important components of the educational campaign was the organization of the Web site by "life stage." Pages were designed specifically for people graduating college and entering the work force, getting married, having a baby, becoming single again, and retiring. These different phases of life are pivotal moments when health benefits should be considered and possibly changed.

Plan for Your Health launched in 2004 during the fall open enrollment season, when many companies allow their employees to change their health benefits plan. Then, each year, the *Plan for Your Health* campaign was "refreshed" with a new theme or focus, and often an additional audience was layered on; the "all about the benefits" campaign (and the targeted Web site, www.allaboutthebenefits.com), for example, was aimed at "young immortals" just entering the work force.

Since its launch, *Plan for Your Health* has established itself as the best online source for health benefits knowledge. Part of the success is due to a solid educational campaign built on extensive, straightforward information on maximizing one's health benefits. Each year, the campaign stayed fresh thanks to new, practical information that was made available to consumers. Most recently, the 2009 campaign offered tips on getting the most value from one's health plan during a slow economy.

The site continues to flourish and will evolve to keep pace with the changing needs of consumers. *Plan for Your Health's* original mission—helping consumers get the most from their health benefits—will remain the campaign's primary goal.

The Challenge: Demystifying a Complex Industry

Ask a consumer if having health insurance is important, and the likely response is a resounding yes. However, most people acknowledge they don't fully understand their health insurance plan. In fact, according to the Institute of Medicine (2004), 90 million Americans have difficulty understanding and using health information, and that difficulty extends to their health benefits.

Evidence that consumer confusion exists is supported by the following common remarks:

"I don't read the fine print."
"I just pick the benefits I had last year."
"If only I understood my plan, I wouldn't feel so powerless."

The lack of understanding in 2004 may have been due in part to the increased growth of new consumer-directed plans that employers had begun offering to employees, adding to the need for greater education. When Aetna (2004) surveyed consumers, the company learned that while the majority of respondents said their health plan is a very important element of their future financial well-being, a significant number admitted they spent more time researching a vacation or buying a car than choosing health benefits.

On this premise, Aetna decided it was time to help consumers understand—and maximize—their health benefits. An opportunity existed for Aetna to become a first mover in the educational space to improve health benefits literacy and make the connection between health benefits and financial health. The campaign platform was established, which would allow Aetna to differentiate itself in the health plan marketplace. The "sweet spot" between the realms of health and finance, and anchored by consumer centricity, became the driving positioning of the *Plan for Your Health* campaign, as depicted in Figure 10-1.

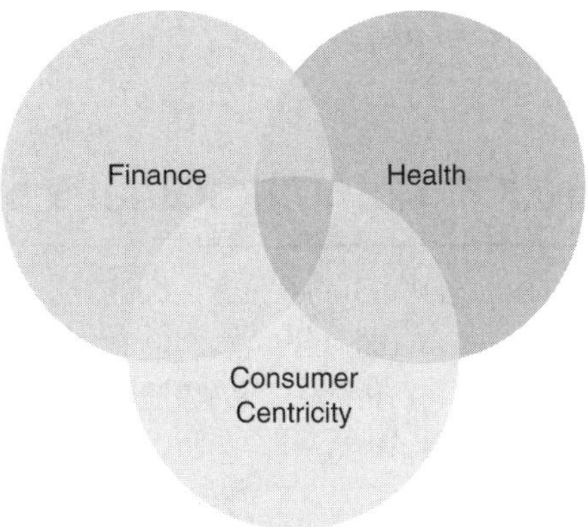

Figure 10-1 The Campaign's "Sweet Spot" Positioning

But *how* does a company go about demystifying something as complex as health insurance? So many different kinds of health benefits plans exist, especially with the recent proliferation of consumer-directed health plans (those that combine a fund for healthcare expenses with an underlying health insurance plan).

Add to that the language: The jargon common among health insurance plans may as well be its own language. The average person can have a difficult time discerning between a point-of-service (POS) plan and a preferred provider organization (PPO) plan or how a health savings account (HSA) differs from a flexible spending account (FSA).

The Mission: Demonstrate the Value of Understanding Health Benefits

Acknowledging the potential for consumer confusion, Aetna decided to pursue a campaign to enlighten consumers on health benefits. The goal was defined: Empower consumers, especially women, to understand their health benefits options. Once they understand their benefits, they will be able to make the best use of them and maximize the value that their health benefits offer. An additional objective was to help people understand how health benefits are an integral part of one's financial portfolio.

To accomplish this goal, it would be important to make health benefits interesting and relevant to the consumer, and to educate people on the basic workings of health insurance.

There was an advantage to Aetna as well. If Aetna could create this awareness, and become known for helping people get the most value from their health plan, it would help strengthen brand preference. Being the industry educator could help differentiate the company and sway more women, who typically make healthcare decisions for themselves and their entire families, toward choosing Aetna.

Clearly, making the world of health benefits accessible and understandable to consumers would be a win-win situation. Consumers would come to understand their health benefits, for which they pay good money. Plus, Aetna would enhance its reputation as a company that makes the effort to help consumers derive the most value from their health benefits plans.

The Plan of Attack (a.k.a. Communications Strategy)

The goal had been defined. The target audience was identified. What needed to happen next was the "how" of the effort. What strategy could make this vision a reality? First, the company needed an agency that could help develop and implement an action plan.

Aetna created a request for proposal (RFP) and sent it to leading public relations agencies in the healthcare arena. After reviewing numerous submissions, Aetna narrowed the field to three agencies, eventually selecting Ketchum Public Relations as the agency to help create the campaign strategy and implement the consumer education campaign.

Adding Credibility: Selecting a Third-Party Partner

Because Aetna sought to create a true public education campaign, it was decided that the effort should be a joint initiative with a third-party partner. There would be no attempts to market or sell Aetna's plans or products as part of the initiative, so it made sense to work with another like-minded organization whose leadership saw value in helping consumers gain an understanding of health benefits. Working with a third-party organization also diminished the likelihood that the campaign might be perceived as marketing.

Numerous organizations were considered. Ketchum narrowed the search and received interest from the Financial Planning Association(FPA, see Figure 10-2). Like Aetna, FPA advocated for consumer understanding of health benefits, as well as benefits in general, as a part of their financial portfolio. Together, Aetna and FPA could launch a campaign to help consumers, especially women, make well-informed choices to protect their health and their finances now and well into the future.

Consumer Survey to Gauge Health Benefits Literacy

The next step was quantifying the problem. What was the average consumer's baseline of knowledge? Aetna needed to measure just how much consumers already knew about health benefits before refining and launching the joint campaign with FPA. Responses from a survey would give insight about consumers and their understanding of health insurance choices. The hope was that the survey findings also would provide a compelling news hook upon which to launch the campaign.

Figure 10-2 Aetna chose the Financial Planning Association to co-launch its campaign.
Courtesy of Financial Planning Association

Aetna and FPA worked with a respected online research company to conduct a national survey of women ages 24–44 who had health insurance. The women were surveyed about the type of coverage they had and their awareness and knowledge of health benefits choices. The women also were asked about researching and choosing health plans, and their overall satisfaction with health plans.

Survey Says...There's a Need for Consumer Education!

The survey results were revealing. Data showed that many women did not know even basic information regarding their health insurance plan (35% were not at all or somewhat knowledgeable) (Aetna, 2004). Even though almost all women (81%) who were offered a choice in health plans said they researched the plans, the majority (60%) of them reported spending no time to less than 2 hours learning about their health insurance options.

Additionally, more than half of respondents said they faced a challenge in selecting their plan, saying that the information available was confusing or hard to understand. Despite this lack of understanding, 63% of women said their health insurance plan was a very important element of ensuring their future financial well-being, above 401(k) plans or life insurance.

These findings provided the perfect platform to launch a campaign. In other words, the need for public education about health benefits was crystallized. As such, the survey results proved to be the central media hook for the campaign's announcement.

Why would the news hook work? It was the perfect "problem/solution" setup. Aetna and FPA identified a problem: a lack of public understanding about health benefits. And together, the two organizations created the solution: an easy-to-use Web site that offered practical information and handy tools to help people understand and make the most of their health benefits.

PlanforYourHealth.com Launch

In September 2004, Aetna and the Financial Planning Association launched the *Plan for Your Health* campaign, with the Web site www.PlanforYourHealth.com as its focal point. The campaign was announced as a response to survey results that had identified that more than half of women surveyed faced challenges in making health benefits decisions. While nearly two-thirds of women were responsible for family healthcare decision, 35% did not know basic information about health benefits.

The Life Stages Approach: "Reachable, Teachable Moments"

In devising the best way to organize the site's content, Aetna worked closely with Ketchum on a focused Web strategy. After much discussion, the two organizations decided to take a "life stage approach."

What does that mean? People have different health benefits needs at critical times in their life. For example, someone who is newly married has to decide whether to maintain his or her own health insurance or go on his or her spouse's plan. A couple with a new baby faces considerations about insuring the newest member of their family, and if it's their first child, they have to move to a "family plan." There are also issues specific to critical life events, like retirement, entering or graduating from college, losing a spouse to death or divorce, and so on.

Essentially, planning for health benefits at pivotal moments in life can significantly impact financial health. And, women are more likely to pay attention to health benefits information at these specific moments in time when it is relevant to their lives. Therefore, categorizing the Web content by life stage would ensure the most consumer-friendly means to communicate its content.

A One-Stop Shop: What to Include on the Site

How do you boil down the health insurance industry into an easy-to-navigate site that helps people understand their health benefits? What kinds of material do you include? How do you demonstrate the intersection of health benefits and finances?

The life stages approach was essential to the site's navigation strategy. The goal was to make the information as digestible as possible to the right people at the right time in their life. Consumers had many questions, and there was a general lack of knowledge. It also was clear that very few people understood all the industry jargon that was used in the world of health insurance.

One important piece of the site that was developed was the glossary—an entire listing of commonly used health and financial benefits terms with clear, plain-language definitions. These terms were organized in alphabetical order; each week a "term of the week" was highlighted on the home page of PlanforYourHealth.com, and the terms were hyperlinked to articles throughout the site.

The site also included a rotating feature story on the front page, tied to the life stage approach. Additionally, visitors to PlanforYourHealth.com could access a Q&A section with commonly asked questions about health insurance, as well as two interactive tools to help people figure out how important life changes will affect their health benefits options.

Because the goal of the site was to help guide consumers through important health benefits choices that could impact their financial futures, it made sense to provide tips on navigating health benefits in relation to overall financial well-being. Additionally, the campaign provided information to help women choose the best health benefits options for themselves and their families.

A logo with a tagline was developed to encapsulate the site's mission: "Plan for Your Health: Your best online source for health benefits knowledge."

Adding Sizzle: Choosing a Celebrity Spokesperson

As part of the launch, Aetna and FPA sought a celebrity spokesperson to strengthen the campaign. The ideal person? Someone accepted by consumers as an expert in the financial field, and someone respected by the target audience.

The answer turned out to be Neale Godfrey, bestselling financial advice author and financial consultant. She endorsed the mission of *Plan for Your Health*, encouraging women to invest time in their health benefits decisions, just as they would any other financial choice. As part of the launch, Ms. Godfrey stated:

> *We want to empower women at all stages of life to take control of their health benefits and financial decisions. The tools and information provided by* Plan for Your Health *will be helpful to anyone who is interested in better understanding their health benefits decisions (Aetna, 2004).*

Ms. Godfrey's support of the program, coupled with the endorsement of FPA, represented at the launch by Elizabeth Jetton, CERTIFIED FINANCIAL PLANNER™ professional (CFP®) and then-FPA president, helped bring greater media attention and credibility to the campaign.

Getting Ink: Hosting a Media Event

To generate targeted media coverage of the launch, the *Plan for Your Health* team hosted a media event in New York City. The timing was just prior to the launch to allow journalists, many from leading monthly women's interest magazines, to get a sneak peek at the survey results.

Approximately a dozen writers and editors attended the luncheon event, where Aetna presented the survey results. Both Neale Godfrey, celebrity endorser, and Elizabeth Jetton, CFP and then-FPA president, shared insights on the problem at hand. Cheryl Pegus, MD, then-Aetna medical director, spoke about the importance of understanding one's health benefits. Aetna then unveiled the *Plan for Your Health* campaign, showing the PlanforYourHealth.com Web site as the campaign's centerpiece.

Not only did the event lead to stories about the initiative, it also cultivated relationships with key reporters and editors who could follow the life of the campaign moving forward.

Timing Is Everything

The launch of *Plan for Your Health* immediately preceded the time known as open enrollment, the once-a-year opportunity when many US employers allow their employees to change their benefits plans. The idea was to educate people—bring them up to speed on health benefits—so they could make an informed choice on a health plan. The secondary goal was to generate as much coverage in consumer media outlets, when employees across the country were being asked to choose their plan, to drive brand preference for Aetna.

Reaching Consumers: The Results

At the end of the first year, the campaign had generated 401 million media impressions and driven 234,500 visits to PlanforYourHealth.com. Aetna also surveyed its employer customers, and noted similar success. In fact, 50% to 60% of all employer customers had a more positive view of Aetna after the campaign.

Keeping It Fresh

Year Two was upon the *Plan for Your Health* team. What could be done with the campaign in 2005 that was new and different to infuse new life into the effort? The company wanted a differentiating campaign to further the goal of educating consumers, while strengthening Aetna's leadership in healthcare consumerism.

With the help of Ketchum's guidance and FPA's willingness to go in a new direction, Aetna decided to continue pursuing a life stage approach in Year Two, with a focus on the milestone of having a baby. So, for the first part of the second year of the campaign, the focus turned to new parents, and "Bringing Home Baby" was born. The new campaign would target women and couples who were expecting or about to adopt, or who had just welcomed a new baby (or multiple babies) into their lives.

Baby-Proofing Your Benefits

One element of the Bringing Home Baby campaign was the announcement of results from a new consumer survey. As with the launch of *Plan for Your Health*, the survey findings provided a platform from which to address a problem and offer a solution to consumers. In the survey Aetna and FPA found that researching the health benefits needs for one's expanding family is a task that often falls to the bottom of consumers' to-do list (Aetna, 2005a).

Furthermore, 44% of expectant mothers reported that they had not created a new family budget to include expenses related to having a new baby. Even those moms who had taken the time to prepare a new budget had overlooked the cost of health benefits, and almost half had neglected to include the cost of noncovered medical expenses.

The press release on the new Bringing Home Baby initiative quoted pediatrician Marjorie Schulman, MD, a senior medical director at Aetna. The release also quoted then-president of FPA, Elizabeth Jetton, CFP professional. Both individuals' quotes enhanced the credibility of the campaign. To inject further expertise, Aetna and FPA engaged mother and daughter Sandy and Marcie Jones, co-authors of the book *Great Expectations: Your All-in-One Resource for Pregnancy and Childbirth*.

New content was developed for the Web site, including the following:

- The Baby Expense Calculator, to help expectant parents estimate the cost of pregnancy and their new baby in the first year
- Tips for finding and interviewing a pediatrician
- Expectant family, and adoptive family, health benefits and financial checklists
- Common questions asked by expectant parents

Market-Specific Events to Help Drive Awareness

To add a new element in year two of the campaign, Aetna and FPA planned consumer public relations events in Philadelphia and Dallas. The summer events took place at major metropolitan hospitals and included the celebrity author referenced above, Dr. Sandy Jones; a local representative from FPA; Aetna's Dr. Schulman; an Ob/Gyn from the hospital; and a local media celebrity.

Local women and couples expecting a baby were invited to the informational session to hear from the experts. The events helped draw attention to the new initiative, both through consumer attendance and media coverage.

Readying for Retirement

With the arrival of fall, the campaign shifted gears to a new life stage—that of retirees. A new campaign on planning for retirement was launched. Based on past success, Aetna and FPA once again teamed up with a third-party organization with similar goals. For the retirement campaign, the partner chosen was Women's Policy, Inc. (WPI), a nonprofit organization that champions the interests of women on significant social, economic, and health issues.

To launch "Planning for a Healthy Retirement," Aetna and FPA once again conducted a survey to gauge how prepared women were for retirement. Results showed a significant lack of planning for health care or health benefits in retirement. The findings were announced at a Capitol Hill briefing in conjunction with WPI. Speakers included two influential members of Congress, as well as Dexanne Clohan, MD, then-national medical director for Aetna, and FPA's Jonathan Guyton, a specialist in retirement planning.

Survey Says...Retirement Planning Needs Improvement

The *Plan for Your Health* retirement survey showed that of Americans ages 45–75, nearly 20% spent no time in the past year actively planning for retirement, and more than 30%

didn't know what to anticipate for healthcare needs (Aetna, 2005). To help gain media interest in the survey, Aetna included a humorous statistic in the press release: "Thirty-one percent of preretirees would rather clean their bathrooms or pay bills than plan for retirement" (Aetna, 2005b).

In response to the survey, Aetna and FPA expanded the *Plan for Your Health* Web site, adding tools, tips, and content to provide a framework for planning a healthy and financially secure retirement. A new interactive tool called the Healthy Retirement Readiness Tool was featured on the site. It assessed where preretirees and retirees stood in the planning process, matched advice to their current level of retirement planning, and offered realistic next steps. It also directed users to vignettes about people in similar life stages, adding personal perspective to all levels of retirement planning.

Reality Check: Is the Campaign Meeting Real Women's Needs?

In early 2006, following what appeared to be two successful years of the campaign, Aetna sought to confirm that the *Plan for Your Health* public education campaign was making the right impact on the correct target audiences. Thus, the Real Women Panel was born, with the overriding goal of creating a panel of real women to discuss their personal perceptions and challenges with health benefits. The panel met quarterly and meetings were held virtually, making it easy for Aetna to ask for further information from the women as they provided their responses.

Not only would this gauge how well the campaign had been performing up to this point; it also would provide input to develop future initiatives that would be meaningful to consumers. The findings proved to be very useful. New information was obtained, which helped lead to recommendations for future campaign ideas. One specific idea that resulted from the panel, for example, was the creation of e-mail newsletters. The women suggested that they would like information about open enrollment or a reminder about sending in receipts for flexible spending accounts, and so on. Overall, the research group proved to be helpful in informing the campaign's direction.

Helping People Prepare for Disasters

As part of Year Three of the campaign, a new focus was placed on disaster preparedness. Numerous natural disasters had been in the news, and they provided an opportunity to help consumers be more prepared to handle any issues relating to health and financial benefits should a disaster strike. In response, new content was developed for PlanforYourHealth.com to highlight the importance of being prepared. The site offered practical tips on what to do in advance and how to get necessary medical coverage and manage health benefits following a disaster.

Pursuing a New Audience: Reaching "Young Immortals"

In 2005, the campaign targeted new parents, and then retirees. In 2006, an additional audience was identified as a key population who needed education about benefits. *Plan for Your Health* began to focus specifically on "young immortals," a common term for people in their late teens or early 20s who have recently graduated high school or college and are on their way to the workforce. A new campaign targeting this youthful audience, as well as their parents, took shape. It was called "all about the benefits."

Given the effort to reach young immortals, Aetna needed a new site with a completely different URL. The site, www.allaboutthebenefits.com, was created to help young adults figure out what they need to know about health benefits as they transition from school to "the real world."

The site was designed with a more hip look and gave information to visitors on bridging from a parent's family health plan to one of their own. It also suggested questions to ask about health benefits on a job interview. Like PlanforYourHealth.com, the site also helped young immortals understand health insurance lingo, make sense of health benefits options, and budget for health expenses.

For a new twist, allaboutthebenefits.com provided entertaining, humorous videos, as well as a podcast—two ways of reaching this audience in a way they prefer. The experts must have agreed with the approach; the program and the Web site won four industry awards.

Engaging Consumers Through the *For Dummies*® Brand

For the open enrollment season, Aetna and FPA wanted a new, fun vehicle to help Americans become smarter about their health benefits. One idea was to develop a custom *For Dummies*® guide, in conjunction with Wiley Publishing, that would explain health benefits in the consumer-friendly format that the well-known *For Dummies* brand is known for.

Given how different an approach this was for Aetna, a significant amount of research was undertaken to assure there was a brand fit. At the time, the *For Dummies* brand had 70% awareness among adults, and there were 125 million *For Dummies* books in print. *For Dummies* reference books are written for people who find the technical complexities of topics from computers and cooking to health benefits overwhelming, and they want clear, easy-to-understand information. It was agreed that creating a customer guide about health benefits would be a good strategy, and *Navigating Your Health Benefits For Dummies*® was born.

The custom booklet was the first *For Dummies* guide to offer the general public a way to make informed decisions about health benefits. The 64-page guide was a hard-copy resource available free to consumers on PlanforYourHealth.com. The content was designed to help readers navigate every step of their health benefits cycle, from choosing a plan to appealing claims decisions and taking advantage of discount opportunities.

Co-authored by Aetna's then-national medical director Charles Cutler, MD, and Tracey Baker, CFP professional and former chair of FPA's National Capital Area Chapter, the guide took the guesswork out of what can be a confusing process. The approach didn't talk down to readers, but rather used simple language and a healthy dose of humor to explain health benefits in a compelling, easy-to-understand manner.

Since 2006, more than 250,000 copies of the guide have been distributed to consumers and Aetna's employer customers. The guide was honored with five industry awards.

Reaching Latinos

In 2007, the goal was to expand the campaign to the Latino population. To reach this important and growing audience, two initiatives were developed as the cornerstones of the campaign.

First, Aetna and FPA created a mirror site to PlanforYourHealth.com that was completely written in Spanish. The new site, PlanifiqueParaSuSalud.com, was a total "transcreation" of the original site. The goal was not merely to *translate* the language, but to *transcreate* it, that is, adapt the site in a meaningful way to make it relevant to the Latino population.

Second, the *For Dummies* guide, *Navigating Your Health Benefits For Dummies*, was transcreated into a Spanish version, *Guía de Beneficios de Salud Para Dummies.* Again, Aetna and FPA teamed up with Wiley Publishing to produce the guide. Aetna used Akorbi Language Consulting to transcreate the guide and assembled a team of Aetna Spanish-language experts to ensure that the Spanish version was not merely a translation of the English guide, but a true transcreation that provided meaningful information to the target audience.

Site Continues to Be Refreshed

In the midst of the specific initiatives, like the two mentioned above to reach Latinos, PlanforYourHealth.com continued to be refreshed on a regular basis to encourage repeat visits, as well as "stickiness" on the site. That is, when consumers visited the site, the hope was they would stay for a significant amount of time.

One of the more significant updates to the site in 2007 was the addition of material about personal health records (PHRs). The impetus for this topic actually came from Aetna's business, whose leadership was hearing that Aetna members did not grasp the full value of PHRs. In response, a three-story series with content focusing on PHRs was developed, with information on how to use and maximize a PHR. Thematically, the content also complemented the existing material about disaster preparedness, since one of the most important things one can do to be prepared for a disaster is to have a complete accounting of one's health history.

In the fall of 2007, more new content was added just in time for open enrollment. The new material featured tips for choosing a plan, and included the launch of the first "two-way conversation" with visitors to PlanforYourHealth.com. Consumers could submit a question and an Aetna or FPA expert would respond.

Helping the Uninsured

In 2008, the public education campaign pursued an exciting new direction: empowering underserved populations. The centerpiece program of 2008 was called "Insure Your Health," and was designed to raise awareness among the 11 million Americans who are eligible for SCHIP (State Children's Health Insurance Program) or Medicaid benefits, yet remain uninsured.

To accomplish this goal, Aetna and FPA worked closely with Magic Johnson Enterprises (MJE). Aetna had recently announced an alliance with MJE to target ethnically diverse communities to improve health literacy and encourage people to make informed choices about their healthcare options. Together, the parties produced a state-by-state guide to raise visibility of free and low-cost health insurance programs that are available to millions of Americans.

Launched during Cover the Uninsured Week, the *Plan for Your Health* team and Magic Johnson Enterprises kicked off a campaign to inform eligible Americans about these programs. The booklet, *Insure Your Health: A State-by-State Guide to Finding Free or Low-Cost Health Insurance Programs,* was offered for free at PlanforYourHealth.com or by calling a toll-free telephone number, and was also distributed at numerous community-based events. Electronic copies of the guide could be downloaded in English at the Web site, and were later offered in Spanish.

The campaign included a partnership with The Links, Inc., a women's organization committed to enriching, sustaining, and ensuring the cultural and economic survival of African-Americans. This organization provided information about *Insure Your Health* in their outreach to underserved communities. Also, the guide and additional *Plan for Your Health* material were distributed at a booth at The Links National Assembly, the group's annual conference.

The guide also was extensively promoted via earned media. Radio and transit (bus and train) public service announcements (PSAs) were also used to promote the guide in Los Angeles, Washington, D.C., and Atlanta. These PSAs featured Mr. Johnson encouraging listeners or viewers to order a copy of the guide for themselves.

The Insure Your Health campaign, which was honored with an industry award, used data from a national survey to shape and announce the program. Two particularly interesting statistics included:

> *More than three-quarters of respondents (78%) said that although they were currently uninsured, they felt that it's important to have health insurance.*
>
> *Over one-third of respondents (37%) felt that their lack of health insurance had worsened their health (Aetna, 2008).*

Helping Latinos Talk with Their Doctor

In the summer of 2008, the *Plan for Your Health* campaign focused on Latinos again, this time with a new initiative to help this population communicate better with doctors. With 21 million Americans having limited proficiency in English, the goal was to help Spanish-speaking Americans get the most out of a visit to the doctor. The information was posted on PlanifiqueParaSuSalud.com and in English on PlanforYourHealth.com.

The campaign was called "Hable con su Médico" ("Talking to your Doctor") and was developed to help improve doctor–patient communication through guidelines on how to take control of one's health (Figure 10-3).

Make your doctor visits more successful

Prepare

- Ask if your doctor speaks Spanish or bring a translator to the visit.
- Write down the medicines you take, or bring them with you.
- Make a list of questions.
- Bring your insurance card.

Share

- Know your family's medical history.
- Mention recent changes in your health.

Visit **www.PlanforYourHealth.com.**

Ask

- If you don't understand, ask.
- Find out if your insurance covers what your doctor recommends.

Act

- Take notes during your appointment.
- Follow the doctor's instructions.
- Learn to eat healthy, drink a lot of water and exercise every day.

Visit **www.PlanforYourHealth.com.**

20.31.329.1 A (10/10)

Figure 10-3 The campaign included wallet-sized cards with tips for talking to your doctor. "Plan for Your Health: A Public Edudcation Campaign to Build Awareness and Gain Consumer Preference" © 2010 Aetna. Reproduced with permission from Aetna Inc.

The summary version (in English) of the tips follows:

- **Prepare**: Helpful tips on getting ready for your next visit to the doctor
- **Share**: How to share health-related information that is important to tell your doctor
- **Ask**: Advice on important questions to ask your doctor
- **Act**: Suggestions on ways to follow your doctor's recommendations and improve your overall health

The overall premise? Better communication with one's doctor can lead to better health. The campaign was recognized with two industry awards.

Weathering the Tough Economy

At the time of open enrollment 2008, the US economy was in a deep recession. To help consumers, many of whom had lost their jobs, weather the economy, *Plan for Your Health* focused on helping Americans save money on their health. The premise was that by making the most of one's health benefits, and making smart decisions in open enrollment and throughout the year, a consumer could maximize the value of his or her health plan.

New content was developed for PlanforYourHealth.com. The feature story acknowledged that people were cutting costs everywhere possible, including clipping more coupons and taking fewer vacations. Yet what many people *didn't* know is that their health benefits could *also* save them money. By taking a few small steps, it was possible to put thousands of dollars back into one's bank account. The site then offered practical tips for stretching one's healthcare dollars.

At this time, Aetna "refreshed" the look of the PlanforYourHealth.com site to help consumers find tips, tools, and information even more quickly and easily. The new design featured a "Life Stage Spotlight," which rotated content to showcase the different life stages—career, marriage, family, living single, and retirement.

Continuing the Economy Theme with a Refreshed *For Dummies* Guide

As the economy continued to soften into 2009, Aetna and FPA determined that the campaign should maintain a focus on the economy. They decided that a refreshed version of *Navigating Your Health Benefits For Dummies* would be the perfect tool to share new money-saving tips with consumers. So Aetna and FPA again teamed up with Wiley Publishing to release an updated version of the free consumer guide.

Aetna medical director Wendy A. Richards, MD, was chosen to be the new co-author along with FPA member Tracey Baker, CFP professional, for *Navigating Your Health Benefits For*

Dummies, 2nd Edition. The handy guide was revised significantly, with a new chapter on maximizing health benefits at the beginning of the booklet.

Following huge consumer demand for the first edition published in 2006, the second edition was designed to be even more helpful to consumers, with easy-to-understand tips on everything from how to navigate health benefits after a layoff to how to make the most of benefits in a down economy. It even included a tear-out page with "Ten Money-Saving Tips," and a brief introduction from Magic Johnson.

Why *Plan for Your Health* Worked: Momentum from Inception to Today

The campaign has been considered successful by both Aetna and FPA. Not only did several specific initiatives within the overall campaign win awards, the overall campaign was honored with four prestigious industry awards from three separate organizations. These awards included:

- A PRSA Bronze Anvil
- A SABRE Award (The Holmes Report)
- A Thoth Award (PRSA National Capitol Chapter)
- A Finalist and Award of Excellence in the PRSA Silver Anvils

As of April 2010, the campaign has generated 1.986 billion consumer media impressions since the launch in fall 2004.

What made *Plan for Your Health* successful was a carefully crafted, long-term strategic approach to educating consumers. The timeline below depicts each phase of the campaign, showing the growth and expansion of the campaign over time.

Year One: Gauging health benefits literacy. The initial survey provided the platform, clearly demonstrating a need for better consumer understanding of health benefits.

Year Two: Impact of life events on health benefits. A life-stage approach—the "Reachable, Teachable Moments" strategy—was implemented, featuring information on how health benefits needs change at pivotal moments in life.

Year Three: Evolution from awareness to action. The campaign helped people prepare for disasters, engaged young immortals, and provided a free *For Dummies* guide to help consumers make the best decisions about health benefits.

Year Four: Educate and activate targeted populations. Campaign materials were transcreated into Spanish including the Web site as well as the *For Dummies* guide.

Year Five: Empower underserved populations. *Plan for Your Health* published *Insure Your Health,* a free guide to help uninsured Americans access free or low-cost health coverage. An initiative to help Spanish-speaking consumers get the most out of their doctor's visit was also completed.

Year Six: Maximizing benefits in a challenging economy. The well-received *Navigating Your Health Benefits For Dummies* guide was republished as a second edition, with a new focus on money-saving measures to maximize health benefits in a tough economy.

The Evolution of *Plan for Your Health* and Looking Ahead

Consumer feedback over the first 6 years of the campaign has reinforced the key tenets of the program. There continues to be interest in general information on the Web site, such as the glossary and the content that simplifies various aspects of health benefits. Consumers also remain interested in changing insurance options, such as COBRA and individual health plans, both of which will continue to evolve as healthcare reform, enacted in 2010, is implemented.

In terms of timing, both consumers and the media continue to be very interested in the topic of health benefits during the fall open enrollment season. As a result, the campaign will continue to leverage this moment in time to launch new initiatives and Web site content.

Linking Health Benefits Literacy to Health Literacy

During the campaign, such elements as the "Hable con su Médico" content related more to *health* literacy than to *health benefits* literacy. Health literacy is defined as "the degree to which individuals have the capacity to obtain, process, and understand basic health information and services needed to make appropriate health decisions" (US Department of Health and Human Services, 2000). Aetna increasingly focuses on health literacy and is at the forefront of health insurers in terms of working to communicate with members in plain language. Health literacy will become a more integral component of *Plan for Your Health* in the future.

Adapting for the Future

Looking ahead, the campaign will need to evolve and adjust to keep pace with the changing needs of consumers. The Web site will need to be reconfigured to remain relevant in an ever-changing world. Also, Aetna will need to adapt the means of outreach in order to accommodate new media. Yet, the overarching mission—helping consumers get the most from their health benefits—will remain the campaign's primary goal.

Summary

In 2004, Aetna set out to create greater consumer understanding of health and financial benefits. The company teamed up with the Financial Planning Association to launch a multiyear public education campaign called *Plan for Your Health*. The centerpiece of the campaign, the Web site www.PlanforYourHealth.com, was developed to help people make smart health benefits and financial planning decisions.

Directed primarily at women, the campaign was designed to reach consumers at different life stages—those pivotal times when health benefits needs may change. Therefore, content revolved around health benefits needs when getting married, having a baby, graduating from college, getting divorced or becoming widowed, and retiring. The site also contained general information on health benefits, such as a glossary of health insurance-related terms and useful tools to help consumers make the most of their health plan.

Each year, the campaign was refreshed to target specific life stages, and new initiatives were launched to help consumers get the most value from their health benefits.

Discussion Questions

1. Why did Aetna and FPA launch the *Plan for Your Health* campaign in the month of September? Discuss why the timing was optimal from a business perspective.
2. What was the rationale for the life stages approach on the Web site? Discuss two of the life stages that became specific initiatives within the overall campaign.
3. Who is the campaign's primary target audience and why?
4. What was the news hook used in the initial campaign launch? Was this tool used later in the campaign?
5. Provide an example of a campaign "refresh" from one year to the next.
6. How did Aetna and FPA ensure they were providing the right kind of information on their site, that is, information that consumers really wanted to learn?
7. What new and different communications vehicles did the campaign incorporate into the "all about the benefits" campaign?
8. Discuss the communications vehicle used to help uninsured consumers learn about free or low-cost healthcare options.
9. What elements did the campaign add in order to appeal to Spanish-speaking consumers?
10. Talk about the dynamics of the campaign's lifecycle. How did the campaign evolve from Year One to Year Six?

References

Aetna. (September 22, 2004). National survey finds more than one-half of women face challenges in making health benefits decisions, prompting experts to find solutions [Press release]. Available at: http://www.planforyourhealth.com/misc/prarchive. Accessed: May 18, 2011.

Aetna. (July 13, 2005a). Have you baby-proofed your benefits? [Press release]. Available at: http://www.planforyourhealth.com/resources/bringhomebaby.pdf. Accessed: May 18, 2011.

Aetna Inc. (October 20, 2005b). New national survey shows lack of planning for health care or health benefits in retirement [Press release]. Available at: http://www.planforyourhealth.com/resources/finalretirement.pdf. Accessed: May 18, 2011.

Aetna. (April 28, 2008). Plan for Your Health and Magic Johnson Enterprises help uninsured Americans take the first step to better health [Press release]. Available at: http://www.aetna.com/news/newsReleases/2008/0428.html. Accessed: May 18, 2011.

Institute of Medicine. (2004). *Health literacy: A prescription to end confusion*. Washington, DC: The National Academies Press.

US Department of Health and Human Services (2000). *Healthy People 2010: Understanding and improving health* (2nd ed.). Washington, DC: U.S. Government Printing Office.

Chapter 11

"It's All Coming Together" –Communications Strategy for the Medicare Part D National Education and Enrollment Campaign

By Kathleen Harrington and Jeff Nelligan

LEARNING OBJECTIVES

By the end of this chapter, the reader will be able to:

- Describe a national campaign with local execution and provide examples of how a campaign can be led by headquarters, but implemented by regional staff.
- Understand the importance of building strong organizational partnerships to provide additional communication channels to reach a target audience.
- Describe the multiple channels and materials of a successful national education and enrollment campaign.
- Differentiate between earned media and paid media.
- Describe the benefit of local earned media vs. national coverage for an education and enrollment campaign.
- Appreciate the need for simultaneous development of program elements to maximize a short time frame.

Introduction

What kind of initiative seeks to and succeeds in enrolling 37 million individuals, spread throughout a vast nation, in a program affecting a sensitive and personal matter—health—and 6 months into its inception, gains an 80% satisfaction rate in polling done by the prestigious Kaiser Family Foundation?

The Medicare Part D national education and enrollment campaign.

This chapter explores the strategies and tactics contributing to the success of the national education and enrollment campaign, including the importance of building strong organizational partnerships and the critical role of national and local earned media.

Background–A Program Without Precedent

After intense congressional debate regarding the design and delivery of the drug benefit, the Medicare Prescription Drug, Improvement, and Modernization Act of 2003 (MMA) was signed into law in November 2003. The effort to provide prescription drug coverage to 37 million Medicare beneficiaries was vast in scope and involved approaches that were entirely new to Medicare. The new program would rely on the private sector offering stand-alone drug plans that would compete against themselves and be at risk for the costs of the benefit. There was little if any precedent in public sector for such a program, relying as it did on private-sector competition. Consequently, implementation of Medicare Part D involved many challenges for the federal government, state government partners, health plans, and beneficiaries.

Standard Benefit Design and...What Is a "Doughnut Hole"?

The statute outlined the standard benefit package while providing insurance companies the option of offering a modified benefit along with the standard benefit. The standard benefit design included an initial deductible of $250 in 2006, a monthly premium, a co-pay of 25% on drug costs up to an initial coverage limit of $2250. At that point, beneficiaries were responsible for paying the entire cost of their drugs until they reached $3600 in out-of-pocket costs. This coverage gap, which soon came to be known as the "doughnut hole" added another level of confusion for beneficiaries throughout the education campaign.

In addition, insurance company plans also had the option of creating their own benefit design for the standard coverage as long as the plans were actuarially equivalent, covering the same amount of drug costs on average. Plans took full advantage of the benefit design flexibility. For example, a majority of plans eliminated completely or in part the standard deductible, substituted flat co-payments for coinsurance and adopted tiered cost-sharing. There was substantial variation in drug plan designs with regards to choice and payment issues.

Negative Surround Sound–Sufficient Private-Sector Participation?

Initially there was much concern about insurance company participation or sufficient plan offerings. But that concern was quickly proven unnecessary. The engagement level of the private sector exceeded expectations, and beneficiaries had a wide choice of plans with considerable variation in terms of premiums charged, cost-sharing arrangements, availability and drugs, and various cost management tools. Sixty-five different organizations chose to participate in the prescription drug plan marketplace. Ten large insurance plan organizations participated in 34 regions covering all the states; other organizations participated in at least 30 of the 34 regions. Most of each participating organization offered three plan options in each region. When enrollment officially began, there were more than 1400 Part D plan options on a national basis. There were 15 to 20 organizations offering plans for a total of 40 to 45 plan options on average within each state.

Geography was another Part D variable. The MMA defined a competitive market structure resulting in private drug plans competing in 39 established regions. Each participating organization had to offer at least one plan in each area. In fact, most offered at least three.

Part D–Reality Is Where You Sit

Another complicating factor in implementation was the relationship of Part D to other existing prescription drug coverage plans. The choice of coverage for each individual was also dependent on their current prescription drug coverage. While most Medicare beneficiaries had no prescription drug coverage at all, some did have coverage through various means, each requiring some level of education and active decision to switch to Part D or stay in their current drug program.

For example, most beneficiaries with some form of retiree health coverage, which included prescription drugs, would be best served by maintaining that coverage. The same was true of individuals with VA or Tricare coverage. Dually eligible beneficiaries who were receiving prescription drug coverage from Medicaid were now required to switch to Part D plans. Autoenrollment, that is, CMS enrolling the beneficiary in a new plan, eased that situation, but it still created much confusion for beneficiaries. Beneficiaries currently enrolled in a Medicare Advantage plan that offered drug coverage might want to explore a stand-alone Part D plan depending on their current offering. Finally, individuals in a Medigap plan with prescription drug coverage had to evaluate offerings because prescription drug coverage would not be available in the future under Medigap. In other words, beneficiaries had to clearly understand their current situation to make an informed decision on Part D.

Extra Help–Low-Income Subsidy

The Low-Income Subsidy, or LIS, was financial assistance available to beneficiaries with incomes below 135% of the federal poverty level. The Social Security Administration, which engaged its massive field resources on this effort, was charged with the outreach and enrollment of eligible beneficiaries in the LIS program. CMS and SSA aligned campaigns to maximize all efforts and work to communicate with one voice to Medicare beneficiaries and those who cared for them about this extra financial assistance.

The program complexity compounded the communications challenge of educating the millions of Medicare beneficiaries, their families, the circles of community support, and networks of senior citizen services.

Timeline and Challenge

The final rule,for the Part D benefit, was published by the Secretary of Health and Human Services on January 28, 2005. In September of that year, contracts were signed with Part D providers and the information on individual plans became available to beneficiaries in October 2005. The enrollment period started on November 15, 2005, and ended on May 15, 2006. It was on this November start date that actual plan marketing could start. The Medicare public and the army of government and partner organizations we had engaged to assist people with Medicare could see the names of the insurance plans, the premiums, and the benefit designs—the many variables in choosing a new insurance product offered by the government.

Consider that CMS had less than 2 years—2004 and part of 2005—to implement a major new program, including the design, oversight, and enrollment into an unprecedented healthcare plan delivered by the private sector. While the government had some experience with private organizations from Medicare Advantage and its predecessor, Medicare+Choice, these programs were very limited and never enrolled more than one of six beneficiaries. Part D was directed at all Medicare beneficiaries. The tight time frame mandated that all parts of the program be developed simultaneously: operations, systems, regulatory, and communications. The logic of a test and refine model, whether it was with systems or messages, was a luxury the timeline prohibited. The challenge was enormous. All involved knew that the success of the Medicare drug benefit would ultimately be judged by the number of Medicare beneficiaries successfully enrolled and satisfied with their prescription drug coverage. Consumer engagement was essential for beneficiaries to make informed decisions.

The era of a consumer-centric Medicare program—rather than a program run top-down from Washington—had begun. This theme was and remains exceedingly important as reform of Medicare becomes inescapable and inexorable in any future political scenario.

The First Strategic Imperative: Build the People Infrastructure

The challenge of enrolling Medicare beneficiaries in the Part D plan that best suited their individual needs by the final enrollment day of May 15, 2006, loomed large. The political controversy surrounding the MMA and the Part D program in particular complicated the environment especially at the national level where major philosophical differences about the delivery model and cost of the new program continued to dominate the postenactment dialogue and news coverage. CMS's disappointing experience with the prescription drug discount card enrollment effort offered some key lessons and strategic direction for the Part D campaign.

This national environment and the prescription drug discount card experience guided us to the first and most important strategic imperative in our campaign planning: the campaign would be nationally defined but locally executed. Building one team—blending the headquarters and regional staff—to ensure mutual respect and harmony, maximum sharing of information, and leveraging of resources was very important part of the campaign communications strategy.

Headquarters provided the strategy, campaign targets, key messages, tools, collateral materials and training, and the 10 CMS regional offices were to develop local field operations tactics and partnerships to meet the unique needs and challenges of the communities they served. This was a significant and sometimes difficult cultural shift for the bureaucracy. The more active consumer facing role was relatively new for the agency. CMS had to develop a web of relationships with organizations that directly touched the lives of seniors and people with disabilities at the local level. To their credit, the regional staff quickly and successfully assumed the new responsibilities and a successful partnership between headquarters and the 10 regional offices quickly emerged.

The regional teams included a campaign manager, field operatives, media relations, and partner relationship managers. Teams met daily huddled in rooms covered with maps indicating key partners, target areas, and gaps in resources. Each region designed its field operations strategy, managed local media relations, developed strategies for all campaign assets, including the Medicare buses, and built the partnerships necessary to reach beneficiaries where "they live, work, play, and pray."

Local strategies were driven by locating and engaging sufficient partners to assist in education and enrollment activities. Measurement and reporting were essential elements of the campaign. Each team had to be data driven—identifying and training sufficient numbers of partners willing and capable to educate and/or enroll people with Medicare. Data drove all action. For example, during the enrollment period, the campaign manager would review the enrollment numbers down to the county level on the CMS databases. Resources would be redeployed as necessary to make certain we were reaching as many seniors as possible.

Two national training sessions were held in Washington, D.C., for headquarters and regional staff on campaign management skills. Much teaching time was spent on the art of partnership development: identification of common interest, nurturing relationship, ensuring that the relationship is valuable for both organizations, and emphasizing the importance of being data driven—identifying our metrics and developing capacity to measure and report.

The formalized internal communications program was critical to success. Daily scrums, weekly conference calls with individual teams, and monthly nationwide videoconferences were held including some of our major partner organizations to report on progress, help one another with particular issues, and generally support the morale of a very dedicated group of civil servants all of whom were learning direct-to-consumer marketing tactics from a fire hose.

The Second Strategic Imperative: We Can't Do This Alone

While the MMA specified the role of the SSA in educating and enrolling beneficiaries in the LIS program, it was silent on any additional resources to complete the Part D education and enrollment campaign in Part D. It became quickly apparent that additional communication channels would be necessary to successfully enroll 95% of Medicare beneficiaries in a Part D plan. This was the beginning of the consumer-centric strategy. We enlisted sister agencies at HHS and other federal government agencies who touched the lives of seniors to assist us in the outreach. The response from other agencies was tremendous, especially the Administration on Aging (AoA.) The AoA was invaluable and became a full partner in the campaign at the national and local level. Their local Areas on Aging were instrumental in connecting our regional campaign people with social service staff in the local communities. The result of this and other partnerships was a web of partnerships at the local level—all delivering the same messages and assistance to our shared constituency, seniors, and people with disabilities and their families.

Other federal agencies that directly touched the lives of senior citizens, such as USDA with the farm service and HUD with senior housing, worked together distributing materials and having events on sites to educate and enroll Medicare beneficiaries in the new program.

Similar partnerships were developed at the state and local levels. Regional campaign teams worked with State Units on Aging, and Medicaid offices. Local mayors' offices were very involved in bringing this new benefit to their constituents. The private and nonprofit sector partnerships were expansive and creative. The partnerships ranged from religious groups to local social clubs, from financial planners to ethnic and civil rights groups. By the end of the campaign we had more than 50,000 organizations in the partner data base, an astonishing number.

The backbone of the one-on-one counseling operation was the State Health Insurance Programs (SHIPS) across the country. The SHIPS, funded by HHS, provide counseling from professional staff and highly trained volunteers on Medicare issues throughout the year. The leadership and volunteer force of the SHIPS were completely engaged and committed to the success of this program. In fact, they largely bore the responsibility of one-on-one counseling efforts of the campaign. They also trained many of the other volunteer groups to do benefit counseling and education. For example, every week in Ft. Smith, Arkansas, SHIPS volunteers would come to a local school and sit with the trained junior high school students as they counseled their grandparents on the benefit. This popular program expanded so that every senior who wanted counseling could come to the school and learn about Part D from an increasingly expert junior high school volunteer, who was coached and mentored by a professional SHIPS counselor.

Third Strategic Imperative: Medicare Was Now a Consumer-Centric Program

This was a critical reorientation of the program. With the need for each beneficiary to make an informed consumer choice came the realization that the traditional one voice messenger from Medicare would not work. We had to speak to beneficiaries where they lived and though the voices of trusted sources of information. This reorientation drove most of the campaign strategy from the design of our infrastructure, our tools, our relationships with other parts of government, to our paid and earned media.

Medicare's consumer-centric approach continues today with its emphasis on wellness, prevention, and chronic disease management.

National Headquarters Role–Strategy, Tools, Resources

Medicare Web Site

It was evident that choosing a Part D benefit plan would be an individual choice. One size was definitely not going to fit all, especially when it became obvious that the private insurance plans were going to participate and offer a significant range of options. Other personal variables affected the choice as well, including: geographic location, personal finances, how individuals obtained prescriptions prior to Part D, health status, and drug needs. The variables for each individual were plentiful, and it became quickly obvious that a tool would be needed that could align an individual's needs with plan options that would meet those needs. Professional staff at CMS began the development of what was to become a very sophisticated Web site that an individual could access to assist them in seeing and comparing all the plan options that would meet their needs. This tool—which became the largest US Government transactional Web site—was innovative, complex, and ultimately very successful in helping seniors, their family, friends, caregivers, and thousands of partner organizations review plan options and make informed decisions. Thousands of partner organizations trained their volunteers in this tool to assist seniors through one-on-one counseling during enrollment period. During 2006, the Web site averaged 12 million hits a week; in 2007, 13 million hits a week.

Medicare & You Handbook

Every year, CMS develops a new handbook on the Medicare program that is distributed to all Medicare beneficiaries. It details the program at great length (average length is 108 pages), and the agency is told in focus groups that it is an important reference as beneficiaries use the program throughout the year. In addition to the many other duties during that first enrollment period, the handbook had to be produced outlining the new benefit. Again, the dedicated staff of CMS met the daunting challenge of describing a benefit that, while standard, allowed for great flexibility in choice.

1-800-Medicare

CMS had employed telephonic assistance strategies in the past during open enrollment season, but the effort of this staff for Part D was heroic. The volume of calls was unprecedented (in 2006, average daily calls hovered around 210,000 a day), and CMS staffed up significantly to meet demand. The combination Web and telephonic volumes were far more than expected, and for the most part the systems met the need and consumers were pleased.

Indeed, the number of customer service representatives on an average week day in 2006 exceeded 550. Even with this workforce, wait times averaged 2 minutes 45 seconds. Weekend traffic during the first extended enrollment period was only slightly less. As late as 2008, there was an average of 105,000 calls per day during the enrollment period.

Training of Counseling Partners

CMS traditionally provides training for its sophisticated partners, primarily the State Health Insurance Programs, but the role of the training operation expanded significantly. Now, CMS also had to train the thousands of organizations across the country, with their thousands of volunteers, to outreach to Medicare beneficiaries or their caregivers. This required a training triage program with three levels of curriculum, materials, and outlets. The training was happening almost simultaneously with program announcements, requiring constant writing, translating, and developing level appropriate materials. Training Web casts were held on specific subject areas on a weekly or bi-monthly basis; training kits were sent out to over 10,000 partner organizations with update materials being sent on a regular basis; and questions were constantly coming into CMS requiring more in depth information.

The training staff was closely aligned with the regional campaign teams that informed headquarters of information needs from the field or areas that needed more clarity.

Print and Media Campaign: Paid Media Driving a Message of Community

CMS started a general education campaign 6 months prior to the official start of enrollment. While this was a good opportunity to begin to educate the public on a new benefit that would be available to them in the next months, it was challenging because the standard benefit design was very complex and unorthodox. It also required each beneficiary to examine his or her own needs and circumstances in a way they had not done so in the past with the traditional Medicare program.

The first effort to describe the benefit for public consumption was a small brochure that would be inserted into newspapers. As the drafting began it was clear that the small brochure would have to become longer to cover all the necessary details of the benefit. Hindsight is brilliant and if we had only known that by enrollment time the standard benefit design would be almost moot perhaps we would not have had to spend so much time and effort on educating the public on a benefit design in a plan that few would ever purchase. The result was a compelling 8-page color brochure that was inserted in Sunday magazines and that we used as a handout at town hall meetings and other public venues.

In addition, we did some print advertising to drive awareness of the benefit and to counter the negative attention the benefit had received during the congressional debate. It was straightforward recognition advertising using the traditional Medicare audience placement strategy.

We followed the similar strategy with the first flight of television advertising. The buy was based on a senior market, and the goal was awareness building of the benefit and upcoming enrollment season.

About midway into the education portion of the campaign—3 months before enrollment began—we changed the campaign message and expanded the target audience to include baby boomers, the adult children of people with Medicare. We altered the theme and pivoted to a message of helping people with Medicare make smart choices about a new and somewhat complicated insurance benefit. The next flight of television advertisements included a message of community spirit and helping those around us—family, neighbor, friend—make a decision that will best meet their needs. Our goal was to turn enrollment into a family and civic event. The ad was beautiful, award winning, and definitely invigorated the campaign and brought more partners, especially at the local level, into the campaign.

Radio advertising was also a part of the media strategy with special focus on the Hispanic and African-American radio audiences. We employed guests artists including Bill Cosby and Sherman Hemsley in the African-American spots, and the Hispanic radio advertising was done in both English and Spanish.

Earned Media: Taking It to the People

After describing this effort, some have likened it to a presidential campaign. Our response is that it is similar, but instead of a few battleground states, we had 50 plus the territories. While resources were generous, they were also finite, and we determined that we would not depend on television advertising in the final enrollment period. Instead we deployed an intense earned media strategy that was combined with our field operations and partner enrollment event strategy. Additionally, we determined that local coverage was our goal; we did not seek national coverage during the enrollment campaign: we took it to the beneficiaries where they "live, work, play, and pray."

Our regional campaign teams were organizing local town hall meetings featuring local celebrities or political figures, especially mayors, who drew local media coverage. This was very successful in building up awareness and local media interest in assisting us in educating beneficiaries. In fact, some television stations did education telethons and radio stations did call-ins with questions on Medicare Part D. Local media engaged and made a significant contribution to the education of people with Medicare. We targeted midsize market dailies and weekly newspapers for coverage of our events and were very pleased that the coverage was apolitical and simply covered the details of the benefit and what it meant to beneficiaries.

The one unsolicited and somewhat surprising national media coverage was a spot on Saturday Night Live encouraging seniors to get on the drug train. It was amusing and nicely targeted our audience of adult children of seniors.

To assist the regional teams in obtaining local media coverage, we engaged four large buses, which we wrapped in Medicare signage and fully equipped with all the necessary technology to do a local press conference and broadcast. A team from headquarters worked with the field in scheduling these buses, a logistical feat in itself, which were usually manned with the Secretary of HHS, a Cabinet member, the Administrator of CMS, a member of Congress, a mayor, or other high profile guest. The media covered the comings and goings of the bus, which usually included a press conference and an enrollment event.

The colorful nature of the bus and the entertainment value always resulted in nightly, local television coverage and a fun enrollment event for beneficiaries. The rear of the bus often was featured on the nightly news pulling out of town with its trademark song blasting "On the Road Again." Tens of thousands of miles were logged by the four buses, manned for days by dedicated public officials, enrolling seniors along the way, never getting off the road until May 15, 2006.

Summary: "It's All Coming Together"

"It's all coming together." This was the slogan for the first ever Medicare Part D education and enrollment campaign. Looking back is it obvious that this slogan was used both with hopeful exuberance and anxious concern during the 18-month period prior to the end of the first official enrollment period for the new Part D Medicare prescription drug benefit. The effort to provide prescription drug coverage to 37 million Medicare beneficiaries was vast in scope and involved approaches that were entirely new to Medicare.

Moreover, the effort, as viewed by the beneficiaries, was an astonishing success. The June 2006 Kaiser poll was the first good news. The numbers would only get better. A September poll by J.D. Power and Associates found that 75% of respondents were pleased with Part D, the highest poll number the organization had ever received for any kind of insurance program. In December, a *Wall Street Journal* Harris Interactive pool recorded satisfaction at 87%.

These are astounding numbers that have no precedent in any service or product the government has ever provided, much less the private sector.

This summary does not do justice to the creativity and dedication of the amazing team of professionals at CMS and our federal, state, and local sister agencies who made certain that 95% of Medicare beneficiaries had some form of prescription drug coverage by the end of the first Part D enrollment period.

Discussion Questions

1. What was the goal of Medicare Part D? Did it achieve its aim?
2. What was the role of headquarters vs. the regional offices in implementing the campaign strategy? Why was this role distinction a potentially difficult change for the bureaucracy?
3. Describe the consumer-centric strategy. What was the impetus of this strategy?
4. Describe the various media materials and elements used to connect with consumers throughout the campaign. Which in your opinion was most effective?
5. Why was the campaign message changed at the midway point of the print and media education campaign?

Chapter 12

Spurring Action on Heart Disease in Women: How a Nonprofit Can Strategically Partner with a Government Campaign

By Lisa M. Tate

LEARNING OBJECTIVES

By the end of the chapter, the reader will be able to:

- Understand the purpose for a public campaign centered on women's heart disease and women's heart health.
- Trace the beginnings of the cause—a marketing campaign devoted to women's heart health.
- Describe how a strategic partnership between the public and private sectors (in particular, government and nonprofit sectors) and how this led to a comprehensive approach for increasing audience penetration and education and expanding the marketing efforts of the cause.
- Identify other ways in which formed alliances serve to benefit their audience and this cause.

Introduction

Heart Disease is the leading cause of death in women and has been since 1984. For decades, heart disease has been identified as a man's disease, and although heart disease was and still is the leading cause of death in women, other gender neutral diseases (cancer, AIDS) and challenges plaguing Americans (e.g., the economy, unemployment, education, war) received nationwide attention. Because of these pressing matters, concern around this growing epidemic was minimized, leaving thousands of American women at risk of developing this condition or leaving those who had heart disease feeling stigmatized and left to suffer alone in silence.

Prior to the start of the new millennium, the facts were staggering. Since 1984, the number of cardiovascular disease deaths for females has exceeded those for males every year, and a 1997 survey commissioned by the American Heart Association (AHA) showed that:

- Only 8% of the female respondents identified heart disease as their greatest health concern.
- Less than 33% of females identified heart disease as the leading cause of death. More women aged 25 to 44 years identified breast cancer as the leading cause of death than women 65 years or older.
- Women aged 25 to 44 years indicated they were not well informed about heart disease.
- Although 90% of the women reported that they would like to discuss heart disease or risk reduction with their physicians, more than 70% reported that they had not (Mosca et al., 2000).

Because women did not have a clear understanding about the facts of heart disease, conversations with their physicians often led to a misdiagnosis (Cohen, 2007), resulting in delayed diagnosis and improper treatment for women suffering with heart disease. In the late 1990s, the numbers of women living with or dying from heart disease served as a clear warning sign that immediate action was needed.

The Dawn of a New Decade in Women's Heart Health

When Nancy Brinker lost her sister, Susan, to breast cancer, she started Susan G. Komen for the Cure, a cause-marketing movement that connected donations from private corporations with researchers and medical centers with the goal of eradicating breast cancer. At the same time, heart disease in women was *still* the leading cause of death and was climbing nationwide, but was largely orphaned due to the lack of a leading champion and advocate. Bearing witness to the mobilization of society around the breast cancer movement and the growing concern around heart disease in women, the timing seemed right for individuals, organizations, medical facilities, and the federal government to address the paucity of information around women's heart disease and to reverse the negative trend impacting women's heart health. At the end of the last decade, individual advocates and groups began to mobilize around research and identify needs in response to this growing health crisis, but the beginnings of this movement were quite fragmented.

WomenHeart and the Building of a Coalition Around Women's Heart Health

In 1999, three courageous survivors of heart disease from opposite ends of the United States founded WomenHeart: The National Coalition for Women with Heart Disease, the nation's only patient-centered organization with the mission to improve the health and quality of life of women living with or at risk for heart disease. These women-turned-activists saw an opportunity to lessen the stigma of women living with heart disease and recognized that more must be done to reach the tens of thousands of other women who faced the same challenges. Today, WomenHeart boasts 518 *WomenHeart Champions*—women living with heart disease who are trained at WomenHeart's annual Science & Leadership Symposium at Mayo Clinic as community educators and advocates—who educate millions of women every year about their risk for heart disease, operate the nation's only network of patient support groups providing peer-to-peer support to women living with heart disease, and coordinate a national advocacy initiative to support the funding for programs, policies, and research to better the lives of women living with heart disease.

Because WomenHeart started as a small nonprofit organization, co-founders Nancy Loving, Jackie Markham, and Judy Mingram realized a more concerted effort from the health community was required to advance its cause. Nancy Loving, a Washingtonian, made multiple visits to Capitol Hill and to government agencies to engage leadership in support of women's heart health.

Eventually, those conversations led to action. In March 2001, the National Heart, Lung, and Blood Institute (NHLBI) convened more than 70 health experts to discuss women's health issues, and the outcome of this meeting was a resounding call for greater public awareness around women's heart health. Based on the recommendations, the NHLBI, in collaboration with Department of Health and Human Service's Office on Women's Health, WomenHeart, and the American Heart Association, formed a think tank to strategize on increasing awareness, education, and resources for women's heart health issues. From the findings of the think tank, the NHLBI hired Ogilvy Public Relations and *The Heart Truth*/Red Dress® national public awareness campaign to educate women about their risk for heart disease was born.

Campaign Design

In September 2002, *The Heart Truth*® campaign was launched. NHLBI's simple, yet profound campaign offered a dual message of personal and universal appeal for all women. The single catch phrase: "Heart Disease Doesn't Care What You Wear—It's the #1 Killer of Women" reminded all women about the importance of heart health, and the visual representation of a red dress pin symbolized women's commitment to eradicating heart disease. The first public service ad campaign featured *WomenHeart Champions* in red dresses to lend credibility to the cause and to illustrate that the face of women's heart disease does indeed come in all shapes and sizes. To extend the symbolic power of the Red Dress® campaign, in 2002, top American fashion designers developed the red dress collection for Mercedes Benz Fashion Week in New York. The first Red Dress Collection debuted February 2003; since then, every February designers and celebrities return to the tents at Bryant Park in Manhattan to contribute garments and their talents to one of the premier shows of the fashion season, and all for a good cause.

The Progression to the National Stage

The Heart Truth campaign was embraced by former First Lady Laura Bush, the Founding Ambassador of the campaign. In 2003, Mrs. Bush included women's heart health in her speaking platform as a part of her Women's Health and Wellness Initiative. Mrs. Bush traveled the country and lent her voice to educate women about heart health and heart disease. Like many *WomenHeart Champions*, Mrs. Bush is credited for saving a women's life. After hearing Mrs. Bush speak at a hospital in Kansas City, Missouri, one woman realized she was experiencing heart attack symptoms and sought immediate treatment.

While Mrs. Bush served as the prominent voice for millions of women, WomenHeart has female heart survivors from all walks of life who serve as spokespersons in their communities. These *WomenHeart Champions* are "stilettos on the ground" who coordinate grassroots efforts to support, educate, and provide advocacy outreach in their neighborhoods.

The Role of WomenHeart Today and the Collaborative Efforts

Today, WomenHeart is the only national network of women heart disease survivor patient volunteers dedicated to educating, advocating, and supporting women's heart health. WomenHeart provides in person and online patient support services, shapes public policy, increases awareness, and provides education and information for the 42 million women living with or at risk for heart disease in the United States. The more than 500 *WomenHeart Champions* in 48 states are heart health ambassadors who put a face on women and heart disease. Each year, the *WomenHeart Champion* roster grows by 60, as women with heart disease are invited to apply, through a nationally competitive application process, to attend this one of a kind 4-day Science & Leadership Symposium at Mayo Clinic in Rochester, Minnesota. Thanks to the generosity of Mayo Clinic Women's Heart Clinic and other sponsors, the program prepares participants to become community educators, advocates, and national spokespersons who rally for prevention, early and accurate diagnosis, and proper treatment of heart disease for all women, not only in their communities, but throughout the country. Attendees leave the Symposium renewed with purpose and resolve.

For WomenHeart, each class of *WomenHeart Champions* that completes the Science & Leadership Symposium adds to the national voice of women heart patients that bring heightened visibility and awareness to heart disease as the leading cause of death in women, allowing the organization and the campaign to connect with women throughout the country. *WomenHeart Champions,* many of them considered the picture of good health, are "the face and voice of heart disease"; when they share their compelling stories and the stories of their "Heart Sisters" with other women, physicians, and the media, it expands the awareness and creates greater understanding about women living with heart disease. *WomenHeart Champions* serve as visible representation of the organization's mission in their communities and extend WomenHeart's reach into their neighborhoods by sharing resources to ensure that other women in the community can recognize the symptoms of heart disease, and if diagnosed, will be aware of the local support to which they can turn.

WomenHeart's network extends far beyond its *WomenHeart Champions* and support networks. With more than 50,000 members and e-newsletter subscribers, WomenHeart reaches women and healthcare providers in urban and rural settings, and underserved communities through its Web site, www.womenheart.org, a portal named the top heart health Web site in 2010 by *O Magazine*. The site averages 50,000 unique visits per month. Additionally, the online support community averages 730 posts by women heart disease survivors weekly. Nearly 77 WomenHeart Support Coordinators hold monthly support meetings for women living with heart disease. These grassroots networks serve as a lifeline for women to share their stories and lessons learned from living with heart disease and support one another as a source of strength and support.

In Washington, D.C., WomenHeart works closely with Department of Health and Human Services Office on Women's Health, NHLBI, and many corporate partners to develop programs and initiatives meant to increase awareness around heart disease and women's heart health and improve both policy and programs serving women living with heart disease.

The Value of Public–Private Partnerships

Beyond women's heart health, the importance of this campaign signifies that combined efforts of the public and private sectors have a greater impact than any one organization could achieve alone. In retrospect, the ability to launch a comprehensive campaign to advance the cause of women's heart health required:

- *Government participation*—Government agencies and leadership used their platforms to raise national public awareness on a grand scale.
- *Nonprofit organizations*—Organizations such as WomenHeart to play a role in disseminating information, serving as advocates, and engaging citizens at the grassroots level.
- *Private corporations*—Businesses and corporate entities provide financial support and resources, and serve as a marketing platform for cause-marketing efforts.

The campaign's success can be attributed to the collaborative nature of the sectors; although each sector has the ability to educate and support its constituents, it is safe to say the alliance formed cast a wider net of support, educating individuals on a national, and eventually, an international stage.

The Campaign's Impact on Women's Heart Health

While the nationwide launch of *The Heart Truth* campaign in September 2002 was the rallying call that women's heart disease was on the rise and a concerted effort was needed to stave off the progressing numbers, the campaign propelled the message nationwide. Thanks to the symbolism of the campaign and the alliance forged between the government and non-profit sectors, the following advances have been made to thwart women's heart disease:

- Thanks to *The Heart Truth*®/Red Dress Campaign and the Red Dress symbol, awareness of women's heart disease has increased 57% (NHLBI, 2010).
- Thanks to increased grassroots campaigns led by the NHLBI, WomenHeart, and the US Department of Health and Human Services Office on Women's Health, and the American Heart Association, physicians and clinicians have become more aware of the disparities between men's heart health and women's heart health and have specific clinical practice guidelines for the diagnosis and treatment of heart disease in women.
- In 2010, President Barack Obama proclaimed February as American Heart Month, to recognize and reaffirm America's commitment to fighting cardiovascular disease (White House, 2010).
- Education by all organizations in the fight against heart disease shows a marked improvement in the numbers: from 1 in 3 deaths in 2003, to 1 in 4 deaths in 2004; a reduction of approximately 17,000 women whose heart condition might have been a fatality had it not been for a consistent stream of communications and support (NHLBI, 2007).

Other Collaborative Efforts

Heart for Women Act

WomenHeart, in collaboration with the American Heart Association, Association of Black Cardiologists, and Society for Women's Health Research are mobilizing volunteers, members, and advocates to urge Congress to pass the Heart Disease Education, Analysis, and Research, and Treatment (HEART) for Women Act. The HEART for Women Act is legislative policy drafted to take a comprehensive approach in the prevention, diagnosis, and treatment of heart disease in women. Passage of the Heart for Women Act will:

- Provide gender and race-specific information for clinicians and researchers; data that is already being reported by gender will require stratification by race and ethnicity as well—this includes clinical trial data, pharmaceutical and medical device approval data, medical errors data, hospital quality data, and quality improvement data.
- Authorize grants to educate healthcare professionals about the prevalence and unique aspects of care for women in the prevention and treatment of cardiovascular diseases.

- Improve screening for low-income women at risk for heart disease and stroke, expanding the WISEWOMAN program of high blood pressure and high cholesterol testing to underserved women all 50 states (American Heart Association, 2009).

10Q Report

As reflected in the 1997 AHA survey mentioned earlier, results show women did not discuss heart disease or risk reduction with their physicians. Although advances have been made in educating patients about the symptoms of heart disease, women have often stated that when communicating concerns to their physicians, the physicians haven't taken them seriously.

In an effort to identify and address some of the research gaps in better understanding women and cardiovascular disease, WomenHeart and the Society for Women's Health Research (SWHR), a national organization whose mission is to improve the health of all women through research, education, and advocacy, joined forces to address critical issues in women's heart health by drafting the 2011 10Q Report, an updated version of a comprehensive expert opinion piece meant to address important unanswered questions in women's heart health. The 10Q Report, due to launch in June 2011, will serve as an alert to members of Congress, administration officials, researchers, healthcare providers, and women that identifying answers to these 10 questions will have a significant effect on the morbidity, mortality, and quality of life for women living with heart disease.

9-1-1 Campaign

While overall death rates from cardiovascular disease have decreased in recent years, there is an alarming trend among women under age 55 of rising mortality rates. Often, women exhibit additional symptoms, such as nausea, vomiting, shortness of breath, dizziness, and indigestion; these are all warning signs that can be associated with heart attacks in women, but sometimes these symptoms are misdiagnosed, resulting in delayed treatment. In 2010, the Department of Health and Human Service's Office on Women's Health, WomenHeart, the NHLBI, and 20 other leading national health organizations devoted to improving women's heart health, joined forces to develop a national public service announcement campaign to bring attention to the need for women to better understand the signs and symptoms of a heart attack and to call 9-1-1 if they think they are having a heart attack. Launched in 2011, the *Make the Call. Don't Miss a Beat* national public service announcement (PSA) campaign will raise awareness of this major public health issue on a national scale by maximizing the resources and relationships with these national medical and patient-centered organizations at the grassroots level. In addition to the 50 *WomenHeart Champions* who have been trained to be the face of the campaign by personally delivering the message to their local media outlets, other partnering organizations such as the Association of Black Cardiologists and the National Association of State and Territorial Health Officers will support this effort through training of healthcare professionals and dissemination of campaign messages. Additionally, materials and training will be distributed nationally to the 9-1-1 operator network and emergency medical technicians. The goal of this campaign is to increase education and awareness about the signs and symptoms of heart attack so that women will know when to call 9-1-1 if they suspect they or another woman is having a heart attack.

Summary

Nonprofit and government agencies perform a valuable service to citizens and society. Individually, they address the constituents they serve, but as we have seen in this chapter, through the collaborations of such entities as the NHLBI and WomenHeart, these organizations were able to extend their reach, increase audience penetration, and engage others through cause-marketing efforts.

Discussion Questions

1. What was the mission of WomenHeart, and what methods did the founders employ to promote the cause?
2. Define the term *WomenHeart Champions*, and describe their role in promoting women's heart health messages in their local communities.
3. What were the specific roles of government agencies, nonprofits, and private corporations in the alliance that was formed to promote *The Heart Truth*/Red Dress® campaign?
4. What has been the impact of *The Heart Truth*/Red Dress® campaign on women's heart health?
5. Describe an example of a partnership between two nonprofit agencies given from the text. What was the objective of the partnership, and how did the collaboration better enable the two entities to reach that goal?

References

American Heart Association. (2009). *Heart Disease Education, Analysis and Research, and Treatment for Women Act.* Available at: http://www.americanheart.org/presenter.jhtml?identifier=3039322. Accessed: April 13, 2011.

Cohen, E. (February 01, 2007). *Heart disease often misdiagnosed in women.* CNN. Available at: http://www.cnn.com/2009/HEALTH/10/19/undiagnosed.women.problem/index.html?iref=allsearch. Accessed: April 13, 2011.

Mosca, L., Jones, W. K., et al. (2000). American Heart Association Women's Heart Disease and Stroke Campaign Task Force: Awareness, perception, and knowledge of heart disease risk and prevention among women in the United States. *Archives of Family Medicine*, *9*, 506–515. Available at: http://archfami.ama-assn.org/cgi/content/full/9/6/506. Accessed: April 13, 2011.

NHLBI. (2007). *Heart disease deaths in American women decline.* Available at: http://www.nhlbi.nih.gov/new/press/07-02-01.htm. Accessed: April 13, 2011.

NHLBI. (2010). *The Heart Truth campaign overview*. Available at: http://www.nhlbi.nih.gov/educational/hearttruth/downloads/pdf/campaign-overview.pdf. Accessed: April 13, 2011.

White House. (2010). *American Heart Month*. Available at: http://www.whitehouse.gov/the-press-office/presidential-proclamation-american-heart-month. Accessed: April 13, 2011.

Chapter 13

Reaching Targeted Audiences in an Evolving Media Environment

By Roba Whitely, with Kristin Paulina and Kathleen Donohue Rennie

LEARNING OBJECTIVES

By the end of the chapter, the reader will be able to:

- Understand the importance of clearly defining a target audience to successfully reach and effectively sustain communication efforts.
- Understand how marketing research can be leveraged to refine communication strategies to better connect with key audiences.
- Leverage emerging technologies and develop two-way communication channels as outreach platforms with key stakeholders.
- Discuss the multiple facets of a fully integrated brand-building communications campaign.

Introduction

Helena Jennings of Mississippi is a retired widow living on a budget. She cannot afford health insurance and is too young to be eligible for Medicare. While she periodically needs medication, she will often forgo filling her prescriptions. Her story, like those of others throughout the country, has become even more common in a slow economy, with people forced to put their health on hold while they focus on more immediate needs, such as paying their mortgage or buying groceries for the family.

Individuals and families are worried about the impact of healthcare costs on their finances, both for today and in the future. According to a survey conducted for the American Institute of Certified Public Accountants by Harris Interactive (2010), medical costs are one of the two most common financial concerns among Americans.

With an understanding of this concern, several of the nation's leading pharmaceutical companies joined together in 2005 to create a prescription savings program that would help Helena Jennings and many other hardworking Americans and their families gain access to immediate and meaningful savings on prescription products right at their neighborhood pharmacies. The program, Together Rx Access, provides eligible individuals with free-to-get and free-to-use Together Rx Access cards.

More than 300 brand-name prescription products are included in the program, and most Together Rx Access cardholders save 25–40% on brand-name prescription products. Cardholders' savings vary depending upon the particular drug purchased, amount purchased, and the pharmacy used. And, cardholders can also save on a wide range of generics. Medicines in the program include those used to treat high cholesterol, diabetes, depression, asthma, and many other common and chronic conditions.

The Together Rx Access card, which does not require a doctor's approval or any eligibility documentation, is accepted at the majority of pharmacies nationwide and in Puerto Rico. Cardholders simply bring the card to their pharmacist along with their prescription, and the savings are calculated right at the pharmacy counter.

"Together Rx Access was built on the belief that all Americans deserve access to quality health care, including prescription medicines, and that improving access to health care for uninsured individuals and families requires collaboration between the public and private sectors," stated Roba Whiteley, executive director of Together Rx Access.

The Together Rx Access card was modeled on the successful Together Rx card. In that program, seven companies—Abbott Laboratories, AstraZeneca, Aventis Pharmaceuticals, Bristol-Myers Squibb Company, GlaxoSmithKline, Johnson & Johnson, and Novartis Pharmaceuticals Corporation—offered savings to eligible seniors who lacked prescription drug coverage. The program enrolled over 1.5 million seniors, and it sunset in December 2005 with the implementation of Medicare Part D. Seniors who used the Together Rx card collectively saved more than $1 billion on their prescription medications.

Today, the companies participating in the Together Rx Access Program include: Abbott Laboratories; Bristol-Myers Squibb Company; GlaxoSmithKline; Janssen, a Division of Ortho-McNeil-Janssen Pharmaceuticals, Inc.; King Pharmaceuticals, Inc.; LifeScan, Inc.; McNeil Pediatrics, a Division of Ortho-McNeil-Janssen Pharmaceuticals, Inc.; Ortho Dermatologics, a Division of Ortho-McNeil-Janssen Pharmaceuticals, Inc.; Ortho-McNeil, a Division of Ortho-McNeil-Janssen Pharmaceuticals, Inc.; Ortho-McNeil Neurologics, a Division of Ortho-McNeil-Janssen Pharmaceuticals, Inc.; Ortho Women's Health & Urology, a Division of Ortho-McNeil-Janssen Pharmaceuticals, Inc.; Pfizer Inc; PriCara, a Division of Ortho-McNeil-Janssen Pharmaceuticals, Inc.; Stiefel, a GlaxoSmithKline company; Takeda Pharmaceuticals North America, Inc.; Tibotec Therapeutics, a Division of Centocor Ortho Biotech Products, L.P.; ViiV Healthcare; and Vistakon Pharmaceuticals, LLC.

With more than 50 million people being uninsured in America (US Census Bureau, 2010), the goal of the Together Rx Access Program is to provide access and affordability to eligible uninsured individuals and families so they can get the medicines they need to take care of their health. By building strong relationships with healthcare professionals, patient advocates, legislators, the media, and others through traditional and social media as well as online and e-communication, Together Rx Access has gotten the word out to those individuals who can benefit the most from the program's savings.

"The Together Rx Access Program has been a blessing...helping me to better afford my prescription medicines. I've recommended the program to my uninsured family and friends," noted Ms. Jennings.

Communications Challenges: Reaching a "Difficult to Reach" Audience

Through its initial research about the uninsured population, Together Rx Access recognized that the program would face challenges in reaching, and effectively sustaining communication with, uninsured individuals and families—a multifaceted and diverse group of Americans. At the end of 2008, as the nation's unemployment rate began to rise and health benefits were lost or reduced, fewer individuals and families were able to afford health insurance. As a result, America's uninsured became even more difficult to define. And, as the faces of individuals and families without healthcare continued to change, misperceptions about the uninsured population and the best ways to reach them grew.

Uncovering Misperceptions About the Uninsured

The Together Rx Access team learned early on that a "one size fits all" approach would not work when reaching out to the uninsured population. It is a *myth* that the uninsured are a homogeneous group with shared traits. The *reality* is that the uninsured are economically and ethnically diverse. Research shows that the uninsured population is composed of two-income families, single parents, the self-employed, recent college graduates, and low-wage workers, among others. According to the Kaiser Family Foundation (2010), the majority of uninsured people, almost eight out of 10, are actually from hardworking families.

Most uninsured individuals are under 44 years of age (US Department of Health and Human Services, 2005). Ethnic minorities make up more than half of the uninsured population (Families USA, 2007).

Since limited market research was available about the uninsured population at the time the program was introduced, the Together Rx Access team conducted comprehensive research and in-market testing (see Box 13-1). In doing so, it uncovered a number of interesting facts that confirmed existing research and shed new light on how to interact with and engage those who were eligible for the program. The Together Rx Access team learned the following:

- By and large, people without prescription coverage are hardworking individuals from all walks of life who were looking for a break, but not a handout.
- Women tend to be more involved than men in making decisions about the medicines they and their families take.
- Although the majority of people without coverage are under 40 years old, the older set (41–64) are much more engaged in health care and are therefore more likely to respond to messages regarding the program.
- Many uninsured are Web users who turn to the Internet for information on health care.

While much was uncovered about the uninsured population, after careful analysis, no direct link was found between the various segments of the uninsured population, except for the fact that all lacked healthcare insurance. With no obvious commonality among the segments of the uninsured population, no single communication method or vehicle could be used to build a relationship with those who could benefit from the program. To drive enrollment efficiently, Together Rx Access needed to find ways to reach those who would most likely respond to the program and its messages.

Through dialogue with uninsured individuals and families during the program's launch and early years, Together Rx Access confirmed that personal, one-to-one communication is the most effective way to engage individuals and families who are uninsured. A personal conversation with a Together Rx Access representative, healthcare professional, or legislator about how to complete the application form helps reassure potential cardholders of the program's benefits and often helps resolve barrier questions, such as "What's the catch?" and "How much will it cost?" Such questions may prevent some people from enrolling in this and other prescription assistance programs.

Box 13-1 Market Research Helps Refine Communications Messaging

In addition to in-market testing and research, the communications platform for Together Rx Access was constructed on findings from focus groups conducted among potential Together Rx Access cardholders to gauge reactions and gather feedback on advertising concepts for the Together Rx Access card.

The primary objectives of the program's consumer research were:

- To examine attitudes toward, and awareness of, existing prescription drug savings cards
- To gather feedback on three advertising concepts for the Together Rx Access card and the extent to which the concepts would motivate potential cardholders to either call the Together Rx Access toll-free number or visit TogetherRxAccess.com

(continues)

Box 13-1 Market Research Helps Refine Communications Messaging *(continued)*

Four focus groups were conducted among potential cardholders, which were segmented by how much participants spent each month on prescription medications.

Focus group participants had the following characteristics:

- Healthcare decision makers
- Aged 18 to 64
- Not eligible for Medicare
- Regularly taking prescription medication
- Having no prescription drug coverage
- Not a current participant in Together Rx Access

The groups were conducted in professional focus group facilities by a trained focus group moderator who specializes in communications research. All focus group conversations were framed by a discussion guide. Altogether, 33 individuals participated, categorized by gender and ethnicity as follows: 21 women, 12 men, 15 Caucasian, 9 African-American, and 9 Hispanic American.

The focus group findings that were most helpful in message development included:

- Uninsured participants preferred the use of the term "a break" when describing how the card could help them with prescription costs. They agreed that "a break" sounded less like someone is helping them and more like they are using the card to help themselves.
- The use of the term "hardworking people" to describe those eligible for the card was perceived as favorable by potential cardholders who do believe they work hard and know how difficult it can be to make ends meet.
- The overarching message, "A free card for people without prescription drug coverage" was well received. It explains what the card is and who can benefit without talking down to uninsured individuals or implying a value judgment.
- The statement, "free-to-get, free-to-use" (without "there's no catch") also resonated. Most participants believed that there was some sort of fee associated with prescription savings cards. This belief makes consumers skeptical. They feel that a fee negates any discounts they would see on their medication costs. "Free-to-get, free-to-use" alleviated this skepticism.
- Participants generally preferred the focus to be on "savings" rather than "help." Savings does not imply a handout or assistance. Many also liked to know they could get "instant savings at the pharmacy counter."
- Most respondents liked seeing the prescription drug company logos and names. They also liked hearing the card was provided as a public service, lending credibility.

Communicating Through Skepticism

In addition to overcoming obstacles in segmentation, Together Rx Access also faced varying degrees of skepticism from the uninsured about the intentions of the program, as well as from those in the media, industry, and government. In the early stages of the program's launch, many in these audiences thought the card's attributes and ease of eligibility sounded "too good to be true." Because of that, many asked questions focused on finding a loophole or "catch," such as enrollment costs, monthly dues, or hidden fees. The Together Rx Access team focused (and continues to focus) on these "too good to be true" myths, communicating about them directly with all key audiences and emphasizing that the program results from the goodwill of member companies.

Embracing a Changing Media Environment

Since the launch of Together Rx Access, the media environment has been evolving. Social, two-way conversations about health and healthcare issues are continually increasing. And social media increasingly became a preferred method of communication among Together Rx Access' key audiences, with the traditional one-way push of information through TV, newspapers, and magazines becoming less significant. Interest in accessing and exchanging information through online communities, social networks, and blogs grew—and continues to grow—among consumers of all ages and demographics, including potential cardholders, the media, healthcare professionals, and legislators (see Figure 13-1). It was (and is) important that Together Rx Access embrace new communications media to reach the uninsured and those who they trust as credible sources of information and guidance.

Communications Outreach: Building Brand and Collaboration

The key to successfully building any strong brand is starting with a solid messaging framework and diligently adhering to that framework. At the outset, Together Rx Access established brand messaging that the program's communication team kept consistent across all communications vehicles. In this way, all messages were informed by the knowledge and insights gained through research about the target audience and the composition of the uninsured population.

Central messages about the program's benefits are clear, concise, and easily understood. And, most importantly, they are integrated throughout all communications and used consistently in marketing, advertising, public relations, and advocacy materials. In addition, all materials are available in English and Spanish.

Adherence to Together Rx Access brand messaging is strictly monitored, guided by a comprehensive messaging guide that defines program details. In this way, all communications across member companies, within the program, and out to key audiences are clear and consistent. For potential cardholders, the most important messages include:

- The card is free-to-get and free-to-use.

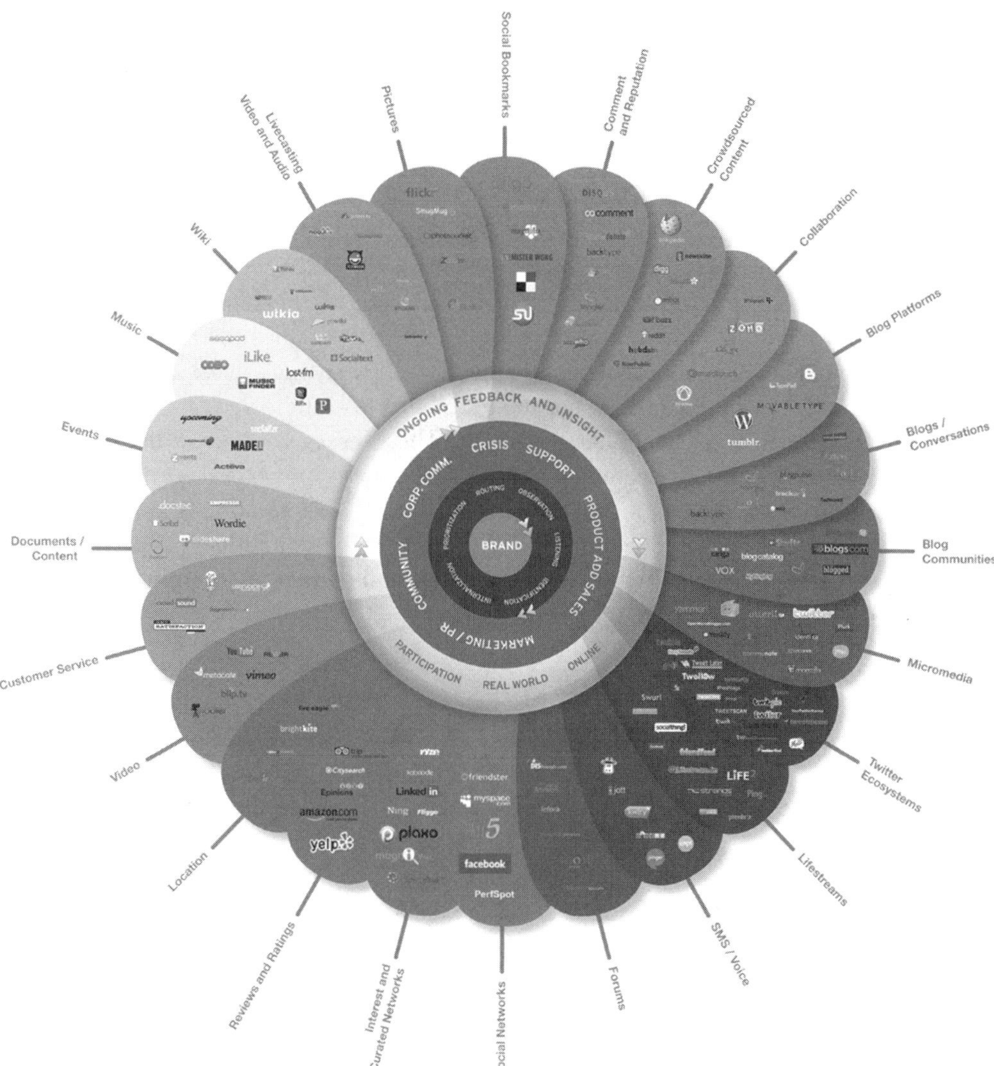

Figure 13-1 The Conversation Prism
Brian Solis, www.briansolis.com and JESS3

- Enrollment is fast and easy.
- No documentation is required.

An easy enrollment process that takes just minutes is an important feature for busy individuals. "No documentation required" resonates well with target audiences who express frustration about the forms and backup documents often required for health care. Not surprisingly, upbeat messages generally have the most impact. Stories from actual Together Rx Access cardholders help demonstrate the value of the program and prove that the program is "the real deal" (see examples in Box 13-2). People also relate to messages that compel them to action, such as "enroll online or call a toll-free number." Precise messaging was (and is) also essential to the task of differentiating the Together Rx Access brand from prescription discount cards that are available either through other organizations or by location (state, counties), sometimes at a fee. In addition to being free-to-get and free-to-use, a distinct characteristic of Together Rx Access is that it is the only program that provides savings on prescription medicines from multiple companies, which is helpful to people who are living with one or more chronic diseases. Additionally, Together Rx Access offers a quick start savings card that allows eligible cardholders to access savings instantly without waiting for the card to be delivered in the mail.

Integrated and consistent messaging also helped appropriately position the brand as a public service created as a philanthropic initiative by the member companies. As part of this, consumers and others were educated about the fact that while Together Rx Access provides immediate help with prescription savings, it does not offer a complete healthcare solution. In short, the card provides for savings, not healthcare coverage. This message is critical in demonstrating that member companies are dedicated to helping individuals and families without prescription drug coverage obtain the medicines they need while a larger solution is being pursued by policy makers. The message demonstrates member companies' commitment to *corporate social responsibility* by participating in the Together Rx Access Program and helping to address an immediate need and a critical societal issue (see Box 13-3).

Box 13-2 Together Rx Access Cardholders

Jan Brooks

As a single mother of two teenage boys, Jan Brooks of Dahlonega, Georgia, found herself in a heartbreaking situation several years ago. Jan was in a car accident and broke her neck in three places. As if the pain from the injury wasn't enough of a hardship, Jan had no healthcare coverage. Following the accident, Jan applied for various state programs, but did not qualify because of her age. She nearly gave up on her quest for prescription assistance until one day, when lying in bed and watching television, she saw a Together Rx Access advertisement and decided to call the toll-free number.

Jan remarked on how easy it was to enroll and start saving on her prescription medicines. "The process is so simple. I spoke with a customer service representative who mailed me an application, which arrived in 3 days. I filled it out and mailed it back in." Jan received the Together Rx Access card just 10 days later and was able to use the card that very day. Said Jan, "Together Rx Access has saved my life."

Lynn Biggs

Lynn Biggs and her husband have weathered difficult times. Five years ago, Lynn, who suffers from diabetes, underwent a partial leg amputation. Following her surgery, the couple experienced a string of bad luck: losing jobs, their health insurance, their savings and, ultimately, their home. Homeless for some time, the Biggs had to rely on help from family and friends to survive.

(continues)

Box 13-2 Together Rx Access Cardholders *(continued)*

Though they eventually found their own place to live and received help through disability income, they still struggled to afford their medicines. While they sought help through various prescription assistance programs, the Biggs were either ineligible or the programs did not cover their medicines. The unsuccessful search for assistance left them feeling frustrated. Relief came when their online research linked them to the Together Rx Access Program.

Lynn was grateful to finally find a program that would provide immediate help. She and her husband enrolled in minutes using the Together Rx Access Web site. According to Lynn, the savings were significant. She was now "able to pay for more food."

Box 13-3 Definition of Corporate Social Responsibility

A voluntary approach that a business enterprise takes to meet or exceed stakeholder expectations by integrating social, ethical, and environmental concerns together with the usual measures of revenue, profit, and legal obligation (BNET Business Directory, 2010).

Strategic Collaborations

Once the brand messaging was solidified, the Together Rx Access team identified opportunities to collaborate with third-party organizations and key opinion leaders with an interest in expanding prescription access within local communities and nationwide. Consistently focused outreach to community leaders; healthcare professionals; federal, state, and local legislators; and advocacy groups to generate support is an integral part of Together Rx Access' efforts to build awareness for the program and its benefits. This outreach has resulted in requests for collaborations that involve state-specific outreach, advocacy communication, and medical relations initiatives that are then implemented on a customized basis. For example, Together Rx Access collaborated with the government of Puerto Rico on the launch of the Together Rx Access PARA PUERTO RICO card (see case study). The program also collaborated with the State of Georgia and the State of Louisiana in similar outreach efforts.

Other examples of successful collaborations include working with organizations within the public and private sectors, such as the American Diabetes Association, National Head Start Association, United Way, and Easter Seals, as well as drug store chains including Snyders, Duane Reade, and Kerr Drug. Many of the collaborations involve developing communications materials customized to the particular group's target audience including press releases,

Web site content, newsletter articles, brochures, flyers, posters, and webinars. The drug store alliance featured training for retail pharmacists and technicians as well as supplying retail kits with materials for display at pharmacy counters. Throughout all efforts, adherence to brand messaging is emphasized and repeated.

Puerto Rico Case Study

Summary

On August 19, 2009, the government of Puerto Rico and Together Rx Access joined forces to launch the Together Rx Access PARA PUERTO RICO card to help thousands of eligible uninsured Puerto Ricans access immediate and meaningful savings on prescription medicines and products right at the pharmacy counter. The collaboration used existing communications channels within the government to identify and reach uninsured residents who would benefit from the prescription savings program.

Research

Chronic diseases, including heart disease, cancer, and diabetes, are the leading causes of death and illness in the Caribbean and Latin America (Pan American Health Organization, 2009). Research indicated that uninsured Puerto Ricans, especially those individuals suffering from chronic diseases, are in need of access to prescription medicines to help manage these conditions. In Puerto Rico, cardiovascular diseases including heart disease, hypertension, and high cholesterol are responsible for more than 30% of all deaths (PAHO, 2001). In addition, more than 20% of Puerto Ricans suffer from chronic respiratory diseases such as asthma (PAHO, 1998).

Planning

The objective of the Together Rx Access PARA PUERTO RICO collaboration was to increase awareness of the free prescription savings card among hundreds of thousands of uninsured Puerto Ricans, many of whom might benefit from the program's savings. A secondary objective was to garner attention as a value-added program for healthcare professionals, community activists, patient advocates, and other leaders who could help raise awareness of the program among uninsured residents and their families.

Strategies included the following:

- Develop and execute a robust media campaign aimed at broadcast, print, and social media to drive messages about the program's availability throughout Puerto Rico.
- Leverage relationships with third-party groups and legislators to show support for the program.
- Communicate Together Rx Access cardholder stories to provide a human interest angle.

Execution

Tactics

The collaboration was launched via a press conference on August 19 at the Department of State in Old San Juan. The press conference welcomed Secretary of State Kenneth D. McClintock and Secretary of Health Dr. Lorenzo González, along with Roba Whiteley, executive director of Together Rx Access (see Figures 13-2 and 13-3). Testimonials from two local cardholders were read in Spanish.

A press release announcing the launch of the Together Rx Access PARA PUERTO RICO card was distributed via wire service on August 19 (English version on PR Newswire and Spanish version on Puerto Rico Hispanic Newsline). As a way to maximize coverage, the press release was also posted in English and Spanish on PitchEngine, a social media distribution site.

Aggressive media outreach to secure attendance at the conference was proceeded by ongoing follow-up to ensure media coverage among all outlets.

Challenges and Materials

The primary challenge Together Rx Access faced in coordinating the launch was the language barrier. All media outreach and press materials had to be in Spanish. As a result, a Spanish-speaking representative from a Together Rx Access member company spoke at the beginning

Figure 13-2 **Together Rx Access PARA PUERTO RICO Press Conference**
Alejandro Ferrer Rivera

Figure 13-3 Together Rx Access PARA PUERTO RICO Press Conference
Alejandro Ferrer Rivera

of the press conference. Another challenge was building familiarity with current island politics surrounding Puerto Ricans' wide-ranging views about statehood versus independence. All communications carefully classified the collaboration as with the government of Puerto Rico. Lastly, the weather proved to be uncooperative. A hurricane predicted to occur the week of the conference threatened to postpone the announcement. However, while initial reports put the storm close to Puerto Rico, it ultimately stayed away from the island and the press conference moved forward.

Launch materials included a press release, cardholder testimonials, and a four-color advertisement (in Spanish) that was placed in top daily papers, including *El Vocero, Primera Hora* and *El Nuevo Dia*, for publication on the day of the announcement.

Evaluation

The announcement generated more than 600,000 media impressions in print publications, in addition to broadcast coverage and a widely distributed Associated Press article that resulted in numerous additional placements. Press conference attendees included Associated Press; TV networks—Telemundo Univision, WAPA-TV, Si-TV, and WIPR-TV; and Noti Uno radio station, as well as three major print publications—*Primera Hora, El Nuevo Dia*, and *El Vocero*.

A comprehensive, positive article appeared in the *Daily Sun* with a photo of Secretary McClintock from the press conference. An article in *El Vocero*, with the headline "Relief to the Patient's Pocket," also highlighted the press conference, and mentioned that the governor supported the program because it is a tool that helps people without insurance. Together Rx Access was also included in lengthy articles about Dr. González's health agenda in *Primera Hora* and *El Nuevo Dia*.

Online and social media coverage included postings of the release on 291 Web sites. In addition, the news reached 21,909 Twitter users.

The three ads placed in the local papers included a toll-free number that resulted in 3512 calls the day of the announcement. Publication of the Web site address resulted in a peak in Web traffic for the month on August 19 with 9313 visits, 20,051 page views, and an 84% increase in visits.

Communications Tools: Meeting the Uninsured Where They Are

Because the uninsured population is significantly fractured, Together Rx Access used in-market research to identify segments within the population most likely to hear the program's messages, and the best ways to communicate those messages.

Face-to-Face Communications

As previously noted, Together Rx Access realized very quickly that face-to-face interaction is the best way to initially engage individuals who may benefit from the savings available with the card. Face-to-face communications allow for honest discussion about misconceptions and create dialogue that educates people through any "too good to be true" concerns.

With its grassroots team, Together Rx Access began selecting venues at the local level where potential cardholders could be engaged face-to-face. The venues met focused criteria: (1) in cities and rural towns with high numbers of uninsured residents; (2) had large audiences, with a percentage of the attendees uninsured, or in need of assistance; (3) had audiences that were receptive to receiving health information or requesting health services; (4) included events where people take their time visiting booths, waiting in line, or filling out information; and (5) in locations that offered a family-friendly atmosphere. The events selected fell into two categories, enrollment events and brand awareness events.

Enrollment Events

At enrollment events, Together Rx Access "brand ambassadors" (see Box 13-4) interact with attendees to distribute program information and enroll eligible individuals onsite. Many of these events are minority-focused, as African-Americans and Hispanics combined have a higher uninsured rate than Caucasians (DeNavas-Walt, Proctor, & Smith, 2010). Also, African-Americans tend to have higher rates of certain chronic conditions, such as hypertension, heart disease, and diabetes (Dotty & Holmgren, 2005). In addition, language barriers may result in lack of health care for Hispanic consumers (Weech-Maldonado, Fongwa, Gutierrez, & Hays, 2007).

Box 13-4 Definition of Brand Ambassador

A representative of the Together Rx Access Program who attends events with the specific goal of communicating the benefits of the prescription savings program to attendees, face to face. The brand ambassador provides information, answers questions, and helps potential cardholders enroll in the program.

A targeted Together Rx Access Hispanic Enrollment Marketing Program was launched in Los Angeles in April 2006. Teams of trained bilingual brand ambassadors interacted with Hispanic consumers at retail locations, health clinics, and special events in local communities. As a result of events held in Los Angeles and Phoenix, nearly 15,000 Hispanic consumers were enrolled in the program in 2006. Overall, these efforts, which continued for 3 years, contributed to more than 130,000 Spanish speaking individuals enrolling in the program.

The grassroots team validated it was personal conversations with reassurances of the program's benefits that allowed representatives to answer the commonly asked question, "What's the catch?" By actively helping eligible individuals learn about the free-to-get and free-to-use, "no catch" card and complete the application form, Together Rx Access can overcome many of the barriers that previously stood in the way of audience acceptance and use of the prescription savings card.

Web Site and Web Enrollment Outreach

Individuals can also enroll in the program using the Together Rx Access Web site. The enrollment process takes about 5 minutes. The cardholder can use the program membership number provided via Web enrollment at the pharmacy immediately, while waiting for the card to be delivered in the mail, which occurs in about 10 days. Enrollment and other key information is available on the Together Rx Access Web site in Spanish.

In an effort to encourage online enrollment among potential cardholders, Together Rx Access uses a cost per acquisition campaign. This is an online advertising model where payment for the ad is based solely on qualifying actions, in this case, enrollments. Together Rx Access invites networks, such as Permission Data and Cool Savings to bid on impression levels on targeted buys. The program pays only for completed enrollments.

Since 2005, the cost per acquisition campaign has resulted in 63% of all program enrollments to date. Additionally, the cost per enrollment has decreased over 30%, making this a cost-effective method of reaching uninsured individuals and encouraging enrollments.

Brand Awareness Events

Research to find existing events and organizations that could help reach the broadest and most appropriate audience for Together Rx Access resulted in Minor League Baseball (MiLB) being selected as a viable outreach opportunity. MiLB has a strong reputation for offering a fun, family-oriented atmosphere, with affordable ticket prices and children's activities both on and off the field. Time between innings gave Together Rx Access face-to-face interaction opportunities and allowed for distribution of program materials.

Together Rx Access began its three-year MiLB tour in 2006, sponsoring select games in key markets, as shown in Figure 13-4

- Red Barons, Wilkes-Barre, PA (June 10, 2006)
- Jacksonville Suns, Jacksonville, FL (July 18, 2006)
- Durham Bulls, Durham, NC (double-header, August 12, 2006)
- Reading Phillies, Reading, PA (double-header, August 19, 2006 and April 6, 2007)
- Rome Braves, Rome, GA (May 11, 2007)
- Kane County Cougars, Geneva, IL (May 18, 2007)
- Carolina Mudcats, Zebulon, NC (June 8, 2007)
- Fresno Grizzlies, Fresno, CA (June 22, 2007)
- Somerset Patriots, Somerset, NJ (June 29, 2007)
- Red Wings, Rochester, NY (July 13, 2007)
- Bridgeport Bluefish, Bridgeport, CT (July 28, 2007 and July 26, 2008)
- Inland Empire 66ers, San Bernardino, CA (June 21, 2008)

From the moment fans entered the stadium at each of the sponsored games, the Together Rx Access brand was visible throughout the ballpark via banners and posters (see Box 13-5).

Figure 13-4 Together Rx Access Minor League Baseball Tour
Together Rx Access

Every fan received a free, blue Together Rx Access baseball cap featuring the program logo and toll-free enrollment number. The vast majority of fans wore the hats, creating a sea of blue at each venue. A Together Rx Access flyer was distributed with each hat to provide additional information about the program and to direct individuals to the Web site. Several fans requested batches of flyers to share with uninsured family members, friends, and colleagues.

Before the game, traditional first pitch ceremonies provided opportunities for delivering key program messages and calls-to-action for the fans. A Together Rx Access representative, usually the program's executive director, provided opening remarks, and led award presentations to representatives of community-based organizations, honoring them for their outstanding work in helping uninsured individuals.

Throughout games, the announcers read information about the program and the Together Rx Access television commercial was shown on the video boards. Between innings in select cities, Together Rx Access sponsored a trivia contest for fans, with winners given a Together Rx Access t-shirt along with a PBS baseball documentary DVD.

In each of the markets, Together Rx Access secured interviews for the executive director with local media, including *Rome News Tribune*, *Atlanta Journal Constitution*, *Rocky Mount Telegram*, ESPN 1240 AM, and local bureaus of Associated Press and the *Wall Street Journal*.

As the game sponsor, the Together Rx Access brand and Web site were mentioned in a number of advertisements placed by the teams and featured in local print and broadcast outlets. All of these efforts led to valuable brand building and awareness among the fans.

Box 13-5 Creation of Together Rx Access Mascot and Baseball Cards

The Together Rx Access mascot was introduced to fans at the Reading Phillies game in April 2007. He was an immediate hit, especially with children who wanted his autograph. Shaped like a prescription savings card, but with arms and legs to walk around the ballpark concourse, "Rex," as he was aptly named, drove increased traffic to the Together Rx Access table in an inviting, fun manner. He energized the brand image, reminding individuals about the program long after the games were over.

Given the popularity of baseball trading cards, Together Rx Access created a baseball card for Rex to hand out to fans at the games. As is tradition among baseball fans, Rex also signed cards of adoring fans upon request. The front side of the card included a photo of Rex holding a baseball and bat (see Figure 13-5), while the back side included key program information, such as the eligibility requirements and the toll-free number and Web site (see Figure 13-6). Fans were receptive to taking the baseball cards as they were small and could fit into a pocket.

Figure 13-5 Rex baseball card (front)
Together Rx Access

Figure 13-6 Rex baseball card (back)
Together Rx Access

Traditional Media Outreach

As with most awareness campaigns, the traditional national media are key to reaching target audiences. As Together Rx Access is a consortium of several companies, all of its messages are delivered through one voice—the executive director. Over the years, Together Rx Access has cultivated relationships with various reporters who cover topics ranging from general health to prescription assistance to personal finance. Interviews have been scheduled for the executive director with national media, including: Associated Press, *Forbes*, *Los Angeles Times*, Bloomberg Radio, ESPN, *U.S. News & World Report*, and the *Wall Street Journal*, among others.

Together Rx Access milestones and program announcements are consistently communicated to traditional media. As an example, in 2008, millions of individuals around the country were affected by job reductions, salary cuts, or the loss of health benefits, including prescription coverage, adding to the already soaring uninsured population in the United States. In response to the economic crisis facing the country, Together Rx Access member companies expanded the program's eligibility income levels to help even more uninsured individuals and families save on the medicines they need to stay healthy and to manage chronic disease. The expansion was announced to the media via a satellite media tour and aggressive media outreach (see Eligibility Expansion case study).

Together Rx Access also reaches out to syndicated health and general information columnists to encourage mentions of the program in relevant articles. These columns are a great resource, as they are picked up on a regular basis by smaller, local newspapers. These types of stories are particularly appealing to outlets that have downsized reporting staff and are looking for easily used and relevant content. For instance, Together Rx Access has been included in the Savvy Senior and Annie's Mailbox columns.

Eligibility Expansion Case Study

Summary

The Together Rx Access Program helps Americans who have no prescription drug coverage and are not eligible for Medicare lead healthier lives by offering them meaningful savings on prescription products. In 2008, the companies that participate in Together Rx Access determined that the economic crisis facing the country called for an expansion of the eligibility criteria for the program so more people could save on the medicines they need to take care of their health.

Research

Together Rx Access conducted extensive research into the economic situation related to healthcare access, spending, and prescription costs. The research revealed three things:

1. According to the Kaiser Family Foundation (2009), for every 1% rise in the unemployment rate, the number of uninsured Americans increases by about 1.1 million.

In 2008, the unemployment rate in the United States had risen by 3.3% which, by some estimates, may have resulted in more than three million additional Americans without health insurance (US Labor of Bureau Statistics, 2009).

2. The loss of prescription coverage may affect an individual's ability to access the medicines needed to stay healthy and to manage chronic conditions. Results from a Kaiser Family Foundation survey conducted in February 2009 showed that 53% of American households had cut back on health care due to cost concerns in the past 12 months. One in five (21%) surveyed said they had not filled a prescription, and one in six (15%) said they had cut pills in half or skipped doses to make their prescriptions last longer.
3. Results from another survey showed that approximately 36.1 million working-age (19–64) adults and children went without prescription drugs because of cost concerns in 2007, an increase of 11.4 million people from 2003 (Felland & Reschovsky, 2009).

Planning

Objectives

The main objective is to increase awareness of the Together Rx Access Program, its sponsors, and the program's expanded income levels to help even more uninsured individuals save on their prescription medicines. A secondary objective is to demonstrate the commitment of the member companies to helping uninsured people take care of their health during a time of increased need.

Strategies

The following four strategies are being used:

1. Develop and execute a robust media campaign aimed at broadcast, print, and social media to drive messages about the program's expanded eligibility income levels.
2. Help drive enrollment by using the economic crisis as a news hook to generate interest among media and encourage them to deliver the program's call to action: Web site and toll-free phone numbers.
3. Leverage relationships with third-party healthcare organizations and legislators to tell others about the program and its expansion.
4. Communicate Together Rx Access cardholder stories to provide a human interest angle.

Execution

Tactics

The following efforts in media relations were made:

- A satellite media tour (SMT) was held on March 19 with Roba Whiteley, executive director of Together Rx Access, and Jan Brooks, a Georgia cardholder, who provided a personal perspective of the card's ease of use and benefits (see Figure 13-7).

Contact: Mariesa Kemble
Sam Brown Inc.
608-850-4745
mariesak@sambrown.com

TOGETHER Rx ACCESS® PROGRAM EXPANDS ELIGIBILITY CRITERIA, RESPONDS TO CHALLENGING ECONOMIC TIMES

Alexandria, VA, March 19, 2009 – Together Rx Access®, a prescription savings program sponsored by many of the nation's leading pharmaceutical companies, announced today that it has expanded the Program's eligibility income levels to help even more uninsured individuals and families save on the medicines they need to stay healthy and to manage chronic conditions. Under the new income levels, nearly 90 percent of uninsured Americans will now be eligible for the Together Rx Access Program.

"Millions of individuals around the country have been impacted by job reductions, salary cuts, or the loss of health benefits, specifically prescription coverage, adding to the already soaring uninsured population in the United States," said Roba Whiteley, executive director of Together Rx Access. "By expanding the Program's income levels, the Together Rx Access member companies are responding to the needs of hardworking Americans during these challenging times."

The enhanced income levels for which individuals are eligible for the Together Rx Access Program are now:

- $45,000 for a single person (formerly $30,000)
- $60,000 for a family of two (formerly $40,000)
- $75,000 for a family of three (formerly $50,000)
- $90,000 for a family of four (formerly $60,000)

Figure 13-7 Together Rx Access Eligibility Expansion Press Release
Together Rx Access

- A traditional press release was distributed via PR Newswire and via the social media site PitchEngine on March 19.
- Aggressive media outreach was conducted to medical/health reporters at top daily national newspapers and magazines, pharmaceutical and general health trade magazines, and local newspapers in states of participating companies' locations.
- An English and Spanish audio news release was developed and distributed on March 25 to radio networks: USA Radio, Radio America, Salem Radio, and CNN en Espanol.
- A mat release, with the headline, "Managing Your Money: Smart Ways to Save on Healthcare," was distributed on April 7. A mat release is a packaged article (copy and image) that is distributed to media outlets for publication.
- An advertisement (see Figure 13-8) announcing the expansion was placed in *USA Today*, *MedAdNews*, *CQ Weekly*, *Pharmaceutical Executive*, and *The Pink Sheet*.

The following efforts were made in government affairs and medical advocacy:

- Communicated expansion news to all members of Congress via a letter from Roba Whiteley, executive director of Together Rx Access.
- Created three special editions (targeted to key audiences) of a quarterly e-newsletter, distributed to legislators and their staff, patient advocates, healthcare professionals, and cardholders
- Prepared numerous newsletter articles about the eligibility expansion for national, state, and local health professional and patient advocacy organizations including Emergency Nurses Association, Easter Seals, United Way of Central Jersey, and North Louisiana Area Health Education Center

Challenges and Materials

There were some initial concerns regarding moving forward with a satellite media tour without a celebrity to help encourage interest and book interviews. After careful consideration, the decision was made that the news alone would drive interest, as the program's expansion would enable nearly 90% of uninsured Americans to be eligible for the program. Also, the addition of a cardholder with a compelling personal story added to the news value, bringing a "human" side to the news.

Evaluation

During the SMT, Roba Whiteley participated in 27 interviews, 16 of which were live. The rest were taped to air later in the day or on radio or Web news programs. Four of the interviews were with national outlets; 22 were with stations within key target markets. The SMT was a tremendous success, booking an impressive number of interviews without a celebrity (a typical SMT books an average of 10–15 interviews). One hundred percent of the interviews included key program messages, such as "sponsored by many of the nation's leading pharmaceutical companies,"

Because times are tough...

...we've made prescription savings available to more Americans.

Together Rx Access has expanded its income levels so that more hardworking Americans are eligible to save on their prescriptions.

Saving on prescription medicines is now easier than ever. For example, a family of four whose income is $90,000 or less may now qualify—compared to $60,000 in the past.

The Together Rx Access® Card is free and easy to use, and offers savings on over 300 brand-name medicines and thousands of generics. With over 1.8 million already enrolled, the Program's success continues to grow. In fact, thousands enroll each week. Isn't it time to find out if you and your family are eligible? **Just visit TogetherRxAccess.com or call 1-877-789-2325.**

Sponsored by many of America's leading pharmaceutical companies.

Abbott
Bristol-Myers Squibb
Janssen
Wound Management
King Pharmaceuticals
LifeScan
McNeil Pediatrics
Novartis
Ortho Biotech
Ortho-McNeil
Ortho-McNeil Neurologics
OrthoNeutrogena
Ortho Women's Health & Urology
Pfizer
PriCara
Takeda
tibotec
Vistakon

©2009 Together Rx Access, LLC. Together Rx Access and the Together Rx Access logo are registered trademarks of Together Rx Access, LLC.

Figure 13-8 Together Rx Access Eligibility Expansion Ad
Together Rx Access

the Web site address and toll-free number. Several of the stations posted the interview or the contact information on their Web sites for viewers to obtain additional information.

Media outreach resulted in an interview for Roba Whiteley with a *U.S. News & World Report* reporter who wrote an article on the publication's Health & Money blog. A brief article about the expansion was also included in the Health Buzz section of the magazine. In addition, Ms. Whiteley participated in interviews with reporters from *The Pink Sheet* and Associated Press. As a result of the Associated Press interview, Together Rx Access was included in three articles focusing on prescription assistance programs. These articles were picked up by numerous newspapers, Web sites, and blogs. Together Rx Access was also featured in broader stories about prescription savings on CNN's Dr. Gupta's *House Call*, and in the following print publications: *Detroit Free Press, Washington Post, Birmingham News, BioCentury, Buffalo News, News-Gazette, News-Leader, and Salt Lake Tribune.*

The ad reach included the following readership figures:

- *USA Today*, 31,000 daily
- *Congressional Quarterly*, 10,438 daily
- *The Pink Sheet*, 4,500 weekly
- *Pharmaceutical Executive*, 18,000 monthly
- *MedAdNews*, 16,513 monthly

The mat release generated a readership of more than seven million.

Expanding Face-to-Face Communication, Building Networks

Just as face-to-face communications is central in the program's outreach to potential cardholders, word of mouth communication is also instrumental in helping Together Rx Access maximize conversations and build networks with advocates—individuals who interact on a daily basis with uninsured individuals and who are viewed as trusted sources of information. These individuals include state and federal legislators, healthcare professionals, and patient advocates. As a way to keep advocates informed about the program and how it can help those most in need within their local communities, Together Rx Access:

- Participates in desk-side briefings with legislators or staff
- Exhibits at annual conferences, health expos, and town halls
- Conducted an advertising campaign geared to Washington, D.C., staffers
- Hosts community leader forums

In the last 5 years, Together Rx Access has participated in nearly 150 desk-side briefings, educating legislators and their staffs about the program. These meetings have been extremely valuable, providing legislators with another resource to offer their constituents who need assistance accessing prescription medicines. After seeing first-hand the value the program brings to the community at no costs to the local or state government, many legislators and their staff continue to make Together Rx Access materials available to constituents.

Participation at annual conferences, health expos, and town halls has further supported brand awareness by leveraging the expertise of Together Rx Access in reaching uninsured individuals. Together Rx Access has had the opportunity to share its discoveries with leading organizations, including the Democratic Governors Association (DGA), Partnership for Quality Medical Donations (PQMD), National Health Council, Families USA, National Association of Workforce Boards, Council for Affordable Health Insurance, National Conference for the Un and Underinsured, PAP Annual Conference, Center for Health Transformation (CHT), National Conference of State Legislators (NCSL), American Legislative Exchange Council (ALEC), National Foundation for Women Legislators (NFWL), National Association of Latino Elected & Appointed Officials (NALEO), and others.

The program's Washington, D.C., advertising campaign, which included three phases of outreach, was designed to drive and maintain awareness of Together Rx Access among policy makers, their staffs, and other opinion leaders. The final phase, conducted April through November 2008, used print, online, and transit (bus shelters, taxi tops, and metro lights) advertising to highlight the "success stories" of four cardholders. Through creative advertising, Together Rx Access also had a strong presence at the two National Conventions in 2008. Four-color ads were placed in the following legislative journals: *Congressional Quarterly*, *Politico*, *National Journal*, *Denver Post*, *St. Paul Pioneer Post*, and *Roll Call*. A readership study from *Roll Call* found that recall of the Together Rx Access convention presence finished second within the healthcare category, and fifth out of 18 of overall *Roll Call* advertisers.

In addition, Together Rx Access has hosted 50 community leader forums, which are informal sessions where community leaders convene to learn more about Together Rx Access. The goal of these events is to engage leaders and solicit their help in reaching out to the individuals they serve who can be helped by the program. Together Rx Access staff members also encourage community leaders to identify additional methods of reaching those individuals who may benefit from the easy-to-use savings card. These forums are generally attended by 30 to 40 community leaders, which may include religious leaders, leaders of civic and business groups, hospital and clinic officials, representatives from social services agencies, mayors, county leaders, and so on. Additionally, Together Rx Access invites a special guest to attend and speak to the audience at each event. In most cases, this guest is a local legislator with strong ties to the community.

Social Media Platforms

Social media was first recognized in 1997 with the start of SixDegrees.com (Boyd & Ellison, 2007), and became popular in 2007 (State of the Media, 2007). It exploded in 2009 (P. Bhagat, personal communications, 2010) developing into a two-way/multiple engagement communications tool with Facebook and Twitter. More than 96 million active Internet users, from all generations and demographics, are now using these platforms to communicate with others about various topics, learn new information, and share personal stories and experiences (Power of the People, 2009). Together Rx Access recognized the value of entering this space, as many audiences, including uninsured individuals, were beginning to access it to obtain information and locate resources for healthcare needs, including prescription assistance. The program identified early on that two-way communications via the Internet and online social media communities allow individuals to take a more active role in seeking and sharing information about their health. In addition, Together Rx Access cardholders are Web savvy, with more than 50% of enrollments resulting from Web-based outreach.

In 2009–2010, Together Rx Access began interacting with its audiences via these platforms using the following social media tools:

- Facebook: Together Rx Access fan page was launched in July 2009. Within the span of a year, the fan base grew significantly. Weekly messages ending with a question encourage fans to comments about topics of interest to them. The Together Rx Access page also provides links to other organizations that help uninsured individuals.
- Twitter: Together Rx Access Twitter page was launched in March 2010. As of March 2011, more than 1200 followers are receiving general health, chronic disease, available health resources, and program information tweets. Also, retweets of relevant health information from other individuals/organizations and media are delivered consistently. By retweeting, the program is building a base of advocates who spread information about Together Rx Access to others.
- TogetherONE: An online savings community was launched in April 2010. TogetherONE.com, which is free and open to everyone, encourages communication among community members who can share tips on how to make the most of a budget, find new uses for household items, and learn ways to save on prescription medicines, groceries, and other items they may need for a healthy life. As of March 2011, more than 3200 individuals had joined the community. This number is expected to grow as the economy continues to struggle and people try to find ways to make ends meet, while taking care of their health and the health of their families. TogetherONE is also sending monthly e-newsletters to its community members that highlight savings tips.
- Social media press release: In March 2010, Together Rx Access began sending viral press releases to media and social media bloggers. These social media releases offer content that can be shared easily, including videos, photos, links to other Web sites, and member company logos. Together Rx Access also cultivates relationships with social media journalists and bloggers to generate additional viral awareness of the program. At the same time, the program continues to enhance its ongoing relationships with traditional media who are now more frequently using social media vehicles and resources.

E-Communication and Online Innovations

In an effort to regularly update audiences about the program and to remind individuals that the program is available to provide assistance when people need it most, Together Rx Access developed two electronic communications vehicles—e-newsletters and webinars.

The e-newsletters are distributed quarterly and focus on a single topic, such as the launch of TogetherONE and other Program news and milestones. The content includes bullet points of relevant information to support the topic, as well as links to available resources within the program, including drug list, pharmacy locator, and "tell a friend." As of March 2011, the e-newsletters are being sent to nearly 200,000 individuals each quarter.

Since April 2008, Together Rx Access has conducted 70 webinars, reaching thousands of health and advocacy organizations, ultimately extending awareness and advocacy of the program. Of note is the growing interest from national organizations to host webinars for their leadership, states, or program staff members.

Communications Successes: Metrics and Tracking

From the time of its launch in January 2005 to March 2011, the Together Rx Access Program has enrolled nearly 2.5 million cardholders. Awareness and advocacy were built (and continue to build) with core audiences, engaging many of them to speak to family members, friends, colleagues, and constituents about the benefits of Together Rx Access.

Measuring and tracking the communications successes of the program has been based upon three main criteria:

- Measuring metrics against two main program objectives: enrollment and savings
- Measuring and tracking the effectiveness and efficiency of all outreach tactics
- Measuring brand awareness and perception

Enrollment and Savings

As of March 2011, Together Rx Access had nearly 2.5 million cardholders, including more than 350,000 children. Momentum in enrollment has been steady, with thousands of individuals enrolling each week, evidence of the program's continued value. In addition, card users have saved more than $120 million on their prescription medicines.

Effectiveness and Efficiency of Tactics

The success of the communications tactics implemented by Together Rx Access is based on how effective each tactic is in reaching target audiences with key messages, coupled with efficiency in penetrating target states and communities to reach a specific cross-section and wide range of consumers within a certain time period. Audience impressions, materials distribution, and message impact are also factors used to determine the success of a specific event, campaign, tool, or initiative. Maximum impact and reach are common goals, as demonstrated by these examples:

- Together Rx Access representatives attended more than 1500 health and job fairs targeting minority communities in cities that include Dallas, Houston, Atlanta, Orlando, Miami, New Orleans, and Harlem (all target markets), welcoming more than 120,000 enrollees in total. These events build goodwill and essential alliances with faith-based and advocacy organizations, as well as minority community groups.

- Hundreds of awareness and advocacy collaborations have been created with healthcare professionals, patient advocacy groups, community leaders, and others.
- Over four million Spanish language materials have been distributed. Online enrollment and other key resources are available on the Web site in Spanish.
- The distribution of quarterly e-newsletters to cardholders, government representatives, and advocacy and healthcare leaders proved to be a cost-effective communications tool to promote Together Rx Access successes/messages to key audiences.

Brand Awareness and Perception

Numbers typically are an easy way to identify and track brand awareness. For example:

- Over the last 5 years, Together Rx Access has earned more than 900 million positive media impressions, from outlets such as Associated Press, *Los Angeles Times*, *U.S. News & World Report*, *Wall Street Journal*, *Forbes*, Bloomberg Radio, and ESPN.
- More than 3000 health professionals and patient advocates have been reached through the Together Rx Access webinar program. The webinars have resulted in the distribution of tens of thousands of program materials to those in a position to help others learn about helpful resources.

With regard to perception, Together Rx Access communicates quarterly with nearly 200,000 individuals, including cardholders, legislators and their staff members, and health and advocacy professionals about the program. The fact that these individuals choose to regularly receive program communications speaks highly of the value of the information.

Additionally, Together Rx Access Program representatives and member companies are viewed by the media, legislators, and advocacy groups as subject area experts on issues relating to the uninsured population, prescription access, and private-sector solutions.

Summary

In January 2005, several of the nation's leading pharmaceutical companies launched the Together Rx Access Program. As the only multimanufacturer model for prescription savings, the Together Rx Access Program communicates the commitment of the member companies to improving access to and affordability of medicines to help people take better care of their health. In March 2009, in response to the challenging economy, member companies expanded the program's eligibility income levels. The program has enrolled nearly 2.5 million cardholders. Awareness and advocacy have been (and continue to be) built via traditional, electronic, and social communication with core audiences, engaging many of them to speak to their family members, friends, colleagues, constituents, and those they serve about the benefits of Together Rx Access.

In conclusion, through the use of thoughtful and targeted communications strategies and tactics, the Together Rx Access Program has been successful in its ability to connect with, communicate, and activate a difficult-to-reach segment of the population.

Discussion Questions

1. How important was research to understanding the uninsured audience?
2. Why is clear messaging essential to building and sustaining brand strength?
3. What impact did cardholder stories have on brand awareness and enrollment? Why?
4. Identify other ways or tactics that Together Rx Access can use to continue to reach its audiences.
5. Did Together Rx Access successfully meet its target audiences? How so?

References

American Institute of Certified Public Accountants. (2010). *Uninsured medical expenses rival retirement as Americans' top financial concern: AICPA survey*. Available at: http://www.aicpa.org/Press/PressReleases/2010/Pages/UninsuredMedicalExpensesRivalRetirementAsAmericans'TopFinancialConcernAICPASurvey.aspx. Accessed: March 18, 2011.

Bhagat, P. (2010). 2010: When social media will become more mainstream. *Global Thoughtz blog*. Available at: http://socialmedia.globalthoughtz.com/index.php/2010-when-social-media-will-become-more-mainstream/. Accessed: March 18, 2011.

BNET Business Directory. (2010). *Business definition for: Corporate social responsibility*. Available at: http://dictionary.bnet.com/definition/corporate+social+responsibility.html. Accessed: March 18, 2011.

Boyd, D. & Ellison, N. (2007). Social network sites: Definition, history, and scholarship. *Journal of Computer-Mediated Communication, 13*(1), article 11. Available at: http://jcmc.indiana.edu/vol13/issue1/boyd.ellison.html. Accessed: March 18, 2011.

DeNavas-Walt, C., Proctor, B., & Smith, J. (2010). The Census Bureau. *Income, poverty, and health insurance coverage in the United States*: 2009. Available at: http://www.census.gov/prod/2010pubs/p60-238.pdf. Accessed: March 18, 2011.

Doty, M. & Holmgren, A. (2006). The Commonwealth Fund. *Health care disconnect: Gaps in coverage and care for minority adults*. Available at: http://www.commonwealthfund.org/usr_doc/941_Doty_hlt_care_disconnect_disparities_issue_bri.pdf. Accessed: March 18, 2011.

Families USA. (2007). *Quick facts about disparities*. Available at: http://www.familiesusa.org/issues/minority-health/minority-health-quick-facts.html. Accessed: March 18, 2011.

Felland, E. & Reschovsky, J. (2009). Center for Studying Health Systems Change. *More nonelderly Americans face problems affording prescription drugs*. Available at: http://www.hschange.org/CONTENT/1039/. Accessed: March 18, 2011.

Kaiser Family Foundation. (2009). *Data spotlight: Unemployment's Impact on Uninsured and Medicaid*. Available at: http://www.kff.org/charts/042808.htm. Accessed: March 18, 2011.

Kaiser Family Foundation. (2009). Kaiser Health Tracking Poll. *Public opinion on healthcare issues*. Available at: http://www.kff.org/kaiserpolls/upload/7866.pdf. Accessed: March 18, 2011.

Kaiser Commission on Medicaid and the Uninsured. (2010). *Five facts about the uninsured*. Available at: http://www.kff.org/uninsured/upload/7806-03.pdf. Accessed: March 18, 2011.

Pan American Health Organization. (1998) *Health in the Americas* (Vol. II). Available at: http://www.paho.org/english/HIA1998/PuertoRico.pdf. Accessed: March 18, 2011.

Pan American Health Organizations. (2001). *Country health profile data 2001*. Available at: http://www.paho.org/english/sha/prflpur.htm. Accessed: March 18, 2011.

Pan American Health Organization. (2009). *PAHO rallies new partners for chronic disease prevention* [Press release]. Available at: http://new.paho.org/hq/index2.php?option=com_content&do_pdf=1&id=972. Accessed: March 18, 2011.

The Project for Excellence in Journalism. (2007). *The state of the news media*. Available at: http://stateofthe-media.org/2007/online-intro/. Accessed: March 18, 2011.

Universal McCann. (2009) *Power to the People social media tracker*. Available at: http://universalmccann.bitecp.com/wave4/Wave4.pdf. Accessed: March 18, 2011.

U.S. Bureau of Labor Statistics. (2009). *Employment situation: February 2009* [News release]. Available at http://www.bls.gov/news.release/archives/empsit_03062009.pdf: Accessed: March 18, 2011.

U.S. Department of Health and Human Services. (2005). *Overview of the uninsured in the United States: An analysis of the 2005 current population survey*. Available at: http://aspe.dhhs.gov/health/reports/05/uninsured-cps/index.htm. Accessed: March 18, 2011.

Weech-Maldonado, R., Fongwa, M., Gutierrez, P. & Hays, R. (2007). *Language and regional differences in evaluations of Medicare managed care by Hispanics*. Available at: http://www.cfah.org/hbns/archives/viewSupportDoc.cfm?supportingDocID=464. Accessed: March 18, 2011.

Chapter 14

The Society for Women's Health Research—Advocacy and Communications at Work

By Phyllis Greenberger and Mary V. Hornig

LEARNING OBJECTIVES

By the end of this chapter, the reader will be able to:

- Describe how advocacy extends beyond lobbying legislators and regulators.
- Discuss the impact that a focused nonprofit organization can have on improving women's health and changing the way health research is conducted in the United States.
- Understand the importance of representing a broad range of healthcare stakeholders, including researchers, providers, and policy makers, in order to succeed with congressional entities.
- Engage the public and consumers through communications and educational campaigns to become more involved in a variety of women's health topics.
- Discuss the myriad challenges facing the country related to health care and women's health research.

Introduction

The nonprofit advocacy organization, the Society for Women's Health Research (SWHR), based in Washington, D.C., is widely recognized as the thought leader in research on sex differences, and it is dedicated to improving women's health through advocacy, education, and research.

Through its efforts over the last twenty years, SWHR has changed the way research is conducted in the United States. Women are now included in medical research, and scientists are looking at the different ways health and disease affect men and women and the reasons why. SWHR attributes its advocacy and communications successes to using evidence-based policy in multi-pronged education efforts, as well as to its inclusion of a mix of healthcare providers and policy makers dedicated to improving women's health. Each of SWHR's campaigns to effect change has been rooted in documentation and communication of the women's health and research issues. Further, SWHR's advocacy and communications efforts extended beyond lobbying legislators and regulators, which many people consider synonymous with advocacy. To a large degree, SWHR's advocacy includes education of and continuous communication with federal legislators and their staff; scientists who are employed by the federal government, academia, and industry; and the public. This chapter explores the various campaigns and initiatives SWHR has undertaken over the years to change policies regarding medical research, including congressional advocacy, coalition building, and consumer education.

Founding of the Society for Women's Health Research

SWHR, the only organization dedicated to exploring differences in research as it relates to men and women ("sex-based biology"), is the brainchild of Florence Haseltine, PhD, MD. When Dr. Haseltine began working at the National Institutes of Health (NIH), she was told that her "role was to champion the field of obstetrics and gynecology," which at that time was underrepresented in research. As former Congresswoman Patricia Schroeder once said, "There are three gynecologists and 39 veterinarians at the NIH" (Haseltine, 2006). The need for more research into conditions affecting women hit home when a friend of Dr. Haseltine's, Rosa DeLauro, developed ovarian cancer. Between 1985 and DeLauro's election to Congress in 1990, NIH had little to offer in terms of in-house expertise and funding of academic scientists.

In the spring of 1989, Dr. Haseltine gathered friends and colleagues from medical and scientific organizations across the country to address this critical issue. They met at the American College of Obstetricians and Gynecologists (ACOG) and agreed on the need not only for more gynecological research at the NIH but also for research regarding women's health in general. This meeting gave rise to SWHR. Dr. Haseltine recognized the success of the HIV/AIDS community in effecting change at the NIH and their push for the hiring of additional scientists to study AIDS and believed this model would also work for increasing the NIH focus on obstetrics/gynecological issues as well as other issues related to women's health. Dr. Haseltine also met frequently with public opinion and policy leaders to communicate her concerns and to set the stage for SWHR's future advocacy efforts.

In 1990, owing to biases in biomedical research, the health of American women was at risk. SWHR's all-volunteer first board of directors made it their priority to confront this injustice. They worked with the Congressional Caucus for Women's Issues, its executive director Leslie

Primer, and Congressman Henry Waxman (D-CA) to persuade the Government Accounting Office (GAO), now the Government Accountability Office, to address the issue. They recommended that GAO evaluate NIH policies and practices regarding the inclusion of women and minorities in clinical trials.

The audit was released at an NIH reauthorization hearing in June 1990. It concluded that the NIH policy announced in October 1986 to encourage the inclusion of women in clinical trials had not been well communicated or understood within NIH or the research community, was applied inconsistently across institutes, and only was applied to extramural research (not to research conducted within the NIH) (NIH, 1986). The GAO report concluded that there was "no readily accessible source of data on the demographics of NIH study populations," so that it was impossible to determine if the NIH were enforcing its own recommendations (NIH, 1990).

For Dr. Haseltine, "this was a 'tipping point'" (Haseltine, 2006). Those who worked on the issues could disappear, but this topic was not going to go away, and 20 years later, enormous changes have taken place. Along the way, SWHR expanded research in obstetrics and gynecology, and Dr. Haseltine's original concerns have been addressed. Contained in this story are clues to the success SWHR has enjoyed in its advocacy and communications efforts. First and foremost, SWHR's leaders sought evidence to make their point; they used an Institute of Medicine (IOM, 1992) report that demonstrated federal funding for research in obstetrics and gynecology was an inadequate tool to garner additional evidence in the form of the GAO audit. Second, SWHR ensured that its dedicated leadership included a mix of healthcare providers and others concerned with research and healthcare equity, which provided a range of perspectives. Included in the initial gathering at ACOG and on the first SWHR board were physicians and researchers specializing in cardiology, mental health, and obstetrics/gynecology, as well as nurses, lawyers, and public policy advocates involved and interested in women's health and sex differences. Since its inception, SWHR has focused on all aspects of women's health and women's health research.

While advocating for change in the field of women's health research, the early SWHR leaders also developed the organization's mission, which remains at the core of SWHR's mission today: to improve the health of women through research. The goals to achieve this mission reflect the evidence-based nature of SWHR's efforts. One of the goals is to identify those areas of research that will have an impact on the health of women, and another is to effect changes in policies and behavior through advocacy and communication to improve the health of women based on research outcomes.

Early Efforts and Successes: Strategy of Congressional Advocacy

SWHR's first advocacy and communication efforts were addressed almost exclusively to Congress in an attempt to change policies and regulations at federal agencies. Working cooperatively with key organizations and policy makers on Capitol Hill and communicating with them on a regular basis was one of the reasons for SWHR's initial success. Within months of the June 1990 GAO audit, the NIH published guidelines that required that women be included in clinical research and established the Office of Research in Women's Health (NIH, 1990). Because these guidelines were not fully implemented, SWHR successfully fought for passage of the 1993 NIH Revitalization Act, which codified these requirements and also required that phase III clinical trial results be analyzed by sex. The act also permanently established the NIH Office of Research on Women's Health. Securing permanent authorization for offices of Women's Health in other federal health agencies continues to remain a goal of SWHR.

Next came important changes at the Food and Drug Administration (FDA). Following the successful tactic of securing information via a GAO audit, SWHR asked GAO to examine the inclusion of women in the clinical trials used by FDA in evaluating drugs for marketing approval. This 1993 report found that while women were sometimes included in drug trials, they were significantly underrepresented (U.S. Government Accounting Office, 1993). Even when women were included, data were not analyzed to determine if women's responses to drugs differed from those of men. The report found that insufficient numbers of women were included in preapproval clinical trials of drugs and charged FDA with improving women's representation; it concluded by recommending that FDA should ensure that drug companies consistently include "sufficient numbers of women in drug testing to identify gender-related differences in drug response and that such sex differences are explored and studied" (U.S. Government Accounting Office, 1993). Again, evidence prevailed. Later in 1993, the FDA reversed its 1977 guidelines and published a new *Guideline for the Study and Evaluation of Gender Differences in the Clinical Evaluation of Drugs* that encouraged the inclusion of women in phase I and II (safety and dosing) studies and required inclusion in efficacy studies. The guideline also requires analysis of data on sex differences, as well as those based on race and ethnicity.

During the early years, SWHR's efforts were handled by an all-volunteer board of directors, including Phyllis Greenberger, MSW, who was SWHR's main contact with Capitol Hill and successfully worked with Congress to introduce a variety of women's health-related legislation. In 1993, when staff was needed, the board chose Ms. Greenberger to establish the office. Ms. Greenberger, who remains SWHR's CEO today, has been involved with SWHR's efforts since its inception. Under her leadership, SWHR continues to secure evidence of research inequity that directly affects women's lives before arguing forcefully for needed legislative or regulatory change. At SWHR's urging, GAO was asked to audit NIH practices again and in 2000, GAO issued a follow-up audit to its examination of practices at NIH, concluding that "NIH has made less progress in implementing the requirement that certain clinical trials be designed and carried out to permit valid analysis by sex, which could reveal whether interventions affect women and men differently." Another GAO report sought by SWHR concluded that "The FDA has not effectively overseen the presentation and analysis of data related to sex differences in drug development" (U.S. Government Accounting Office, 2001a).

An additional GAO audit sought by SWHR and issued in 2001 on FDA records revealed that eight out of the last 10 drugs withdrawn from the market caused adverse events more often in women than in men (U.S. Government Accounting Office, 2001b). Four of these drugs were more often prescribed to women than to men, which explained higher number of adverse events in women. The other four appeared to present a true sex difference in the incidence of adverse events. The GAO report concluded that "The FDA has not effectively overseen the presentation and analysis of data related to sex differences in drug development" (U.S. Government Accounting Office, 2001b).

SWHR needed to represent a broad spectrum of healthcare researchers, providers, and policy makers in order to succeed with government and congressional entities. In 1999, SWHR established the national Women's Health Research Coalition (WHRC). It now comprises more than 600 advocates from a broad range of academic, medical, and scientific institutions, as well as health-related associations and organizations to encourage coordination and funding for women's health research. Today, SWHR still ensures that its voice represents a broad spectrum of healthcare researchers and providers and policy makers. Similarly SWHR reaches out to healthcare providers and researchers in every field in conducting the many Capitol Hill briefings it holds each year. These briefings inform policy makers and their staff about contemporary women's health issues and the need for increased research funding for women's health and the study of biological sex differences affecting the prevention, diagnosis, and treatment of disease.

Advocacy and Communication Within Scientific Communities

The successes generated by advocating and communicating with Congress gave rise to new challenges for SWHR. First was appropriate staffing and composition of the board of directors. As a nonprofit entity, SWHR functions under the governance of a board of directors. Within 5 years of her hiring, SWHR CEO Phyllis Greenberger formed a team of administrative, fundraising, government relations, and scientific staff, whose efforts gradually replaced much of the work that had been accomplished by the all-volunteer board. Board members are still called on to represent SWHR, particularly in scientific venues, and to add their networking to that of SWHR staff's for advocacy and communication efforts. Periodically the board and staff review SWHR's mission and strategies to ensure that its work continues to focus on how it can make improvements in women's health and promote increased funding for sex-difference research.

Second, the inclusion of women in clinical trials corroborated SWHR's belief that, in matters of health and disease, men and women are different. However, scientists needed to be convinced of this fact so they would design studies to explain these differences. SWHR's response to this challenge was multipronged: it sought and received independent, unbiased validation of research on sex differences, hosted interdisciplinary conferences on sex differences in biology, and successfully sought funding for novel interdisciplinary sex differences research.

Ms. Greenberger led a 6-year campaign to secure funding for the formation of an IOM Committee on Understanding the Biology of Sex and Gender Differences. The strength of long-term relationships that she had forged through the years, coupled with her constant communication regarding the need for research into sex differences, were instrumental in securing the necessary funding from private and public sources. SWHR then submitted a proposal to IOM to validate the concept of sex differences. In 2001, IOM published a landmark report from this committee, entitled, *Exploring the Biological Contributions to Human Health: Does Sex Matter?*, and answered the question with a resounding, "yes." This IOM report established that:

- Every cell has a sex.
- Sex begins in the womb.
- Sex affects behavior and perception (IOM, 2001b).
- There is sufficient knowledge of the biological basis of sex differences to validate the scientific study of sex differences and to allow the generation of hypotheses with regard to health.
- Naturally occurring variations in sex differentiation can provide unique opportunities to obtain a better understanding of basic differences and similarities between and within the sexes" (IOM, 2001b).

SWHR sponsored five regional scientific advisory meetings (SAMs) to educate scientists and policy makers about the IOM report and worked diligently to communicate IOM findings. From 2000–2006, SWHR convened innovative conferences on sex and gene expression (SAGE) that explored how the biological variable of sex influences the expression of genetic information from embryonic development through adulthood. The SAGE conferences brought together leading established researchers and outstanding new researchers in biochemistry, genetics, and molecular, developmental, and cellular biology. Many of them came to believe that more than an annual conference was needed: working with SWHR staff, these leaders in sex differences research founded the Organization for the Study of Sex Differences (OSSD) in 2006. This nonprofit scientific membership society promotes the field of sex and gender differences research by facilitating interdisciplinary communication and collaboration among scientists and clinicians of diverse backgrounds.

Today OSSD has established itself as the home for the study of sex differences. The OSSD Web site (http://www.ossdweb.org) provides daily updates on the latest research on biological sex differences, and a bimonthly newsletter features recent articles on a specific topic within the field. The official electronic journal of OSSD, *Biology of Sex Differences*, is currently accepting submissions. OSSD's annual meeting brings together leading experts on sex differences research for face-to-face discussions on a wide range of topics, methodology, and future research directions.

Another outgrowth of the 2001 IOM report, *Does Sex Matter?* was the establishment of SWHR's Isis Fund for Sex-Based Biology Research. The SWHR Isis Fund promotes scientific communication and collaborations through interdisciplinary networks focusing on distinct areas. The first network, which was established in 2001 and concluded in 2007, concentrated on "Sex, Gender, Drugs, and the Brain." Other networks address sex differences in metabolism, musculoskeletal health, and cardiovascular disease, and several additional networks are in the preliminary stages of development.

Additionally, SWHR now hosts "What a Difference an X Makes: The State of Women's Health Research," an annual scientific conference bringing leading researchers, clinicians, physicians, and nonprofit professionals together to share new findings and groundbreaking studies in sex differences research. Recent conference topics included pain and the musculoskeletal system, the brain, the immune system, hypoactive sexual desire disorder (HSDD), cardiovascular disease and therapeutics, and obesity and comorbidities.

Other advocacy and communications efforts within the scientific community included analyzing sex differences research efforts at NIH. In May 2005, SWHR released a groundbreaking report that showed NIH support of research on biological health differences between women and men was lower than the growing evidence of the importance of sex differences warrants. It also showed that the institutes with the largest budgets appeared to be supporting the least research on sex differences. SWHR discussed this report with many NIH institute leaders and communicated its findings to other interested parties. Again, SWHR discovered that presentation of the facts, such as the IOM report or SWHR's examination of NIH granting practices, goes a long way toward persuading both people and organizations to change. In large part because of SWHR's education and communications, several of the NIH institutes, including the National Institute on Drug Abuse, the National Institute for Mental Health, the National Institute for Environmental Health Sciences, the National Institute on Aging, and the National Institute for Dental and Craniofacial Research, have recognized the need for sex differences research and have installed programs to fund research on sex differences.

Increasingly, those who fund biomedical research have become interested in sex as a biological variable. Researchers have found sex differences in every tissue and organ system (Becker et al., 2008). The field advanced to such a degree that SWHR and the Medtronic Foundation established the "SWHR-Medtronic Prize for Scientific Contributions to Women's Health" to recognize annually a woman scientist or engineer for her contributions to the field. The $75,000 prize is intended to encourage research on issues uniquely related to women's health, which almost always involves determining how and why women's health differs from men's. SWHR also administers the RAISE Project, which has a goal of increasing the status of professional women through enhanced recognition of their achievements in science, technology, medicine, and mathematics.

Advocacy and Communication with the Public

SWHR's first major public educational effort was the "Woman Can Do" campaign, initiated to educate and recruit more women to become involved in medical research. After the regulatory changes mandating women's participation in research, SWHR learned that researchers had difficulty finding women to participate in research studies. In 2003, nearly 90 other organizations joined SWHR's Alliance for Women in Clinical Research to educate women about medical research and ways they can participate. The campaign continues today and additional information can be found on the Woman Can Do Web site (http://www.womancando.org). SWHR continues to advise researchers, research establishments, and the FDA about ways to eliminate the barriers to recruiting and retaining women in research and clinical trials.

SWHR conducts many other consumer education and communications campaigns on a variety of topics, has a press service distributing news on women's health to over 10,000 media outlets, conducts periodic media briefings and roundtables, and holds workshops for clinicians. In 2006, SWHR published the first consumer book ever to discuss the impact of sex differences on health, entitled, *The Savvy Woman Patient: How and Why Sex Differences Affect Your Health.* The book is a guide to the health conditions and treatments unique to women of all ages and focuses on how women's health differs from men's. SWHR also annually presents their Excellence in Women's Health Research Journalism Awards to honor journalists who excel in providing the public with valuable and accurate health research information.

In addition to providing the latest research on conditions that affect women differently from men, SWHR's education and communications efforts also emphasize that women need to become advocates for themselves and their families. SWHR is founded on the belief that health can be improved through research efforts, and this new knowledge must be communicated and translated into individual care, which requires an up-to-date, current exchange of information between healthcare providers and their patients.

SWHR works to provide women, who make about three-fourths of the healthcare decisions in the United States, with advice that communication with healthcare providers is a two-way dialogue and with the information that allows them to participate in decisions affecting themselves and their family members. SWHR's educational programs and written materials, as well as its Web site, also serve as resources for practitioners and individuals involved or interested in women's health issues.

SWHR will soon begin working with the Office of Women's Health at the FDA and the Drug Information Agency on their joint program on recruitment and retention of women in clinical trials. SWHR also provides information regarding clinical trials to the public on its Web site.

Current Challenges and Opportunities

While proud of its many accomplishments, SWHR is looking ahead to the myriad challenges facing the country related to health care, health insurance reforms, and the push for personalized medicine. Its current advocacy priorities include:

- Funding for research in women's health
- Clinical trials
- Comparative effectiveness research
- Sex-based biology
- Drug labeling

SWHR is committed to ensuring that women's health remains a high priority on the national agenda, that sex differences become more widely recognized as vital to healthcare treatment options, and to advocating for increased funding for related research. Both the size of SWHR's staff and the roster of volunteer leaders have grown over time to assist in these efforts. Medical, nursing, research, and scientific experts from a wide range of disciplines have been involved with SWHR's advocacy and communications outreach. Staff can now call on OSSD Council officers and members, current and past members of SWHR's networks, authors of chapters in the *Savvy Women Patient*, and presenters from past SWHR conferences, as well as board members for the medical and technical knowledge that undergirds the organization's advocacy and communications efforts. As we enter the second decade of the 21st century, SWHR will continue to partner with the widest possible range of healthcare providers and policy makers to gather evidence-based knowledge and then communicate it to Congress, the scientific research community, and to healthcare providers and the public.

Summary

The Society for Women's Health Research (SWHR) is a nonprofit advocacy organization now recognized as the thought leader in research on sex differences. It was founded 20 years ago and remains dedicated to improving women's health through advocacy, education, and research. SWHR credits its original advocacy and communications strategies coupled with the inclusion of a mix of healthcare providers and policy makers dedicated to improving women's health with its ability to:

- Change the way research is conducted in the United States.
- Force the inclusion of women and minorities in medical research.
- Alter how scientists now look at the different ways health and disease affect men and women and the reasons why.

Beginning with a request that the GAO evaluate NIH policies and practices regarding the inclusion of women and minorities in clinical trials, SWHR has for the last 20 years sought solid evidence to make its points regarding women's health and research. In addition to documenting and communicating a variety of these issues, SWHR's advocacy and communications efforts have extended beyond the traditional lobbying of legislators and regulators to include education and continuous communications with federal legislators and their staff; scientists employed by the federal government, academia and industry; and the public.

As SWHR forced changes at other federal agencies, including the FDA, the volunteer organization morphed into a professionally run nonprofit led by current President and CEO, Phyllis M. Greenberger, MSW. Under Ms. Greenberger, SWHR was able to represent a broad spectrum of healthcare researchers, providers, and policy makers to succeed with governmental and congressional entities, culminating in the establishment of the national WHRC, which now includes over 600 advocates from a wide range of academic, medical, and scientific institutions as well as health-related associations and organizations to cooperatively encourage coordination and funding for women's health research.

SWHR's hard-won successes related to the inclusion of women in clinical trials confirmed its belief that in matters of health and disease, men and women are different, and SWHR initiated advocacy and communications efforts within the scientific community to convince scientists they needed to design studies to explain such differences. SWHR pushed for independent, unbiased validation of research on sex differences, hosted interdisciplinary conferences on sex differentness in biology, and successfully sought funding for novel interdisciplinary sex differences research. In 2006, SWHR founded the OSSD to promote the field of sex and gender differences research by facilitating interdisciplinary communication and collaboration among scientists and clinicians of diverse backgrounds. SWHR also created the SWHR Isis Fund for Sex-Based Biology Research to promote scientific communications and collaborations through interdisciplinary networks focusing on distinct areas of study. The annual conference, "What a Difference an X Makes: The State of Women's Health Research," is SWHR's annual scientific conference that brings together leading researchers, clinicians, physicians, and nonprofit professionals to share new findings and groundbreaking studies in sex difference research.

SWHR's other advocacy and communications efforts within the scientific community included analyzing sex differences research at the NIH, which resulted in several of the NIH institutes recognizing the need for sex differences research and implementing programs to fund research on sex differences.

SWHR has made great inroads in championing women's health research and the scientific study of sex differences. Those who fund biomedical research have become interested in sex as a biological variable, and researchers have found sex differences existing throughout the human body.

Finally, SWHR has and maintains extensive advocacy and communications efforts with the public. Its first major effort of this type was the "Women Can Do" campaign to educate and encourage more women to become involved in medical research. SWHR's Alliance for Women in Clinical Research continues to educate women about medical research and ways they can participate. SWHR also conducts several other consumer education and communications campaigns on topics related to women's health, conducts media briefings and roundtables, and holds workshops for clinicians. *The Savvy Woman Patient: How and Why Sex Differences Affect Your Health* was published by SWHR in 2006 and was the first consumer book to discuss sex differences. SWHR's communications efforts also emphasize that women need to become advocates for themselves and their families by working with their healthcare providers in making healthcare-related decisions. SWHR's Web site, educational programs, and materials also serve as resources for healthcare practitioners and individuals interested in women's health issues.

As the leader in the study of sex differences and an outspoken advocate for women's health research and funding, SWHR is focused on the current challenges related to health care, health insurance reforms, and the call for personalized medicine. Because of its successful advocacy and communications strategies, SWHR has grown from an all-volunteer to a nationally recognized, professionally run organization with a wealth of scientific expertise and research behind it. Through advocacy and communication efforts, SWHR will continue to collaborate with a variety of healthcare providers and policy makers to gather more evidence-based knowledge and communicate it to Congress, the scientific research community, healthcare providers, and the public.

Discussion Questions

1. Why was the background of SWHR's founders and board critical to the success of SWHR?
2. What role did advocacy and communications play in SWHR's efforts to promote women's health and sex differences research?
3. What successful communications and advocacy skills did SWHR's leaders exhibit?
4. Who does SWHR communicate with today and why?
5. What best practices in healthcare communications and advocacy do you see in the history of SWHR?

References

Becker, J. B. et al. (2008). *Sex differences in the brain: From genes to behavior.* New York, NY: Oxford University Press.

Haseltine, F. Forward. (2006). *Savvy woman patient: How and why sex differences affect your health.* Herndon, VA: Capital Publishing, Inc.

IOM (Institute of Medicine). (1992). *Strengthening research in academic OB/GYN departments.* Washington, DC: National Academy Press.

Institute of Medicine. (2001). *Exploring the biological contributions to human health: Does sex matter?* Washington, DC: National Academy Press.

NIH (National Health Institutes). (1986). *NIH guide for grants and contracts.* Bethesda, MD: Author.

NIH (National Institutes of Health). (1990). *Problems in implementing policy on women in study populations* (Rep. GAO/T-HRD-90-50). Washington, DC: U.S. Government Accounting Office.

U.S. Government Accounting Office. (1993). *Women's health: FDA needs to ensure more study of gender differences in prescription drugs testing* (Rep. GAO-HRD-93-17). Washington, DC: Author.

U.S. Government Accounting Office. (2001a). *Women sufficiently represented in new drug testing, but FDA oversight needs improvement* (Rep. GAO-01-754). Washington, DC: Author.

U.S. Government Accounting Office. (2001b). *Drug safety: Most drugs withdrawn in recent years had greater health risks for women* (Rep. GAO-01-286R). Washington, DC: Author.

Chapter 15

Changing Obesity Policies and Behavioral Risk Factors Through Social Marketing: Case Study of the Chicago 5-4-3-2-1 Go! Program

By W. Douglas Evans

LEARNING OBJECTIVES

By the end of this chapter, the reader will be able to:

- Understand the relationship between social marketing and ecological approaches to health.
- Understand how social marketing has been applied in community-based settings to prevent and control childhood obesity.
- Describe the evidence base for social marketing in changing childhood obesity community-level policies and reducing behavioral risk factors.
- Apply social marketing strategies on an introductory level to promote community-level policy change.

Introduction

In recent years, an ecological approach to nutrition and physical activity promotion has become widespread in community-based obesity prevention programs (Green & Kreuter, 2005). Ecological approaches are concerned with changing the social and physical environments in which people live to reduce health risks for conditions such as obesity. Social marketing, defined here as the application of commercial marketing methods using the four *P*s to benefit consumers and society, is a promising ecological approach to obesity prevention (Kotler & Lee, 2008). Social marketing can be used both to influence "downstream" individual decision making to reduce obesity health risks and as part of an "upstream" policy change process (Evans, Christoffel, Necheles, & Becker, 2010).

Recent community-based research has studied social marketing campaigns as a policy change tool to create healthier social and physical environments. For example, Shape Up Somerville is a citywide campaign to increase daily physical activity and healthy eating through programming, physical infrastructure improvements, and policy work (Chuggish & Kinder, 2008). The campaign targeted all segments of the community, including schools, city government, civic organizations, community groups, businesses, and other people who live, work, and play in Somerville, MA. The effort began as a community-based research study at Tufts University targeting first through third graders in the Somerville public schools and expanded to encompass the Somerville community environment. With funding from the Centers for Disease Control and Prevention (CDC), this environmental change intervention decreased BMI *z*-scores in children at high risk for obesity. These results are significant given the "obesigenic" environment in which the intervention was implemented (Economos, Hyatt, Goldberg, et al., 2007).

In Chicago, the 5-4-3-2-1 Go! obesity prevention program has explored the relationship between ecological approaches to obesity prevention and social marketing. The program was successful both in increasing fruit and vegetable and water consumption among individual parents, and in building and promoting use of citywide, neighborhood, and school-based nutrition and physical activity resources (Becker, Longjohn, & Christoffel, 2008). Social marketing can promote and create conditions where community actors are empowered to engage in collective action to improve community resource, systems, and policies that serve as obesity protective and preventive factors (Evans, Christoffel, Necheles, & Becker, 2010).

In this chapter, we discuss the role of social marketing in childhood obesity prevention, its relationship to and significance for policy-based interventions, and offer recommendations for research and action. While this chapter focuses mainly on social marketing and its applicability to childhood obesity, the perspective that we offer may be more broadly applicable to adult obesity and related chronic disease prevention issues. Social marketing can influence social and physical environments and government policies in addition to individual behavior, and thus may be broadly applicable within an ecological model of health.

Obesity Ecology, Social Marketing, and Policy Change

Ecological View of Obesity and Related Risk Factors

In recent years, numerous intervention programs have been developed to address community-level risk factors for obesity. As noted, such programs often take an ecological view of obesity risk factors (Green & Kreuter, 2005; McLeroy, Bibeau, Steckler, et al., 1988), which view the community as one environment in which conditions can be modified to lower risk. These programs can be classified in a number of ways, but for illustrative purposes, community intervention programs can be classified as seeking to influence factors such as:

- Physical environment (e.g., availability of fresh fruits and vegetables or low-fat milk; recreational opportunities, and point of decision prompts for healthy choices)
- Family and social environment
- Community outreach and mobilization (e.g., engaging community-based organizations and resources)
- Social capital (to facilitate community outreach, healthy environments, and encouragement of healthy activities that control weight)
- Social marketing and health communication campaigns

A generalized conceptual framework (shown in Figure 15-1) suggests that interventions designed to enhance social capital, to mobilize communities, and to conduct social marketing can mutually reinforce each other in enhancing the physical environment and the family and social environment to prevent obesity. The impact of interventions is a function of their intensity (e.g., reach, frequency, and duration). The effects of interventions on obesity are mediated by changes in knowledge, attitudes, and beliefs; intentions to engage in behaviors; and to maintain behaviors that can prevent obesity.

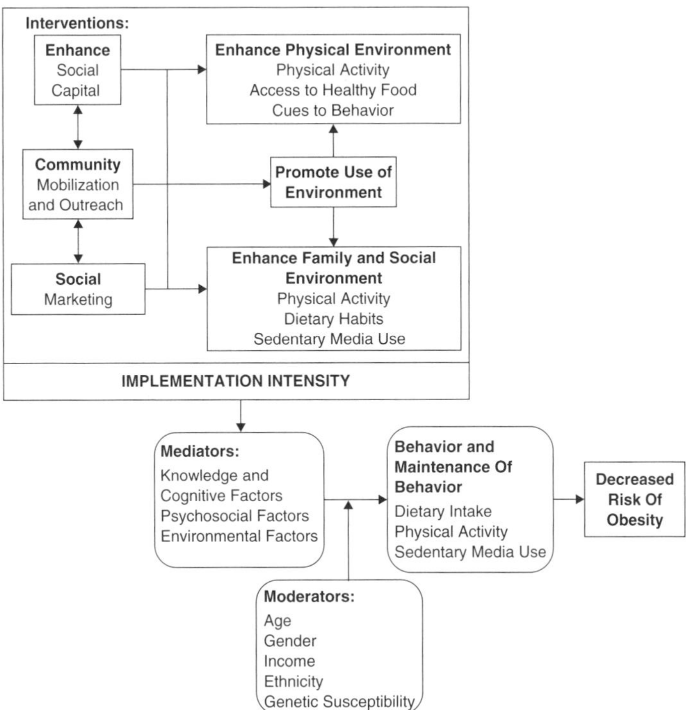

Figure 15-1 Interventions Obesity Chart

Examples of these behaviors include increased use of opportunities for physical activity available in one's community, or improved dietary practices such as reducing portion size, decreasing consumption of high-energy-dense foods and sugared beverages, and substituting more nutritious, low-energy-dense foods such as fruits and vegetables (IOM, 2005). As discussed below, social marketing can contribute to behavior change by directly reaching and influencing individuals and by changing their social and physical environments to create incentives to change. The latter approach can be successfully affected through changes in government policies that create healthier environments and provide individuals with social, economic, and other benefits that encourage them to change their behavior and reduce obesity risk factors.

Social Marketing for Policy Change

Often marketing and communication programs are conceived as individual behavior change strategies. Product marketers target individual shoppers within audience segments to maximize sales and market share. Historically, social marketing efforts to change modifiable health behaviors, such as preventing HIV/AIDS, have focused primarily on downstream individual behaviors such as promoting condom use (Evans & Hastings, 2008). Until recently, upstream efforts to change policies and larger environmental factors have received less attention in social marketing literature.

However, the notion of influencing upstream environmental factors and intervention strategies such as policy change, as well as downstream individual behavior, is now prominent in public health. In the 1980s and early 1990s, the exclusive focus on downstream behaviors was criticized, and there was a call for more attention on social environmental conditions that could promote behavior change over the longer term (Dearing and Rogers, 1996; Wallack et al., 1993). Social marketers responded by recognizing the upstream agenda (Hastings et al., 2000).

The National Cancer Institute's American Stop Smoking Intervention Study (Project ASSIST) offers a good example of upstream social marketing. The purpose of ASSIST was to influence health policy by changing public acceptability of tobacco use and social norms in order to influence public policy (National Cancer Institute, 2005). ASSIST used media advocacy—the strategic use of mass media as a resource for advancing a social or public policy initiative—to stimulate policy initiatives to restrict youth access to tobacco, promote clean indoor air laws, increase excise taxes, and restrict or ban advertising and promotion of tobacco (Evans, Ulasevich, & Stillman, 2006). ASSIST branded tobacco control policies as the prosocial choice, and created a social movement to control and prevent tobacco use. Engagement with the social movement through writing letters to elected officials, attending tobacco control events, and donating funds to tobacco control organizations offered individuals a way to contribute. The resulting groundswell of support led to policy changes such as smoke-free restaurants, which in turn further influenced social norms in favor of tobacco control (Evans, Ulasevich, & Stillman, 2006). This example may provide a model for future obesity prevention social marketing to affect policy change. Engaging citizens in a social movement was part of the strategy in Shape Up Somerville, and, as described later in the chapter, it is part of the 5-4-3-2-1 Go! program in Chicago (Chuggish & Kinder, 2008; Evans, Christoffel, Necheles, et al., 2010).

Readiness for Obesity Policy Change

A policy change strategy, similar to what has occurred in tobacco control, has been proposed as a way of addressing obesity in the US population (Koplan & Dietz, 1999). The rationale guiding a policy change approach is that public and private policies reflecting community norms may be influential in affecting the underlying determinants that shape the health of individuals in communities and environments governed by such policies (Bell & Standish, 2005; NIH, 2005).

There has been increasing support in the literature for using a policy advocacy approach to address the obesity epidemic (Blackburn & Walker, 2005; Dodson, Fleming, and Boehmer, et al., 2009; Finkelstein, French, Variyam, et al., 2004). There is also evidence of strong public support for various types of policy change strategies for preventing obesity (Evans, Finkelstein, Kamerow, et al., 2005). For instance, opinion surveys have found that Americans generally prefer social policy strategies and government interventions that include school-, community-, and media-based strategies such as offering health information, providing healthier options in school vending machines and cafeterias, and increasing health nutrition and physical education options (Evans, Finkelstein, Kamerow, et al., 2005). Increasing tax on unhealthy food marketed to children and restricting marketing practices targeting children have received less support (Finkelstein, French, Variyam, et al., 2004). Fewer studies have evaluated the level of support for public and private policy changes aimed at preventing adult obesity, despite a call by researchers for including macro-level policy interventions as a way of addressing both childhood and adult obesity (Koplan & Dietz, 1999; Swinburn, Gill, & Kumanyika, 2005). In general, public and private policies aimed at adult obesity prevention can take a number of forms, including regulation and incentives. Policy changes that encourage employers to provide facilities and opportunities for physical activity and reimbursements for prevention and treatment of obesity are two strategies that have been recommended by the surgeon general (USDHHS, 2001). Employer or health insurer incentives to individuals for maintaining weight or health could be another policy strategy that could help to prevent obesity in adults.

To date, however, the degree to which people may favor such healthcare and workplace policy interventions is unknown. Knowing the degree to which people favor such policies would be a first step toward policy change. Further, knowing the factors that predict people being in favor of such policies may be also helpful in building support for public and private policies or give an indication as to which segments of the population may favor or oppose a particular policy change strategy. Previous studies examining factors that influence choice for various childhood obesity policies have examined sociodemographic factors. For instance, higher income, higher educational level, and gender (i.e., women) have been found to be factors that predict favorability toward policy interventions aimed at regulating school vending machines and school cafeteria lunches (Evans, Renaud, Finkelstein, et al., 2006). In addition to sociodemographic factors, other factors that may be important predictors of whether or not a person favors certain social policies over others may be beliefs about what causes obesity and the level of obesity-related health risk to which they believe themselves to be exposed.

The health communication literature suggests that message framing about individual versus social responsibility for a health problem may be important predictors of belief formation and behavior change (Williams-Piehota, Cox, Silvera, et al., 2004).

For instance, emphasizing the social context in which eating a healthy diet occurs (e.g., family, one's community) has been found to be a better predictor of healthy dietary change than emphasizing the individual or personal responsibility (Williams-Piehota, Cox, Silvera, et al., 2004). Likewise, the degree to which people believe themselves to be at risk for disease has also been thought to be an important determinant of behavior (Rosenstock, Strecher, & Becker, 1988). For instance, patients who believe themselves to be at risk of certain cancers may be more likely to seek appropriate cancer screening. Thus, it may also be the case that individuals who believe themselves to be at risk for obesity-related diseases may be more in favor of policy suggestions that curtail and prevent obesity. Finally, the degree to which one is overweight may also be an important predictor of whether or not someone favors one type of policy over another, as certain policies may provide greater incentives for those who are overweight/obese (e.g., offering ways to save money by losing weight).

Need for Community Resources, Systems, and Policy-Level Interventions

There is now considerable agreement that escalating rates of obesity can be tied to characteristics of the environments in which people live (Drewnowski, 2004; Hill, Wyatt, Reed, et al., 2003; Jefferey & Utter, 2003; Swinburn, Egger, & Raza, 1999). As such, environmental changes with policy as one component of the intervention will likely be required. Accordingly, social marketing for obesity prevention is grounded in a socioecological framework that acknowledges that the factors that influence pediatric and adult obesity are present at multiple levels, including policy (Haire-Joshu, 2002; McLeroy, Bibeau, Steckler, et al., 1988; Stokols, 1996).

One lesson from community studies is that changes in the physical environment should be accompanied by active promotion and point of decision prompts to engage in healthy behaviors. For instance, signs placed by elevators and escalators can increase the percentage of people who use nearby stairs by more than 50% (Community Preventive Services Task Force, 2005).

Reducing environmental barriers can encourage physical activity. For instance, a study in London, England, found that improved lighting on footpaths increased footpath use by 34–101% (Painter, 1996), and a study in Toronto, Canada, found that the creation of bike lanes increased bicycle use by 23% (Macbeth, 1999). One recent review adds that point-of-purchase prompts may have greater impact on food choices in settings such as worksites where fewer alternatives were available (Seymour et al., 2004). Similarly, a systematic review by the Community Preventive Services Task Force (2005) found that increasing access to places for physical activity in worksites (eight studies) or low-income communities (two studies: Brownson, Smith, Pratt et al., 1996; Lewis et al., 1993), combined with information activities, increased by a median of 48% the proportion of adults who exercised three or more times a week.

Social Marketing and Childhood Obesity Prevention

Social marketing has been used in the context of community-based obesity prevention programs to promote behaviors such as increased parent-child communication and improved family health. Many social marketing efforts—such as nutrition and physical activity messages promoted by the 1% milk campaign in California, the CDC's *VERB: It's What You Do* campaign, and the *5-4-3-2-1 Go!* campaign in Chicago—have targeted parents in order to encourage them to change the home health environment and talk to their children about health behaviors (Evans, Necheles, Longjohn, et al., 2007; Huhman, Price, & Potter, 2008; Reger, Wootan, Booth-Butterfield, et al., 1998).

Many such programs use community outreach as well as mass media components for a multichannel message strategy. In that context, marketing efforts may address multiple risk factors in the social and physical environment, such as the effects of community environments, food and physical activity resource availability, and food advertising on children's health behavior (Evans, 2008). They may also address parents as a pathway through which to reach children.

Parents of children and adolescents can be reached with targeted social marketing campaigns aimed at changing social norms about food preference and choice, social desirability of exercise, and healthy weight. Risk factors such as excessive media use (e.g., TV watching, video game playing) can be targeted with messages aimed at both parents (to encourage their involvement) and children (to change their preferences) varying by children's stage of development (Evans, 2008). Some examples of social marketing help to illustrate possible approaches.

Social Marketing as Part of Ecological Approaches

Social marketing can be integrated into multilevel ecological approaches to health promotion, using multiple *P* intervention strategies to support changing the environment around the audience, fostering change in community norms by delivering health messages, as well as encouraging individual behavior change. Social marketing goes beyond individual-focused health communication and uses multiple interventions at the various ecological levels (Evans, Christoffel, Necheles, et al., 2010).

Family

Parents serve as important nutrition and physical activity role models, for better or worse. Their behavior fosters child emulation of eating, exercise, and leisure habits, such as playing sports, entertainment, and media use (Calvert, 2008; Huhman, Price, & Potter, 2008). Parental modeling can serve as either a risk or protective factor for childhood obesity. To foster beneficial modeling, social marketing can encourage parents to adopt protective behaviors by depicting positive parental role models creating a healthy home environment (Evans & Hastings, 2008). Parents who model healthy rather than unhealthy behaviors, such as keeping fruits and vegetables in the household instead of junk foods, or limiting consumption of such foods, can lay the foundation for their children to incorporate healthy habits at home and in school and community environments.

Community

Social marketing can be used to *promote* engagement and positive role modeling of residents, community leaders in the faith and not-for-profit sectors, and local health and healthcare organizations. Community mobilization has long been a major component of social marketing, including coalition building and empowerment of youth to tackle public health challenges such as tobacco control (Evans, 2008). Youth empowerment at the community level was used as an intervention component of the 5-4-3-2-1 Go! childhood obesity prevention initiative (Evans, Necheles, Longjohn, & Christoffel, 2007).

Policy and Society

Social marketing has demonstrated its ability to influence health policy, as exemplified by programs such as the National Cancer Institute's American Stop Smoking Intervention Study (ASSIST) (Evans & Hastings, 2008). Social marketing can change policy makers' frame of reference for social issues, such as the social acceptability of smoking, contributing to legislation and policy that change the environment. Such approaches can be integrated with behavior change messages to individual consumers and need to be strategically applied in obesity prevention as in fields such as smoking (Evans, 2008).

One lesson from the tobacco control movement and its success in reducing smoking rates is that multicomponent programs are required to effect lasting and meaningful population-level behavior change (USDHHS, 2004). Researchers in other public health domains, such as substance abuse prevention, have similarly theorized that comprehensive programs that include two or more elements will prove more effective (Flay, 2000). Meta-analyses of social marketing campaigns have shown they generally yield larger effect sizes in behavioral outcomes when combined with other levels of intervention, such as programs in schools and communities, as well as policy change (Snyder & Hamilton, 2002). The same may well be true in obesity prevention as well. The following case study represents one approach to comprehensive, multicomponent social marketing to reduce multiple obesity risk factors in the social and physical environment, in an effort to change individual behavior and promote collective action in a major US city.

Case Study of The 5-4-3-2-1 Go! Program

Beginning in 2004, the Consortium to Lower Obesity in Chicago Children (CLOCC; www.clocc.net) developed a public health education initiative to bolster ongoing local efforts addressing Chicago's childhood obesity epidemic through healthy eating and physical activity. CLOCC is a citywide coalition of nearly 1000 organizations representing virtually all social sectors. CLOCC and its partners developed the 5-4-3-2-1 Go! social marketing initiative. Following a community-based participatory approach, 5-4-3-2-1 Go! was led by local partner organizations, community leaders, and young people across Chicago to develop and disseminate the initiative. The campaign is based on healthy eating and active living messages for children: Consume five or more fruits and vegetables, four servings of water, and three servings of low-fat dairy a day; spend no more than 2 hours watching television or similar sedentary behavior; and engage in at least 1 hour of physical activity per day. These messages are disseminated widely through community channels and form the core of an environmental change strategy.

The 5-4-3-2-1 Go! initiative uses a healthy lifestyles *branding* strategy aimed at improving family food choices and increasing use of community physical activity resources (Evans, Price & Blahut, 2005). It is aimed initially at six vanguard community areas that are linked to census boundaries in Chicago: Englewood, Humboldt Park, Lower West Side, Rogers Park, West Garfield Park, and West Town. These areas were targeted based on high pediatric obesity prevalence (Mason, et al., 2006), research conducted by the Sinai Urban Health Institute (SUHI, 2006), local resources, and an existing relationship with CLOCC.

The 5-4-3-2-1 Go! initiative has become a component of the City of Chicago's strategic efforts for addressing obesity by Chicago's Department of Public Health and Chicago Department of Youth Services. Through a partnership with the not-for-profit Communities In Schools of Chicago (CISC), CLOCC has also integrated 5-4-3-2-1 Go! activities and messages into the public school system.

Community Background

The 5-4-3-2-1 Go! initiative is in part a response to the "obesigenic environment" prevalent in the six target communities, that is, a social and physical environment that inhibits healthy lifestyles (Hill, Wyatt, Reed et al., 2003). Environmental factors that may contribute to unhealthy nutrition and reduced levels of physical activity (Booth, Pinkston, & Poston, 2005; Popkin, Duffey, & Gordon-Larsen, 2005) include inability to consume sufficient quantities of fruits and vegetables due to lack of convenient access to supermarkets and high costs; restaurant offerings in lower-income areas that present a barrier to eating a healthy diet outside of the home (Lewis et al., 2005; Morland et al., 2002); and obesity-related social capital, such as community participation, social agency, and feelings of trust and safety to use community nutrition and physical activity resources (Onyx & Bullen, 2000).

The creation of 5-4-3-2-1 Go! was also prompted by specific barriers and potential opportunities in the target communities. As noted in a series of focus groups conducted with community leaders, service providers, and residents, there is very limited access to fresh fruits and vegetables and few supermarkets or farmer's markets, few healthy restaurant options, safety concerns about use of parks and recreational facilities due to gangs, and lack of widespread information about alternative access to better nutrition and physical activity options. These same focus groups also found high levels of community demand for resources such as a Web site where information on community resources could be disseminated, promotion of community events and resources such as health fairs and after-school activities, and interventions such as the Greater Chicago Food Depository "Produce Mobiles" that bring surplus fruits and vegetables directly to communities.

The resulting 5-4-3-2-1 Go! concept is to brand a culturally relevant and "source authentic" (i.e., delivered by authentic voices and true to community norms and values) message platform based on nutrition and relevant health promotion science. Youth ambassadors from Chicago communities participate in interpreting and adapting the message to compelling forms of media, and in disseminating the message to the communities' children and parents. Thus messages and delivery channels are "by and for the people" and are aimed at changing nutrition and physical activity practices and altering the local obesigenic environment (Young, Anderson, Beckstrom, Bellows, & Johnson, 2004). This follows from similar community-based approaches used in the tobacco control movement, specifically in youth- and community-engagement components of the American Legacy Foundation's *truth* campaign to prevent adolescent smoking (Holden, Evans, Hinnant, et al., 2005).

Program Development

The 5-4-3-2-1 Go! initiative is based on current lifestyle recommendations and guided by CLOCC's formative research on community attitudes, beliefs, lifestyle, health information-seeking practices, and service in target communities. The investigators conducted focus groups in all six CLOCC vanguard communities (total of 12, 2 per community) with community service providers, such as lay health workers and community recreation groups. The purpose of the focus groups was to collect input on redesigning the CLOCC Web site to support health promotion activities such as its 5-4-3-2-1 Go! message. The focus groups also addressed communication infrastructure (how community members communicate about health issues), social support for nutrition and physical activity, community activities and resources for physical activity, and food access and availability.

The study identified potential barriers, such as the "digital divide" in access to health information (Fox, 2005), as well as supports, message strategies (e.g., promoting site to community-based organizations), and community readiness for change. Results of these groups and ones with community youth were used in development of specific 5-4-3-2-1 Go! messages, message delivery strategies, and for the development of an evaluation strategy.

Social Marketing Strategy

5-4-3-2-1 Go! objectives are to:

- Raise awareness of the local opportunities and community-based services available to promote healthy lifestyles
- Drive intent to participate in activities that promote healthy lifestyles
- Increase year-round involvement in activities that promote healthy lifestyles
- Raise awareness of Chicago as a city that is tackling the obesity epidemic
- Raise awareness of CLOCC's work among corporations, community groups, and grassroots organizations (CLOCC partners and nonpartners) to engage them in program activities and initiatives

The strategy behind 5-4-3-2-1 Go! is to create a new healthy lifestyles brand in Chicago that does the following:

- Uses a name and logo that embodies the brand essence: "Eating right and being healthy is as easy as *5-4-3-2-1 Go!*"
- Communicates positive messages that resonate across different ethnic communities
- Uses high school volunteers—"Go! Teams"—to serve as community ambassadors
- "Comes to life" at programs and events and through earned news media coverage
- Enjoys support of key political, civic, and community leaders
- Rewards youth and adult involvement
- Optimizes awareness and participation by becoming part of as many current neighborhood and citywide programs as possible
- Builds on local community residents' pride in being Chicago residents

The 5-4-3-2-1 Go! brand includes key messages about daily nutrition and physical activity—consume 5 servings of fruits and vegetables, 4 servings of water, and 3 servings of low-fat dairy per day; limit screen time to 2 hours per day; and engage in at least 1 hour of moderate physical activity per day.

To achieve these goals, a 5-4-3-2-1 Go! campaign was developed and implemented beginning in 2007. The ongoing campaign uses 5-4-3-2-1 Go! messages in public service announcements (PSAs) on television, in games taught by high school volunteers to thousands of grade school children, in trainings held for YMCA camp counselors and other community child care workers, in clinical pediatrics settings for resident physician training and goal-setting by patient families, and in community events. Thus it addresses multiple ecological levels within Chicago communities and seeks to change the social and physical environment at multiple levels. These activities form the community-based social marketing intervention.

CLOCC's approach in 5-4-3-2-1 Go! is to use the basic principles of the marketing mix, or four *P*s of marketing—place, price, product, and promotion—and adapt them to the target communities (Borden 1964). For example, all messages and materials are in Spanish and English. Authentic sources and marketing that aligns with community health information sources and role models from the community can help to build the 5-4-3-2-1 Go! brand.

Many important lessons can be learned from *5-4-3-2-1 Go!* that should be considered when developing public health education campaigns focused on healthy eating and physical activity.

- *Source credibility and message receptivity*—Social marketing and message theory emphasizes the importance of source credibility and positive cognitive and affective reactions to health messages (Petty and Cacioppo, 1986). Formative research for the 5-4-3-2-1 Go! confirms this and points to the importance of nutrition messages that take urban lifestyles, health information sources, and healthy eating barriers into account in developing culturally relevant messages and delivery systems. Go! teams composed of adolescent youths representing positive, source-authentic role models for young children are a central strategy.

- *Culturally relevant health information sources*—Many urban communities rely on health information from trusted local sources rather than physicians or mass media sources. Spanish-speaking communities, in particular, obtain such information from their own media and targeted service providers such as local clinics or faith leaders. The 5-4-3-2-1 Go! intervention demonstrates the value of using local health information sources to reach urban target audiences.
- *Multipronged outreach strategies.* Given that many urban audiences use local health information sources with relatively low reach (e.g., community newspapers), 5-4-3-2-1 Go! is using a multipronged outreach and message delivery strategies. By using multiple sources targeting community members in their homes, through businesses or churches, and at public events, 5-4-3-2-1 Go! maximizes reach using cost-effective strategies.
- *Community partners and "influentials"*—Another critical approach to extending reach is through such partners as community-based organization and the city of Chicago. CLOCC works with partners to leverage resources and enhance acceptance in target communities. Community leaders can influence government policy to change local obesigenic environments. They can also serve to reinforce 5-4-3-2-1 Go! messages, and act as additional channels to support Go! teams, earned media, and www.clocc.net.

Outcome Evaluation: Program Effects on Behaviors, Community Resources, and Policy

The 5-4-3-2-1 Go! campaign was evaluated in a community trial with participants from six Chicago communities where the full campaign was implemented (Evans, Christoffel, Necheles, et al., 2010). Some elements, such as the PSAs, had broader reach. Parents of children aged 3–7, the primary campaign target, were eligible for the study. Parents were randomly assigned to receive a brief in-home counseling session on benefits of, and overcoming barriers to, 5-4-3-2-1 Go! behaviors (treatment) or no counseling (control). The campaign was later implemented in these same communities, and both groups had the opportunity to be exposed to campaign messages in the community.

The objectives of the study were to evaluate the effectiveness of the 5-4-3-2-1 Go! campaign in preventing and controlling obesity risk behaviors. The study examined the effects of brief counseling delivered by trained staff to randomly chosen study participants based on the campaign messages on the five targeted behaviors. Their behavior changes were compared 1 year postexposure to those of control participants. Both groups had the potential to be exposed to the community-based intervention, and all of these potential effects were measured through an in-person questionnaire based on validated and program-specific nutrition and physical activity knowledge, attitudes, beliefs, and behavior items. The study also measured reactions to the 5-4-3-2-1 Go! brand, family media use, and exposure to other obesity interventions, social capital, and obesity-related policies and in the 5-4-3-2-1 Go! communities.

As expected, the study found most parents and children in the study were not meeting recommended levels of 5-4-3-2-1 Go! behaviors. As has been observed in many experimental, regional, and national studies of behavioral risk factors for adult and childhood obesity, there is significant room for risk reduction (Zenk, Schulz, Hollis-Neely, et al., 2005). In multivariable analyses, 5-4-3-2-1 Go! had some statistically significant effects on obesity risk behaviors.

5-4-3-2-1 Go! counseling resulted in improvements in parental fruit and vegetable and water consumption 1 year after campaign inception (Evans, Christoffel, Necheles, et al., 2010). A possible mechanism for this is that the messages and materials left behind with parents as part of the brief counseling, which included refrigerator magnets, water bottles, and other day-to-day items, served as reminders for shopping trips. This and other possible mechanisms deserve further investigation. Thus one hypothesis, that parental exposure to *5-4-3-2-1 Go!* messages is associated with positive parental behavioral outcomes targeted by the campaign, was confirmed for those outcomes. As African-American and Hispanic families were the primary beneficiaries, the campaign suggests how to address obesity in communities suffering from significant health disparities.

Analysis of community message exposure effects showed that exposure to 5-4-3-2-1 Go! community messaging in schools was associated with increased parent water intake (Evans, Christoffel, Necheles, et al., 2010). This suggests opportunities for future research and obesity prevention programming working on collaboration between community-based campaigns and school-based efforts.

Despite these positive effects on parents' self-reported behaviors, a second hypothesis that parental message exposure would be associated with parental reports of positive behavioral outcomes for their *children* was not confirmed. This indicates that additional research is needed to explore whether and if so how changes leading to parental behavior change can lead to child behavior change. It also suggests that closer examination of the accuracy of parental reports of child behaviors may be needed, as well as validation studies that directly examine children's behavior through observation and self-report.

Summary

Implications for Ecologically Focused Obesity Prevention Programs

The 5-4-3-2-1 Go! campaign and other examples discussed in this chapter suggest strategies for ecologically focused obesity prevention programs to integrate social marketing. For example, there are opportunities to prevent childhood obesity at the family, school, and community levels (Evans, Blitstein, Lynch, et al., 2009).

At the individual level, *promotion* and *product* strategies can directly reach individuals and nudge them to change nutrition and physical activity habits for the better (e.g., reduce processed and low-nutrient density, high-fat foods; promote convenient ways to increase energy expenditure such as neighborhood walking or household activities). Advertising to individuals can depict socially desirable role models realizing social benefits (e.g., more friends, better appearance) and functional benefits from a healthy active lifestyle. The *product* is the packaging of these behaviors and their benefits.

At the family level, programs can reduce childhood obesity risk factors by changing parental behavior. The *price* of getting children active can be reduced through community sports and recreation programs in local neighborhoods (integrating *place*) at times convenient for busy working parents. *Promotions* aimed at individual parents can suggest small changes in food choice, such as buying one less package of processed snack foods and one more fruit or vegetable item (e.g., grapes) each shopping trip.

Social marketing can also operate at the school-level of ecology, and there are many examples of successful school-based campaigns to change student's nutrition and exercise patterns through environmental changes such as cafeteria and vending machine interventions as well as promotional advertising (Haire-Joshu & Nanney, 2002). These strategies use varying combinations of *place* (i.e., where food is purchased in school), *price* (i.e., food prices in vending machines), and *product* (i.e., food availability) strategies and can be integrated with in-school posters aimed at students promoting healthy active lifestyles (Thackeray, Neiger, Leonard, et al., 2002).

At the community level, social marketing has shown evidence of effectiveness in promoting nutrition and physical activity among parents and children. Evans (2008) described the characteristics of effective community-based social marketing campaigns including source authenticity for the audience, use of relevant social models, and use of multiple outreach channels including co-branding with popular community events and venues (Evans, 2008). The *VERB* campaign used media and community outreach to reach youth and was effective in increasing pre-adolescent physical activity (Berkowitz, Huhman, & Nolin, 2008; Huhman, Potter, Wong, et al., 2005).

These strategies can be combined in integrated multilevel family, school, and community social marketing interventions. The 5-4-3-2-1 Go! campaign is an example of the multilevel approaches that we see as possible. It was designed to affect parental behaviors within the context of obesigenic environments in low-income Chicago communities (Mason, Meleedy-Rey, Christoffel, et al., 2006). As described in detail elsewhere, the campaign is designed to address five risk behaviors: eat five of more servings of fruits and vegetables, four servings of water, three servings of low-fat dairy, two hours or less of screen time, and one hour or more of physical activity daily (Becker, Longjohn, & Christoffel, 2008; Evans, Necheles, Longjohn, et al., 2007). The campaign employs the full marketing mix (Kotler, 2001), including price (e.g., making it easier to be active and eat well), place (reaching people where they live and shop), product (e.g., healthy behaviors they can do), and promotion (e.g., the 5-4-3-2-1 Go! message).

Future Directions

Future interventions need to draw on lessons from comprehensive programs such as 5-4-3-2-1 Go!, *VERB*, and Shape Up Somerville. The public health literature increasingly shows that multilevel programs using social marketing as part of a comprehensive set of interventions strategies including policy, school, workplace, community, interpersonal, and individual levels are most likely to affect complex health challenges such as obesity. As this chapter points out, there are an increasing number of campaign examples and intervention strategies to draw upon. New programs should use innovative combinations of these strategies tailored to community contexts.

Additionally, the policy-advocacy and social-movement-building functions of social marketing should be emphasized. The tobacco control movement, especially Project ASSIST, showed the power of social marketing in this arena (NCI, 2005). Media advocacy is now poised to catalyze collective action for obesity prevention with the presence of mobile health and social media tools, including social networking applications, that provide platforms to rapidly disseminate messages and encourage shared ownership of social and health challenges such as obesity (Evans, Christoffel, Necheles, et al., 2010; Uhrig, Bann, Williams, et al., 2010).

Finally, more research is needed on best practices for comprehensive obesity prevention programs. The 5-4-3-2-1 Go! evaluation provides initial evidence of how community-based social marketing can impact obesity. More research is needed on which combinations of program components are most effective in specific contexts and with varying priority populations. The role of mobile and social media should be explored, both for delivery of low-cost, high-reach social marketing for populations using these media such as adolescents and young adults (Cole-Lewis & Kershaw, 2010), and as tools for research and evaluation (Evans, Davis, & Zhang, 2008).

Discussion Questions

1. What are the best strategies for disseminating and replicating evidence-based childhood obesity prevention social marketing programs such as 5-4-3-2-1 Go!?
2. How can social marketing be most effectively integrated into future multilevel, ecologically focused childhood obesity prevention programs?
3. How can mobile and social media be used most effectively for childhood obesity control and prevention?
4. What opportunities are there for rigorous research and program evaluation to build the evidence base on social marketing for childhood obesity prevention?

References

Becker, A. B., Longjohn, M., Christoffel, K. K. (2008). Taking on childhood obesity in a big city: Consortium to Lower Obesity in Chicago Children (CLOCC). *Progress in Pediatric Cardiology*, *25*(2):199–206.

Bell, J., & Standish, M. (2005). Communities and health policy: A pathway for change. *Health Affairs (Millwood)*, *24*(2):339–342.

Berkowitz, J., Huhman, M., & Nolin, M. J. (2008). Did augmenting the VERB campaign advertising in select communities have an effect on awareness, attitudes, and physical activity? *American Journal of Preventive Medicine*, *34*(Suppl 6):S257–S266.

Blackburn, G. L., & Walker, W. A. (2005). Science-based solutions to obesity: What are the roles of academia, government, industry, and health care? *American Journal of Clinical Nutrition, 82*(1 Suppl):207S–210S.

Booth, K. M., Pinkston, M. M., & Poston, W. S. C. (2005). Obesity and the built environment. *Journal of the American Dietetic Association,105*, s110–s117.

Brownson, R. C., Smith, C. A., & Pratt M., et al. (1996). Preventing cardiovascular disease through community-based risk reduction: The Bootheel Heart Health Project. *American Journal of Public Health, 86*(2):206–213.

Calvert, S. (2008). Children as consumers: Advertising and marketing. *Future of Children: Children, Media, and Technology, 18*(1):205–234.

Chuggish, S., & Kinder, G. (2008). Shape Up Somerville: District tackles childhood obesity. *Education Digest: Essential Readings Condensed for Quick Review, 73*(8):32–36.

Cole-Lewis, H., & Kershaw, T. Text messaging as a tool for behavior change in disease prevention and management. *Epidemiologic Reviews* [Online advance access]. Available at: http://epirev.oxfordjournals.org. Accessed: April 5, 2011.

Dodson, E. A., Fleming, C., Boehmer, T. K., Haire-Joshu, D., Luke, D. A., & Brownson, R. (2009). Preventing childhood obesity through state policy: Qualitative assessment of enablers and barriers. *Journal of Public Health Policy, 30*, S161–S176.

Drewnowski, A. (2004). Obesity and the food environment. *American Journal of Preventive Medicine, 27*(3s):154–162.

Economos, C., Hyatt, R., Goldberg, J., Must, A., Naumova, E., Collins, J., & Nelson, M. (2007). A community-based environmental change intervention reduces BMI z-score in children: Shape Up Somerville first year results. *Obesity, 15*: 1325–1326.

Evans, W. D., Christoffel, K. K., Necheles, J., Becker, A. B., & Snider, J. (2010). Outcomes of the *5-4-3-2-1 Go!* Obesity Prevention Trial. *American Journal of Health Behavior,* 35(2):189–198.

Evans, W. D., Blitstein, J., Lynch, C., de Villiers, A., Draper, C., Steyn, N., & Lambert, V. (2009). Childhood obesity prevention in South Africa: Media, social influences, and social marketing opportunities. *Social Marketing Quarterly, 15*(1):22–48.

Evans, W. D., & Hastings, G. (2008). *Public health branding: Applying marketing for social change.* Oxford, UK: Oxford University Press.

Evans, W. D. (2008). Social marketing and children's media use. *Future of Children: Children, Media, and Technology,18*(1):181–204.

Evans, W. D., Davis, K. C., & Zhang, Y. (2008). Social marketing research with new media: Case study of the Parents Speak Up National Campaign evaluation. *Cases in Public Health Communication and Marketing, 2*, 1–18.

Evans, W. D, Renaud, J., Finkelstein, E., Brown, D., & Kamerow, D. (2006). Changing perceptions of the childhood obesity epidemic. *American Journal of Health Behavior, 30*(2):167–176.

Evans, W. D., Necheles, J., Longjohn, M., & Christoffel, K. K. (2007). The 5-4-3-2-1 Go! intervention: Social marketing for nutrition. *Journal of Nutrition Education and Behavior, 39*(2)(S1):S55–S59.

Evans, W. D., Ulasevich, A., & Stillman, F. (2006). The ASSIST newspaper tracking system. In F. Stillman, C. Schmitt, & W. Trochim (Eds.), *Evaluation of Project ASSIST: A blueprint for state-level tobacco control.* Bethesda, MD: National Cancer Institute Press.

Evans, W. D., Finkelstein, E. A., Kamerow, D. B., & Renaud, J. M. (2005). Public perceptions of childhood obesity. *American Journal of Preventive Medicine, 28*(1):26–32.

Evans, W.D., Price, S. and Blahut, S. (2005). Evaluating the truth® Brand. *Journal of Health Communication,10*(2):181–192.

Finkelstein, E., French, S., Variyam, J. N., & Haines, P. S. (2004). Pros and cons of proposed interventions to promote healthy eating. *American Journal of Preventive Medicine, 27*(3 Suppl):163–171.

Flay, B. R. (2000). Approaches to substance use prevention utilizing school curriculum plus social environment change. *Addictive Behaviors,25*, 861–885.

Fox, S. *Digital divisions: Pew Internet and American Life Project.* Available at: http://www.pewInternet.org. Accessed: April 5, 2011.

Green, L. W., & Kreuter, M. W. (2005). *Health program planning: An educational and ecological approach* (4th ed.). New York, NY: McGraw-Hill Higher Education.

Haire-Joshu, D., & Nanney, M.S. (2002). Prevention of overweight and obesity in children: Influences on the food environment. *Diabetes Educator, 28*(3):415–422.

Hill, J. O., Wyatt, H. R., Reed, G. W., & Peters, J. C. (2003). Obesity and the environment: Where do we go from here? *Science, 299*(7):853–855.

Holden, D., Evans, W. D., Hinnant, L., & Messeri, P. (2005). Modeling psychological empowerment among youth involved in local tobacco control efforts. *Health Education and Behavior, 32*(2):264–278.

Huhman, M., Price, S., & Potter, L. D. (2008). Branding play for children: VERB™ It's What You Do. In W. D. Evans, & G. Hastings (Eds.), *Public health branding: Applying marketing for social change.* London, UK: Oxford University Press.

Huhman, M., Potter, L., Wong, F., Banspach, S., Duke, J., & Heitzler, C. (2005). Effects of a mass media campaign to increase physical activity among children: Year-1 results of the VERB campaign. *Pediatrics, 116*, e247–e254.

Institute of Medicine. (2005). *Preventing childhood obesity: Health in the balance.* Washington, DC: The National Academies Press.

Jefferey, R. W., and Utter, J. (2003). The changing environment and population obesity in the United States. *Obesity Research, 11*(Suppl):12s–22s.

Koplan, J. P., & Dietz, W. H. (1999). Caloric imbalance and public health policy. *Journal of the American Medical Association, 282*(16):1579–1581.

Kotler, P., & Lee, N. (2008). *Social marketing: Influencing behaviors for good* (3rd. ed.). Thousand Oaks, CA: Sage.

Kotler P. (2001). *A framework for marketing management.* New York, NY: Prentice-Hall.

Lewis, L. B., Sloane, D. C., Nascimento, L. M., Diamant, A. L., Guinyard, J. J., Yancey, A. K., & Flynn, G. (2005). African Americans' access to healthy food options in south Los Angeles restaurants. *American Journal of Public Health, 95*(4):668–673.

Lewis, C. E, Raczynski, J. M., Heath, G. W., Levinson, R., Hilyer J. J., & Cutter, G. R. (1993). Promoting physical activity in low-income African American communities: The PARR project. *Ethnicity and Disease, 3*(2):106–118.

Macbeth, A. G. Bicycle lanes in Toronto. *ITE Journal, 69,* 38–46.

Mason, M., Meleedy-Rey, P., Christoffel, K. K., LongJohn, M., Garcia, M.P., & Ashlaw, C. (2006). Prevalence of overweight and risk of overweight 3- to 5-year-old Chicago children, 2002–2003. *Journal of School Health, 76*(3):104–110.

McLeroy, K. R., Bibeau, D., Steckler, A., and Glanz, K. (1988). An ecological prespective on health promotion programs. *Health Education Quarterly, 15*(4):351–377.

Morland, K., Wing, S., Roux, A. D., and Poole, C. (2002). Neighborhood characteristics associated with the location of food stores and food service places. *American Journal of Preventive Medicine, 22*(1), 23–29.

National Cancer Institute (NCI). (2005). Shaping the future of tobacco prevention and control [NCI Tobacco Control Monograph Series No. 16]. Bethesda, MD: Author.

National Cancer Institute (NCI). (2005). *ASSIST: Shaping the future of tobacco prevention and control* (NIH Pub. No. -5-5645). Bethesda, MD: U.S. Department of Health and Human Service, National Institutes of Health, National Cancer Institute.

Onyx, J., & Bullen, P. (2000). Measuring social capital in five communities. *Journal of Applied Behavioral Science, 36*(1):23–42.

Painter, K. (1999). The influence of street lighting improvements on crime, fear, and pedestrian street use after dark. *Landscape and Urban Planning, 35*, 193–201.

Popkin, B. M., Duffey, K., & Gordon-Larsen, P. (2005). Environmental influences on food choice, physical activity, and energy balance. *Physiology and Behavior, 86*, 603–613.

Reger, B., Wootan, M., Booth-Butterfield, S., & Smith, H. (1998). 1% or less: A community-based nutrition campaign. *Public Health Reports, 113*(5):410–419.

Rosenstock, I. M., Strecher, V. J., & Becker, M. H. (1998). Social learning theory and the health belief model. *Health Education Quarterly, 15*(2):175–183.

Seymour, J. D., Yaroch, A. L., Serdula, M., Blanck, H. M., & Kettel Khan, L. (2004). Impact of nutrition environmental interventions on point-of-purchase behavior in adults: A review. *Preventive Medicine, 39*, S108–S126.

Sinai Urban Health Institute. Catalyzing public policy to improve community health. Available at: http://www.sinai.org/urban/originalresearch/rwj/index.asp. Accessed: April 5, 2011.

Snyder, L. B., & Hamilton, M. A. (2002). Meta-analysis of U.S. health campaign effects on behavior: Emphasize enforcement, exposure, and new information, and beware the secular trend. Hillsdale, NJ: Lawrence Erlbaum Associates.

Stokols, D. (1996). Translating social ecological theory into guidelines for community health promotion. *American Journal of Health Promotion, 10*(4):282–298.

Swinburn, B., Gill, T., & Kumanyika, S. (2005). Obesity prevention: A proposed framework for translating evidence into action. *Obesity Review, 6*(1):23–33.

Task Force on Community Preventive Services. (2005). Physical activity: Increasing physical activity through information approaches, behavioral and social approaches, and environmental and policy approaches. *The Guide to Community Preventive Services* (pp. 80–112). New York, NY: Oxford.

Thackeray, R., Neiger, B., Leonard, H., Ware, J., & Stoddard, G. (2002). Comparison of a 5-a-day social marketing intervention and school-based curriculum. *American Journal of Health Studies, 18*(1):46–50.

Uhrig, J. D., Bann, C. M., Williams, P. N., and Evans, W. D. (2010). Social networking web sites as a platform for disseminating social marketing interventions: An exploratory pilot study. *Social Marketing Quarterly, 16*(1):2–20.

United States Department of Health and Human Services. (2001). *The Surgeon General's call to action to prevent and decrease overwieght and obesity*: U.S. Department of Health and Human Services, Public Health Service, Office of the Surgeon General.

United States Department of Health and Human Services. (2004). *The health consequences of smoking: A report of the Surgeon General*. Atlanta, GA: Department of Health and Human Services, Center for Disease Control and Prevention, Office on Smoking and Health.

Williams-Piehota, P., Cox, A., Silvera, S. N., et al. (2004). Casting health messages in terms of responsibility for dietary change: Increasing fruit and vegetable consumption. *Journal of Nutrition Education and Behavior. 36*(3):114–120.

Young, L., Anderson, J., Beckstrom, L., et al. (2004). Using social marketing to guide the development of a nutrition education initiative for pre-school aged children. *Journal of Nutrition Educaiton and Behavior, 36*, 250–257.

Zenk, S. N., Schulz, A. J., Hollis-Neely, T., et al. (2005). Fruit and vegetable intake in African-Americans: Income and store characteristics. *American Journal of Preventive Medicine, 29*(1):1–9.

Chapter 16

Health Reform: The New Era of Prevention

By William A. Tatum

LEARNING OBJECTIVES

By the end of this chapter, the reader will be able to:

- Explain how the success of advocacy campaigns hinges on successful engagement of members of Congress, the media, and advocacy partners.
- Describe elements of an advocacy campaign, such as policy forums, model legislative language, policy recommendations and papers, and advertising and campaign materials.
- Understand the importance of articulating a clear, concise evidence-based message to the appropriate decision makers and opinion leaders.
- Engage the public to become active participants in a reform debate.

Introduction

Partnership for Prevention (or just *Partnership*) was founded in 1991 by visionaries who saw the need for an organization dedicated to advancing "prevention as a whole" as a priority in health policy. Partnership is a national nonprofit membership organization composed of leaders in the business community, nonprofit organizations, and local and state governments advancing evidence-based prevention in policies and practices. The organization seeks to create a "prevention culture" in America, where the prevention of disease and the promotion of health, based on the best scientific evidence, is the first priority for policy makers, decision makers, and healthcare practitioners who can make a difference in this area. Partnership accomplishes its critical mission by:

- Analyzing leading scientific research to identify effective policies and practices that should be adopted to accelerate progress toward better health for all Americans

- Convening diverse healthcare stakeholders to assess evidence-based disease prevention and health promotion policies and practices and to work toward achieving mutually agreeable objectives and solutions
- Educating decision makers about innovative prevention policies and health promotion practices, providing useful, analytical tools to aide their implementation and advocating for the adoption of these approaches in the private and public sectors

Partnership addresses a range of important health issues, including tobacco control and cessation, nutrition and physical activity, alcohol abuse and misuse, clinical and community preventive services, worksite health promotion, and immunization policy. The organization is uniquely positioned to influence policy makers as it stands alone in its dedication to prevention across all risk factors and diseases, in both clinical and population settings. Owing to its expertise in evaluating a cross-cutting approach to prevention, Partnership believes that a prevention-centered health system will not only save lives and money, but it will enhance individual quality of life.

This chapter highlights the efforts of Partnership to position prevention as the primary focus of health reform in the United States over the past two decades. It outlines the communication strategies and recommendations for policy changes Partnership undertook to achieve several important provisions in the recently enacted Public Law 111-148, the Patient Protection and Affordable Care Act.

Background

> *As the 20th century neared its end, the United States enjoyed the dubious distinction of having the highest healthcare costs in the world while being the only major democracy with a substantial fraction of the population still lacking basic medical insurance. On several occasions in this century, Congress seriously considered plans to provide universal health coverage. In each case, determined opposition led by physicians, big business, and Republican lawmakers blocked the proposals. With the election of President William Clinton, however, all of the auguries seemed to favor major reform. (Bok, n.d).*

The Clinton health care plan was a 1993 healthcare reform package proposed by the administration of President Bill Clinton and closely associated with the chair of the task force devising the plan, First Lady Hillary Rodham Clinton. The Task Force on National Health Care Reform was created in 1993 and its goal was to come up with a comprehensive plan to provide universal health care for all Americans, which was to be a cornerstone of the administration's first-term agenda. The core element of the proposed plan was an enforced mandate for employers to provide health insurance coverage to all of their employees through competitive but closely regulated health maintenance organizations. That same year, Partnership outlined the essential principles of health reform and prevention in a paper entitled, *Prevention Is Basic to Health Care Reform*. The Prevention in Health Care Reform Advisory Group, created by the California Wellness Foundation, devised recommendations from Partnership's paper around the three essential elements of prevention in health reform. Led by principal investigator, Helen Halpin Schauffler, PhD, MSPH, the three components were: public policy for health promotion and disease prevention; community-based health promotion and disease prevention; and clinical preventive services. According to the Health Care Reform Advisory group, the specific objectives in making these recommendations were to:

- Implement an integrated model of health promotion and disease prevention that coordinates the prevention efforts and information systems of health plans, community-based organizations, public health agencies, and government to attain the goals set forth in *Healthy People 2000: Health Objectives for the Nation*
- Adopt comprehensive public policy for prevention at the federal, state, and local levels
- Increase the availability and effectiveness of community-based health promotion and disease prevention
- Increase the appropriate use of clinical preventive services for all Americans (Schauffler, 1994)

The advisory group wanted the government to set national priorities and define goals, standards, and systems of accountability for measuring and monitoring system performance:

> *At present (1993) public policy for prevention is fragmented and fails to make use of the variety of policy tools available to influence health-promotion behaviors of individuals and institutions. Until very recently, most health insurance plans in the United States did not cover any preventive screening services, health education, or immunization in the benefit packages. As a result, many Americans have not received the clinical preventive services they need, thus contributing to the high levels of preventable morbidity and mortality in the population. Our goal in developing the recommendations is to address these failures in the present system and move toward a comprehensive and integrated approach to health promotion and disease prevention in health care reform (Schauffler, 1994).*

Early into the debate, Partnership and the advisory group were firm believers that a comprehensive, long-term multifaceted approach, which included public policy, community prevention, and clinical preventive services, was essential for sustainable reform in the Clinton plan.

However, opposition to the Clinton plan was heavy from conservatives, libertarians, and the health insurance industry, and they criticized it as being overly bureaucratic and restrictive of patient choice. Opposition to the Clinton plan was initiated by William Kristol and his policy group Project for the Republican Future, which is widely credited with orchestrating the plan's ultimate defeat through a series of now legendary "policy memos" faxed to Republican leaders (Edsall, 2007).

> *The conservative Heritage Foundation argued the Clinton Administration is imposing a top-down, command-and-control system of global budgets and premium caps, a superintending National Health Board and a vast system of government sponsored regional alliances, along with a panoply of advisory boards, panels, and councils, interlaced with the expanded operations of the agencies of Department of Health and Human Services and the Department of Labor, issuing innumerable rules, regulations, guidelines, and standards (Moffit, 1993).*

The effort also included extensive advertising criticizing the plan, including the famous "Harry and Louise" ad paid for by the America's Health Insurance Association, (formerly the Health Insurance Association of America (HIAA) (Coh, 2007).

> *"Harry and Louise" was a $14 to $20 million year-long television advertising campaign that ran intermittently from September1993 to September 1994. Fourteen television ads and radio and print advertising depicted a fictional suburban middle-class married couple despairing over bureaucratic and other aspects of healthcare reform plans, and urged viewers to contact their representatives in Congress (Johnson & Broder, 1996).*

In August 1994, Democratic Senate Majority Leader George J. Mitchell introduced a compromise proposal that exempted small businesses and would have delayed requirements of employers until 2002. However, "even with Mitchell's bill, there were not enough Democratic Senators behind a single proposal to pass a bill, let alone stop a filibuster" (Pantel & Rushefsky, 1997). A few weeks later, Mitchell announced that his compromise plan was dead, and that healthcare reform would have to wait at least until the next Congress. "The 1994 mid-term election became a "referendum on big government" — Hillary Clinton had launched a massive health-care reform plan that wound up strangled by its own red tape" (Thomas, 2006). On November 8, 1994, Republicans, led by Newt Gingrich, gained control of both the House of Representatives and the Senate and ended prospects for a Clinton-sponsored healthcare overhaul.

At the same time, Partnership made a strategic decision to highlight the importance of clinical and community prevention in America. To that end, Partnership created the Congressional Prevention Caucus (CPC), a bipartisan, bicameral caucus to raise the level of knowledge in the Congress about disease prevention and health promotion and identify strategies that can lead to a healthier nation. In 1998, the CPC was chaired by Senators Tom Harkin (D-IA) and John Chafee (R-RI) and US Representatives James Moran (D-VA) and James Leach (R-IA). Since its inception, the CPC and Partnership have cosponsored a number of health promotion and disease prevention-related activities on Capitol Hill including the following:

- Health screening fair for congressional members and staffs—Participants received blood pressure, diabetes, and cholesterol screenings and learned about a variety of prevention issues including nutrition and exercise.

- Congressional briefings—Partnership educated congressional staff on a wide variety of prevention issues, including tobacco legislation, prevention research, obesity, injury prevention, and *Healthy People 2010* so members of Congress could make informed decisions regarding prevention legislation.
- "Dear Colleague" letters—The CPC and *Partnership for Prevention* developed and disseminated "Dear Colleague" letters to inform members of Congress about important prevention issues. Each letter focused on a specific and timely issue as well as provided information about prevention strategies that members can suggest to their staffs and constituents.

In 1999, Partnership convened a working group on setting a national prevention agenda. The meeting focused on the following areas: injury and violence, substance abuse, sexually transmitted diseases, physical activity, tobacco, maternal and child health, and environmental and occupational health. The goal of the meeting was to choose a short list of high-impact policies—policies that will have a great effect on preventable mortality and morbidity in the nation. The chief criteria for selecting the highest-impact polices were burden, effectiveness, and cost. The working group defined the short list of high-impact national prevention polices as:

- Require all states to set the legal blood alcohol limit to .08; provide states with incentives and grants to reduce alcohol-related crashes using roadblocks and increased police enforcement
- Enact a comprehensive and effective firearms policy
- Raise the federal excise tax on all alcoholic beverages, and raise the tax rate on beer to be equal to wine and spirits
- Create incentives for the state to offer comprehensive physical education classes in K–12 schools
- Increase the deferral tax on tobacco products
- Grant the US Food and Drug Administration (FDA) authority to regulate tobacco products, including tobacco advertising
- Ban smoking in public areas throughout the nation
- Require federal government sponsored health plans to cover the set of clinical preventive services recommended by the US Preventive Services Task Force

In 2003, Partnership formed the National Commission on Prevention Priorities (NCPP) to produce a comprehensive study ranking the relative value of 25 clinical preventive services for the US population. NCPP provides decision makers with evidence-based information about preventive services that offer the greatest health impact and are most cost-effective, guidance about where improving delivery rates will offer the greatest returns on investment, and a resource for building demand for a prevention-focused healthcare system. Three years later, NCPP released its clinical rankings study, *Priorities for America's Health: Capitalizing on Life-Saving, Cost-Effective Preventive Services*, which significantly increased policy makers' attention and awareness about the value of clinical preventive services.

The study found more than 50% of Americans go without some of the most valuable preventive services in medicine, services that can prevent disease and death. According to "Priorities for America's Health," the three most valuable preventive health services that can be offered in medical practice today, each of which save more money than they cost and provide enormous health benefits, are:

- Discussing daily aspirin use with at-risk adults to prevent cardiovascular disease
- Immunizing children to prevent and eradicate disease
- Intervening with tobacco users to help them quit

Sponsored by the Centers for Disease Control and Prevention (CDC) and the Agency for Healthcare Research and Quality (AHRQ) within the US Department of Health and Human Services (HHS), the study looked at all the preventive services currently offered by healthcare providers and developed a ranking of 25 recommended services based on those that provide the greatest health benefits, both in terms of saving lives and improving quality of life, while offering the most value for the healthcare dollars. "Currently, about 95% of health care dollars in the United States are spent on treating diseases, with relatively little attention paid to preventing diseases, which should be a national priority," said David Satcher, MD, PhD, former US Surgeon General. "The landmark study highlights the importance of shifting focus to preventive care, which can provide an enormous positive impact on health and well-being, while also more effectively allocating our precious health care dollars. Basically, these are the preventive health services that offer the biggest bang for the buck."

In 2007 Partnership's NCPP released, *Preventive Care: A National Profile on Use, Disparities and Health Benefits*, a follow-up to the 2006 study. The report highlighted how increasing the use of just five preventive services would save more than 100,000 lives every year in the United States. That included 45,000 lives that would be saved each year if more adults took a daily low-dose aspirin to prevent heart disease. The report also found that a few measures—such as more adults getting flu shots and being screened for cancer—could save tens of thousands of lives each year in the United States.

The study found serious deficiencies in the use of preventive care for the nation as a whole, and particularly troubling shortfalls among racial and ethnic populations. "This report illustrates that the health benefits would be great if more people took preventive actions," said Dr. Julie Gerberding, former director of the Centers for Disease Control and Prevention. "More illnesses would be avoided, fewer lives would be lost, and there would be more efficient use of our limited health care resources. It's important that all of us make a concerted attempt to focus our energies and efforts on preventing disease, not just treating it." In a prereformed healthcare system, low utilization rates for cost-effective preventive services were rampant. Among the 12 preventive services examined in this report, seven were being used by about half or less of the people who should have been using them. Racial and ethnic minorities were getting even less preventive care than the general US population. With the public release of this seminal study, Partnership communicated clearly and loudly to key audiences that expanding the delivery of preventive services of proven value would enable tens of millions of Americans to live longer, healthier, and more fulfilling lives.

Creating the Platform for Health Reform

Partnership realized that the typical centerpieces of healthcare reform efforts were financing of health insurance coverage and access to care. While financing and access are critical and necessary elements of healthcare reform, by themselves they fall short of achieving the overarching goal: improving the health of all Americans. Indeed, much of the criticism of the healthcare system was that for all we spend, America's health outcomes lag behind those of other nations that spend much less. To that end, Partnership produced its *Principles for Prevention-Centered Health Reform*. The organization believed that the following prevention policy principles, if enacted in conjunction with national health reform efforts, would have a significant and lasting impact on the health of the American people:

Clinical Preventive Services Should Be a Basic Benefit of Proposed Healthcare Financing Reform

- *Financing mechanisms should make high-value clinical preventive services accessible to all who need them*—This should be accomplished by ensuring all Americans have access to quality, affordable health care and by increasing the capacity of community-based providers, such as community health centers, rural and migrant health centers, free clinics, and public health departments, to deliver these services to people who are not adequately served by the traditional healthcare system.
- *Financing mechanisms should encourage patients to use preventive services*—Health insurers and healthcare purchasers should encourage individuals to use preventive services by avoiding financial disincentives such as applying high levels of cost-sharing to such services. Governments should also encourage consumer demand for high-value services by supporting public education efforts about preventive services.
- *Financing mechanisms should offer incentives to healthcare providers to deliver clinical preventive services*—Incentives such as tax benefits and preferential payments for healthcare delivery organizations can be used to encourage investments in systems and strategies that are proven to result in improved health outcomes. These might include such practices as: offering health risk assessments and behavioral counseling for diet and exercise, tobacco use, and alcohol and substance abuse; establishing linkages with community-based programs that provide preventive services; and having in place decision supports and patient advisories to ensure consistency in the delivery of preventive care and chronic disease management services. Another desired practice is the use of proactive "practice teams" that provide ongoing coaching for patients regarding preventive practices and management of their chronic conditions.

- *Financing mechanisms should offer incentives to employers that reward their active engagement in employee health promotion*—This can be accomplished by providing companies with incentives to, for example, establish evidence-based worksite health programs that promote health and screen for disease, adopt policies for maintaining a healthy workplace, provide health insurance coverage for preventive services, and require health plans and providers with whom they contract to use electronic health records.

Community Preventive Services Should Be an Integral Part of Healthcare Financing Reform

- *Congress should enact policies that create healthy environments and encourage healthy behaviors*—Healthcare professionals and policy makers have identified a wide range of policies that would lead to healthier diets, higher levels of physical activity, reduced tobacco use, and lower levels of inappropriate use of alcohol. Partnership has previously recommended, for example, that Congress give the Federal Trade Commission the authority to regulate advertising of "junk food" to children and give the Food and Drug Administration the authority to regulate tobacco. In addition, Congress should look beyond traditional public health programs and consider legislative changes in such areas as agriculture, transportation, advertising, and education, all of which influence behaviors that affect health. One important strategy is to give communities incentives to ensure the built environment (e.g., the availability of parks, walking trails, and safe neighborhoods) promotes healthy lifestyles. The goal should be to make healthful choices easy options for all Americans to adopt.
- *Financing mechanisms should offer incentives to organizations that influence the health of populations to deliver community preventive services*—Forward-looking health reforms should create incentives for public health departments, as well as for other institutions such as school districts and parks and recreation departments, to deliver evidence-based community preventive services to bring about public health and environmental changes that promote good health. One suggested approach is to reward county and state public health departments that meet strict performance standards with higher levels of federal funding.
- *Financing reforms should increase support for research on community-based and clinical prevention*—Increased federal funding for public health systems research and health services research will enhance our ability to translate knowledge about prevention into effective policy and practice. Additional research will increase our understanding of which community and clinical preventive services are most effective and most cost-effective and in which settings.
- *Financing mechanisms should support the development of system performance standards related to prevention and the subsequent evaluation of performance*—Prevention-centered health reform requires that the nation develop performance standards to measure progress in promoting good health and preventing disease. The performance measures should address both clinical and community preventive services and should help guide future decisions by Congress to ensure that our investment in prevention yields maximum results.

In the lead-up to the 2008 November elections, Partnership joined the Partnership to Fight Chronic Disease and other groups to launch a national TV and online advertising campaign that urged women to get answers from the candidates about health care, specifically how each candidate plans to prevent chronic diseases. The 30-second TV spot and 45-second online spot featured Hollywood celebrities such as Mary-Louise Parker, Lauren Bacall, Katey Sagal and Phylicia Rashad urging viewers to find out where the candidates stand on disease prevention and to "Vote like your health depends on it."

The ad called on women voters, a particularly influential group in the election, to ask important questions about health care and demand action on an issue that is not only one of the most threatening health concerns to women, but is also jeopardizing the affordability of health care in the United States. By raising awareness of the tremendous costs of chronic diseases and the strong impact they have on healthcare cost, quality, and access in this country, the ad sought to encourage a substantive, bipartisan discussion of this issue in the context of broader discussions of healthcare reform. Both the McCain and Obama campaigns engaged in the health reform debate. In its summer meeting, Partnership's board of directors recognized a historic opportunity, regardless which candidate won, to make prevention an integral part of a health reform campaign in the new administration. The board made a number of fundamental commitments: the creation of policy papers; hiring senior leadership in communications and government affairs, and hosting a December policy forum.

Recognizing the time was ripe in our nation's history for the enactment of meaningful healthcare reform, Partnership intensified its efforts to effectively convey prevention and health promotion messages to policy makers and opinion leaders after the election of President Barack Obama. On December 11, 2008, Partnership hosted a major forum on health reform, "Rhetoric to Reality: The Urgency of Health Reform," that featured discussion from some of the most influential players in healthcare. The event was co-sponsored by AARP's Divided We Fail, the Partnership to Fight Chronic Disease, and the Emory Institute for Advanced Policy Solution. More than 220 attendees participated in "Rhetoric to Reality: The Urgency of Health Reform," where leaders from business, healthcare, media, and Capitol Hill talked about what was at stake for health reform in 2009 in light of the changes in Congress and the Administration, and how feasible it would be to build consensus for comprehensive reform. David Broder, syndicated news columnist, participated in the first panel entitled, "The Appetite and Atmosphere for Health Sector Transformation." Mr. Broder wrote about the event in his column in *The Washington Post*, reflecting on the breadth of support for reform among all stakeholders in healthcare as represented by speakers at the event. "Today, [the] status quo has become unendurable for almost everyone. The budgets of families, businesses, and government at all levels are being wrecked by the rising cost of health care," he reported.

At the policy forum, Partnership unveiled a new publication of health reform recommendations entitled, *Real Health Reform Starts with Prevention*. The findings made clear to Congress and other target audiences the efforts that could strengthen disease prevention and health promotion and reduce medical costs.

The report's recommendations focused on three areas: increased utilization of clinical preventive services, promotion of community preventive services, and an increased impact of prevention through research and performance measurement. Partnership's recommendations were drawn from a series of policy papers commissioned from leading national public health authorities. The authors included: Kurt Stange, professor of Family Medicine, Epidemiology & Biostatistics, and Sociology and Oncology at Case Western Reserve University; Steven Woolf, professor in the departments of Family Medicine, Epidemiology and Community Health at Virginia Commonwealth University; Douglas Kamerow, chief scientist at RTI; Jonathan Fielding, Los Angeles County director of Health and chairman of the Board of Partnership for Prevention; Ron Goetzel, director of Emory University's Institute for Health and Productivity Studies; Arkansas Surgeon General Joe Thompson; and Larry Lewin, health consultant and founder of The Lewin Group. The papers covered such diverse topics as modernizing Medicare to improve the delivery of preventive services, determining the content of a package of preventive services, linking the clinical care and public health systems, strengthening the role of the nation's public health system, reorganizing the Department of Health and Human Services, and expanding worksite health promotion programs.

Under these proposals, federally funded insurance programs would provide highly cost-effective clinical preventive services with no deductibles or co-pays, while Congress would provide incentives to states, healthcare providers, and employers to deliver such services. The recommendation to cover preventive services in federally sponsored health insurance programs would apply to Medicare, Medicaid, the Department of Defense, and the Veterans Administration, as well as the private-sector health insurance offerings included in the Federal Employees Health Benefits Program. The covered services would be those recommended by the US Preventive Services Task Force and the Advisory Committee on Immunization Practices. Meanwhile, a stand-alone revenue source would be established to fund state and local efforts to create healthy environments and promote healthy lifestyles, while a Public Health Advisory Commission would be created to recommend how that funding should be allocated. The newly created Public Health Advisory Commission would also recommend strategies to hold the public health system accountable for achieving the *Healthy People* goals sponsored by the Department of Health and Human Services. Partnership also recommended increased investment in research on effective clinical and community preventive services, as well as improved data systems to monitor progress in meeting Healthy People goals.

Initial Success

In January 2009, Partnership collaborated with Dr. Helen Halpin from University of California-Berkeley School of Public Health to finalize model legislative language for prevention-center health reform. The language was designed to bring to center stage two additional priorities that were central to successful healthcare and public health reform: (1) adopt "improving the health of the American people" as a primary goal of any health reform legislation, and (2) define prevention broadly to include evidence-based clinical preventive services, community-based prevention and public health interventions, and social and economic policies central to health improvement. Partnership shared the document with key legislators and congressional staffers. The language was devised to provide congressional offices a "prevention standard" when incorporating legislation into health reform proposals. The following nine components represent key elements of a prevention standard:

- Provision of high-value, evidence-based personal, clinical preventive services, fully covered in the core benefit package based on the findings of the *US Preventive Services Task Force (USPSTF)* and the *Advisory Committee on Immunization Practices (ACIP)*
- Support for evidence-based community prevention and public health interventions at the national, state, and local levels, based on the findings of the *Task Force on Community Preventive Services*
- Identification of social and economic policy changes that are clearly tied to health improvement
- Financial incentives to health organizations, employers, health insurers, and individuals to adopt effective prevention interventions, and rewards for the adoption of proven wellness programs
- Commitment to strong and sustained support for stable public health funding to support the essential services of public health (defined below) at the national, state, and local levels and building the infrastructure needed to perform these functions
- Assurance of the capacity for data collection and reporting for health status tracking, problem identification, and monitoring of implementation
- Strategies for assuring the training and deployment of a public health workforce and a primary-care workforce, skilled in prevention and public health, adequate to meet the population's needs
- Sustained public awareness interventions that contribute to an improved public understanding of the centrality of prevention to health and health care
- Research to identify the most efficient and effective prevention services, programs, and policies

The Struggles

As the health reform debated intensified over the summer 2009, Partnership continued to educate members of Congress about the need to include evidence-based prevention policies in comprehensive health reform, despite contentious town hall meeting in opposition to health reform. Based on the findings of a Partnership study, the government affairs team publicly posed to Congress the following question, "If you could save 100,000 lives, would you?" Partnership raised this question to legislators because many of the clinical preventive services that were essential to saving 100,000 lives were underutilized because of deductibles, co-pays, and lack of coverage. During the debate, Partnership wanted to inform Congress that they had the opportunity to remove obstacles as part of health reform legislation. Partnership suggested to Congress they could:

- Provide coverage in all federal health plans
- Encourage coverage in nonfederal plans
- Eliminate deductibles and co-pays for the most effective services
- Educate the public about the importance of getting clinical preventive services

Partnership continued to attend meetings with Hill staffers on prevention and health reform legislation. The wellness and prevention policies discussed included:

- Creating a national prevention and health promotion strategy to improve health with a dedicated funding stream for public health and prevention
- Expanding the charge of the US Preventive Services Task Force and the Community Preventive Services Task Force
- Promoting the use of evidence-based clinical preventive services
- Improving the health of communities by providing grants to implement evidence-based community preventive services
- Providing new investments to increase prevention research and the number of health workers

In August, Partnership sent a "Call for Action" to its members, board, and Council of Advisors urging them to contact their members of Congress to support prevention as a critical key component of meaningful health reform.

In the fall 2009, Partnership for Prevention and Trust for America's Health (TFAH) launched a new ad campaign entitled, "Health Care vs. Sick Care." The ad copy read:

> *Americans are not as healthy as they could be or should be. High rates of preventable diseases, like heart disease, stroke, and type 2 diabetes are one of the biggest reasons the US has skyrocketing healthcare costs. We will continue to struggle with healthcare costs until we do a better job of keeping people healthier. Smart, strategic investments in proven prevention programs can have a real payoff in dollars, workforce productivity, and quality of life. With an investment of $10 per person per year in proven community-based program to increase physical activity, improve nutrition, and prevent smoking and other tobacco use, the country could save more than $16 billion annually within 5 years. That's a return of $5.60 for every $1 invested. Real health reform starts with prevention.*

The ad emphasized the importance of including prevention as a central pillar of health reform. It featured visuals of people riding bikes, juxtaposed with an individual in a wheelchair, underscoring that real health care must involve keeping people healthy in the first place, instead of just focusing on treating them after they get sick. The return on investment figures in the ad were from TFAH's *Prevention for a Healthier America: Investments in*

Disease Prevention Yield Significant Savings, Stronger Communities, published in July 2008 and based on a literature review by the New York Academy of Medicine and an economic model by the Urban Institute.

Partnership continued to run the ad in a deliberate effort to brand the prevention debate as a basic choice. But the organization also recognized it was important to demonstrate in all advocacy efforts with Congress that there was strength (and safety) in numbers. Therefore, Partnership ran the ad multiple times in the congressional-focused publication *Congress Daily*, but this time included the logos and support of 15 other organizations.

Is the Past Prologue?

The House of Representatives passed the healthcare reform bill by a vote of 220-215 on November 8, 2009. With the passage of H.R. 3962, the Affordable Health Care for America Act, comprehensive health reform legislation included a robust array of provisions that increased access to clinical and community preventive services and programs. During committee consideration of the legislation, Partnership worked closely with Rep. Lois Capps (D-CA) to win passage of an amendment expanding coverage and eliminating cost-sharing requirements for preventive services under Medicaid. Other provisions Partnership had advocated that were incorporated into the bill included:

- Expanded coverage that includes clinical preventive services recommended by the US Preventive Services Task Force
- Elimination of cost-sharing requirements for preventive services in Medicare as well as Medicaid
- Codification and strengthening of the US Preventive Services Task Force as well as the Task Force on Community Preventive Services
- Direction to establish a national prevention and wellness strategy
- Creation of a multiyear, dedicated annual appropriations stream for public health and prevention
- Establishment of restaurant menu labeling for chains with more than 20 sites
- Expanded research on worksite wellness programs
- Authorization for a new grant program to assist small employers in establishing wellness programs
- Authorization for programs to prevent and reduce the prevalence of excess weight and obesity among children
- Expanded workforce training programs to eliminate critical public health workforce shortages

On Christmas Eve 2009, the Senate passed its version of health reform by a 60 to 39 vote along party lines. While the bill was less comprehensive and financially generous than the

House version, it did represent the "radical shift towards prevention and public health" that President Obama had sought. In fact, the prevention provisions contained in the House and Senate versions of health reform reflected in large measure all of Partnership's major health reform recommendations.

It was fortunate indeed the Senate acted when it did. The surprise election less than a month later (January 19, 2010) of Republican Scott Brown to fill the seat of the late Massachusetts Senator Edward Kennedy shocked the White House and Democratic leadership, which had planned to strengthen the Senate legislation in a Conference Committee with the House of Representatives. The election of a 41st Republican Senator meant the Democratically controlled Senate no longer had the necessary two-thirds super majority necessary to overcome the Republican filibuster that had previously stalled the legislation until its Christmas Eve passage. With Republican calls to "start over," it was obvious it would not be possible to ask the Senate to vote on a new health reform measure. The only viable choice left to the President was to ask the House of Representatives to set aside the reform measure they had labored on throughout 2009 and pass the Senate bill, clearing it to become law with the President's signature.

On March 21, 2010, the House of Representatives voted 219 to 212 to approve H.R. 3590, the "Patient Protection and Affordable Care Act." H.R. 3590 enacted vital health insurance reform, expanded Medicaid and made affordable health insurance available to tens of millions of American families. The bill reoriented our nation's high cost, "sick care" system into a healthcare system that provided funding and priority to evidenced-based clinical and community prevention. Additionally, the bill established a dedicated public health and prevention fund providing $15 billion over 10 years to help bring community prevention to every American family. Two days later, President Obama signed the bill and it became Public Law 111-148 (Figure 16-1). At the historic bill signing, President Obama said, "We are a nation that does what is hard, what is necessary, what is right. This bill delivered the core principle that everybody should have some basic security when it comes to their health care" (Henry, n.d.)

Lessons Learned

The work of health reform does not end with a bill's enactment; indeed, the hard work of utilization, implementation, and oversight begins. Partnership learned a number of valuable lessons during the health reform debate, including:

- *Cost matters*: The single most difficult challenge in securing support for our recommendation to eliminate cost sharing and expand coverage for recommended clinical preventive services was cost. Congressional staff had a great interest in whether Partnership had information on the cost of expanding services or, in the best of all worlds, whether there was evidence of cost savings. Whether or not provisions were included in legislation or offered as amendments was often determined by the cost estimate provided by the Congressional Budget Office. Whether the issue is clinical or community prevention, Partnership and other organizations are currently developing a capacity to estimate more effectively the financial costs of prevention.

One Hundred Eleventh Congress of the United States of America

AT THE SECOND SESSION

Begun and held at the City of Washington on Tuesday, the fifth day of January, two thousand and ten

An Act

Entitled The Patient Protection and Affordable Care Act.

Be it enacted by the Senate and House of Representatives of the United States of America in Congress assembled,

SECTION 1. SHORT TITLE; TABLE OF CONTENTS.

(a) SHORT TITLE.—This Act may be cited as the "Patient Protection and Affordable Care Act".

(b) TABLE OF CONTENTS.—The table of contents of this Act is as follows:

Figure 16-1 **Public Law 111-148**
http://democrats.senate.gov/reform/patient-protection-affordable-care-act-as-passed.pdf

- *Politics trumped policy*: In 2009, Partnership supported a variety of briefings for its CPC members and discovered that the intense partisanship of the health reform debate precluded its use as a forum for forging political consensus around the health reform prevention issues.
- *Product produced progress*: The success of advocacy is dependent upon repetition of messages and engagement with Capitol Hill, advocacy partners, and the media. The key to Partnership's success in becoming a valued ally in the health reform campaign was our production of the policy papers, drafting model legislative language, and developing effective communications campaigns materials such as the universal (REAL HEALTH REFORM) prevention logo. These products helped identify the Partnership brand and created a powerful platform to articulate our prevention message with Congress, partners, and the media.

The Future

The passage of Public Law 111-148 marked the end of an important chapter in American policy and public health history. It represents the passage of one of the most significant pieces of domestic legislation of the 21st century. It expands access to healthcare services, including lifesaving/cost saving clinical preventive screenings for millions of Americans. It puts into effect a $15 billion mandatory fund that is dedicated to prevention, wellness, and public health. It represents an inventory of important tools that the medical community must put to use with the same commitment and energy with which they greet new drugs and therapies. However, we are at a critical crossroads. We have seen a generation's worth of ground lost to the risk factors that threaten the longevity of our children and the vitality of our economy. We have also seen the promise of how, by investing in keeping people healthy, we have the potential to provide a better future for generations to come. Implementation of the hundreds of new requirements on government, employers, and insurance companies will determine the ultimate success of PL 111-148. No less important will be the willingness of individuals, families, and communities to take advantage of new opportunities to fashion healthier, more livable, and more prosperous communities. It is a campaign for life that does not end with the passage of a single bill.

Summary

An integrated healthcare advocacy plan needs to identify effective policies and practices that can be adopted to accelerate change. The communicator's role is to convene healthcare stakeholders to assess evidenced-based research and move toward developing win-win solutions for everyone involved. Additionally, it is imperative to educate the appropriate decision makers and opinion leaders with clear, concise, evidence-based messages that aid their ability to advocate for the cause.

Discussion Questions

1. Explain how Partnership for Prevention accomplishes its mission of creating a "prevention culture" in America.
2. List and describe three examples of how the Congressional Prevention Caucus (CPC) and Partnership for Prevention educated members of Congress about disease prevention and health promotion.
3. Why was the National Commission on Prevention Priorities (NCPP) formed? Explain how research studies are leveraged to support advocacy campaigns.
4. Why would Partnership convene a major forum on health reform? What would a forum, such as the "Rhetoric to Reality" forum, enable an advocacy organization to achieve?
5. Describe the role of the ad campaign launched by Partnership and Trust for America's Health (TFAH) entitled "Health Care vs. Sick Care" in the advocacy campaign. What did it accomplish?

References

Bok, D. The great health care debate of 1993–94. Harvard University. Available at: http://www.upenn.edu/pnc/ptbok.html. Accessed: July 13, 2010.

Cohn, J. (2007). Hillary was right—The health care plan that dares not speak its name. *The New Republic.*

Edsall, T. B. (2007, January 18). Happy hours. *The New York Times.* Available at: http://www.nytimes.com/2007/01/18/opinion/18edsall.html?ex=1326776400&en=4ac5968a31842091&ei=5088&partner=rssnyt&emc=rss. Accessed: July 24, 2010.

Henry, E. Obama signs healthcare bill: Senate takes up house changes. Available at: http://articles.cnn.com/2010-03-23/politics/health.care.main_1_health-care-obama-and-democratic-leaders-health-insurance?_s=PM:POLITICS. Accessed: July 22, 2010.

Johnson, H., and Broder, D. S. (1996). *The system: The American way of politics at the breaking point.* Boston: Little, Brown and Company.

Moffit, R. (1993). A guide to the Clinton health plan. Heritage Foundation.

Pantel, K. & Rushefsky, M. (1997). "Congress and Healthcare." Politics, power, and policy making: The case of health care reform in the 1990s. (Pp. 107). Armonk, NY: M.E. Sharpe, Inc.

Schauffler, H. H. (1994). Health promotion and disease prevention in health care reform. *American Journal of Preventive Medicine, 10*(5):1–3.

Thomas, E. (2006). Decline and fall. *Newsweek.* Available at: http://www.newsweek.com/2006/11/19/decline-and-fall.html. Accessed: July 27, 2010.

Index

Note: Figures and tables are indicated by *f* and *t* respectively following page numbers.

A

D

E

F

G

I

J

N

O

P

Q

R

S

T

U

V

W

X

Y

Z